Working-Class America

# Working-Class America

ESSAYS ON
LABOR, COMMUNITY, AND
AMERICAN SOCIETY

EDITED BY

Michael H. Frisch and Daniel J. Walkowitz

University of Illinois Press URBANA AND CHICAGO

Illini Books edition, 1983

© 1983 by the Board of Trustees of the University of Illinois
Manufactured in the United States of America

P 4 3

*This book is printed on acid-free paper.*

LIBRARY OF CONGRESS CATALOGING IN PUBLICATION DATA

Main entry under title:

Working-class America.

(The Working class in American history)
Includes index.
1. Labor and laboring classes—United States—
History—Addresses, essays, lectures. 2. Trade-
unions—United States—History—Addresses, essays,
lectures. 3. United States—Social conditions—
Addresses, essays, lectures. I. Frisch, Michael H.
II. Walkowitz, Daniel J. III. Series.
HD8066.W65          305.5'6          81-23971
ISBN 0-252-00954-1                    AACR2

# Contents

# Introduction

The essays in this volume represent some of the best work of a new scholarly generation in the field of American labor and working-class history. They are all original essays drawn from doctoral theses or major research projects, some of which will shortly be appearing in important new books.

These essays have been brought together into a collection with several purposes in mind. First, the volume presents a kind of early report from the frontiers of research where young scholars are fashioning the basis for an influential new understanding of the history of the working class in American society. The collection also demonstrates how the close study of concrete historical situations involving quite diverse groups, settings, and problems can contribute to and shape general interpretations. Finally, these essays illustrate something of how historical understandings change and grow in the process of being carried across intellectual generations. The extraordinarily fertile work of the last generation has fundamentally altered our sense of what is significant in labor history. The essays collected here are strongly influenced by this scholarship and bear the imprint of some of its seminal works. But the past two decades of scholarly ferment have generated more questions than could be answered and, given the dual influence of fresh discoveries and the perspective of a new generation's social, political, and intellectual experiences, young historians have naturally begun to refashion older questions and to ask new ones of their own. In order to appreciate the new directions in which this work has moved, it may be helpful to say a few words about how these essays relate to what has preceded them.

Approaches to labor history have changed profoundly since the field of study emerged in the early twentieth century. Under the direction of scholars such as John R. Commons, Phillip Taft, and Selig Perlman, early labor history tended to be formal and institutional. In a country where labor had been politically embattled and largely invisible in the historical record, these Wisconsin economists legitimized the trade-union movement as historically worthy and politically prominent.

The Wisconsin school focused on the history of the trade union movement, celebrating it as the expression of a pragmatic economic interest
group struggling toward organization, collective bargaining, and improved working conditions.[1]

By the 1960s this framework came under criticism as conceptually
and empirically limited. Scholars as diverse as Herbert G. Gutman,
David Brody, and David Montgomery had begun to write labor history
as an aspect of a social history of working people responding to a
process of industrialization itself involving broad changes in both
society and culture. They and others emphasized new dimensions of
labor history, particularly the need to examine working-class communities, organized and unskilled workers, and ethnic and racial minorities, all of which had traditionally been slighted in the earlier
narrow economic concentration on the evolution of "mature" trade
unionism.[2]

New directions in American labor history were complemented in the
late 1960s and early 1970s by the enormously influential work of the
English Marxist historians, Eric J. Hobsbawm and Edward P. Thompson, and by the European-inspired advances in what came to be called
the "new social history."[3] By the middle seventies, labor history in the
United States principally focused on working-class social history. The
"from the bottom-up" community-centered case study was now as
characteristic of the field as trade-union histories and labor economics
had once been. These developments were never hailed as the "new
labor history," perhaps because they were not as dependent on the
innovations in quantification and methodology that seemed so profoundly "new" in economic, social, and, to some extent, political
studies. But the evolution of labor history involved no less dramatic a
reconceptualization of the objects and methods of historical study.

Readers of this collection have available to them elsewhere a series of
thorough and recent review essays from a variety of perspectives survey-
ing these changes in critical depth.[4] We take it as a given that the
working-class history emergent in the 1960s and 1970s came as a
necessary corrective to what preceded it, and that its accomplishments
have been substantial. Since our collection represents the work of what
might be considered a new generation of labor historians, it will be
most useful in this introduction to discuss how a new orientation is
coming to be refined, extended, and to some extent redirected in the
work of contemporary scholars.

Our reading of the range of work presented to us for inclusion in this
volume suggests that many current historians are striving to develop an
understanding of working-class history integrated in what can be
thought of as horizontal and vertical dimensions. First, to judge from

the essays in this collection, many younger scholars seem concerned about the tendency of local studies, especially those influenced by the new social history, to fragment our understanding of the working class by isolating for intensive study particular dimensions of its structure and experience. Ironically, intellectual fragmentation of this sort mirrors the ways in which contemporary society segments experience and understanding, separating home from workplace and both from community, thereby confusing and obscuring the operation of class in industrial society. By treating phenomena such as social mobility and the family as discrete structures, historians have isolated workers from their full social context, depriving these concerns of the sense of historical process from which their meaning arises. Such social history obscures how social relations stem from production, and the unequal power that flows, in turn, from these relations. Perhaps this may explain why the new social history has found it so hard to focus on the various forms of struggle and organization in working-class communities.

In contrast, the essays in this collection integrate multiple dimensions of the working-class experience within a framework that reveals their interconnections. The combination allows the authors to trace the usually elusive processes of social transformation in concrete settings. Rather than sharing in the common invocation to interdisciplinary social history, these essays are in this sense more accurately characterized as multidimensional and thematic.

Our survey also suggests that many scholars today are endeavoring to integrate working-class history in a vertical sense into a broader discussion of interclass relations. Building on the recent explorations of a working-class culture whose very existence had been denied in the heyday of middle-class consensus history in the 1950s, this scholarly generation inquires as well into the historical relationship between these patterns and the evolving contours of American culture more generally. Industrial capitalism divided the experience of different classes, introducing a substantial segmentation of culture and consciousness. But this was an uneven process, proceeding at different rates and in different ways in economic, social, and political spheres. Accordingly, our authors see in working-class history a changing mix of class-specific values and experiences on the one hand, and those shared among classes in American culture more generally on the other.

As a group these essays strive to achieve this dual integration, but they differ thematically and pursue different interpretations. Rather than force this thematic diversity into artificial categories, the volume is organized chronologically. Let us suggest, however, four basic themes, dimensions which readers can use as a framework in approaching the collection. Although each essay could be cross-indexed under several or all of these headings, we will only identify the individual essays most expressive of each focus.

The exploration of the changing forms and nature of working-class culture—the most direct extension of the social-historical researches of the last decade—is the first dimension. Many of the essays individually explore familiar aspects of the working-class family, associational life, and ethnic culture, while others excavate less well developed areas such as leisure activities or the culture of the workplace. Each of these essays connects culture with class politics, relating cultural formations to the more particular struggles of both organized and unorganized workers against the constraints of class.

Jonathan Prude's essay on New England family-based textile mills during the first third of the nineteenth century, for example, details the social system of family and owner-worker relations as they are shaped by the pressures of early industrialization and traditional expectations. Elizabeth and Kenneth Fones-Wolf study evangelical religion—a subject that has been most fully explored for the nineteenth century—and trace its complex uses in trade-union politics and organization early in the twentieth century.

For Francis Couvares, the development of Pittsburgh's park system and the changing character of participatory and spectator sports are central to the political and class struggle in that city at the turn of the last century. Susan Benson extends our range of study, too, in her discussion of the work culture of female department-store clerks, who control and organize the workplace through implicit codes of conduct. Each of these essays represents the best tradition of recent historical anthropology: they analyze culture not merely as a passive series of isolated and quaint habits or customs, but as it is actively used within society. In these essays, to paraphrase the anthropologist Sidney Mintz,[5] society is the arena and working-class culture is the complex of attitudes, traditions, and associations elaborated by workers in their struggle to make their history in that arena.

A second theme of the collection is the effort to ground working-class history in a more precise history of capitalism. This development parallels the direction of the broadened study of working-class culture. In a sense, the narrower scope of the Wisconsin school proceeded from an interpretation of industrialization that focused on the transformation of artisanal craft economy into one based on mechanization, the factory, and industrial organization. As we have noted, labor history in the 1960s expanded considerably our understanding of these processes.

This later historiography viewed class as a set of changing historical relationships and not as a fixed group stratification—as a process, not as a series of results. To the extent that one takes the term at all seriously, then, a social history of the American working class must be set within the evolving social relations of capitalism.

Nonetheless, these social relations have been difficult to explore. Much cultural history and, for all its methodological sophistication, much of the recent social history, has been enclosed within the concept of the "industrial" revolution—the factory and technological change—as the dominant reality of industrial life, often relying on the all-explaining tautologies of "modernization." These formulations tend to be organized by misleading and rigid dichotomies—the division between pre-industrial and industrial workers, between traditional and modern, between workplace and home, between male producers and female consumers, and so on. These dichotomies undermine history as process; they cannot account for the complex ways in which there is continuity even in change, the ways that conflicting groups—including dominant as well as submissive ones—mediate each other's responses and give shape to one another.

The essays in this collection recast these categories to fit the socially complex transitions from commercial to industrial to monopoly capitalism, suggesting how these changes were understood, engaged, and responded to by working people. The result is a more subtle and descriptive economic history. Christine Stansell's and Sean Wilentz's essays, for example, both proceed from an understanding of the metropolitan economy of mid-nineteenth-century New York as itself a significant new form of industrial organization. In Wilentz's essay we see how artisanal rituals addressed the constraints and demands of this changing urban political economy, while Stansell demonstrates how this framework helps us to appreciate the centrality of women's outwork and sweated labor as a fundamental yet otherwise invisible dimension of early industrialization. In a later period, the complexities of the varying forms of capital in the garment trades help Steve Fraser explain how the history of the Amalgamated Clothing Workers reflects its socially complex constituency and its relation to the state. Finally, Couvares's Pittsburgh study argues the importance of structural economic bases for understanding the shaping and commodification of mass leisure.

The collection's third dimension is its concern with political ideas and culture, a concern both growing from and yet qualifying the focus on class culture and capitalism. This interest in political ideas and activity has not generally characterized labor history; this interest was patronized as utopian and immature in the most traditional works and dismissed as superficial and tangential by recent historians more concerned with social structure. It is in this context that the essays most explicitly seek the vertical integration discussed earlier; they acknowledge the need to understand political ideas and forms of expression rooted in a broader American history as a central element in working-class experience. This renewed interest in political ideas and ideology, however, should not be confused with the current reaction against social history. Recent neoconservative fashion has dictated a rejection of the concern with minorities, women, and radicals as frivolous, holding this to be a sort of intellectual virus contracted during the 1960s and curable now through heavy doses of a more serious traditional history, one stressing the role of elites and the expression of their power in political life. These essays involve no such recantation; they do not argue that politics needs to be put back into social history. Rather, their intention is to dissolve the division between the two.

Seen as the arena in which social power is consciously exercised, struggled over, and allocated, this political inquiry is also broadly based: the essays deal with the politics of space, family, and neighborhood. Discussions such as those by Couvares on Pittsburgh's parks or by Benson on the department-store sales counter demonstrate that the history of the working class under capitalism involves a struggle for power mounted and expressed in a variety of public and private forms.

But the essays are perhaps most distinctive in addressing the more conventionally understood sphere of political values, institutions, and behavior. Many of them ask how a broader American political culture mediated the effects of class divisions introduced so relentlessly by the growth of capitalism. In the process, political ideas introduced values, language, and organizational forms that working people employed along a wide spectrum ranging from resistance to accommodation.

It has been all too easy to assume that the symbols and institutions of American politics have always been as defiantly bourgeois as they have become in the mid and late twentieth century, to assume that the working class faced and faces, in these forms, only the hegemonic power of an ascendant bourgeois ideology. The history in these essays, in contrast, shows that republican ideology served perhaps longer than any other dimension of American culture as a legitimization of working-class values; these political ideas could be a bulwark against the corrosive power of capitalism to refashion American culture in its own image. Many of the essays testify to the ways in which political analysis is becoming an increasingly critical tool for understanding the social transformation of the working class and its society. Sean Wilentz elucidates how changing artisan participation in New York City parades reveals the importance of republican values in working-class culture. A distinctly different tradition of republicanism later appears in Joshua Freeman's discussion of New York transportation workers in the 1930s, where a nationalist Irish republicanism intersects with radical politics. Steve Fraser's essay, in turn, considers the role of Jewish radical political culture, as it gives political direction to the New York garment workers' union. Leon Fink's essay on the Knights of Labor is the collection's most explicit example of this dimension. With reference to the historiography on both the Knights and the American working class more generally, Fink argues for the central importance of political activity to the Knights, and shows how it helps to clarify their historical meaning as a movement.

The fourth dimension of the collection closes the circle, recalling the original trade-union focus of the labor economists and showing the centrality this deserves when recast within a more broadly conceived working-class history. Labor historians today are turning to the history of trade unionism to a degree that was not true even several years previously, when the focus of so many dissertations was on community social history. The renewed focus is also partially a reflection of the heightened interest of labor historians in the more recent twentieth-century past. Through the mid-1970s, the most innovative studies in working-class social history tended to concentrate on the industrializing era through the turn of the century; the post-World War I era remained by and large the preserve of more traditional trade-union historians, labor economists, and students of industrial relations. We can only suggest why this was so: labor historians focused on the last half of the nineteenth century in part because census records used in the new social history were available for that period and in part because the nascent labor movement may have seemed to New Left scholars, shaped by the political activism of the 1960s, to hold greater historical relevance for labor radicalism than the more formal era of the AFL-CIO. Regardless, our essays indicate these preferences are all fading. As a result, powerful new approaches to twentieth-century labor history are emerging. The Elizabeth and Kenneth Fones-Wolf study of Labor Forward, for instance, explores on a national basis the complex relationship between craft unionism, religious traditions, radicalism, and the American Federation of Labor at a crucial twentieth-century turning point. The essays by Fraser, Freeman, and Nelson Lichtenstein bring to the study of some modern unions virtually all of what the social-historical sensitivity has taught us to observe: they examine the relationship of workplace to community, of class to ethnicity, of worker militance to political radicalism, of labor to the new corporate state, and they show the centrality of all of these to the history of particular trade unions.

These twentieth-century essays make explicit what we think the entire collection tends to demonstrate: the heightened capacity of working-class history to offer insights into the very nature of American society and the processes of capitalist transformation. This redefined labor history is not all history; but it is also a good bit more than just another subcategory for the bibliographers, another product pushed through the tireless mill of academic specialization. Building as it does on previous work and setting out in new, more integrative directions, the working-class history we see embodied in these essays gives every promise of contributing to what for decades has been the unrealized potential of social history: to move beyond the history of groups, institutions, and events, and to approximate in a deeper sense an understanding of the history of a society.

One final comment on our process of selection. The collection has been assembled on two criteria: the quality of the individual essays and the degree to which they represent the thematic and historiographical direction of current work. Our choices, of course, had to be based on what kind of work was being done and what was made available to us. We think the essays in this collection represent the first-rate scholarship and imaginative, powerful analysis of current working-class history, but the selections also tell us something about remaining lacunae in the field. While we can see the full integration of labor and women's history in the writing of historians such as Stansell and Benson, the new trends of labor history have not yet blended with Black and Hispanic history, to the detriment of both. In addition, major groups of workers remain largely neglected, from white-collar professionals to the uniformed services and the largest male group of all, construction workers. Finally, one looks to the next generation of labor historians for study of post-World War II America—a world where workers and their families struggle in the context of multinational corporations, new patterns and demands for consumption, and a State variously an ally, employer, or warden.

Clearly much still needs to be done. Yet that is not to minimize the considerable achievement presented in the following essays. While we have arrived at a rough chronological balance in the collection, we elected to lean to thematic coverage, in the hope that the conceptual framework that develops through the volume will prove useful to those interested in pursuing such historical research themselves in diverse settings. More generally, we think this the best way to introduce readers to the extraordinary richness of current work and to its value for understanding the complex heritage of American working-class history.

NOTES

1. See John R. Commons et al., *History of Labour in the United States*, 4 vols. (New York, 1918-35); Selig Perlman, *A History of Trade Unionism in the United States* (New York, 1922), and *A Theory of the Labor Movement* (New York, 1928); and Phillip Taft, *The AFL in the Time of Gompers* (New York, 1957).

2. David Brody, *Steelworkers in America: The Nonunion Era* (Cambridge, Mass., 1960); Herbert G. Gutman, *Work, Culture, and Society in Industrializing America: Essays in American Working-Class and Social History* (New York, 1976); and David Montgomery, *Beyond Equality: Labor and the Radical Republicans, 1862-1872* (New York, 1967), and *Workers' Control in America: Studies in the History of Work, Technology, and Labor Struggles* (New York, 1979).

3. See, for example, Edward P. Thompson, *The Making of the English Working Class* (London, 1963); Eric J. Hobsbawm, *Primitive Rebels: Studies in Archaic Forms of Social Movement in the Nineteenth and Twentieth Centuries* (Manchester, 1959), and *Labouring Men: Studies in the History of Labour* (London, 1964); George Rude, *The Crowd in History* (New York, 1964); Charles Tilly, *The Vendee* (Cambridge, Mass., 1959); and Louise A. Tilly and Joan W. Scott, *Women, Work, and the Family* (New York, 1978).

4. For example, see David Brody, "The Old Labor History and the New: In Search of an American Working Class," *Labor History*, 20 (1979), 111-26; Mike Davis, "Why the U.S. Working Class Is Different," *New Left Review*, 123 (1980), 3-46, and "The Barren Marriage of American Labor and the Democratic Party," *New Left Review*, 124 (1980), 43-84; David Montgomery, "To Study the People: The American Working Class," *Labor History*, 21 (1980), 485-512; and in response to Montgomery from the point of view of the first generation, Robert Ozanne, "Trends in American Labor History," *Labor History*, 21 (1980), 513-21.

5. Sidney Mintz, Foreword to *Afro-American Anthropology: Contemporary Perspectives*, ed. Norman Whitten, Jr., and John F. Szwed (New York, 1970).

Working-Class America

# The Social System
# of Early New England Textile Mills:
# A Case Study, 1812-40

JONATHAN PRUDE

"A cotton factory is a school for the
improvement of ingenuity and industry. . . ."
—Samuel Ogden, 1815

"[Our employee] James Fenton ran away
yesterday and Samuel Greene has gone to
day. . . . If it is suffered to pass another will go
tomorrow and so on until they are all gone. . . ."
—Samuel Slater to Almy and Brown,
Mar. 20, 1797

## I

In 1812, in the rural Massachusetts township of Dudley, fifty miles
southwest of Boston, five local entrepreneurs built a woolen mill,
several tenements, and a store. Initially titled Merino Village, this
manufacturing compound suffered reversals and in time even passed
on to other proprietors. But in one form or another it remained a
presence in Dudley's history throughout the next two generations.[1] In
1813, Samuel Slater—the celebrated English immigrant to Rhode
Island who in 1793 had helped construct America's first successful
water-powered spinning mill—arrived in Oxford, abutting Dudley to
the east, and opened a cotton factory. Along with its workshops, store,
cottages, and boardinghouse, this establishment was styled the East
Village. By 1828, Slater had added the South Village woolen mill and
the North Village thread factory, both in Dudley—his three enclaves
lying north of the Merino Village in a triangle roughly four miles
around and all of them, like the Merino Village, surviving downturns
and setbacks to endure through the succeeding decades.[2]

We remain curiously ignorant about such "manufactories." As vanguard institutions of the American factory system, New England's antebellum textile mills have, of course, received abundant scholarly attention. But most writers have lavished their energies on the large, self-consciously famous "boardinghouse" establishments: the factories of Lowell, Waltham, and other urban or rapidly urbanizing manufacturing centers; the factories which, beginning with Waltham's prototype Boston Manufacturing Company in 1814, undertook a fully integrated production process encompassing machine-weaving as well as machine-spinning; and (perhaps their best-known feature) the mills which sought to recruit into their workrooms and carefully supervised boardinghouses single young women from the "virtuous rural homes" of middling yeomen.[3] The social and economic importance of these mills—even their reputation among contemporary European literati— cannot be disputed. But focusing so exclusively on their story has distorted our perception of early textile factories and thus, given the pioneering role of these factories, skewed our understanding of basic patterns in early American industrialization.

This is because scattered through the antebellum Northeast were also mills like the Slater and Merino factories. Usually small and moderately capitalized, these factories were not rooted in cities but "studded thickly along . . . wild and rapid streams" of rural communities—and so carried the phenomenon of textile industrialization far into the Yankee hinterland.[4] These were also factories which, for many years, commonly "put out" various tasks to farming households outside the mill villages: the task of picking clean the raw fibers used by early mills, for example, and the task of weaving mechanically spun yarn into cloth.[5] And finally, these were factories which followed the "Rhode Island" or "family" plan—inaugurated by Slater himself in the 1790s— of recruiting workers from across the social and economic spectrum and of hiring households as well as unattached individuals.[6]

The distinction between family and boardinghouse factories was, to be sure, neither permanent nor rigid. After 1840 pressures within the industry and the influx of immigrant operatives combined to meld the two types; and even in the 1820s and 1830s some mills combined traits of both genres. By all indications, however, rural family enterprises like the Slater and Merino villages comprised the typical format of textile manufactories throughout the early nineteenth century, and hence were the typical setting for America's earliest factory employees.[7] The scholarly inclination to overlook these country mills is thus an anomaly that needs to be corrected.

This is the most general and obvious rationale for the study that follows. But an equally pressing reason to explore the Slater and Merino villages concerns the relations between labor and management that developed within these compounds. To most scholars, the key indices of employer-employee interaction in early Yankee mills have been strikes or some other overt gestures of protest. Thus they have either stressed the relative absence of such incidents and concluded that "labor militancy was rare" because operatives "worked hard and for the most part without complaint"; or they have used the few upheavals that did transpire to argue that millworkers were militant in the orthodox labor historian's sense of the word: capable of mounting large, explicit confrontations.[8] The Slater and Merino villages suggest another perspective. On the one hand, only one insignificant turnout occurred in these factories before 1840; and exploring the history of these mills throws light on why large-scale confrontations were uncommon among antebellum operatives generally and family mill operatives particularly. On the other hand, Slater and Merino workers were not passive. Quite the contrary: there developed between employees and employers in these four compounds intricate patterns of give and take, of managerial demands evoking operatives' efforts to win greater earnings and (what was equally important) greater independence, of struggles and compromises. Reflecting relationships among workers as well as between workers and their supervisors, expressing goals and strategies that never changed and others that evolved, these patterns defined the fundamental social system of the Slater and Merino villages.

And they do more besides. While the Slater and Merino villages were not the first American textile manufactories, employers and employees working in these enclaves still ranked among the earliest new-world participants in factory labor. As a result, their complex choreography of friction and accommodation should actually be viewed as an early installment in a critically important educational process: a kind of learning which is unavoidable in industrializing societies; which initial generations of every American occupation affected by industrialization had to undergo; and which—in different ways and degrees—in fact often provided the prelude and backdrop to whatever overt militancy some American industrial workers achieved. Put briefly, what early textile employers and employees taught themselves was how to respond to one another. They deciphered—or, more accurately, they created—the rules of the game for being industrial employers and employees. And by doing so they implemented a pivotal lesson in the social meaning of industrial capitalism.

## II

The size and structure of society in the Slater and Merino villages can be set out fairly easily. Available data suggest that between the early 1820s and the early 1830s the Merino labor force grew from around 60 to 108, of whom 40 percent were men, 50 percent were "women and girls," and 33 percent were attached to families. The aggregate roster of the three Slater compounds increased from 54 operatives in 1813 to around 260 in 1840, and in the East Village—requiring fewer skilled adult employees than a woolen factory—men accounted for 25 percent of the employees, women and children hovered around one-fifth and one-half, respectively, and two-thirds were attached to families living inside the compound. To these statistics we should add the ten to fifteen managerial officials—all adult, all male—resident in each village. And we should also add the various mill-village inhabitants—of both sexes, all ages, and totaling perhaps 20 percent of each compound's labor force—who coresided with working parents, siblings, or children but did not themselves hold berths.[9]

But how did this social structure function? What were its dynamics and lines of force? We may begin unraveling these issues by exploring management and the regimen it sought to impose. And the point of departure here is the highly personal character of the Slater and Merino administrative structure. For a striking fact disclosed by the records is that several Merino owners served supervisory stints at their mills, and that even in the early 1830s—after Boston investors had purchased stock—the entire proprietary retinue met regularly at the Dudley factory.[10] It is striking too that Samuel Slater, despite business interests scattered throughout New England, frequently visited his southern Massachusetts mills. Along with his sons, who began shouldering administrative duties around 1825 and who took control of the villages after their father's death in 1835, Slater intervened frequently: establishing wage guidelines, evaluating work turned out, setting requirements for "steady," punctual, "industrious and temperate" workers, providing favorite employees with cash gifts, scolding others for "unfaithfulness"—all enough to communicate a continuing personal involvement with the "hands."[11]

Below the proprietors were the agents, charged with overall daily supervision of the villages, and the room overseers, responsible for the "business" of each factory room. Hired mainly from mercantile positions or administrative posts in other mills, and working for the most part in secluded offices, the former officials were not intimate with the rank and file under their authority. But agents were sufficiently involved in the ongoing operation of these mills to develop ties with some operatives and to be at least known to all of them. Overseers were even more familiar to the labor force. Typically recruited from experienced male operatives (one-third of Slater's East Village overseers were drawn from the payroll of this compound) these front-line supervisors were every day brought into direct, continuous contact with the hands under their charge.[12]

Coupled with this administrative inclination to personal contact—providing an important animus for this tendency and legitimizing its capacity to embrace both strictness and generosity—was management's claim of "interest" in employees. Antebellum mill masters (or commentators writing on their behalf) commonly declared that efforts by managers to prevent tardiness and drinking, for example, were merely "prudent and effectual" attacks "against disorderly and immoral behaviour"; and along with more obvious expressions of altruism—such as Slater's cash presents—these efforts disclosed the industrialists' "kindly and paternal" concern in the workers' "welfare."[13]

Given the frequency with which such interest was proclaimed, it is scarcely surprising that scholars have often described antebellum factory management as paternalistic. In the hands of recent writers the characterization can be used pejoratively (in the sense of overly intrusive) as well as approvingly; and it is conventional scholarly wisdom that, whether judged positively or negatively, paternalism faded after immigrants began entering the mills in the 1840s and 1850s. The rubric itself, however, remains firmly embedded in the scholarship of early Yankee manufactories.[14]

This, in turn, has created difficulties. The administrative order ramifying through mills like the Slater and Merino factories was complex, and if it reflected personal involvement and interest it also reflected an array of contrary themes. We can continue to call these factories paternalistic: the term usefully underscores important dimensions of their regimen. But we need to establish precisely what paternalism meant in these compounds. And this requires examining elements and trends generally ignored by both antebellum commentators and modern historians.

We should note, first, that management's rhetoric of paternalism, while not necessarily hypocritical, was manifestly self-serving. By following the long line of Protestant moralizing that fused righteousness with diligence, mill masters could simultaneously assert concern for their workers' well-being and strive to inculcate values encouraging productivity. Even more important, factory managers used paternalistic slogans to counter the suspicions with which late eighteenth- and early nineteenth-century New Englanders greeted manufactories. Yankees were not insensitive to the tax revenues and jobs textile mills represented.

But from the outset there was worry that American factories would create a permanent, degraded proletariat (as they supposedly had in England), or would disrupt customary riparian privileges, or would find some way to avoid paying local taxes. And over time concern also grew that industrialists accustomed to "ruling . . . their mills" might "step out into the community with the same air. . . . What is this but tyranny?"[15]

Invoking paternalism could not forestall all these anxieties. But in an era when milldams blocking local streams were often met with lawsuits and occasionally with physical attacks, when tight labor markets (an issue even more fundamental and far more often confronted) left many manufacturers struggling to find hands—at such a time it made sense to assure New Englanders that factories gave operatives the same "moral protection of their character" as "virtuous rural homes." And some country mill masters (including Slater) pushed further. They offered what amounted to a counterimage of rustic New England in which factories offset the "ignorance, weakness, and barbarism" they saw as imminent in rural life. In part, it was said, mills effected this cure by providing markets for foodstuffs and thus galvanizing an otherwise "sluggish" farming population. But it was also argued that paternalistic managers provided relief from the "neglect" many children suffered in rural homes, and that "interested" employers helped poor and unskilled workers by providing both jobs and a "strict though mild and paternal scrutiny" to instill good habits.[16]

By every indication, the Slater and Merino mills rang the changes on paternalism in all these ways—and in one other way as well. In company with other country factories, the North, South, East, and Merino villages found particular utility in using assertions of paternalistic interest to justify intrusions into the operatives' family life. There can be little question that domestic relationships were vitally important in the Slater and Merino compounds. Often it was kinship that drew operatives into the mills: "My sister is coming ther to work this week," announced a prospective Merino employee, "and I will come in two weeks."[17] Once within the enclaves, moreover, workers attached to families usually coresided (sometimes with boarders) in small cottages provided by the factories. But more than a physical locus, the family provided a close-knit haven, a continuing refuge, from the pressures of factory discipline.[18] While mill supervisors apparently relied on parents to keep order over their children after working hours, there is no evidence families systematically cooperated with management's efforts to produce industrious young employees. And while, over time, domestic ties were doubtless strained by mill-village life, it is clear families persisted as significant institutions for many Slater and Merino operatives. But what the family did not do—what it was not permitted to do—was work together. Siblings sometimes labored in close proximity, but Slater and Merino managers appear to have systematically separated parents and children during the working day.

Probably the mills feared that adults placed near their offspring would challenge the overseers, or, if overseers themselves, would cause friction by favoring their own youngsters. Their concern, coupled with the emerging pattern of awarding skilled "male" jobs to unmarried men or to teenagers promoted from below, increasingly forced fathers to remain idle, leave the villages for jobs elsewhere, find work on neighboring farms, or content themselves with outdoor duties for the mills. Coupled with the antebellum prejudice against wage-earning mothers, management's suspicion of parental authority inside the mills led to complete exclusion of married women from the Slater and Merino labor force in the years prior to 1840.[19]

These were the developments establishments like the Slater and Merino villages sought to justify with paternalism. Managers, it was said, could undermine daytime parental authority because they were themselves acting *in loco parentis.* Apprenticeship offered an obvious precedent for this role, but, save for a few paupers and some trainees in management and cassimere weaving, Slater and Merino officials avoided "unfree" laborers.[20] Instead they took schoolmasters as their model, arguing that mill families "delegated" temporary authority to their employers just as Yankee households surrendered authority to teachers.[21] Again, the rationale by no means precluded resentment, but it may well have dampened its intensity.

Such was the self-interest behind management's rhetoric. But we must also consider structural limitations of paternalism in the Slater and Merino villages—and the consequent distinction between the form managerial interest took in these compounds and the pattern existing in "Waltham" mills. Unlike the latter enterprises—with their carefully monitored tenements, curfews, and mandatory church attendance[22]— the four Slater and Merino compounds made little effort to control their employees' lives after quitting time. Because these establishments were relatively isolated, most workers depended upon company housing for residences and on company stores for provisions. But it was rarely required that workers use only factory retailers; boardinghouses (for unattached laborers) evidently posted few rules; and because of their reliance on the after-hours authority of parents, family cottages were supervised not at all.

Reliance on family government may also explain the mills' relaxed attitude toward religious and secular instruction. Though often pious themselves, and though doubtless pleased to find operatives occasionally participating in local revivals and churches (most often those run by Methodists and Baptists), Slater and Merino managers built no chapels within the villages and left "devine services" entirely optional. And so with secular instruction: efforts were made to establish schools in or near the villages during the 1820s, but since attendance was not mandatory and since most operative-households preferred wage earners to scholars, mill children generally escaped formal education.[23]

From another perspective, it was the market that limited paternalism. Whatever their claims to serve the workers' welfare, decisions to expand or trim the Slater and Merino rosters, for example, were dictated almost entirely by sales. Generally between 1810 and 1840, conditions permitted expansion. But the Slaters laid off employees during commercial downturns, and the Merino Village closed completely during the 1816 depression.[24] Moreover, as factories grew more numerous and competitive during the 1820s and 1830s, Slater and Merino managers began jettisoning less profitable elements of their payrolls even during good times. Most dramatically, they dismissed their part-time outworking employees during the 1820s, replacing them with more efficient full-time pickers (mainly children) laboring inside the factory villages, and full-time power loom operatives (mainly young women) posted in the mills. Indeed, by 1830 even the skilled woolen handloom weavers resident inside the South and Merino compounds had been largely supplanted by operatives "tending" water-driven weaving machines. And in the winter of 1828, feeling increasingly pressed by rival mills, Slater pointed out to his supervisors that "as days are now short and cold and much time is taken up by . . . [outdoor workers] . . . in thrashing their hands," agents should "discontinue [i.e., dismiss] all you can."[25]

Impersonal economic factors shaped the income as well as the number of Slater and Merino employees. Proprietors might occasionally distribute cash presents, but the formal bargains management offered were always confined by guidelines—increasingly rigid as time went on—designed to protect profit margins.[26] In themselves these formulas did not preclude comparatively high wages—a fact the mills naturally emphasized in their recruiting campaigns. While skilled men earned two to four times more than women and children, and while the presence of youngsters kept overall Slater and Merino wages about 10 percent below comparable "boardinghouse" statistics, the average price of labor in these villages—fifty-one cents per day in 1832—encompassed rates surpassing most nonindustrial pay scales.[27] But this is misleading. Absenteeism and another economic factor—living expenses—quietly undermined operatives' earnings. Skilled machinists and mule spinners, especially those unattached to households, could earn $200-$300 above room and board. But members of families whose male heads were unemployed or held only outdoor jobs were sometimes rudely shocked to find that after a year's labor they were actually "owing the mill."[28]

The lack of involvement in nonworking hours and the force of economic pressures were two factors that significantly diluted management's personal interest. Technology was another. By 1830, perhaps 70 percent of the workers on the Slater and Merino payrolls tended machines driven "perpetually" or partially by water. For these employees (mainly women and children), the personal authority of the overseer was mediated through the unprecedented stricture of mechanically imposed work-rhythms. It is likely children managed to play between their chores, and all "tenders" enjoyed some respite—daily for lunch, occasionally for repairs. We should also recall that operating machines was initially considered "not half so hard" as many agricultural chores.[29] But the demands of the pounding looms and spindles pressed with cumulative weight upon millworkers and, like a number of other pressures, became more intense with passing years. Again we may cite the shift from handlooms to power looms. Beyond this, beginning around 1817, managers sought to improve their competitive position by increasing both the number and speed of machines assigned to operatives.[30]

Finally, there was the bureaucratic dimension of the mills: the established procedures and bylaws which, however freighted with moralism, inevitably introduced a flavor of formality and even distrust into employer-employee relations. Although "[R]ules and regulations" ran like stiff girders all through the industrial order, they were especially obvious in management's treatment of time. It was not, after all, the length of the factory schedule that was new; during harvests rural Yankees labored the same twelve-hour days, six-day weeks early textile mills required. Similarly, management's stress on punctuality expressed values long since put forward by Benjamin Franklin and countless Puritan divines. What was new in the mills was the rigidity with which the schedule and norms were promulgated. In factories, seventy-two-hour weeks were a constant requirement, even during winter months when the mills ran past dusk and had to rely on candlelight. Moreover, because they generally paid employees by the hour, managers reckoned each worker's attendance with unprecedented care. Transcribed in coded shorthand into an array of interlocking ledgers and Time Books, daily punctuality of Merino employees was measured to the nearest three hours—twice as accurately as the attendance of most nonindustrial employees. The Slater books were equally precise before 1817; thereafter, as a further emblem of mounting stringency, the standard became the nearest ninety minutes.[31]

Such, then, was paternalism in the Slater and Merino villages: on the one hand, interested and intimate; on the other hand, impersonal, self-serving, and bounded—in some respects increasingly bounded—by technology, bureaucracy, and the vicissitudes of the market. This complex evolving alloy of attitudes and disciplines comprised the stance management came to hold within these manufactories. This is what pressed upon the workers and, by pressing, evoked reactions that shaped the social system of the North, South, East, and Merino Villages.

III

But to understand precisely how operatives learned to respond to the industrial regimen we must first consider how they responded to one another. The strength and scope of relationships among workers, the degree to which they felt isolated or bound into group loyalties—all this critically affected how they coped with factory life. Often, as we have seen, employees were linked by kinship. But camaradarie in the mills, if it existed at all, rested on ties stretching beyond the household. It is the nature of extradomestic bonds that requires attention here.

Such bonds obviously existed. In the glimpses of daily life provided by the Slater and Merino records we find millworkers standing in for absent colleagues; and we find friendship leading on to something more—65 percent of East Village operatives who married during their stints took another village resident as mate.[32] But the critical question is whether these liaisons gave workers a continuing sense of unity, and here glimpses are inadequate. The problem requires systematic investigation of factors which, though perhaps only occasionally apparent to workers, constantly conditioned extrafamilial relations.

One such factor was the extraordinary heterogeneity of the labor force: a pervasive lack of common denominators that weakened links among nonrelatives. Some of this diversity has already been signaled by the range of skills and income levels among the workers. The lines between family and nonfamily operatives, and between operatives from different families, are also relevant here: even as they provided after-hours relief from managerial supervision, kinship ties tended to deflect energy from more inclusive alliances among workers. But beyond these were further divisions, less immediately obvious but in some ways deeper, sharper, and even more corrosive.

It is significant, for example, that workers lacked common geographic origins and so typically entered the villages as strangers. Most Slater and Merino employees in this period were native-born Americans, sharing both a common language and general traditions of republicanism and Protestantism. But drawn by advertisements and

word of mouth ("I have heard you was in want of some one . . ."),
operatives came from all over southern New England, sometimes from
New York, and even from Delaware. Few were local. Less than 33
percent of Slater and Merino operatives can be definitely shown to have
arrived from communities immediately surrounding these factories.[33]

To their varied geographic provenance, employees added a mixed
sociological background. There was no "average" millworker in the
Slater and Merino villages. Some operatives (exact numbers are not
possible) entered the factories because they supposed—despite the
tainted reputation of manufactories and the low net earnings befalling
some employees—that millwork would provide an interesting and
profitable interlude. Comprised principally of individuals rather than
families, this relatively prosperous contingent included young adults
waiting upon inheritances, property owners and craftsmen seeking
funds to enlarge their estates, and women like those the boardinghouse
mills claimed to employ before immigrants arrived: "respectable"
women who became operatives to sample the independence of their
own wage-earning jobs, to provide financial help to their families, to
increase their dowries and find husbands, or perhaps simply to escape
the endless round of chores on country homesteads.[34]

Unlike boardinghouse proprietors, however, family mill masters like
the Slaters and the Merino owners acknowledged from the outset that
they also employed "destitute . . . and very poor" workers who embraced factory berths out of economic necessity.[35] This, of course,
dovetailed neatly with the orchestration of paternalistic rhetoric explored earlier: many mills guaranteed to preserve their workers' character; family factories also claimed to assist and reform New England's
more needy citizens. So it was the Slater and Merino villages hired
landless laborers, both rural and urban, often with their families and
some with extra children "[made] up from the neighbors." And they
engaged yeomen whose "small and poor farms" no longer provided
support, artisans and small shopkeepers overwhelmed by debt, and
teenagers from poor or middling households, expecting little or no
patrimony and obliged to start out on their own.[36]

A third group was composed of veterans: employees who arrived
already seasoned in millwork and who, by all indications, moved on to
other factories after leaving the Slater and Merino compounds. In the
earliest New England mills such operatives had been skilled Irish and
English workers. At least by 1815, however, veterans also included
native-born workers. These were skilled and unskilled Americans,
single men and women (the latter especially after power looms were
introduced), widows depending on wages earned by their children,
whole families ("I can spine or weave and one boy that can spine one

gerl that can wave on a pour loom . . .")—who were all convinced
millwork offered the highest wages they could expect but who also,
sometimes, were trapped on a treadmill of low net earnings and unable
to move easily to other employment. Their extended commitment to
factory work did not necessarily make these workers the permanent
factory proletariat Americans feared; by all accounts, experienced employees moved not only between mills but also in and out of millwork,
and few ended their working lives as factory hands.[37] Yet veterans
deserve notice as people committing many years to the mills.

Middling, poor, and veteran—combined with the other differenti-
ations etched into the work force, such divisions, while doubtless
overlapping, must have affected relations among the operatives. Arriving from widely scattered communities, their experience within the
compounds varying according to job, income, and the presence of kin,
Slater and Merino operatives could only have found the lack of common backgrounds and expectations a further hindrance to fellowship.

These were the consequences of the workers' heterogeneity. But there
were also other barriers to camaraderie. Contact among operatives
inside the mill buildings, for example, was constrained by the ceaseless
attention required in tending machines, by the patrolling overseers,
and by the deafening racket—"like frogs and Jewsharps all mixed
together"—thrown up by the technology.[38] Then too, the characteristic
transiency of Slater and Merino workers (both novices and veterans)
further reduced opportunities to develop ties. Operatives did not commonly limit their engagements to a single season, but periodic managerial efforts to balance reduced sales with reduced payrolls and—as we
shall later have reason to stress—the workers' own restlessness combined to keep stints quite brief. Employment periods increased somewhat over time, but in 1830 only 10 percent of the East Village payroll
remained at that enclave three or more years, most (51 percent) remained nine months or less, and about 6 percent (10 percent in the
Merino Village) stayed less than half of any given month.[39]

A further critically divisive feature of life in these villages was the
absence of settings where operatives could gather communally after
factory hours. While the isolation of the Slater and Merino mills
encouraged workers to use company housing, the fact that operatives
were dispersed through both tenements and family cottages meant
residences in these compounds never became the social centers into
which Waltham-style boardinghouses—for all their tight supervision—
commonly evolved.[40] Moreover, because the four villages were isolated,
operatives found it difficult to tap facilities in surrounding communities. Indeed, coupled with residency requirements, the logistical
problem of reaching town meetings discouraged adult men in the

villages from participating even in local political activities. It is true (as earlier noted) that some workers trekked to nearby churches; and even without convenient meeting places some collective festivities— July 4th parties, for example—probably took place.[41] But unlike employees in urban factories, Slater and Merino operatives did not find the resources of broader community life ready at hand. As a consequence, these workers could neither draw on nor generate the clubs, societies, and voluntary associations that buoyed wage laborers in more developed milieus.

Thus engendered by the character of the work force and thus amplified by practical obstacles to unity, centrifugal pressures tugged continuously at Slater and Merino employees, limiting the intensity and range of their nonfamilial ties. There are signs, however, that over time the divisions following from the intrinsic variety of the labor force may have grown less pronounced. Though sketchy (and again resisting definitive quantification) the evidence suggests that between 1810 and 1840 veterans in the Slater and Merino villages increased sufficiently to become socially, and perhaps numerically, dominant. Certainly there are indications managers were increasingly determined to hire experienced employees: to avoid the burden of training green hands, Slater stipulated after 1815 that operatives who had already "worked in a Mill would be preferred."[42] It is also demonstrable that during the 1820s increasing numbers of incoming operatives of all skill levels were actually returning to mills they had previously quit: between 1820 and 1830 the proportion of East Village employees who had logged earlier stints in this mill rose from 4.5 percent to just under 33 percent. Together with references to experience at other establishments ("I have worked for the Pocasset Co. over 16 years and I think I should be able to suit you . . .") these clues indicate an expanding presence of workers thoroughly familiar with manufactories.[43]

This in turn evidently promoted a more dense and self-conscious occupational culture. By the 1820s Slater and Merino operatives were routinely manipulating a specialized jargon of "slubbing billys" and "dresser-warpers." Moreover (again despite the absence of convenient meeting places) workers had by this point probably appropriated the English operatives' custom of bracketing the months of candlelit work with "lighting up" and "blowing out" parties. This emerging array of arcane terms and ceremonies did not, of course, equal the heritage of older, established crafts. By 1830 the net consequence of an operative culture expanding amidst the divisive pressures of factory life was no more than limited camaraderie: a fraternalism that was most intense among small groups, that did not preclude broader collaborations but failed to encourage a "habit of solidarity" among nonrelatives.[44] Yet there had been change. Within the confines of limited fellowship, the enlarged corps of veterans and their growing web of common experience promoted a measure of increased mutuality. It was, in sum, a work force pushing toward at least somewhat greater unity that confronted—and slowly began learning how to counteract—the variegated but increasingly stiff, impersonal, and harsh regimen of the Slater and Merino villages.

## IV

The relationship that gradually developed between employers and employees in these four compounds took various forms, some of which were devoid of any trace of friction. This was because one strategy Slater and Merino operatives adopted for coping with the industrial order was simply obedience. And this in turn, of course, was in large measure a consequence of the personal and "kindly" dimensions of management's authority and the resulting loyalty and sense of indebtedness some workers came to feel toward their employers.[45]

But workers also acceded to the formal, bureaucratic strictures of the regimen: time discipline, for example. During Slater's first years in Rhode Island, operatives had sometimes drifted away for a few hours or days to pick berries or to protest delayed wage payments. Others, accustomed to the pre-industrial convention of quitting work at sundown, had bridled when mill masters demanded they labor past dusk on winter evenings: "The first night I lit candles," Slater acknowledged in 1795, "[Benchley] sent for his children to come home" and it took "considerable and warm debate" to retrieve them. By 1812, however, a cultural accommodation had taken place. Attendance continued to dip slightly in autumn as operatives took off occasional hours to help harvest nearby fields. But working long days the year round no longer sparked debates, and, by 1830, the average Merino operative—even counting the 10 percent staying only a half a month—registered 77.9 percent perfect attendance. The comparable figure for the East Village was 91.3 percent, which included a steady 20-21 percent with no absenteeism at all.[46]

Such pliability and loyalty obviously raise the possibility that at least some operatives accepted the legitimacy of industrial rhythms and strictures. And the notion becomes all the more compelling when we remember that churchgoing residents of these villages inclined to worship among the discipline-minded Methodists and Baptists. In the end, however, docility is only a small part of the story. Throughout these years, in widely varying ways, Slater and Merino operatives blended obedience and deference with efforts to push back against the men and rules governing them. Prompted by the novel and increasingly intrusive pressures of factory life, prompted also by the unwillingness of post-Revolutionary Americans to submit entirely to a regimen so frequently labeled "tyranny," perhaps inspired by the hostility Yankees occasionally vented at milldams, or by the cocky independence of first-time wage earners—evoked and encouraged in all these ways, resistance emerged as a fundamental motive of the industrial social system.

Often the opposition was individualistic: the fact that even in the 1830s ties among workers remained limited tended to channel opposition into gestures essayed alone or in small groups. Often too it involved operatives' directly challenging fundamental managerial policies or threatening the mills' existence: the broadening accommodation of Yankees to elements of the industrial regimen did not prevent some employees from being thoroughly repulsed by factory life. And often these two themes intersected. Thus, we find parents protesting the daily separation from their children. Peter Mayo—acting alone, refusing to compromise, almost certainly knowing his resistance precluded continuing employment—was dismissed from the East Village in 1827 for trying to "controul his family whilst [it was] under charge of the Overseers."[47]

And thus we find hints of arson. Rumors abounded in antebellum New England that fires suffered by textile factories were often of "incendiary origin." As a result, while the Merino mill never burned, Slater was never certain the several conflagrations striking his properties were all accidental. His suspicions were never proved, nor were the precise issues that might have prompted such attacks ever explained.[48] But if it did occur, this expression of opposition would have closely resembled the uncompromising attacks on milldams Yankees living around factory villages occasionally mounted. And it would clearly disclose the presence of operatives on Slater's payroll committed only marginally to industrialization and deeply offended by its implications.

From the outset, however, many Slater and Merino employees also resisted in ways that accepted the continuing existence of the mills and their own continuing involvement as operatives. This was accommodation that avoided docility. Here workers—not just men, as was the case with the more aggressive opposition, but women and children too—pushed back, but in measured ways: to bolster their earnings or to assert the precious antebellum republican value of independence, and sometimes both at once. Absenteeism should be cited here, for even as punctuality increased, staying away from the mills remained a satisfying, relatively nondisruptive means of expressing autonomy from factory pressures. After all, the attendance rates quoted earlier suggest

that Slater and Merino operatives in 1830 were still absenting themselves about 15 percent of working hours. Equally important, many
millworkers—again acting alone—supplemented their incomes and
demonstrated their independence by stealing raw materials and finished
goods from their employers. The practice was evidently common
among Slater's earliest Rhode Island employees and may well have
looked back to the "almost traditional" thievery in the eighteenth-
century English textile trade.[49] In southern Massachusetts in the early
nineteenth century stealing did not threaten the solvency of Slater and
Merino mills, but officials had "to rise sometime before the sun" if they
hoped to prevent operatives from making off with management's
property.[50]

This inventory of certain and probable resistance—seeking "controul" over their children, arson, absenteeism, stealing—persisted
through the 1830s. As conditions changed, however, such continuity
was bracketed by important shifts in the complexion of resistance.
With the growing realization that textile mills would not soon fade
away, and with the growing number of veterans dependent on these
manufactories, tactics aimed at rejecting or destroying manufacturing
establishments received less emphasis than efforts to achieve a *modus
vivendi* with the industrial order. But at the same time, management's
mounting stringency prompted new and more varied opposition. Thus
by the 1820s there is reason to suppose Slater and Merino employees
had begun sabotaging their machines—not to destroy the mills but
simply to give themselves temporary respite from engines running
"perpetually" at ever faster speeds. And by 1830, East Village residents
had implemented another response to technology: women power-loom
weavers were routinely pacing themselves so that, despite the looms'
steady speed, they could pursue a psychologically more palatable slow-
to-fast weekly work rhythm.[51]

While rooted (like all resistance) in attitudes shared by operatives,
these emerging responses to machine discipline were still essentially
individualistic gestures. The drift toward at least more fellowship
among workers, however, produced a further evolution: by the 1820s
we find hints of collaborative resistance. Admittedly the clues are
elusive: collective opposition only once involved confrontation, and
(like the workers' extrafamilial activities generally) never found institutional expression. Yet there are traces of whispering campaigns and
slowdowns aimed at excessively demanding overseers. There are hints
too of a strange choreography of funeral attendance, by which operatives took half-days off to bury their friends and relatives but declined
to attend services for managers.[52] And we can detect—if only after the
fact, from shifts in factory routine they induced—the goals and efficacy
of these tactics.

In effect, operatives collaborated to fill a vacuum. Lacking established traditions specifying normal demands in factory work, operatives sought to create norms. Time discipline was once more a focus, for if workers balanced punctuality with persisting absenteeism, they also collectively appropriated management's seventy-two-hour week and turned it to their own purposes. Thus, whereas in 1814 Slater's Smithfield employees were "willing to work as long as they do to [i.e., in] Pawtucket," even if that meant a few minutes longer, by the 1830s in the Merino Village and as early as 1817 in the East Village, demands for work beyond seventy-two hours, even five minutes worth, was "extra," to be purchased with "extra" pay.[53] The stringency with which the mills calculated punctuality was thus paralleled by the workers' invention of overtime.

Comparable boundaries appeared around production. In the years before machine-made cloth undercut their position, handloom woolen weavers in the Merino Village set output ceilings and demanded bonuses for added work. Similarly Slater's mule spinners and power-loom weavers did not reject assignments of more and faster machines during the 1820s, but they insisted the added output be accompanied by higher gross earnings. And women throstle spinners, who operated twice as many machines in 1835 as in 1817, received both more pay and pay at higher rates for "tending extra sides."[54]

Thus developed a kind of balance. The increased stress on opposition which countenanced continued employment in the mills, and especially the emergence of collaborative efforts to distinguish normal from extra demands, suggests that many operatives were coming to accept the industrial order but simultaneously modifying the regimen with their own requirements. Accepting factory life on these terms—giving and taking in ways which both employers and employees could more or less accept but which also underscored the differences between them—this was an established pattern in the Slater and Merino villages by 1820, and significantly colored life and work in the compounds over the next two decades. But once, in 1827, the balance collapsed, precipitating the single expression of overt militancy these villages experienced before 1840.

The incident arose out of Slater's handling of handloom weavers— not the part-time outworkers, for they were too scattered and for the most part insufficiently committed to weaving to protest when they were laid off. Rather, it was the skilled cassimere weavers inside the South Village who rose into action. Responding to competitive pressures, Slater had cut the piece rates of these men in the spring of 1827. While the size of the reduction is unknown, it was evidently too large to be offset with compromises, and the affected weavers quickly voiced a "determination not to weave unless at the old prices . . .": in other words, to strike.[55]

The 1827 turnout should be viewed in two ways. First: as the consequence of pressures playing across life and work in Slater's woolen village. The strike did not arise *ex nihilo*, or even simply as a reaction to a wage cut. The weavers' "determination" arose largely because they were skilled workers and hence particularly inclined to protest economic demotions. Doubtless, too, the weavers drew inspiration from the overall rise of labor militancy in this period; indeed, the operatives' transiency makes it possible that South Village employees had learned from events in other mills—the 1824 strike in Pawtucket, for example, which introduced turnouts to American manufactories.[56] But most of all, the 1827 confrontation arose from the long-building momentum of resistance—the tradition of individual gestures, the collaborative insistence on extra pay for extra work—brewing in the Slater and Merino villages. Here, in fact, is where the South Village incident illuminates a pattern common in overt labor confrontations. For throughout American industrialization, but perhaps particularly during its antebellum phase, strikes typically emerged from a background of employees and employers struggling to establish the lines and limits of their relationship. As in the South Village, so in other workplaces, strikes were usually conservative efforts to forestall changes—whether wage cuts or (sometimes seemingly trivial) amendments in work rules—that workers felt went too far too fast, as though a threshold had been reached that workers were unwilling to cross without a struggle. But as in the South Village also, such eruptions of militancy were usually shaped by—indeed, are often comprehensible only in light of—prior, more subtle histories of fencing between labor and management.[57]

But it is also true that the South Village turnout must be viewed in a second way—as a failure. Despite advancing bonds of common experience among Slater and Merino employees, countervailing factors—the acceptance of discipline, the personal loyalty to managers among some workers, and the various obstacles to unity we have recounted—all remained too strong. The weavers stood alone, and management won simply by replacing them with operatives tending power looms.[58] Nor did the strike even prove a helpful precedent. Despite further wage reductions, there was no significant rise in political activism among Slater and Merino operatives after 1827, no rush to participate in workingmen's conventions or the Ten-Hour Movement during the 1830s and 1840s, and no further strike among any local textile workers until 1858—and this second turnout was as fruitless as the first.[59]

Yet none of this should surprise us. If their turnouts followed patterns common in antebellum labor struggles, textile operatives as a group were still less militant than other workers of the era: skilled urban journeymen, for example, whose craft heritage provided both firmer standards to defend and greater unity with which to wage the defense. Those strikes and other public protests millworkers did mount before 1860, moreover, were concentrated among employees in large, urban factories. In cities operatives could draw support from surrounding social institutions and artisans. And urban boardinghouse mills provided even further inducement. By hiring mainly adult, single, middle-class women and housing them in a few dormitories, Waltham establishments ironically produced a labor force more homogeneous and unified, more uniformly quick to treat wage reductions and tighter disciplines as challenges to their status—in short, more prone to organized militancy than employees of small, rural mills. Yet it is just these hundreds of family factories we must bear in mind. Their record implies that turnouts and other large, overt protests, while not unknown, were not the notation in which most antebellum operatives tended to register resistance.[60]

As we have seen, other notations existed. But at this juncture we should pause to consider whether they succeeded in altering the basic character of the industrial regimen. After all, managerial vigilance in the Slater and Merino mills almost certainly confined, even if it did not prevent, whatever stealing, arson, and machine-breaking that went on. And the various other gestures of opposition had limited impact on daily operations. Even after securing their extra rewards, for example, the output of mule spinners and power-loom weavers increased more than their gross wages in this period by 33.9 percent and 49.2 percent respectively.[61] In an important sense, the operatives' response to industrialization which we have considered to this point, while far from inconsequential, appears to have left mill masters with the upper hand.

But there is more to say. A close reading of Slater and Merino records reveals one response that did force significant compromises from management. It is a response thus far glimpsed only in passing: leaving.

## V

All that we know suggests employees throughout the early New England textile industry were transient. But so, of course, were most Americans. A host of investigations have disclosed significant patterns of geographic mobility beginning at least in the mid-eighteenth century and continuing on past the Civil War.[62] In itself the restlessness of Slater and Merino employees (a necessary corollary of their short work stints) is thus not surprising. Still, the level of movement is remarkable. As Figure 1 indicates, aggregate arrivals and departures of East Village

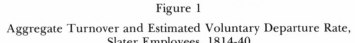

Figure 1

Aggregate Turnover and Estimated Voluntary Departure Rate,
Slater Employees, 1814-40

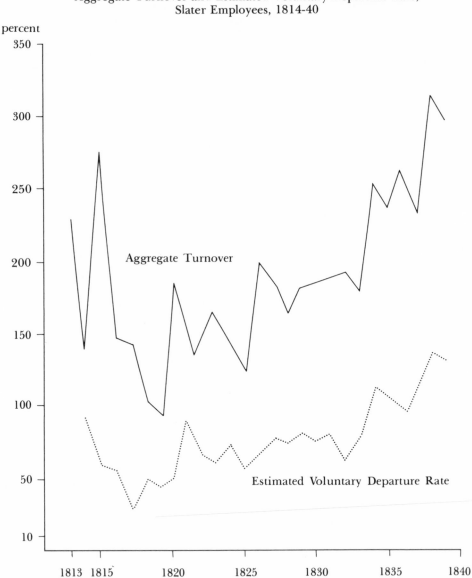

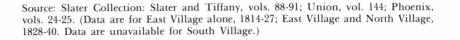

Source: Slater Collection: Slater and Tiffany, vols. 88-91; Union, vol. 144; Phoenix, vols. 24-25. (Data are for East Village alone, 1814-27; East Village and North Village, 1828-40. Data are unavailable for South Village.)

operatives, while varying widely from year to year, dipped below 100 percent of the average annual work force only two times before 1840. Nor did this turnover merely register movement through the payrolls: for just as most employees traveled long distances to reach these compounds, so most—around 80 percent—moved beyond nearby communities after leaving the Slater and Merino rosters.[63]

For our purposes, however, the key rates disclosed by Figure 1 are voluntary departures. While only estimates, these data indicate that exits reflecting the workers' own decisions were numerous. Except for the 1816-20 depression, when operatives clung to jobs they had, at least 45 percent of the East Village average annual work force evidently chose to leave. Samplings from the Merino records yield even higher estimates: 116.4 percent in 1823, 108 percent in 1830.[64]

Besides its volume, other structural aspects of this mobility warrant attention. First, transiency varied somewhat with skill levels and sex. Both skilled mule spinners and women power-loom weavers had below-average voluntary departure rates. The differences were not systematic, however, and were never greater than 20 percent.[65]

Second, transiency ranks among the operatives' more private reactions to industrialization. We have already suggested that movement could undercut ties within the villages; what requires notice here is that workers typically left by themselves or with just a few others. Even families rarely left together. A sampling of children (between eight and sixteen) and fathers showed half of the former and most (56 percent) of the latter left kin behind when they departed. And many arriving workers had left relatives in other factories.[66] This dispersal, of course, did not signal the breakdown of domestic relations any more than did the daily separation of parents and children within the villages. We find, after all, that compared to the unattached employees, workers with kin remained 50 percent longer in these mills, and upon leaving were 30 percent more likely to return; that some household members did travel together; and that scattered relatives often remained in contact and often journeyed to rejoin one another.[67] We should also bear in mind that antebellum Yankee youngsters commonly began a cycle of shifting to and from their homes—seeking schooling and sampling jobs—around twelve or thirteen. Nonetheless, the mobility of family operatives offers some structural indication that policies and pressures of the industrial regimen at least occasionally attentuated domestic bonds. For only among other hard-pressed wageworkers did fathers so frequently leave their families. And while less anomalous, departures of children always implicitly threatened terminal separation: "My daughter . . . about 12 . . . left the service of . . . the Cotton Factory at Waterford; since that time, no intelligence . . . has been received respecting her."[68]

But why did family members leave? Indeed, why did any operative leave? Those using millwork as a temporary expediency departed when their expectations matured. Others left simply because they were accustomed to movement. Or, in rare instances, they left because they had saved enough to buy a business or farm. Or, especially among fathers lacking regular berths and perhaps feeling ineffectual in the villages, they left because they found better work situations elsewhere. Or, especially among children who could expect neither training nor bequests from their parents if they stayed, they left because factory labor was intolerably tedious.[69]

Operatives had left factories for such reasons even in the 1790s, and Slater and Merino workers reflected these promptings right through 1840. Gradually, however, in a manner paralleling other developments we have cited, another motive developed. As mills grew more numerous across New England, as there emerged among Slater and Merino employees cadres of operatives committed to long stretches of factory work, and as these operatives were subjected to stiffer demands, some workers began using movement, not to leave textile work, but to improve their situation within it. Obviously, this was a strategy for prosperous times. Depressions, as already noted, reduced mobility of operatives; and those who did move during slumps generally accepted any available opening and even angled for multiyear contracts.[70] Yet against this we must contrast a mounting inclination of veterans to use good years as hunting seasons for better berths. Again there were precedents: Slater had lost skilled men to another mill as early as 1802. But by the 1820s and 1830s the pattern was commonplace, and had broadened to include women and youngsters. In the East Village in 1834: "[M]ore [power-loom weavers] have given their notice to Leave to go to . . . where they can do better . . ."; in the Merino Village in 1841: workers are "leaving our employ more wages wanted." Nor was maximizing income the operatives' only priority. They moved to secure better working facilities ("faster water"), more compatible supervisors, or more flexible "rules and regulations."[71] Indeed, among workers who rarely voted and whose other forms of resistance had only moderate effect, mobility may well have emerged as the principal means of rejecting "corrupt" dependency on management—of asserting independence and freedom.

But operatives did more than merely seize existing opportunities. They also used movement, or the threat of movement, to bid up the value of their services to create better jobs for themselves. They could do this because mobility presented difficulties for factory masters. While ideologues argued that turnover proved America had no permanent proletariat,[72] managers found the phenomenon burdensome. The

task of assigning incoming workers to suitable jobs, preparing lodg-
ings, and maintaining current records taxed administrative facilities.
And the stream of demands for terminal wage payments created frequent shortages of cash. Most serious, however, was that transiency
aggravated the labor shortage these managers confronted, for it meant
rosters had to be repeatedly replenished. All early manufactories faced
this challenge. But the greater fame of the Waltham factories, and the
somewhat higher wages they offered their all-adult work force, appear
to have given these establishments an edge over family mills in securing
recruits at short notice. Thus, although rarely left short of help for
long, Slater and Merino managers often had to scramble to fill empty
positions: "I have sent out in various directions after weavers," moaned
an East Village agent, "but have not as yet had the Good Luck to get
any."[73]

Here was the workers' leverage. In good times, factories wishing to
retain hands were frequently maneuvered into bidding against other
establishments. So William Richmonds used an offer from the Merino
Village to chivy his Southbridge employer into "paying him his price."
By the same token, mills needing workers, and wishing to hire veterans,
were often challenged to improve on bargains operatives already had:
"I am [given] fair pay . . . where I am now," a prospective Slater
employee wrote in 1827, "[and it] would not be an object for me to
change places unless I can receive as pay one dollar pr. day and
board."[74]

There were, of course, limits to what workers could win this way.
Mills needed operatives. But since some workers continued to face low
net incomes, it is clear that managers were too protective of profit
margins to give all employees what (in Slater's words) "their unlimited
consciences . . . dictate them to ask."[75] Similarly, the fact that the local
mill regimen grew more demanding suggests that officials declined to
dismantle disciplines they believed promoted productivity. Concessions gained through movement were thus confined to the margin,
where proprietors thought compromise was at least potentially afford-
able. Yet even here the stakes were sufficiently high to create fierce
struggles—the most dense and protracted to develop within these
villages—as management sought to control the mobility of millworkers,
and operatives sought to retain freedom of movement.

So it was that the mills introduced contracts. The Merino Village in
1813 and the Slater compounds around 1824 began systematically
imposing twelve-month (April-to-April) work agreements and withholding wages "until the expiration of yr." Such agreements obviously
served several purposes: the deferred payments simultaneously eased
liquidity problems and effectively granted interest-free loans to the

mills. But the basic goals were, first, to reduce movement (if workers traveled only in April, aggregate turnover could not surpass 100 percent) and, second, to funnel what movement there was into predictable, manageable periods each spring.[76]

The effort failed. This was partly because employers proved more interested in obliging workers to honor yearlong engagements than in honoring such arrangements themselves. The mills increased their April hirings; but layoffs continued to follow slumps, and between 1812 and 1840 sales did not slip only in the spring. The more critical resistance, however, came from workers. While springtime voluntary departures grew and while operatives increasingly spoke of yearlong factory "seasons," at least half the exits workers chose to make after contracts were introduced fell in the summer, fall, or winter quarters.[77] Unsettled accounts were no deterrent. Those in debt simply took "French leave . . . in the night." Those with net wages due them frequently denied the legitimacy of management's contracts (". . . I made no engagement . . . for any particular time I should not think any one could have any objections my leaving . . .") and persuaded their next employers to help them secure the money—and in one instance even the clothes—left behind.[78]

Faced with such resistance, the mills could only retreat. By 1830, despite occasional lingering threats to withhold wages from workers until their "time is up," payments in the Slater villages had apparently slipped to quarterly, monthly, and even bimonthly rhythms. Moreover, while operatives occasionally signed on for lengthy stints up through 1840, agreements after 1830 commonly stipulated less than twelve months and contained clauses permitting "either party [to] be released . . ." by giving one month's notice.[79]

Contracts, however, were only one front of the battle. Officials of family mills evidently often sought to lure employees with inflated bargains, aiming to "cut down" their wages after their rosters were filled—to which operatives responded by demanding guarantees of good faith with all offers.[80] More defensively, managers tried to protect their payrolls against other mills by establishing guidelines for wages and by threatening law suits against factories "enticing" employees already under contract. But this too proved useless. Mill masters were too numerous and varied to collaborate on wages, and too often desperate for workers to stop their "inveigling." (Indeed, Slater and the Merino proprietors were themselves accused of improperly approaching employees of brother manufacturers.) But again it was the workers' resistance that was most significant. Civil action against "enticements" usually required sworn statements by employees; since, however, such offers typically meant better jobs, operatives called on to testify would, as Slater's lawyer acknowledged glumly, as soon "cut our throats" as tell the truth.[81]

Finally, management stressed the ethical importance of workers staying put. Along with punctuality, rootedness was, in fact, what managers invoked when they set "steadiness" among the principal *desiderata* of textile operatives. As we have seen, Slater and Merino workers did become quite punctual, and even hoisted management on its own clocks with overtime. But their extraordinary transiency makes clear operatives never accepted the moral necessity of remaining in a manufactory longer than they wished. Even intense religious experiences did not prevent unsteady behavior: workers used mobility to assert their autonomy throughout the revivals that occasionally swept the four villages.[82]

In sum, efforts to coerce operatives into stability had little impact. As this approach faltered, however, the Slater and Merino mills began pursuing a different and more successful tack. Once again the records are only suggestive, but what they imply is a campaign by management to give the villages a good reputation among employees. Part of this program, of course, involved the "kindly and paternal interest" earlier considered. But these factories went further. Unlike boardinghouse administrators, who used fines, firings, and blacklists to enforce discipline,[83] Slater and Merino officials (in company with other family managers) reacted to their more severe staffing difficulties by offering what amounted to a hidden contract: a tacit agreement to avoid such draconian measures.

Every social institution, of course, implicitly specifies which formal regulations will be stressed and which ignored. Indeed, there are signs Slater hesitated to mobilize harsh disciplinary techniques even in the 1790s.[84] But it is surely significant that despite the rising pressure for increased efficiency, the pattern of restraint both persisted and broadened out, becoming a distinctive characteristic of antebellum country factories. Thus, in the Slater and Merino villages between 1812 and 1840 sobriety was required, but drinking was tolerated and a Merino agent had no qualms recommending an operative who had been "the worse for Liquor but once during 12 months." Punctuality was stressed, but existing tardiness went unfined. Obedience was mandated, but only three workers were discharged for "misconduct," and "work badly done" met only sporadic sanctions. Finally, employees leaving before their times were up were neither pursued nor sued and their names were not "sen[t] around": "I shall make some inquiry after them [two runaways]," Slater informed son John in 1825, "tho' I shall not take much trouble to find them."[85]

We should not exaggerate this administrative slack. It did not raise wage levels, or countermand increased workloads, or alleviate the mounting precision with which work time was measured—in short it did not offset the increasing burden of the industrial order. Nor, as we have seen, did it remove the need many operatives felt to resist that order. Yet this pattern of informal leniency may well have represented the greatest victory Slater and Merino workers wrung from their employers, for it guaranteed a small but valuable addition in daily freedom. This is perhaps the final reason strikes were rare in mills like the Slater and Merino establishments. It is also why, from management's perspective, leniency was a successful policy: despite their constant worry about labor shortages, manufactories like the Slater and Merino mills could usually rely on their good reputation to attract sufficient employees.

Here, then, was the final compromise: a bargain yielding advantage to both managers and workers. But the question remains how operatives discovered that certain mills tacitly avoided strict enforcement of rules and regulations. The answer can only be from one another. Circulating through smaller factories, especially in southern New England, veteran millworkers learned "the customs of all the villages roundabout."[86] And at least by the 1830s the same informal networks that communicated news of openings were also ranking managers. Thus a young man informed the South Village: "You may think [it] rather strange why I keep writing to you the reason is that your place has been recommended to me as . . . a good one."[87] We may suspect hypocrisy. It is equally likely, however, that such statements disclose that the transiency of experienced operatives was coming to rest on shared evaluations—and hence providing further reason for separated friends and relatives to remain in contact. While continuing to reflect and effect divisions within the labor force, movement may thus have grown gradually less atomizing, may to some degree have reflected the increased unity of textile workers. Even movement, that is, may ultimately have involved a kind of community.

## VI

We have considered changes in the nature of work and work discipline and accompanying shifts in the structure of the Slater and Merino labor force. We have observed these strands interacting and moving forward to produce increasingly defined patterns of demands and resistance. But what, finally, do we make of these developments? How should we characterize the way employees and employers in the Slater and Merino villages came to deal with one another?

No single formula is entirely adequate. But it is difficult to ignore signs that what we are chronicling is, fundamentally, the emergence of class. It is significant in this context that during the 1820s and 1830s operatives were increasingly perceived from outside the factory villages as a separate, ominous social grouping. Despite industry's claim to protect and improve its employees, New Englanders became steadily more convinced that millworkers deviated sharply from Yankee norms. The very term "operative" achieved currency—probably by the 1830s— to distinguish these wage laborers from other workers. And outside the Slater and Merino mills we find local townspeople in the early 1830s concluding that, despite their own chronic mobility, the "floating and transient" character of textile operatives was most alarming.[88]

But the more significant indication of class was the social system developing within the mill compounds. By 1840 the net result of all the conflicts and compromises was a clear demarcation between the interest of employees and employers. One side wished to maximize output and minimize labor costs; the other side sought a regimen permitting the best price and the greatest independence possible. When every allowance is made for paternalism and concern on the one hand and deference and obedience on the other, this opposition is the axis around which the Slater and Merino mills came to revolve.

There was, to be sure, an imbalance in the consciousness of the competing groups. Managers acted with consistent forcefulness to achieve their goals. Operatives, by contrast, must be seen as comprising a class in itself that acted overtly for itself only to a limited extent. Yet workers quite obviously did find ways to resist between 1812 and 1840, and at least limited forms of cooperation—of community—increasingly underlay their opposition. All this denotes a considerable social achievement.

And one that lasted. Extant Merino records run only to 1845. The more extensive Slater materials suggest that after 1840 heightened competition among textile mills prompted further stiffenings in industrial discipline. The simultaneous influx of immigrants presented new obstacles to unity among the operatives and, as already noted, there was no upsurge of organized militancy. But in more discrete ways—in ways that reflect patterns explored in these pages, in ways that continued to be typical of many antebellum millworkers—operatives in the North, South, and East Villages succeeded in limiting the hegemony of their employers.[89]

## NOTES

An earlier version of this paper was presented to the Smith College Symposium on the "New" New England Working Class History, March 1979. Research for this essay was supported by the National Endowment for the Humanities, the American Antiquarian Society, and the Faculty Research Committee of Emory University. I gratefully acknowledge their assistance. I should also like to thank the consistently helpful comments and suggestions offered by Milton Cantor, Thomas Dublin, Steven Hahn, Alexander Keyssar, and the editors of this volume.

1. Holmes Ammidown, *Historical Collections*, 2 vols. (New York, 1874), I, 435-36. The principal manuscript collection available for the Merino mill is the "Merino and Dudley Wool Company Records, 1811-1845," at Old Sturbridge Village, Sturbridge, Mass. (hereafter Merino Records). The Merino proprietors dissolved their partnership in April 1818, and the Dudley Woolen Manufactory company took over the mill in August of that year. For convenience, however, I have continued to refer to the property as the Merino Village throughout the 1812-40 period.

2. George F. Daniels, *History of the Town of Oxford, Massachusetts* (Oxford, Mass., 1892), pp. 190-91; Jonathan Prude, "The Coming of Industrial Order: A Study of Town and Factory Life in Rural Massachusetts, 1813-1860" (Ph.D. dissertation, Harvard University, 1976), pp. 76-80. The principal manuscript sources for the Slater mills are: (1) the Slater Collection at Baker Library, Harvard University (hereafter Slater Collection) and (2) the Almy and Brown Papers at the Rhode Island Historical Society, Providence, R.I. (hereafter Almy and Brown Papers).

3. See, for example, Thomas Dublin, *Women at Work: The Transformation of Work and Community in Lowell, Massachusetts, 1826-1860* (New York, 1979); Hannah Josephson, *The Golden Threads: New England's Mill Girls and Magnates* (New York, 1949); and Howard Gitelman, *Working Men of Waltham: Mobility in American Urban Industrial Development, 1850-1898* (Baltimore, 1974).

4. John Carver, *Sketches of New England, or Memories of the Country* (New York, 1842), p. 10. As late as 1845, 82 percent of the cotton and woolen mills in Massachusetts and 54 percent of the operatives were located in townships of under 5,000 people. (Derived from the *Massachusetts State Census, 1845* ([Boston, 1846]).

5. Merino Records: Series IV, Part I, D, vols. 80-81, 84-86. Slater Collection: Slater and Tiffany Weave Books A-D; S. Slater and Sons, vol. 191. East Village outworkers initially included pickers, but they were replaced by full-time operatives by 1820. The handloom weavers increased from 135 weavers between 1813 and 1817 to around 280 by the mid-1820s. By the latter years, so-called commercial weavers, controlling their own networks, were acting as subcontractors for Slater, and some of the farming-weaving households were themselves becoming more dependent on weaving. But until the outwork system was disbanded in 1827 (see p. 8) most East Village weaving outworkers continued to regard their employment as peripheral. See Prude, "Coming of Industrial Order," pp. 85-98. Outwork is an important and curiously neglected aspect of industry's interaction with New England's society and economy. Since, however, the present essay focuses on relationships developing within the mill villages, the subject can here be treated only cursorily.

6. J. Brennan, *Social Conditions in Industrial Rhode Island: 1820-1860* (Washington, D.C., 1940), pp. 32-34. Caroline F. Ware, *Early New England Cotton Manufacture, A Study in Industrial Beginnings* (Boston, 1931), pp. 22-23, 199.

7. See n. 4 above. Also Caroline Ware, *Early New England Cotton Manufacture*, p. 202. Elsewhere (p. 199) Ware suggests that "about half" of New England's mills were family factories. But the overall tilt of her discussion would indicate this is simply a misstatement.

8. Barbara M. Tucker, "The Family and Industrial Discipline in Ante-Bellum New England," *Labor History*, 21 (1979-80), 55; Anthony F. C. Wallace, *Rockdale* (New York, 1978), p. 69. Compare Caroline Ware, *Early New England Cotton Manufacture*, pp. 272-76, with Thomas Dublin, "Women, Work, and Protest," *Labor History*, 16 (1975), 99-116.

9. Derived from: Louis McLane, *Report of the Secretary of the Treasury, 1832, Documents Relative to the Manufacturers in the United States* (Washington, D.C., 1833) (*House Executive Documents*, 22nd Cong., 1st Sess., Doc. No. 308), I, 484-85, 526-27, 576-77. Merino Records: Series IV, Part I, D, vol. 75. Slater Collection: Slater and Tiffany, vols. 84, 88-91; Union, vol. 144; Phoenix, vols. 24-25; Webster Woolen, vols. 45-46. The figures for family workers and, in the Slater mills, for women and children also, are estimates based on names, coresiding patterns, and wage rates. The Slater and Merino ventures were probably larger than most family mills (the average factory in Massachusetts employed only fifty-eight workers in 1845). But they were considerably smaller than mills in Lowell and Waltham. (See *Massachusetts State Census, 1845*.)

10. Merino Records: Series IV, Part 1, A, vol. 1, pp. 6, 28.

11. Prude, "Coming of Industrial Order," pp. 147-49, 332-35. Slater Collection: Slater and Tiffany, vol. 93; Samuel Slater and Sons, vol. 235, Samuel Slater to John Slater, Mar. 5, 1826; Mar. 30, 1826; Oct. 23, 1827; Nov. 11, 1827; July 15, 1828; Samuel Slater and Sons, vol. 109, S. Slater and Sons to D. W. Jones, Dec. 30, 1839; Samuel Slater and Sons, vol. 110, S. Slater and Sons to D. W. Jones, May 1, 1837.

12. Prude, "Coming of Industrial Order," pp. 150-56. Merino Records: Series IV, Part I, A, vol. 1, pp. 9-11. Slater Collection: Slater and Kimball, vol. 111. The rank-and-file background of East Village overseers is derived from Slater Collection: Slater and Kimball, vol. 111, and Slater and Tiffany, vols. 88-90.

13. George White, *Memoir of Samuel Slater* (Philadelphia, 1836), p. 108; William R. Bagnall, *Samuel Slater and the Development of the Cotton Manufacture in the United States* (Middletown, Pa., 1890), pp. 68-69. For the assertion that paternalism persisted in the Slater mills after 1840 see Holmes Ammidown, *Historical Collections*, I, 502.

14. Scholarly evocations of paternalism include: J. Coolidge, *Mill and Mansion, a Study of Architecture and Society in Lowell, Massachusetts, 1820-1865* (New York, 1942), pp. 114-15, 164; George Rogers Taylor, *The Transportation Revolution 1815-1860* (New York, 1968), pp. 275-76; and (though he means the term critically) Norman Ware, *The Industrial Worker, 1840-1860* (New York, 1964), chs. VI-VIII.

15. For the controversy over water rights see Morton J. Horwitz, *The Transformation of American Law, 1780-1860* (Cambridge, Mass., 1977), pp. 35, 274 n. 5; J. Conrad, Jr., "The Evolution of Industrial Capitalism in Rhode Island, 1790-1830: Almy, the Browns, and the Slaters" (Ph.D. dissertation, University of Connecticut, 1973), pp. 90-91; J. D. Van Slyck, *Representatives of New England Manufacturers* (Boston, 1879), p. 415; Merino Records: Series IV, Part II, E, Box 23, S. W. Babcock to Mr. Clemens, May 28, 1834. Fear that the mills degraded workers is recorded in Sui Generis: Alias Thomas Man, *Picture of a Factory Village* (Providence, R.I., 1832), pp. 8-9. And fear of losing taxes is cited in Thomas Steere, *History of the Town of Smithfield* (Providence, R.I., 1881),

p. 65. "[T]yranny" is cited from the *Pawtucket Chronicle*, Aug. 29, 1829. See also Samuel Ogden, *Thoughts, What Probable Effect the Peace with Great Britain Will Have on the Cotton Manufacture of This Country* (Providence, R.I., 1815), pp. 6-7, 26. Such concerns directly affected the Slater and Merino factories: complicating their efforts to recruit workers, for example, and fueling community tensions that by 1832 led Slater to break completely with Dudley and Oxford and petition to have his villages set off into the new township of Webster. See Prude, "Coming of Industrial Order," pp. 289-311.

16. H. A. Miles, *Lowell, as It Was, and as It Is* (Lowell, Mass., 1847), pp. 130-31. McLane, *Report of the Secretary of the Treasury*, I, 931. Ogden, *Thoughts, What Probable Effect*, pp. 6-7. White, *Memoir of Samuel Slater*, pp. 108, 207.

17. Merino Records: Series IV, Part II, E, Box 20, Phebe N. Larned to Mr. Permans (?) Feb. ?, 182?.

18. See Slater Collection: Map in Slater and Howard, Box 26. For indications of families maintaining control over children's wages and determining which household members would fill available berths, see Slater Collection: Slater and Tiffany, vols. 89-91. For a distinctly different interpretation see Barbara M. Tucker, "Family and Industrial Discipline in Ante-Bellum New England," pp. 55-74.

19. Some married women "washed towels," others turned out candle wicks in their living quarters, and widows frequently ran the boardinghouses. The point here is simply that married women and mothers did not hold berths. See Slater Collection: Slater and Tiffany, vols. 73, 88-91, 93; Slater and Kimball, vol. 111. Seven out of ten male household heads had berths in 1817; by 1830 the proportion was 35.3 percent. Out of eleven mule spinners and dressers in 1830, eight (72.7 percent) had been promoted or hired as unmarried men.

20. Slater made brief, unsatisfactory attempts to use apprentices in Rhode Island during the 1790s. See Conrad, "Evolution of Industrial Capitalism in Rhode Island," pp. 100-103. The records of Slater's Oxford and Dudley establishments contain only two indenture forms. (See Slater Collection: Slater and Howard, vol. 22.) For Slater's management trainee, see Prude, "Coming of Industrial Order," p. 76. Apprenticeships in the Merino Village were confined to 1813-14. Merino Records: Series I, A, vol. 2.

21. *Manufacturers' and Farmers' Journal, Providence and Pawtucket Advertiser*, Sept. 22, 1823.

22. Miles, *Lowell, as It Was*, pp. 67-70, 128-33, 145-46.

23. For indications of religious involvement of workers and manufacturers see Ammidown, *Historical Collections*, I, 448; Daniels, *History of the Town of Oxford*, pp. 64-80 passim, 88-89; Slater Collection: H. N. Slater, vol. 33, Alex Hedges to H. N. Slater, Sept. 12, 1837: ". . . [T]his being camp meeting week with our Good Methodists will be rather a broken one with the mills . . . ." On day schools see Prude, "Coming of Industrial Order," pp. 207-8, 290-91, 297-99. In Rhode Island, during the 1790s and subsequently, Slater was somewhat more involved in educational and religious activities; and elsewhere some New England family mills provided such facilities into the 1820s and 1830s. On balance the laissez-faire attitude in the southern Massachusetts Slater and Merino villages was thus neither wholly anomalous nor wholly typical. See Conrad, "Evolution of Industrial Capitalism in Rhode Island," pp. 123, 262-64; Brennan, *Social Conditions in Industrial Rhode Island*, pp. 95-96. Peter J. Coleman, *The Transformation of Rhode Island, 1790-1860* (Providence, R.I., 1963), p. 231.

24. Slater Collection: Slater and Tiffany, vols. 84, 88-91; Union, vol. 144; Phoenix, vols. 24-25. There were lay-offs in 1816-19, 1834, and probably 1827. Breaks in the records suggest the possibility of brief shutdowns in 1816 and 1834-35. For the Merino mill see Merino Records: "A Checklist and Guide," p. 1. For an economic history of the textile industry in these years see Caroline Ware, *Early New England Cotton Manufacture*, pp. 79-104, and Arthur H. Cole, *The American Wool Manufacture* (Cambridge, Mass., 1926), I, chs. XI-XII.

25. Conrad, "Evolution of Industrial Capitalism in Rhode Island," pp. 338-44; Prude, "Coming of Industrial Order," pp. 96-98. Slater Collection: S. Slater and Sons, vol. 235, S. Slater to John Slater, Nov. 16, 1828. Compare this to the more generous attitude Slater showed during the 1790s when he discovered that operatives were inconvenienced by tardy wage payments and were "grieving" for lack of stoves in the mills. See Almy and Brown Papers: Box 1, No. 126, Samuel Slater to Almy and Brown, Nov. 23, 1794; Box 1, No. 101, S. Slater to Almy and Brown, Nov. 4, 1793; Box 2, No. 374, Slater to Almy and Brown, Oct. 17, 1796.

26. Slater Collection: Samuel Slater and Sons, vol. 110, S. Slater and Sons to Jones, May 1, 1837.

27. Ratio of wages for men, women, and children derived from Slater Collection: Slater and Kimball, vol. 111; Slater and Tiffany, vol. 73. Comparison to boardinghouse wages is derived from 1830 and 1835 data in Slater Collection: Slater and Tiffany, vols. 84-85, 91; Phoenix, vol. 84; and Robert Layer, *Earnings of Cotton Mill Operatives, 1825-1914* (Cambridge, Mass., 1955), p. 18. Daily rates in Slater and Merino mills are computed from McLane, *Report of the Secretary of the Treasury*, I, 484-85, 526-27, 576-77. Average annual wages for an operative who labored every day for a full working year in 1832 came to $154.20.

28. Slater Collection: Slater and Tiffany, vols. 89-90, 93-94; Slater and Howard, vol. 26, Joseph W. Collier to Slater and Howard, Mar. 26, 1829.

29. *New England Offering*, I, no. 1 (Apr. 1848), 5. Merino Records: Series IV, D, vols. 74-75. Slater Collection: Slater and Tiffany, vols. 84, 89-91; Slater and Kimball, vol. 111.

30. Slater Collection: Slater and Kimball, vol. 111; Slater and Tiffany, vols. 73, 93, 84; Union, vol. 84.

31. Merino Records: Series IV, Part I, D, vols. 74, 78. Slater Collection: Slater and Tiffany, vol. 88. Prude, "Coming of Industrial Order," pp. 11-16. See E. P. Thompson, "Time, Work-Discipline, and Industrial Capitalism," *Past and Present*, 38 (Dec. 1967), 66-97.

32. Slater Collection: Slater and Tiffany, vols. 84, 88-91. *Vital Records of Dudley and Oxford Massachusetts* (Worcester, Mass., 1908 and 1905.)

33. Slater Collection: Webster Woolen, vol. 110, Ashron Loring to D. W. Jones, Sept. 4, 1836. The proportion of locals entering the mills is derived from comparison of payrolls in Slater Collection: Slater and Tiffany, vols. 84, 88-90, and Merino Records: Series IV, Part I, D, vols. 74-75, with Dudley and Oxford enumerations, Fourth and Fifth Federal Censuses (1820 and 1830), Worcester County, Mass.

34. Derived from William R. Bagnall, "Contributions to American Economic History" (unpublished materials, Baker Library, Harvard University), II and III, passim; Van Slyck, *Representatives of New England Manufacturers*, passim; and analysis of local workers found in Daniels, *History of the Town of Oxford*,

Genealogy, pp. 365-753. See also Dublin, *Women at Work*, ch. 3.

35. Almy and Brown Papers: Box 10, No. 1443, Sally Brown to Almy and Brown Nov. 14, 1794.

36. John Slater Papers at the Rhode Island School of Design, Providence, R.I. (hereafter John Slater Papers): R. Rogerson to John Slater, Sept. 2, 1814. White, *Memoir of Samuel Slater*, p. 127. Daniels, *History of the Town of Oxford*, Genealogy, pp. 365-753.

37. Bagnall, "Contributions to American Economic History," II and III, passim; Slater Collection: Slater and Howard, vol. 26, passim, and John Brierly to Edward Howard, Mar. 5, 1829.

38. *Lowell Offering*, IV (June 1844), 170.

39. Derived from Merino Records: Series IV, Part I, D, vols. 74-75. Slater Collection: Slater and Tiffany, vols. 88-89. There may have been seasonality in the demand for textile goods, but most employers were evidently reluctant to release hands regularly and risk being short in busier periods. Certainly Slater and Merino records reveal no systematic seasonal payroll cuts between 1812 and 1840. These factories released workers only during slumps.

40. See Dublin, *Women at Work*, ch. 5.

41. Thomas Leavitt, ed., *The Hollingworth Letters: Technical Change in the Textile Industry, 1826-1837* (Cambridge, Mass., 1969), p. 30.

42. *Massachusetts Spy*, May 27, 1818.

43. Figures on returning workers are derived from Slater Collection: Slater and Tiffany, vols. 84, 88-89; Samuel Slater and Sons, vol. 234, P. Pond to H. N. Slater, July 31, 1839; see also Slater and Howard, vol. 26, passim. For evidence of experienced women see Slater Collection: Webster Woolen, vol. 110, Anne Smith to D. W. Jones, Jan. 15, 1838; Joanne Littlefield to D. W. Jones, Aug. 3, 1838.

44. See Slater Collection: Slater and Howard, vol. 26, passim. Josephson, *Golden Threads*, p. 83. Eric Hobsbawm, *Labouring Men: Studies in the History of Labour* (London, 1964), p. 9.

45. Two workers actually named sons after Samuel Slater (see *Vital Records of Dudley and Oxford*) and when newly appointed agents and overseers arrived at the North Village in 1838, operatives evinced such loyalty to their former supervisors that one newcomer feared "some of the hands will rebell and refuse to do duty under me." Slater Collection: H. N. Slater, vol. 33, Hedges to H. N. Slater, Apr. 11, 1838.

46. Almy and Brown Papers: Box 3, No. 352, Slater to Almy and Brown, July 19, 1796; Box 2, No. 227, Slater to Almy and Brown, June 2, 1795; Box 2, No. 256, Slater to Almy and Brown, Sept. 25, 1795. Autumn slips in attendance and Slater attendance figures are derived from Slater Collection: Slater and Tiffany, vols. 88-91. Merino figures are derived from Merino Records: Series IV, Part I, D, vol. 75. It should be pointed out that the fall harvesting in which Slater's southern Massachusetts workers engaged may have been in fields owned by Slater and undertaken at his orders. And it should be noted further than punctuality increased even within the 1812-40 period: Slater employees were 2.5 percent more punctual in 1830 than in 1813; Merino workers improved 8.7 percent just between 1820 and 1830.

47. Slater Collection: Slater and Kimball, vol. 111.

48. Brennan, *Social Conditions in Industrial Rhode Island*, pp. 32-33. Slater acknowledged that "many are of the opinion" that an 1811 fire in a Providence mill with which he was associated "was set . . . willfully"; he personally could only "think and hope not." Almy and Brown Papers: Box 7, No. 944, Samuel

Slater to Almy and Brown, Oct. 9, 1811. Fire struck his southern Massachusetts holdings in 1820 and 1834; see Daniels, *History of the Town of Oxford*, p. 191. Slater Collection: Samuel Slater and Sons, vol. 235, Samuel Slater to John Slater, Dec. 23, 1834. See also Gary Kulik, "Pawtucket Village and the Strike of 1824: The Origin of Class Conflict in Rhode Island," *Radical History Review*, 17 (Spring 1978), 23-25.

49. Conrad, "Evolution of Industrial Capitalism in Rhode Island," pp. 259-60, discusses stealing by Slater's operatives in the 1790s and the widespread fear among early mill masters that thieves would attack any goods shipped by land. For stealing among eighteenth-century English weavers see Neil J. Smelser, *Social Change in the Industrial Revolution: An Application of Theory to the British Cotton Industry* (Chicago, 1959), p. 66.

50. Slater Collection: Slater and Tiffany, vol. 101, Charles Waite to John Slater, Aug. 8, 1834.

51. "Work Diary," in Gordon Papers, Baker Library, Harvard University, 12 vols. (hereafter N. B. Gordon, "Diary"), vol. 5, June 8, 1831. The rhythm of power-loom weaving is derived from Slater Collection: Slater and Tiffany, vol. 89. See Prude, "Coming of Industrial Order," pp. 225-27.

52. Slater Collection: Samuel Slater and Sons, vol. 235, Samuel Slater to John Slater, Apr. 4, 1820. Funeral attendance is noted in Slater Collection: Slater and Tiffany, vols. 88-91; Samuel Slater and Sons, vol. 235, Samuel Slater to John Slater, Aug. 6, 1834.

53. Old Slater Mill Collection at Providence, R.I.: Caleb Farnum to Samuel Slater, June 9, 1814. (Reference courtesy of Gary Kulik.) Merino Records: Series IV, Part I, D, vols. 74-78. Slater Collection: Slater and Tiffany, vols. 88, 91, 93. For an example of other mills starting to pay "something extra" for work past normal quitting time see Caroline Ware, *Early New England Cotton Manufacture*, p. 69.

54. Merino Records: Series I, A, vol. 2; Contracts with William Taylor, Dec. 19, 1814, and Luther Hammond, May 2, 1815, Slater Collection: Slater and Tiffany, vols. 73, 89, 93; Slater and Kimball, vol. 111.

55. Merino Records: Series IV, Part II, E, Box 20, Slater and Howard to Major John Brown, Mar. 10, 1827.

56. Gary Kulik, "Pawtucket Village and the Strike of 1824," pp. 5-37.

57. For indications of this pattern elsewhere in the textile industry see Caroline Ware, *Early New England Cotton Manufacture*, p. 273; Philip Foner, *The History of the Labor Movement in the United States*, 4 vols. (New York, 1947), I, 105. For the context surrounding confrontations among antebellum shoemakers see Alan Dawley, *Class and Community: The Industrial Revolution in Lynn* (Cambridge, Mass., 1976).

58. Data on the 1827 strike are sparse, but it is clear that, while some hand weaving persisted in the South Village until 1830, this factory had stopped turning out cassimere by handlooms considerably before that. Slater Collection: Samuel Slater and Sons, vol. 191.

59. Slater Collection: Union, vol. 119. Voting data kindly supplied by Ronald P. Formisano. For failure to attend regional mechanics' meetings see *Providence Daily Journal*, Oct. 25, 1831.

60. Some brief confrontations doubtless escaped the public record, but the perspective argued here is generally substantiated by Carrol D. Wright, *Strikes in Massachusetts, 1830-1880*, from the *Eleventh Annual Report of the Massachusetts Bureau of Statistics of Labor for 1880* (1880; reprint ed. Boston, 1889). A general treatment of strikes and a suggestion they did not become important in

antebellum America are found in David Montgomery, "Strikes in Nineteenth Century America," *Social Science History*, 4 (1980), 81-104.

61. Derived from Slater Collection: Slater and Tiffany, vols. 73, 84; Slater and Kimball, vol. 111.

62. Philip Greven, *Four Generations, Population, Land, and Family in Colonial Andover, Massachusetts* (Ithaca, N.Y., 1970); Kenneth Lockridge, *A New England Town: The First Hundred Years* (New York, 1970); Stephen Thernstrom, *Poverty and Progress, Social Mobility in a Nineteenth Century City* (Cambridge, Mass., 1964).

63. The number of arrivals and departures used to compute aggregate turnover was established by comparing payroll listings four times each year (April, July, October, and January). Names of departing workers were compared to 1820 and 1830 enumerations, Fourth and Fifth Federal Censuses, of Dudley, Oxford, Charlton, Ward, Millbury, Sutton, Woodstock, and Southbridge, Worcester County, Mass.

64. Voluntary exits were estimated by subtracting departures coinciding with net reductions in the work force from each year's total exits and computing the remainder as a percentage of the average annual work roster. (The rate of voluntary departure could exceed 100 percent of the average annual labor force because the calculations for this rate are derived from measurements of movement taken quarterly.) The assumption behind this methodology is that net reductions reflected managerial decisions. This in turn assumes management succeeded in finding the number of workers it wanted during any given quarter. As will be indicated Slater and Merino managers worried constantly about being left shorthanded and often had difficulty filling their berths. Nonetheless, available evidence indicates these mills were not left short often or long enough to distort the estimates revealed in Figure 1. The larger shifts in Figure 1 were probably caused by economic pressures. Turnover and voluntary rates trailed off in 1815 when sales began falling. But in 1816 the two rates moved in opposite directions as the East Village dropped fifty workers, while those with jobs chose to remain in place. Slow times continued into 1820, and only in 1821 was prosperity sufficient to permit those wishing to leave to do so. Movement then continued at a fairly even pace until 1826-27, when power-loom operatives were added, forcing up aggregate turnover rates. Both movement and the payroll contracted during the downturns of 1833-34; in 1837 turnover rose as workers were released, while voluntary departure rates declined. Overall, however, we see after 1830 a general rise in movement—a trend continuing through the 1840s and 1850s. See Prude, "Coming of Industrial Order," pp. 351-56.

65. Slater Collection: Slater and Tiffany, vols. 73, 84.

66. Slater Collection: Slater and Tiffany, vols. 88-91; Slater and Kimball, vol. 111. "My family," wrote one incoming Merino father, "will remain in Millbury for the present." Merino Records: Series IV, Part II, E, Box 23, Tyler Chamberlain to Major John Brown, Mar. 11, 1831.

67. Slater Collection: Slater and Tiffany, vol. 88.

68. Joseph F. Kett, *Rites of Passage: Adolescence in America 1790 to the Present* (New York, 1977), pp. 15-29. *Massachusetts Spy*, Nov. 27, 1816.

69. Derived from Bagnall, "Contributions to American Economic History," and Daniels, *History of the Town of Oxford*, Genealogy, pp. 365-753. *Providence Daily Journal and Evening Bulletin*, Sept. 29, 1890.

70. See Slater Collection: Slater and Howard, vol. 26, passim, for letters of

wool workers desperate for jobs during the 1828-29 downturn. There is no evidence, however, that workers generally traded longer contracts for lower rates.

71. Slater Collection: Samuel Slater and Sons, vol. 236, Hedges to John Slater, Aug. 18, 1834. Merino Records: Series IV, Part I, A, vol. 5, Sept. 1, 1841. Desire for nonfinancial improvements is indicated in Slater Collection: Webster Woolen, vol. 110, Ashron Loring to D. W. Jones, Sept. 4, 1836; Slater and Howard, vol. 25, Thomas Haywood to Edward Howard, May 28, 1827. For Slater's earlier experience with intermill mobility see Conrad, "Evolution of Industrial Capitalism in Rhode Island," p. 292.

72. Miles, *Lowell, as It Was*, p. 129.

73. The relative ease Waltham mills had in securing workers is suggested in Caroline Ware, *Early New England Cotton Manufacture*, pp. 201, 214. For logistical inconveniences facing smaller mills, see Slater Collection: Dudley Thread, vol. 26, Phoenix Mill to Mr. James Cooke, June 30, 1831; Samuel Slater and Sons, vol. 236, Hedges to John Slater, Aug. 18, 1834.

74. Merino Records: Series IV, Part II, E, Box 23, S. A. Hitchcock to John Brown, Feb. 26, 1831. Slater Collection: Webster Woolen, vol. 26, J. M. Gibbs to Edward Howard, Nov. 30, 1827.

75. John Slater Papers: Samuel Slater to John Slater, Dec. 23, 1808.

76. Slater may have occasionally used such agreements during the 1790s. See Almy and Brown Papers: Box 3, No. 398, Slater to Almy and Brown, Jan. ? [1796]. For contracts during the 1812-40 period see Merino Records: Series I, A, vol. 2, "Contracts." Slater Collection: Slater and Howard, vol. 22; Slater and Kimball, vol. 111. A variation on year-end payments was to dole out "expenses through the year" and the rest in April, or "15 percent on demand" and the remainder in April. All these approaches, however, differed significantly from the previous policy of paying workers their outstanding wages on demand. See Slater Collection: Slater and Tiffany, vol. 93.

77. Derived from: Merino Records: Series IV, Part I, D, vols. 74-75. Slater Collection: Slater and Tiffany, vols. 88-91. In the East Village the proportion of voluntary departures undertaken in the spring grew from 34.1 percent before 1824 to 50.3 percent between 1825 and 1830; the level never became higher. In the Merino Village, the proportion ranged from 14.0 percent (1823) to 34.1 percent (1830).

78. Almy and Brown Papers: Box 8, No. 1092, Slater to Almy and Brown, Mar. 3, 1814. Merino Records: Series IV, Part II, E, Box 23, Nancy Gossett to [Merino Factory], Mar. 26, 1831. Slater Collection: Slater and Howard, vol. 25, William Buckminster to Edward Howard, May 29, 1827.

79. For continuing threats not to pay workers who left precipitously see Slater Collection: Slater and Kimball, vol. 111. Wage payment schedules cannot be derived precisely from extant records, but see Slater Collection: Slater and Tiffany, vols. 89-91; and vol. 101, Samuel Slater to Sales and Hitchcock, Apr. 25, 1827. For an example of workers signing agreements with "time up" before April see Slater Collection: S. Slater and Sons, vol. 237, Joseph Gregory to John Slater, June 7, 1829. For contracts permitting giving "notice," see Slater Collection: Slater and Kimball, vol. 111. Even with these clauses, workers continued to leave "unexpectedly." See Slater Collection: Webster Woolen, vol. 114, Hedges to S. Slater and Sons, Oct. 25, 1838.

80. Slater Collection: Samuel Slater and Sons, vol. 236, Hedges to John Slater, Apr. 11, 1834; Webster Woolen, vol. 110, Christy Davis to D. W. Jones, Dec. 4,

1836. Merino Records: Series IV, Part II, E, Box 20, James Wolcott, Jr., to John Brown, Sept. 5, 1825.

81. On the failure of textile masters to establish wage agreements see James Montgomery, *A Practical Detail of the Cotton Manufacture of the United States of America* (Glasgow, 1840), pp. 39-40, and Paul F. McGouldrick, *New England Textiles in the Nineteenth Century* (Cambridge, Mass., 1968), pp. 35-38. Merino Records: Series IV, Part II, E, Box 20, James Wolcott to Perez B. Wolcott, Sept. 5, 1825. John Slater Papers: P. C. Bacon to John Slater, Mar. 20, 1831.

82. Philip Greven, *The Protestant Temperament: Patterns of Child-Rearing, Religious Experiences, and the Self in Early America* (New York, 1977), p. 25. Whitney R. Cross, *The Burned-Over District: The Social and Intellectual History of Enthusiastic Religion in Western New York, 1800-1850* (Ithaca, N.Y., 1950), p. 6. For a substantially different view of how revivals affected operatives see Wallace, *Rockdale*, Parts III-IV.

83. Miles, *Lowell, as It Was*, pp. 128-40. Carl Gersuny, "'A Devil in Petticoats' and Just Cause: Patterns of Punishment in Two New England Textile Factories," *Business History Review*, 50 (1976), 131-52.

84. Prude, "Coming of Industrial Order," pp. 66-67.

85. Merino Records: Series IV, Part II, E, Box 23, Edward Howard to Chester Clemons, July 8, 1830. Slater Collection: Slater and Tiffany, vol. 84; Samuel Slater and Sons, vol. 235, Samuel Slater to John Slater, Aug. 19, 1825. For comments on comparable situations among the other small mills of southern New England during the middle and late antebellum era, see Brennan, *Social Conditions in Industrial Rhode Island*, pp. 66-67, 86.

86. Brennan, *Social Conditions in Industrial Rhode Island*, pp. 66-67.

87. Slater Collection: Webster Woolen, vol. 114, John A. Wheelock to J. Wilson, Feb. 6, 1840.

88. Quoted in Prude, "Coming of Industrial Order," p. 309.

89. Prude, "Coming of Industrial Order," p. 340-64.

# Artisan Republican Festivals
# and the Rise of Class Conflict
# in New York City, 1788-1837

## SEAN WILENTZ

### I

One of the most important, if still unfinished, tasks of the new labor historians has been to elucidate the connections between nineteenth-century working-class radicalism and other contemporaneous forms of political awareness. Most illuminating have been the attempts to recover the ways in which plebeian interpretations of republicanism helped to shape the rise of American workers' protest movements. Several recent studies, both national and regional in scope, have argued in a Thompsonian vein that republican images and slogans provided various shades of rebellious opinion with "a transcendent and sanctioning 'notion of right.'"[1] Nineteenth-century workers now seem to have been particularly quick to point out that industrial capitalist innovations violated republican principles regarding personal independence and commonwealth. Labor radicalism, we are told, should not be interpreted simply as a response to changes in work structure, wages, or community life (although all these factors were crucial) but as an effort by workers to prevent what they feared was the imminent collapse of republican ideals and institutions.

The argument as developed thus far is a compelling one, but it is in need of considerable exposition and refinement if it is to be as persuasive as the market determinism of the Commons school once seemed to be. While they have illuminated the cultural and political perceptions of workers, historians of labor (unlike their colleagues in other fields)[2] have paid only passing attention to the eighteenth-century origins of nineteenth-century political discourse. In particular they have been slow to give the work of J. G. A. Pocock on civic humanism and commerce and the complementary studies of eighteenth-century America by Gordon Wood, Eric Foner, and others the attention they deserve.[3]

This failure, a product in part of the lingering biases against political and intellectual history, has led to a curious vagueness in terminology—allowing republicanism to signify everything from a belief in democratic government to the cult of "equal rights"—and to an inability to discuss the rise of labor radicalism as part of the broader social and political history of American ideas. Simultaneously, the existing literature leaves open important questions about the links between republican labor radicalism and other realms of working-class thought and experience. What, for example, were the relationships between republicanism and wage earners' attitudes toward work, craft, and the market? How was the advent of evangelical religion, a central event in the formation and development of the working class, associated with radical republican ideology? Why did republicanism, a political outlook rooted in a world of petty production and early commercial capitalism, continue to inspire labor movements long after the dawn of the industrial age?

Beyond these substantive issues, there remains the need to understand how workers rearticulated widely held republican beliefs into a critique of American capitalism. It is one thing to take account, as have several fine studies, of what Foner calls "the contradiction between republican thought and the expansion of capitalist production and market relations."[4] It is quite another to show how these contradictions arose and why workers grappled with them in the ways that they did. Put another way, the history of American working-class republicanism has yet to be explained fully as a *process* of ideological confrontation, negotiation, and redefinition, a fitful process that changed the meanings of old terms as much as it revived them, and that only gradually pitted employers against employees. To analyze this process, it is vital to examine the common roots of both radical republicanism and the entrepreneurs' republican defense of emerging industrial capitalism and then to see how entrepreneurial republicanism tested and helped to forge—and was in turn tested and forged by—the very different republican notions of labor radicals.

This essay will try to solve some of these problems by taking another look at early industrialization and interpreting a series of events that might once have appeared as anecdotal marginalia of labor history, the public trade rituals and political festivals of the artisans of early national and Jacksonian New York City. Thanks to the work of Natalie Davis, Alfred Young, Maurice Agulhon, and others, it should be clear how much a historical reading of public ceremony can reveal about popular *mentalité*, especially about the political culture of "middling" and poor urban dwellers.[5] By attempting to treat in a similar way the origins and development of American workers' pageantry, historians can discover a great deal about working-class republicanism without having to rely solely on the pamphlets and speeches of the articulate few. By concentrating on the artisans, such a study can consider the most important elements in the earliest avowedly class-conscious American labor movements. By focusing on late-eighteenth- and nineteenth-century New York, America's emerging commercial metropolis and a leading center of early labor movements, it is possible to trace the history of republicanism among both organized workers and the craftsmen-entrepreneurs they so stoutly opposed. Above all, if the history of the craftsmen's rituals is placed within the context of the changes in artisan economic and political life, a pattern of associations emerges, one that clarifies some of the relationships between social disruption and ideological combat. Certain questions must remain open, especially about republican radicalism in factory towns and about the ongoing contest over republicanism and labor after 1840; others, above all the question of religion, must be developed at greater length elsewhere.[6] Within these limits, an examination of ritual and republicanism in New York contributes a frame of reference that helps make sense of ideological trends that were eventually to appear throughout industrializing America.

## II

Let us begin with a brief review of the economic and political history of the New York City trades. Early national and Jacksonian New York is rightly remembered as the premier expanding American port, Melville's island of the Manhattoes in the making, where all streets sloped toward the wharfside forest of masts and the merchants' counting houses.[7] Like other commercial ports of the era, New York also provided work for thousands of artisans and craft workers, who furnished everything from luxury items and maritime goods for leading merchants to humble clothing for the respectable laboring poor. Journalists and politicians pointed with pride to this distinctive group of "plain honest men" of the mercantile city, the fiercely independent, self-styled "leather breeches" who stood between the mercantile elite and the common laborers. Yet even as they appeared to be the embodiment of what Thomas Jefferson called the urban yeomanry, New York's artisans confronted profound social and economic transformations, transformations that eventually generated class identities and conflicts within the trades.[8]

As late as the 1820s, the majority of New York's craftsmen plied their arts in small independent shops, settings where some important features of the ancient artisan system of labor remained intact. Although they never had anything approaching an elaborate guild or corporation system, the artisans produced primarily for a limited local market for limited returns, and followed the age-old route of advancement from apprentice to journeyman to master. As in early modern old-world trades, masters usually paid their journeymen by the piece, on a fixed scale that rewarded those with the highest skills. Although they worked in a capitalist market and relied on wage labor, and while they were free of most of the formal rules and restrictions common to European trades, they preserved the ambiguous dualities of artisan production so cogently outlined by Marx:

> The master does indeed own the conditions of production—tools, materials, etc. (although the tools may be owned by the journey-man too)—and he owns the product. To that extent he is a *capitalist*. But it is not as a capitalist that he is *master*. He is an artisan in the first instance and is supposed to be a master of his craft. Within the process of production he appears as an artisan, like his journeymen, and it is he who initiates his apprentices into the mysteries of the craft. He has precisely the same relationship to his apprentices as a professor to his students. Hence his approach to his apprentices is not that of a capitalist but of a *master* of his craft.[9]

As the New York artisans put it, they worked to refine their arts and to earn their independence and a simple "competence," within a co-operative craft system of "reciprocal obligation" between masters and men.[10]

Life in even the most traditional New York shops was, to be sure, hardly one of contentment and pastoral harmony. Craftsmen's families, especially those of journeymen and small masters in lesser-skilled trades like common shoemaking, could expect to live on the margin of poverty. Any common catastrophe—fire, disease, bad weather, a sudden downturn in trade—could plunge them into economic ruin, a fate recorded in pathetic detail in local bankruptcy registers and church reports. Some masters, especially in the luxury branches of production, earned an enormous rate of profit relative to the wages they paid their journeymen, while others mistreated their employees and apprentices. Nor was the structure of the craft economy static. The decline of slavery and indentured servitude in late-eighteenth-century New York made local masters increasingly dependent on free wage labor; the shifting tides of immigrants from Britain and Europe and of migrants from rural areas kept the state of the artisan labor market in flux. But despite the absence of an apocryphal precapitalist artisan "golden age," these conditions alone were qualitatively different from those that would lead to the artisan class conflicts of later years. Through the Jeffersonian period, New York's trades, already in transition, still remained largely circumscribed by the aspirations and hierarchies of the craft order described by Marx and numerous subsequent historians rather than by the imperatives of a mature and extensive capitalist market.[11]

Beginning gradually in the 1780s, and even more after 1825, this artisan system eroded and collapsed in the face of continued capitalist development in New York. The course of decline was quite similar to that evident in other large commercial cities, notably Philadelphia, but it proceeded in Manhattan on an even grander scale.[12] As New York's merchants, armed with ready capital, established their hegemony over American commerce, so they, along with some farsighted craftsmen-entrepreneurs, altered the relations of workshop production and tied the crafts to the expanding local and national market. Several factors impeded most employers from adopting the methods used by the early factory builders; above all, the high cost of Manhattan real estate and the inaccessibility of water power precluded much mechanization or centralization of work. Instead, the merchant and craft capitalists cut their costs to the bone, bought up large stocks of raw materials on credit, and tapped New York's enormous pool of inexpensive immigrant and rural migrant labor by putting as much assembly work as possible into the hands of sweatshop contractors and outworkers. Not all important New York trades were affected. Some, like shipbuilding, required highly skilled hands and could not be divided easily; butchering remained tied to neighborhood markets and a small shop system regulated by municipal authorities and the butchers themselves; still others—cigarmaking, for example—remained small custom trades until the Gilded Age. But in the city's leading crafts—especially consumer finishing crafts like tailoring and furniture-making which served both local and national markets—contracting and sweating became synonymous with the developing industrial order. In no other American city was manufacturing so thoroughly dominated by such an extensive sweated craft economy; by 1850, when New York emerged as the most productive manufacturing city in the nation, observers pointed to New York as the London of America, the metropolitan capital of sweatshop work and degraded artisan labor. So it would remain through the end of the century.[13]

The importance of contracting, as well as the diversity of the metropolitan market, meant that the experiences of New York's craftsmen diverged in some important respects from the image of the displaced, declining artisan commonly associated with early industrializing cities. Far from causing the thorough elimination or proletarianization of the artisans, as seems to have occurred in the first single-industry towns,[14] the restructuring of craft in New York actually opened up new opportunities for those craftsmen willing and able to adapt to the new regime. Some established master craftsmen, notably those who eventually earned membership in the General Society of Mechanics and Tradesmen, quickly learned how to handle the intricacies of credit financing and the division of labor and made considerable fortunes.[15] For journeymen, some roads to self-advancement and independence remained, as did some of the privileges and financial rewards accorded skilled workers; even in the most debased consumer finishing trades, an ambitious younger wage earner might hope some day to strike out on his own as a subcontractor.[16] Much of the poorly paid labor at the base of the new segmented labor market consisted not of debased artisans but of women and (after 1840) impoverished Irish and German immigrants, groups that played only marginal roles in paid workshop production through the late eighteenth century.[17] When other features of New York's industrialization through the 1840s and after are taken into account—the persistence of a dispersed, small-shop work force in the largest trades, the continued reliance on human power and handicraft methods of work, the lingering importance of the local luxury trade, and the preservation of the artisan system of labor in some crafts—it becomes all the more obvious that the city's craftsmen did not succumb to what have long been thought classic patterns of industrial growth.[18]

The effects of this metropolitan form of industrialization cannot, however, be gauged only by the external measurements of social mobility and shop size. The entire social context of production was at stake—the nature of relations between workmen and employers and between competing employers, the types of work to be done, the importance of craft and skill. In this respect, metropolitan industrialization had an incalculable impact upon New York's leading trades, severing the social relations of production and distribution that had once sustained the artisan economy. The work itself, particularly in the consumer finishing trades, was simplified at every level, stripping the journeymen of their expertise and measure of control over production. In the contractors' shops and outwork cellars, payment by piece became a potent means to insure that hands worked as hard and as long as possible. Even custom trade workers found their work more intense than before, while the most privileged in-shop journeymen preparers in the larger "ready-made" enterprises learned to work under the watchful eyes of a foreman.[19] Cutthroat competition of the likes unseen in the provincial port became a way of life in the colonies of garret operations, leading to complaints from small masters beleaguered by the frenzy of underbidding and from journeymen caught in the downward pressure on wages inevitable in the contracting system.[20] Gimcrack goods deluged the market, a blow to the entire concept of craftsmanship for luxury tradesmen and "common" artisans alike. The apprenticeship system, a sine qua non of artisan production, crumbled as employers replaced formal apprentices with either casual child labor or outworkers. Those masters who survived did so by abandoning their direct roles as producers and "professors" of craft. The greater availability of cheap consumer goods did not necessarily bring greater abundance to wage earners; the sweated outworkers, especially in the needle trades, could barely sustain themselves on the prevailing piece rates of the 1830s and 1840s, while even those fortunate journeymen who could count on steady work were paid rates that only just allowed them to support their families. Discrepancies in material life were reflected in housing and residential patterns as masters and journeymen increasingly lived in different sorts of buildings and eventually in different neighborhoods. The shell of the old artisan system remained; within that shell, the system disintegrated, creating new social tensions between large groups of masters and employees.[21]

While the artisans adjusted to new economic and social realities, their political station and allegiances also changed. Despite the influence of the crafts in the anti-British and democratic revolutionary movements of the 1760s and 1770s, the artisans of Federalist and Jeffersonian New York had to overcome the abiding stigma against "meer mechanicks" as socially—and therefore politically—inferior men. Artisan enthusiasm for tariff protection led them to support the Federalists in the late 1780s, but amidst the political turbulence of the 1790s and with the mounting elitism of the leading New York Federalist merchants and financiers, most artisans drifted into the Jeffersonian fold.[22] Once there, masters and journeymen formed a clear "mechanics' interest," devoted to expanding the suffrage and to protecting the artisans' collective rights while muting the growing social splits within the trades.[23] For the most part, the Jeffersonian-artisan alliance remained sturdy through the mid-1820s, reinforced by artisan fears of a Federalist or neo-Federalist revival, the promechanic rhetoric of the early, artisan-dominated Tammany Society, and the Jeffersonians' liberal stance on suffrage for white males. During the late 1820s, however, the disruption of "one-party" Republican rule and the arrival of professional politics, as practiced by the friends of Andrew Jackson, completely changed the context of artisan political engagement. As the Jacksonians won and consolidated power, locally and nationally, large numbers of craftsmen found their sympathies lay either with the proto-Whig backers of Adams and Clay or with more radical spokesmen. As the mechanics' interest dispersed, those issues that divided employers and employees in the workshop, divisions which the Jeffersonians had successfully kept out of party affairs for a generation, began to appear in political debates as well.[24]

The political dilemmas of the late 1820s and 1830s, coupled with the
ongoing disruption of the crafts, hastened the development of openly
class-conscious groups of employers and wage earners.[25] Only three
journeymen's strikes—by twenty tailors in 1768, by the printers in 1778,
and by the shoemakers in 1785—hit the city before 1795; between 1795
and 1820, journeymen in almost every dividing trade formed "permanent" benefit societies, conducted strikes, and delivered increasingly
biting rebukes—with some flashes of class consciousness—against the
more innovative capitalist employers. Most of these journeymen's
societies abandoned trade-union ends during the hard times between
1815 and 1817, but critiques of capitalist enterprise reappeared, in new
forms, when radical Ricardian interpretations of the labor theory of
value circulated through the city's workshops and taverns in the early
1820s. In 1829, these ideas, spurred by the anti-evangelical efforts of the
city's artisan deists, the polemics of Frances Wright and Robert Dale
Owen, and Thomas Skidmore's writings and speeches on property,
provided the small master and journeymen radicals of the Working
Men's party with the basis for their attacks on the more cynical politics
of the Jackson Democrats and the inequalities of American society.
The party fell apart between 1829 and 1831, a victim of the disputes
between anti-Jackson entrepreneurs, Owenite perfectionists, and Skidmoreite "agrarians" in its ranks; thereafter, the journeymen in the
fastest-changing city trades, wary of party politics and most politicans,
returned to union-organizing, linking the radical political economy
that had surfaced over the previous decade to their strikes over wages
and hours. Between 1833 and 1836, natives and immigrants in the
separate craft unions, endangered by the twin threats of the Jacksonian
inflation and metropolitan industrialization, combined to form the
General Trades' Union, the first effective city central labor union in the
country. All the while, the city's prospering master craftsmen and their
merchant allies counterattacked, using the courts to suppress unions
for conspiracy and backing their case with liberal arguments on the
sanctity of individual rights and the free market. They too had their
own organizations, ranging from individual craft employers' societies
to the General Society of Mechanics and Tradesmen, the Mechanics
Institute, and the American Institute, a pro-Adams, promanufacturing
group founded in 1827 to spearhead the promotion of emerging
Whiggish doctrines on the harmony of economic interests.[26] By the
mid-1830s, the strikes and polemical battles between the GTU and the
employers brought to a head all the basic questions surrounding contracting, exploitation, and the fate of the crafts; as never before, these
were presented by the unionists, joined across craft lines, as battles
between capital and labor. While many other issues of concern to all

artisans—temperance, land reform, and antislavery among them— would later intervene to deflect the departures of the Jacksonian period, New York's craft workers and their employers would find themselves returning to the issues and class identities evident in the 1830s for decades to come.[27]

Three rough stages emerge from this sketch of artisan politics and economics: the first, from the 1780s to the mid-1820s, a period of slow but accelerating division of some of the city's largest trades matched with a fraying political unity among the craftsmen and the first wave of union-organizing and repression; the second, in the late 1820s and early 1830s, when political upheaval and quickening industrialization toppled old political connections and fostered a variety of radical critiques; the third, in the early to late 1830s, when the new alignments of entrepreneurs and wage earners crystallized within the trades. In economic and political terms, it was the gradual rearrangement of established alliances and practices and not their sudden destruction that underlay the industrialization of craft. The changes in artisan ritual in each of these three periods reveal the ideological patterns that accompanied these fitful and uneven transitions.

## III

The richness of New York artisan ceremony in the early national years defies some old assumptions about artisan life in the New World. Here, supposedly, with no guilds to foster a sense of "the Trade," the texture of craft traditions, holidays, and community life was thinner than in British and European cities. John Pintard, the wealthy New York philanthropist, noted the difference in 1822, when he claimed that New York's mechanics had fewer opportunities for leisure and celebration than the English workingmen "with their red-letter days."[28] Despite such impressions, however, craft rituals were constant features of early national New York life. Two mammoth craft processions framed the period, the first in 1788 to urge the adoption of the Constitution, the second in 1825 to celebrate the opening of the Erie Canal. On both occasions, thousands of masters, journeymen, and apprentices marched by trade, carrying emblems of their crafts. Throughout the early nineteenth century, the master craftsmen of the General Society displayed their familiar arm-and-hammer crest and motto—"By Hammer and Hand All Arts Do Stand"—whenever citywide celebrations took place. Individual craft groups like the Society of Shipwrights and Caulkers spent most of their funds and energies on such items as "a skooner to be carried in procession," "musick at celebration of the Grand Canal," certificates, badges, and such "articles emblemmatical [*sic*] of our

Trade" as a ceremonial caulking mallet. Craft benefit societies, along with sympathetic Jeffersonian politicians, founded important holidays for annual celebrations, including Independence Day and Evacuation Day, November 25, honoring the British military's departure from Manhattan in 1783. Special events, including the opening of the Apprentice School and the Mechanics' Institute in the early 1820s, also brought colorful craft exercises sponsored by members of the General Society.[29]

Many of the forms used in these demonstrations and rituals had their distant origins in the British trade spectacles which, along with popular carnivals like Guy Fawkes Day, crowded the calendar of celebration in the seventeenth and eighteenth centuries. In addition to marking the feast days of such patrons as St. Crispin and St. Clement, British craftsmen played important roles in preparing royal entries, state visits, and other public civic ceremonies. In large cities, notably London, these festivities culminated in the annual Lord Mayor's Show, an inaugural parade in which artisan fraternities accompanied the incoming Lord Mayor to his installation. Brandishing craft symbols, master artisans carried examples of their wares while journeymen and apprentices performed their daily tasks in mock workshop pageants. The theatrics of the craft shows were impressive enough; the London diarist Celia Fiennes, writing of a Lord Mayor's Show in about 1700, took special note of the "Stages Covered and Carryed by men and on ye top many men and boys acting out ye respectable trades or Employts of Each Company."[30] Even more important, the festivities provided the craftsmen with the opportunity to document the antiquity of their crafts and the usefulness of the labors. The pageants dramatized, not a consciousness of class, but an intense pride in craft and in the ideally interdependent workshop roles of master, journeyman, and apprentice. The emblems and songs prepared for the day bespoke the craftsmen's pride in what they asserted was their rightful place within what one historian has called that "shadowy image of a benevolent corporate state" that had grown from the matrix of guild regulations. One London tailors' song, composed for the Lord Mayor's Show in 1680, set the theme most common in each of the trade displays: "Of all the Professions that ever were nam'd / The Taylors, though slighted, is much to be fam'd."[31]

The precise connections between these British shows and those of early national New York are not clear. There is only scant evidence that colonial New York artisans shared in or even knew much about craft ceremonial; through the mid-eighteenth century, when British spectacles of "the Trade" were themselves declining, the major public festivities in New York do not seem to have had any important craft component.[32] What is clear is that as soon as New York's artisans had an independent nation and economy to celebrate, they did so with rituals and symbols almost identical to those known to earlier generations of British craftsmen. When the General Society designed its emblem in 1785, it borrowed the London blacksmith's artful slogan and the hammer-and-hand design of several guilds. The elaborate procession of 1788 resembled an old Lord Mayor's Show in almost every detail. Preceded by political dignitaries on horseback, the trades marched with signs which, apart from their allusions to the tariff, would have been familiar to any Elizabethan Londoner. The tailors' banners, like those in English parades, depicted Adam and Eve and bore the legend "And They Sewed Fig Leaves Together." The cordwainers' flag included a view of the good ship Crispin arriving in New York harbor, as if the kindly saint himself had made the voyage from the Old World. Several trades not only carried banners but performed the rolling platform displays that had been the theatrical highpoints of the English festivities. Whether as a continuation of trade traditions or, more likely, as a retrieval of those traditions, the artisans' displays suggested that they continued to respect and cherish long-established images of the crafts.[33]

These forms and images remained typical of New York artisan displays until 1825. The Fourth of July, a day for considerable revelry and solemn speechmaking, found masters and journeymen marching through the streets carrying examples of their work, before gathering to hear speeches from artisans and Jeffersonian politicians. Evacuation Day remained, as the English traveler Thomas Hamilton reported, "a grand gala-day at New York," with a procession of the different trades followed by "profuse and patriotic jollification."[34] The march to celebrate the opening of the Erie Canal repeated many of the motifs of 1788. The Journeymen Tailors' Society returned to a pastoral image with their flag of a "Native" receiving a cloak, above the motto "Naked Was I and Ye Clothed Me." The master, journeymen, and apprentice combmakers featured a miniature workshop, in which "seven of the trade," using the latest simple machines, finished six hundred combs, which they distributed to the spectators. Seven other trades performed similar pageants in motion. The employing and journeymen hatters carried a picture of their adopted patron with the words "St. Clement—Hats Invented in Paris in 1404." The Bakers' Benefit Society frankly copied their banner from the one presented by Edward II to the London Company of Bakers in 1307. While they rejoiced at the latest improvement of American commerce, the artisans, employers and employees, continued to regale themselves in ancient symbols.[35]

What did these themes and theatrics mean? At one level, the artisans' ceremonies clearly evoked the ideal communities of "the Trade." Appearing together on holidays and in processions and pageants, the employers and employees in each craft formed a symbolic body of interdependent artisans. To be sure, the masters remained at the head of the artisan order, a position emphasized in 1825 when highly respected masters from the different trades led various delegations; still, each trade was most eager to stress its harmony, cooperation, and self-respect. Even the most arcane icons contributed to the trade ideal. The biblical and religious allusions in the banners, for example, were no demonstrations of a secret baroque piety; rather, much like those of the earlier English artisan festivals, they offered each trade a collective identity, sometimes underscored by such mottos as the shoemakers' "United We Stand." Just as important were the marchers' contentions that their work was essential for the well-being of all. The tailors' banners, for instance, pointed out not only that their labors were as old as Eden or that they were unknown only to "Natives," but that all God's children need tailors. At times, the artisans advanced what appear to have been vestigial "pre-capitalist" ideals about their relationship with their clients. Utility, the use-value of the handicrafts, and not the luxury or special advantages of the artisans' goods, was their central claim about their products, articulated in the name of the trade as a whole and not as a kind of boastful advertising ploy. As if to summarize their direct services to the city, some delegations in the 1825 march, notably the printers and combmakers, handed out free samples of their work as souvenirs to the crowds of spectators. Several trade banners, like the chairmakers' emblem of a chair with the motto "Rest for the Weary," emphasized both pride in craftsmanship and a collective sense of service to the commonwealth. In all, through the mid-1820s, the trades seemed to celebrate an artisan system of production and distribution quite unlike the divided, entrepreneurial, accumulation-oriented regime that had begun to emerge in the city's workshops. To drive the point home, craftsmen and Jeffersonian spokesmen at various celebrations noted that they had gathered to mark what one master called the "common bond and mutual sympathy," the "ties and attachments . . . interwoven with the strongest feeling of the heart" that were supposedly the marks of the artisan community.[36]

At another level, the artisans' gatherings honored a different set of principles, one which both participants and spectators readily identified as republicanism. The dates the crafts chose for their annual festivities—Evacuation Day, the Fourth of July—were only the most obvious indications of their preoccupation with peculiarly American red-letter days. Even in their occasional ceremonies, the artisans usually decided to assemble on the Fourth of July or November 25, when they would explicitly associate their exercises with a commemoration of the Republic. In the major processions of 1788 and 1825, patriotic banners billowed beside signs of the trades. Republican imagery, most often the American eagle, vied with craft iconography for space on the trade banners. Far from a simple displacement of old forms into a new context, far from proclamations of a hollow, merely symbolic patriotism, these themes expressed powerful sentiments. From the 1790s on, orators at artisan ceremonies opened their speeches with the claim that "the feelings expressed on an occasion like this are unknown to the subjects of kings." Their manifestations of "rational liberty," they continued, renounced old-world "luxury" and "degeneration" in favor of republican simplicity.[37]

Most striking were the ways in which the artisans invoked the key concepts of the Atlantic republican tradition, "independence," "virtue," "commonwealth" (or "community"), and "citizenship." Independence, they explained, stood not only for the freedom to ply their trades outside the shackles of British power, but also for the freedom to work without the internal restraints and corrupt privilege characteristic of monarchies. As they honored the interdependence of their own workshop labors, the craftsmen listened to endless perorations on how American mechanics lived in a land of personal independence and equal rights where, as one General Society member put it, no "offensive government" would turn the artisans into dependent "vassals and slaves." Yet as they spoke of independence, the artisans also shied away from endorsing the pursuit of self-interest for its own sake. Each citizen, artisan spokesmen explained, had to put the interests of the entire community before his own, exercising what they called, in classical republican style, "virtue." "Be virtuous," the Reverend Samuel Miller enjoined his artisan audience in 1795, to be followed two years later by the master sailmaker George Warner's declaration that those who sought personal gain alone were unvirtuous, "distinct from the general interests of the community." Ambition for power or riches, later speakers confirmed, would only leave America, like the republics of antiquity, "enervated by luxury [and] depressed by tyranny," a land where "the [poor] will be found in a state of vassalage and dependence on the [rich]." The only way to secure the Republic, they concluded, was for virtuous men of middling property, those whom Warner described as men who lived in "a state of mediocrity," to be active citizens, engaged in the political process.[38]

By adapting familiar and widely held republican language to their own uses, the artisans were hardly projecting themselves as radical social democrats, as later generations of New Yorkers would understand the term. Speakers at artisan ceremonies displayed nothing but

contempt for the dependent or laboring poor, those whom the Republican John Irving ridiculed on July 4, 1809, as "that uninformed class
. . . who, like dull weeds sleep secure at the bottom of the stream." Nor
were women ever incorporated into the artisan festivals of the period,
even though women had begun to become important in the craft labor
force; both republican precepts and the gender-system of "the Trade"
excluded the idea of a female citizen.[39] Neither the propertied masters
nor the propertyless journeymen challenged the "artificial distinctions
of wealth" they conceded were evident in New York City. Rather, the
artisans formulated an attack on political deference that aimed primarily to deny that men of great wealth and privilege—i.e., the mercantile elite—were necessarily the best citizens. As men who held to the
ideals of both "the Trade" and the Republic, they were most concerned
with sustaining a political order that would soften inevitable social
differences, maintain independence and virtue, and legislate the common good. Within this democratic republican framework, it was
enough to claim, as Warner did, that "systems of oppression" would
triumph in America only if "tradesmen, craftsmen, and the industrious
classes consider themselves of TOO LITTLE CONSEQUENCE to the
body politic."[40]

By equating the qualities of the artisan with the qualities of the
republican, the crafts made their most powerful point: as far as they
were concerned, republicanism and the system of "the Trade" were so
analogous as to be indistinguishable from each other. The New York
artisans were not, to be sure, the only group of Americans to claim the
mantle of true republicanism; such assertions were the very basis of
early national and, later, Jacksonian American political rhetoric.[41] But
the New York trades moved beyond commonplace republican pronouncements by attempting to demonstrate, en masse, that their very
social situation, their lives as cooperative yet independent craftsmen,
made them preternatural republican citizens. On the one hand, artisans,
either masters or journeymen who would one day earn their compe-
tences, were peculiarly virtuous men, imbued with the spirit of independence, fellowship, and commonwealth and free from the economic
dependence that bred corruption. As the mason John Rodman maintained in 1813, men of "domestic industry" were uniquely attuned to
republican politics, and "more conducive to the general happiness"
than others. On the other hand, a republic was the ideal polity for
craftsmen, for it allowed them to practice their arts untrammeled by the
arbitrary economic and political power of any privileged class. It was
"in consequence of our Republican form of government," Samuel
Berrian told the tradesmen on July 4, 1815, that "[y]ears of unprecedented welfare and expanding prosperity have smiled on our national

career."[42] In sum, the festivals projected a particular variant of republican precepts, an outlook best described as artisan republicanism, that celebrated the ideal unity of masters, journeymen, and apprentices and depicted the crafts as more likely republicans than other groups of New Yorkers.[43]

Through the mid-1820s, these artisan republican sentiments continued to unite the craftsmen far more than emerging conditions in the trades would have seemed to justify. By reaffirming the supposed basic harmony and identity of interests of all artisans, employers and employees, the ceremonies managed to blur, at least temporarily, the increasingly vitriolic disputes that had arisen between employer-entrepreneurs and wage earners. Even more important, perhaps, the festivals after 1788—particularly those held on the Fourth of July—ratified the "mechanics' interest" and the artisans' allegiance with the Jeffersonians. It was no coincidence that various craft groups agreed, on several occasions, to listen to prominent Republican politicians, including those notorious wire-pullers Matthew L. Davis and Mordecai Noah.[44] Nor was it surprising that the politicians were most eager to address the artisan festivals. For the trades, the appearance of the politicians underscored their newly won political importance while it insured that they would be treated to suitable remarks about the nobility of the republican crafts. For Jeffersonian politicians, the festivals were a fine opportunity to reach out for support from one of their foremost constituencies and to attack their political opponents as enemies to the Republic and to the trades. George Eacker, the prominent Republican, set the tone in 1801, when he invoked the usual artisan and republican phrases about virtue and corruption to denounce the Federalists as "a monied influence distinct from the general interests of the community," whose insidious plans were stopped only with the election of that well-known "Man of the People," Thomas Jefferson. So various politicians through 1825 clouded the early signs of artisan conflict by calling for a concerted effort to beat back what they described as the greatest threat to the Republic, elitist Federalism and (after 1815) crypto-Federalism.[45]

As powerful as these rituals of mutuality were, however, they could not completely deny the emerging splits within the trades; indeed, numerous hints appeared in the ceremonies themselves to suggest that all was not well in the artisan republic. At least once, in 1811 (and probably more often) journeymen cabinetmakers set aside part of the Fourth of July to meet and celebrate American independence on their own; over the next four years, journeymen shoemakers and shipwrights held their own festivities and dinners. In 1825, benefit societies of journeymen tailors, masons, stonecutters, chairmakers, and coopers marched under their own banners in the Erie Canal procession.[46] None of these efforts appears to have turned into a protest against the masters (indeed, in 1825, the chairmakers' and masons' societies joined with their masters in the same contingent); all celebrated the usual artisan republican principles; their importance was overshadowed by the enthusiastic participation of most journeymen, including the hatters and shoemakers, in ceremonies of "the Trade." Yet the very fact that employees in some of the leading New York crafts chose to hoist their own colors on days otherwise devoted to celebrations of intratrade unity confirmed that a shift in social alignments within the crafts was underway.

Even more telling were the less than subtle changes in the rhetoric of leading master craftsmen during various celebrations. At least as early as 1809, during the celebrated cordwainers' conspiracy trial of union journeymen, master craftsmen blended their paternalism with frankly liberal doctrines on the social necessity of self-interest and pursuit of individual gain; after the war of 1812, both the political economy and the moral code of possessive individualism crept into the masters' ceremonial speeches. Increasingly, employers spoke in anxious tones about conditions in the workshops. To the stereotyper Adoniram Chandler, speaking before the master craftsmen of the New York Typographical Society on July 4, 1816, it seemed necessary to urge his listeners to do more for "the promotion of harmony" by aiding efforts at "the suppression of vice [and] the extension of benevolence." Thomas Mercein, the president of the General Society, reiterated Chandler's points on Evacuation Day, 1820, and went on to stress the need for artisans in large cities, "where their employment and intercourse with the rest of the community is extensive and . . . contracts and responsibilities are constantly entered into," to gain "the capacity and knowledge to understand rights and detect errors." Without departing from artisan republican forms, master craftsmen began to add new lessons to their speeches, lessons on keeping regular and industrious habits, restoring an eroding sense of cooperation between employers and employees, and adapting to the new commercial realities.[47]

These changes in style and content foretold deeper divisions in the trades. Until 1825, it was still possible for masters and journeymen in most of the city's leading crafts to march together and to perform the old trade shows, despite the conflicts in the shops. Such an event would be more problematic in later years when the gap between artisan republican principles and workshop life appeared to widen. Significantly, however, the rituals later used by employers and unionists in Jacksonian New York drew upon many of the themes of the early national artisan festivals. Like the Jeffersonian journeymen who met alone or the masters who encouraged artisans to be more like acquisitive but benevolent businessmen, different groups of artisans perceived the world within the accepted artisan republican framework. The difference was that, in the changed political and economic setting of the late 1820s and 1830s, these perceptions eventually turned the rituals into declarations of class consciousness.

## VI

The years between 1825 and 1831 brought one great massing of the New York trades, a procession in 1830 to honor the July Revolution in France. As in 1788 and 1825, the ostensible purpose of the show was to pay homage to republicanism and the crafts. Instead, it demonstrated how fragmented New York artisan ideology was becoming and how differently various groups had begun to interpret the artisan republican legacy.

The idea for holding the celebration originated in October 1830, when a Committee of Working Men, all of them activists in the Working Men's party, called for a public exercise to express their esteem for their brother mechanics in Paris, who had risen against "an ignorant and bloated aristocracy." As Thomas Hamilton later recounted, the group appealed primarily to "the operative class, or *workies*"; among those involved in the original planning was the deist radical printer George Henry Evans.[48] A month later, when the committee met again, what had begun as a workingman's affair had greatly expanded in scope. The committee, persuaded by some outside the original group, added the names of over 250 additional sponsors "to make the celebration more effective." A few of the new men were also well-known radicals or allies of the Working Men's party; the vast majority were either leading merchant capitalists, master craftsmen, or Jacksonian politicians. Almost immediately, the wealthier, more conservative men began to take control. The committee on arrangements, now chaired by Philip Hone, dropped all references to the Parisian workingmen. The craftsmen were still to be the largest single contingent in the events of the day, but they were to march, as before, as united bodies of masters and journeymen. It was not that the newer members of the committee, described by Thomas Hamilton as members of New York's "more enviable class," were all that eager to celebrate the July days; rather, as Hamilton observed, "finding it could not be prevented, [they] prudently gave in, and determined to take part in the pageant." As the committee on arrangements completed its work, it appeared that any ceremonial trace of radicalism among the artisans would be stifled.[49]

As planned, the formal celebration was to be another artisan republican festival, on the order of the marches of 1788 and 1825. Fittingly, the committee chose that New York republican feast day, November 25, to hold the grand procession.[50] Led by the militia and contingents of prominent politicians and Revolutionary heroes—including the aging James Monroe—the trades turned out in all of their usual regalia. The cordwainers carried a grand standard of St. Crispin being crowned by the Genius of Liberty with the mottos "Industry Rewarded in America" and "Union Is Our Strength." The coopers displayed a banner they had used in 1788 and 1825 and another, smaller banner of a finished hoop and staves, with the words "United We Stand." The printers designed a horse-drawn platform on which two presses turned out an ode to the day, set to the tune of the "Marseillaise"; the chairmakers, not to be outdone, also featured a trade pageant, in which a body of men and boys made a cane-seat chair which they later presented to Monroe. As the three-mile-long procession inched along toward Washington Square, where appropriate speeches were to be delivered, there was no overt sign that the marchers believed in anything other than the old artisan republican verities.[51]

It took a foreigner with an acute political sense like Thomas Hamilton to notice that something was amiss. Having expected to see "a vast multitude animated by one pervading feeling," Hamilton was surprised to find "not the smallest demonstration of enthusiasm on the part of the vast concourse" of spectators and participants.[52] A sullen feeling prevailed, one that became all the more obvious when the contingents filed into Washington Square and the official speech making began. Suddenly the disharmony hidden by the old rituals burst into the open. Samuel Gouverneur, Monroe's son-in-law, had begun to mumble through his predictable keynote speech praising Louis Philippe and the moderation of the French when the crowd became unruly. Shouts of "Raise your voice and be damned to you" mingled with more profane opinions of the speaker, nearly drowning him out. All order had seemed at an end, Hamilton reported, when a portion of the audience leapt to the stage and began to struggle for the podium. As the militia tried to quiet the militants, the dissatisfied crowd below knocked out the supports of the scaffolding, causing the entire stage to crash to the ground. No injuries were reported in the melee, but the official ceremonies were quickly brought to a close with some presentations, songs, and a hurried *feu de joie* by the soldiers.[53]

In the evening, the substance of the disputes among the artisans was revealed at various dinners. In the eighth and ninth wards, leading craft employers assembled with officeholders, merchants, and lawyers to toast the names of Louis Philippe, Napoleon ("the victim of the

Holy Alliance'') and the Orleanist financier Jacques Lafitte. A gathering of master printers drank to those future European revolutionary movements which, like the French, would "stop at the point of temperate liberty." A dinner to honor the local Jacksonian leader Samuel Swartout, grand marshal of the parade, brought similar toasts to the moderation of the Parisians and to the various mechanics' contingents for their "splendid appearance and good conduct" in the parade. Meanwhile, at Masonic Hall, a group of Working Men met in a very different sort of celebration. Robert Walker of the Working Men's party began with a speech which made due note of the French and republican spirit but concluded with a denunciation of unrepublican American monopolies, aristocrats, professional party politics, and other "excrescences fastened by the interested on our glorious constitution." The toasts to "Free Inquiry" and "the Rights of Man" included one by George Henry Evans, in the jargon of his trade, to the workingmen of Paris for the *"job* commenced by them . . . may the *finishing stroke* be applied with equal skill." An address to the Paris mechanics, drafted by the original committee, expressed similar thoughts. Where employers of the "enviable class" saw the July Revolution as a successful vindication of political freedom and antimonarchism, those dining at Masonic Hall hoped the revolution would go further, to offer New York workingmen an example to emulate. "[W]hile Europe is thus convulsed to its centre by the struggle of the oppressed against their oppressors," Walker declared, "shall we the favoured sons of the western hemisphere allow ourselves to be despoiled of those rights which the Constitution of our Country guarantees us?"[54]

It would be inaccurate to interpret these events as a sudden or thorough social and political *prise de conscience* by masters and journeymen. The more respectable meetings avoided making any remarks derogatory to American wage earners or radicals; indeed, the shrewdest of the politicians, like the Jacksonian from New Hampshire, Isaac Hill, made a point of toasting "[t]he great state of New York [and] her democratic Working Men." Political lines were not yet clearly drawn among the more fashionable celebrants, as many who would later be stalwart Whigs supped with leading Jacksonians. The Working Men who, after all, permitted themselves to lose control of planning the events, said nothing about the differences between employers and employees, but stuck to classic "country" republican attacks on Tammany, unequal education, chartered monopolies, and those who opposed "the principles of Thomas Jefferson." A few took the opportunity to urge those present to avoid the most radical doctrines and to ignore cries of "Fanny Wrightism, Agrarianism, or any other *ism* but stick to true republicanism." Like the Working Men's party, the dinner to honor the workingmen of Paris brought together small masters and journeymen with many different dissident points of view; in 1830, few, if any, seemed to interpret their grievances as part of a systematic contest between entrepreneurs and wage earners or between the propertied and the propertyless.[55]

The events did reveal a disintegration of artisan harmony that amounted to a crisis of artisan republicanism. Once more, the craftsmen were able to march, however unenthusiastically, in a procession of the republican trades, to mark their shared respect for certain broad ideals. For some, however, notably the more prominent employers, the French Revolution enshrined, in a foreign land, principles that Americans already enjoyed; the most they could do was to use the familiar language of the crafts and the republic to express their hope that in France, as in the United States, industry would be rewarded and moderation respected. For others, artisan republicanism took on different connotations; far from an exemplary land, America had started to turn away from its first principles by allowing corrupting institutions—monopolies, banks, private schools—and unprincipled party politicians to thwart the independence of the craftsmen. "Move on then, mechanics and working men," Walker told his audience, "and your country shall stand redeemed from the poison of fashion and the canker-worm of party; and in their place shall spring up the tree of genuine republicanism, yielding the choice fruits of real equality of rights." More than a divergence between conservatives and radicals, these clashing interpretations signified a bifurcation of the New York artisan republican tradition, with one side satisfied with the status quo and the other insistent that the status quo—economic and political— was, in Walker's words, "at war with the rights and interests of republican America."[56] This bifurcation was only beginning in 1830; each group was just coming to terms with why their own version was the correct one. Within five years the ongoing redefinition of artisan republicanism would turn into a peculiarly republican, peculiarly American form of class conflict.

## V

The transformation of the rituals of mutuality into declarations of class began in the late 1820s and early 1830s with the activities of the American Institute. Apart from establishing itself as the foremost champion of manufacturing in the city, the institute assumed the task of sponsoring an annual trade fair, to draw attention to what one member referred to as the superiority of "republican ingenuity." Such fairs had been tried before in the mid-1820s by the master craftsmen and philanthropists of the institute's forerunner, the Mechanical and Scientific

Institution; the American Institute men, even more than the MSI, decided to make their own fair a top priority. Their efforts began modestly, with a small gathering in 1828. By 1835, the American Institute Fair had become one of New York's most renowned public spectacles, attracting visitors from New England and the upper South as well as from the metropolitan area. Well-known orators and political figures from around the country, including Edward Everett and Tristram Burges, the politician-manufacturer from Providence, agreed to deliver the annual opening-day speeches. By the end of the Jacksonian period, the institute had set a standard for industrial and trade fairs unmatched in the United States until the opening of the New York Crystal Palace exposition in 1853.[57]

As new forms of public ceremony, the institute fairs expanded upon the entrepreneurial messages delivered by the masters after 1815 and recombined them with older images of the trades. The exhibits were monuments to enterprise and innovation, containing what Philip Hone deemed "every object which the versatility of invention and the ingenuity of our artisans and manufacturers could produce."[58] The speeches themselves more pointedly praised industry, obedience, and individual achievement, and sometimes went to extraordinary lengths to do so. Burges, for example, delivered a didactic opening-day speech in 1830, refuting the errors of the "agrarian" Ricardians' version of the labor theory of value and arguing that their views had "effected the excitement of hostile feelings among men, all equally engaged in one great community and brotherhood of labor for mutual benefit."[59] Those attending the fairs were bid to envision the expansion of manufacturing and protection of private property as consistent with the preservation of social harmony, independence, and economic abundance. At the same time, the institute tried to preserve a sense of both old craft and republican gatherings. Although the displays watered down much of the imagery of "the Trade," the speakers reminded their audiences of the similarities, *mutatis mutandis*, between the institute's efforts and the great fairs of medieval burghers. Most important, the orators insisted that the institute's efforts on behalf of industrial capitalist growth preserved respect for what most called "the dignity of labor" and the republican spirit. By 1840, Cyrus Mason was able to look out over the institute opening-day crowd and declare, "this is the appropriate festival of the working-men of our country."[60]

Quite different festivities began in 1833, under the aegis of the General Trades' Union and its constituent unions. Almost as soon as the GTU elected its officers and adopted a constitution, it decided to celebrate itself with a public procession. New emblems of unity, like the GTU banner of Archimedes lifting a mountain with a lever, announced to all that the union was an entirely new type of organization, one composed solely of journeymen wage earners from various crafts. From that moment on, the GTU took its public ceremonial duties quite seriously. A few months after the inaugural march, when the city fathers called for a parade of mourning to mark the death of Lafayette, some GTU delegates insisted that the union—"the creators of wealth"— be allowed to march before every other civic body; otherwise, a few suggested, the GTU should hold its own independent ceremony. Subsequent GTU anniversary processions in 1834 and 1835 reemphasized the sundering of the trades, as did the meetings of individual unions on such republican feast days as the Fourth of July. The rhetoric on these occasions matched the militant symbolism, as union leaders, sometimes couching their remarks in explications of the labor theory of value, excoriated capitalists and "purse-proud aristocrats" for bleeding the journeymen dry. No longer restricting themselves to the standard Ricardian categories of "producer" and "non-producer," GTU spokesmen like John Finch complained that "while the *Employer* [is] rapidly running the road to wealth, the *Employed* [is] too often the victim of oppression, bound to the vassalage of inadequate reward for his labour." For the first time in public discourses, the wage earners referred to "capital," a "class" of men—speculative financiers, merchant capitalists, and entrepreneur-masters—as their enemy. The journeymen themselves, meanwhile, appeared as men united by their status as wage earners, forming what one journalist described as a new "band of brothers."[61]

Yet while the unionists' parades brought numerous innovations in ritual and meaning, they also retained many of the themes and forms of earlier artisan republican proceedings. Although they marched alone, the journeymen in the different crafts repeated the old trade shows and pageants, in what one reporter called a "highly pleasing spectacle" of craft iconography. Despite their newfound brotherhood, the journeymen continued to march trade by trade, evincing a strong consciousness of the special ties within each individual craft. In the GTU anniversary march of 1834, the Union Society of House Carpenters carried the carpenters' arms with a picture of two workmen at their jobs and the motto "We Shelter the Homeless"; in the same parade, the ladies' cordwainers carried the crest of their trade, supported by two women (one holding a slipper, the other holding a boot), declaring "Protective Industry, a Nation's Wealth." Republican sentiments also ran high whenever the GTU or its constituent unions celebrated. The GTU deliberately chose November 25, the familiar republican red-letter day, to hold its inaugural parade in 1833. On numerous occasions, the unionists listened to clichéd phrases about the glory of America's political institutions, as when Robert Walker told the militant Journeymen Stonecutters' Society that "ours is emphatically a government of the people." With all of their newfound anger and pride, the journeymen went only so far in declaring their separate identity or in charging that the trades had been inalterably changed. In 1834, the unionists, out of respect for the Revolution, eventually ignored pleas to hold their own obsequies to Lafayette and joined the citywide tribute, much as the trades had done on earlier occasions. Union speakers exempted "honest" employers from their attacks and voiced hopes that a sense of harmony, what Finch called a "mutual dependence," between masters and men could be restored. Women craft workers, although now a major segment of the labor force in several trades, neither appeared in the marches nor merited inclusion in the GTU; unskilled day laborers were similarly left to organize on their own. Hardly a mythical, well-calibrated "proletarian" force, the GTU proclaimed a radicalism that conserved some of the aspirations and language of "the Trade" they had long honored, and a sense of distinctiveness vis-á-vis other workers that they had long enjoyed.[62]

Far from the ritualistic vestiges, artisan republican principles coupled with the labor theory of value informed every aspect of the various craft groups' outlooks. As the inflation of the mid-1830s and the strike waves of the period sharpened the lines between entrepreneurs and radical unionists, disputes over the artisan republican legacy became all the more heated. For the journeymen, the activities of the GTU were meant to defend the artisan republic which they found crumbling around them. "Corrupt," "selfish" men, acting as a class with the aid of party professionals to protect their collective interests, were, the journeymen claimed, to blame for their plight. Prosperous masters had joined with aristocratic merchants and bankers by forsaking the workshop and living in luxury from the work of others, without any concern for the commonwealth of all and without creating any value with productive labor. The journeymen were cheated out of proper recompense by a system in which, GTU President John Commerford declared, "capital is rewarded by *filching from labor*," making it impossible for the worker to maintain "the independent character of an American citizen." All that had typified the artisan shop, including what the labor press called "the spirit of cooperation," had been perverted or lost in the intense competition of the new workshop world. Skilled craftsmen, once the quintessential virtuous republicans, now resembled, as one mechanic put it, "mere commodities"; if mechanics and workingmen were to "preserve the inheritance for which their fathers have fought," declared the GTU newspaper *The Union*, they had to "resist the invasion which fictitious capital is making on their privileges." Since the skilled employees were threatened, the journeymen warned, surely the Republic itself was endangered; the union sought to rescue "the great principles upon which our government is founded." To the unionists, the offending masters and merchants were not only selfish capitalists: they were, quite simply, unrepublican traitors to a cause that was older than the nation itself, one that masters and journeymen had once honored as a group. To save the republic, the journeymen organized across trade lines to oppose the defenders of egoistic competition, resurrect the cooperative spirit, and insist that they be paid the full value of their labor—a price they alone, and not the market, could fix. Their weapons, in addition to strikes, included boycotts, journeymen's cooperative shops, and independent, non-partisan political action against centralized banking, paper money, and the state prison contract labor system. In their fusion of a radical political economy and artisan republicanism, a fusion that had long been in the making, the unionists found both the means to interpret the causes and effects of metropolitan industrialization and the power to resist.[63]

In response, the unions' opponents perfected an alternative entrepreneurial vision of the artisan republic. Challenged by the growing class consciousness of the journeymen, employers and their allies drew apposite maxims from the defenders of manufacturing and from classical economists—from Smith to Hamilton to Say—to argue that republican America remained free of exploitation. Exhortations to temperance and personal reform, a common theme in numerous American Institute speeches and tracts, served at once to buttress the individualist self-discipline of the masters' political economy, to enhance the employers' authority in the workshops, and to explain away the union as a cabal of "second-rate," "indolent," "blasphemous" men.[64] In their refutation of the unionists, the masters restated the old faith that America's tradition of "equal rights" prohibited oppression. No titled aristocracy blocked open opportunity to accumulate property: as Tristram Burges declared, anticipating the Whig pamphleteer Calvin Colton, America was a land where every man "is a working man," each with an equal chance to win his competence.[65] If a man did not succeed, it was due either to a personal lack of virtue—usually meaning he was a drunk—or to the occasional, and ameliorable, flaw in American institutions. To alleviate the first, the masters offered a series of efforts, coordinated by the General Society and various evangelical temperance groups, to encourage moral regeneration. To correct the second, they aided a series of reform movements, led by the American Institute, to protect the trades from licensed auctioneers and competition from foreign producers, provide an effective lien law, and widen the artisans' access to credit.[66] Like the journeymen's observations on inequality, the employers' passionate stress on entrepreneurial ethics and opportunity implied a significant ideological shift, especially when they ceased to speak of the cooperative workshop and praised the division of labor. Even so, the ideals of "the Trade" remained strong. As before, the masters described themselves as benevolent small producers, the *patresfamilias* of the crafts. By increasing their profits, they contended, employers could also increase their men's wages, and thus prepare them for independence. The main threat to the artisan republic came from the journeymen whose union, mocked by one pro-employer newspaper as a so-called American system, was the soul of coercive tyranny, interfering with the employers' rights in the market and the nonunionists' rights to buy and sell their labor. To support their claim, some employers hinted that the GTU was the handiwork of a few recent immigrants, refugees from old-world oppression unaware of American liberty, who had persuaded some deluded natives to join their scheming.[67]

It was this bitter dialogue over the meaning of the crafts and the republic that set the new boundaries of class within the trades. While they battled over such seemingly straightforward matters as wages and hours, employing masters and their men resolved the tension within the body of artisan republican ideals. Both sides spoke of harmony and virtue, but where masters looked forward to the continuation of republican independence and reciprocity, the journeymen saw in the new market and in the reformed workshop the breeding ground of corruption and their own permanent dependence. While each group drew on new ideas, neither abandoned artisan republicanism; rather, artisan republicanism, already fragmenting from the 1790s to the 1820s, divided into an individualist defense of the emerging order on the one hand and a radical critique of that order, saturated with the spirit of cooperative labor and production for the commonwealth, on the other. In both cases, the ambiguities of artisan republicanism eased the transition from the world of craft to the industrializing metropolis. By 1836, when a hard-fought journeyman tailors' strike coordinated by the GTU led to reprisals by individual masters and the prosecution of twenty of the strikers for conspiracy, the bifurcation was complete. As employing tailors denounced their men as enemies of equal rights, the journeymen organized a mammoth demonstration in support of the convicted men. Amidst trade signs and emblems, the protesters passed out copies of an ominous "coffin handbill" that summed up their own artisan republicanism: "Mechanics and workingmen! a deadly blow has been struck at your liberty! The prise [*sic*] for which your fathers fought has been robbed from you! The Freemen of the North are now on a level

with the slaves of the South! with no other privileges than laboring
that drones may fatten on your life blood!"[68]

## VI

No single series of events, even events as graphic as the rituals examined
here, can fully explain the origins and rise of urban class consciousness, in New York or around the nation. Throughout the 1830s and
1840s, the older rituals of mutuality continued to be performed by New
York tradesmen not affected by metropolitan industrialization, most
prominently by the butchers. Women craft workers in New York, left
by the GTU to organize on their own, used much of the familiar
artisan republican language in their own defense, even though they
had never taken part in the trade festivities; so too did common laborers
when they organized ad hoc strike groups in the 1830s and formal
societies in the 1840s. While immigrants hardly dominated the GTU,
they did play an important role in its activities, bringing to bear their
own visions of the crafts and the Republic. At the height of the GTU
agitation, some journeymen—even in the most militant trades—preferred either the evangelical chapel or the rough-and-tumble republic
of the streets and taverns to the union meeting room. In the early 1840s,
during the ongoing depression that wrecked the GTU in 1837 and
temporarily cooled the battles between journeymen and masters, much
of the old rhetoric of unity appeared once more, at least superficially,
in the nativist and temperance movements; in 1842, the trades were
once again able to mount a procession, complete with pageants, to
honor the opening of the Croton Reservoir and temperate, "cold water"
artisan republicanism.[69] Unless these and other factors are considered—
above all the ebb and flow of conflict and the persistence of the ideal of
harmony among the artisans after the age of Jackson—important features of class formation in the metropolis are missed. Similarly, it
remains for other historians to examine in detail the transformation of
republicanism in other types of cities, where early factory production
was preeminent.

   With all these caveats, study of the artisan festivals still points
toward new interpretations of the making of the middle and working
classes in New York and the significance of republican ideology to
nineteenth-century American workers and employers. Most clearly, it
affirms the importance of ideological continuity—or, more precisely,
the ongoing counterpoint between continuity and change, consensus
and conflict—and reveals the steps whereby the most active workers
and employers rearticulated old ideas as class perceptions. Neither the
unionists of the GTU nor their opponents were entirely "new men" of

the industrial age; both groups interpreted the new world in light of the ongoing struggle over established principles of the Republic and "the Trade," a struggle shaped by the continuities as well as the transformations of workshop production.[70] The pace of industrialization in the different metropolitan crafts certainly affected the degree to which old truths were turned to new uses; nevertheless, the appearance of old conventions in the most innovative displays show that even those employers and journeymen most engaged in trade disputes remained ever faithful to artisan republican ideals.

The changing meanings of artisan republicanism as expressed in the festivals further alters the way we may interpret political and economic thought and the concept of craft during the early stages of industrial growth. Through the early nineteenth century, the New York artisans' economic liberalism, the "middle-class" possessive individualism so often ascribed to them as a matter of course, was tempered by an older spirit of cooperation in the workshop and republican notions of virtue and commonwealth.[71] The breakdown and eventual bifurcation of this set of ideals signified far more than the evocation of "equal rights" and the spirit of 1776 so often stressed by historians.[72] Through the mid-1820s, artisan republicanism stood for an entire moral order, based on the interlocking concepts of independence, virtue, and citizenship and closely related to the "pre-capitalist" features of artisan production and distribution. The apparent growing disparity between these ideals and life in the workshops and in politics, accompanied by the disintegration of the old Jeffersonian alliance, propelled the journeymen militants, not the mere pursuit of an abstract self-interest or a desire to legitimize their actions. At the same time, these values, as tested by the journeymen and reinterpreted by New York's entrepreneurs and successful master craftsmen, informed the most powerful (and, in their own way, highly idealistic) defenses of the industrialization of the crafts. In neither case did the rhetoric of the artisan republic represent a merely nostalgic yearning for a mythical lost age; rather, both entrepreneurs and radicals judged the emerging social order with concepts they shared, and in so doing transformed those concepts into different, and opposing, class visions.

The rituals after 1830, with their strong artisan republican components, further clarify the meaning of class consciousness in the industrializing metropolis. William Sewell, Jr., in his recent study of "the language of labor" in early-nineteenth-century France, describes how, after the July Revolution, urban journeymen (especially those in the metropolitan Paris trades) turned old corporate ideals of trade fraternity into attacks on bourgeois notions of individualism and the sanctity of the wage relation. Class consciousness, Sewell writes, signified

not so much a confrontation between sharply defined groups of propertied entrepreneurs and proletarians as an attempt by militant workers
to adjust their ideals of "the Trade" and "to erect a complete countersystem" to industrial capitalism, one that would honor labor rather
than property, useful work rather than social privilege, fraternity rather
than selfish competition.[73] Similarly, the class consciousness of New
York's union journeymen was neither utopian fantasy nor a prelude to
"proletarian" revolutionism; rather, it was an American form of radical
countersystem, based on older ideals of harmony and fraternity but
containing a thorough critique of the inequities of capitalism and, as
the journeymen saw it, a fully logical and practicable set of proposals
for a different future than the one their opponents envisioned. Furthermore, the class consciousness of the most active entrepreneurs was not
some fixed liberal "bourgeois" outlook; in defense of the emerging
order, the entrepreneurs also wished to vindicate commonwealth, virtue, and independence. By so defining class consciousness, historians
may at last abandon the pointless search for an idealized "Marxist"
class conflict among the artisans (and the search for explanations for
why such conflicts did not occur) and accept the very real class perceptions and struggles of the 1830s on their own terms.[74]

Beyond the 1830s, a full understanding of the artisan republican
framework of early class consciousness makes sense of the ideologies
evident in later New York labor conflicts. Throughout the nineteenth
century, the clash between liberal, entrepreneurial artisan republicanism and the more radical variants remained central to labor disputes.
Continually, during the labor uprising of 1850, the unemployment
demonstrations of 1857, and the strikes of 1872, native New York craft
workers joined with first- and second-generation immigrants and
turned again to the defense of the rights of free-born republicans as the
basis of their cause.[75] In the first major Labor Day procession, in 1882,
New York wage earners of the Central Labor Union carried placards
and insignias with many of the old themes about the nobility of
productive labor and the artisans' contributions to the commonwealth.[76] The Henry George campaign of 1886, the most significant
political movement in New York labor history, restated practically
verbatim many of the radical artisan republican statements of the
Jacksonian period.[77] Just as strikingly, many of the most articulate and
powerful New York industrialists of the later nineteenth century appreciated pieties about the harmony of the free-labor republic that the
masters of the 1830s would have readily recognized as their own. It was
hardly surprising that the somewhat disillusioned Walt Whitman,
though still clinging to some of the artisan radicalism of his youth,
should have chosen to mark the opening of the American Institute Fair

in 1871 with a ceremonial poem that urged his audience to behold America as "in procession coming," "speeding industry's campaigns / With thy undaunted armies, engineering, / Thy pennants labor, loosn'd to the breeze / Thy bugles sounding loud and clear."[78] Nor was it surprising that Abram Hewitt and Andrew Carnegie—both men with links to the New York General Society of Mechanics and Tradesmen—should have presented updated versions of liberal artisan republicanism as political and economic creeds of the Gilded Age. The idiom of the artisan republic died hard, especially in a city where sweated craft work and the consumer finishing trades remained central to the manufacturing economy; only in the 1890s, amidst numerous shifts in the city's (and the nation's) political and economic structure, did other modes of thought and action gain the ascendancy.[79]

Finally, given the history of artisan republicanism in New York, it seems possible to comprehend the language of labor—and capital—in many cities in industrializing America. While none exactly replicated New York's experience, several lesser commercial-manufacturing cities also industrialized in the uneven, "sweated" pattern evident in the metropolis. Moreover, from Philadelphia to Cincinnati to San Francisco, labor radicals and their opponents battled over republican values, coming to many of the same conclusions as the New Yorkers did.[80] Local conditions must, of course, be taken into account; nevertheless, it seems likely that something approaching the bifurcation of artisan republicanism recurred in major cities throughout the country between 1830 and the 1880s, propelling local movements of masters and men as well as such national organizations as the Knights of Labor. The terms and tactics of battle often changed; the social solidarities (particularly those between the labor movement, women, and unskilled immigrant labor) sometimes shifted. Throughout, however, Americans returned to the debates over republicanism and society so evident in Jacksonian New York, pitting industrial capitalism's defenders—those who repeated the American Institute's claim that "[t]o the effects of a republican form of government existing in the United States it may be attributed . . . that a spirit of commercial enterprise and manufacturing interest prevails"[81]—against trade unionists and radicals—those who reechoed John Commerford's assertion that in a true republic, men would be judged by their labor's worth, as productive citizens, and not be reduced to a dependent class, "the willing tools of other men."[82]

# NOTES

Earlier versions of this essay were presented as papers to the Seminar on the American Working Class, Johann von Goethe Universitaat, Frankfurt, West

Germany, January 1978, and to the Annual Meeting of the Organization of American Historians, New York, April 1978. I am grateful to the commentators on those occasions, Gunter Lenz, Alan Dawley, and Bruce Laurie, as well as to David Brion Davis, Eric Foner, Eugene Genovese, and the editors of this volume for their challenging criticisms and useful advice. I should especially like to thank Alfred Young for sharing his own work in progress and Christine Stansell for perceptive readings of several drafts and inestimable aid in the final stages.

1. Herbert Gutman, *Work, Culture, and Society in Industrializing America* (New York, 1976), pp. 49-53, 87. Other studies which discuss working-class republicanism include David Montgomery, *Beyond Equality: Labor and the Radical Republicans, 1862-1872* (New York, 1967); Alexander Saxton, *The Indispensable Enemy: Labor and the Anti-Chinese Movement in California* (Berkeley, Calif., 1971); Alan Dawley, *Class and Community: The Industrial Revolution in Lynn* (Cambridge, Mass., 1976); Daniel J. Walkowitz, *Worker City, Company Town: Iron and Cotton-Worker Protest in Troy and Cohoes, New York, 1850-1884* (Urbana, Ill., 1978); Bruce Laurie, *Working People of Philadelphia, 1800-1850* (Philadelphia, 1980). See also Leon Fink's forthcoming book on the Knights of Labor, based on his dissertation, "Workingman's Democracy: The Knights of Labor in Local Politics, 1886-1896" (Ph.D. dissertation, University of Rochester, 1977). For parallels with the development of European labor radicalism, see Bernard Moss, *The Origins of the French Labor Movement: The Socialism of Skilled Workers* (Berkeley, Calif., 1977); and William H. Sewell, Jr., *Work and Revolution in France: The Language of Labor from the Old Regime to 1848* (Cambridge, 1980).

2. For example, John M. Murrin, "The Great Inversion, or Court versus Country: A Comparison of the Revolution Settlements in England (1688-1721) and America (1776-1816)," in J. G. A. Pocock, ed., *Three British Revolutions, 1641, 1688, 1776* (Princeton, N.J., 1980), pp. 368-453; Robert Dawidoff, *The Education of John Randolph* (New York, 1979); Daniel Walker Howe, *The Political Culture of the American Whigs* (Chicago, 1979); Michael F. Holt, *The Political Crisis of the 1850s* (New York, 1978); and especially Robert Kelley, *The Cultural Patterns of American Politics: The First Century* (New York, 1979).

3. J. G. A. Pocock, "Virtue and Commerce in the Eighteenth Century," *Journal of Interdisciplinary History*, 3 (1972), 119-34; Pocock, *The Machiavellian Moment: Florentine Political Thought and the Atlantic Republican Tradition* (Princeton, N.J., 1975), esp. ch. 15; Gordon S. Wood, *The Creation of the American Republic, 1776-1787* (Chapel Hill, N.C., 1966); Wood, "Rhetoric and Reality in the American Revolution," *William and Mary Quarterly*, 23 (1966), 3-32; Eric Foner, *Tom Paine and Revolutionary America* (New York, 1976). See also Lance Banning, *The Jeffersonian Persuasion: The Evolution of a Party Ideology* (Ithaca, N.Y., 1978); Drew R. McCoy, *The Elusive Republic: Political Economy in Jeffersonian America* (Chapel Hill, N.C., 1980); John F. Kasson, *Civilizing the Machine: Technology and Republican Values in America, 1776-1900* (New York, 1976); Rowland Berthoff, "Independence and Attachment, Virtue, and Enterprise: From Republican Citizen to Free Enterpriser, 1787-1837," in Richard Bushman et al., eds., *Uprooted Americans: Essays Presented to Honor Oscar Handlin* (Boston, 1979), pp. 77-94. For some apposite remarks on the failure of eighteenth-century social and intellectual historians to merge

their work, see Murrin, "Great Inversion," pp. 371-78; the divisions Murrin discusses have been just as troublesome, if not more so, in nineteenth-century studies.

4. Eric Foner, *Politics and Ideology in the Age of the Civil War* (New York, 1980), p. 10.

5. See, for example, Natalie Zemon Davis, *Society and Culture in Early Modern France* (Stanford, Calif., 1975), chs. 1, 4, and 6; Alfred F. Young, "Pope's Day, Tars and Feathers, and 'Cornet Joyce, jr.': From Ritual to Rebellion in Boston, 1745-1775" (unpublished ms, courtesy of the author); Maurice Agulhon, *La République au Village* (Paris, 1969); Agulhon, *Marianne au Combat: L'Imagérie et la Symbolique Républicaines de 1789 à 1880* (Paris, 1979). I have also found instructive John Brewer, *Party Politics and Popular Ideology at the Accession of George III* (Cambridge, 1976); Mona Ozouf, *La Fête Révolutionnaire* (Paris, 1976); Alain Faure, *Paris Carême-Prenant: Du Carnaval à Paris au XIXe Siècle* (Paris, 1978).

6. On popular religion, evangelicalism, and republicanism, see my forthcoming *Chants Democratic: New York City and the Rise of the American Working Class, 1790-1865*.

7. The most thorough study of the early-nineteenth-century New York economy remains Robert G. Albion, *The Rise of New York Port, 1815-1860* (New York, 1939).

8. Howard B. Rock, *Artisans in the New Republic: The Tradesmen of New York City in the Age of Jefferson* (New York, 1979), pp. 151-82, 238-63, discusses the trade economy in depth, but Rock's treatment of the "middle-class," "entrepreneurial" attitudes of the artisans should be read with caution. See Richard Twomey's review in *Pennsylvania Magazine of History and Biography*, 104 (1980), 133-34. For typical contemporary references to the artisans, see *American Citizen* [New York] Mar. 11, Apr. 13, 1801. For Jefferson's remark, see Thomas Jefferson to James Monroe, May 5, 1793, quoted in Staughton Lynd, *Class Conflict, Slavery, and the United States Constitution* (New York, 1967), p. 265.

9. Karl Marx, *Capital*, trans. by Ben Fowkes (New York, 1976-  ), I, 1029.

10. *Independent Mechanic* [New York], Apr. 6, 1811, Jan. 4, 1812; Thomas Mercein, *An Address Delivered on the Opening of the Apprentices' Library* (New York, 1820), p. 3; M. M. Noah, *An Address Delivered before the General Society of Mechanics and Tradesmen on the Opening of the Mechanics' Institute* (New York, 1822), p. 17. See also *Longworth's Directory of the City of New-York for 1805* (New York, 1805), for several ditties on "just" business practices in the trades, as contrasted with the perceived code of the mercantile houses. The following, dedicated to the stone masons, is illustrative:

—I pay my debts,
    I steal from no man, would not cut a throat
to gain admission to a great man's purse,
    or a whore's bed; I'd not betray a friend
to get his fortune; I scorn to
    flatter a blown up fool above me or crush
the wretch below me.

In all, a far cry from the individualist, acquisitive ethics characteristic of later generations of New Yorkers.

11. Insolvency Assignments, New York City, 1800-1831, Historical Documents Collection, Queens College, New York, #1815-41, #1816-32, #1817-430,

#1819-31, #1819-97, and passim; Ezra Stiles Ely, *Visits of Mercy, Being a Journal of the Stated Preacher to the Hospital and Alms House in the City of New-York, 1811* (New York, 1812), pp. 162-63; Richard B. Morris, *Government and Labor in Early America* (New York, 1946); Raymond A. Mohl, *Poverty in New York, 1783-1825* (New York, 1970), pp. 14-34 passim; Gary B. Nash, *The Urban Crucible: Social Change, Political Consciousness, and the Origins of the American Revolution* (Cambridge, Mass., 1979), pp. 10-17, 102-28, 233-63, 312-38. Suggestive accounts of the expectations and aspirations of artisans in colonial and early national Philadelphia appear in Sharon V. Salinger, "Colonial Labor in Transition: Indentured Servants in Eighteenth-Century Philadelphia" (paper delivered to the annual meeting of the Organization of American Historians, New York, Apr. 1978); Billy G. Smith, "'The Best Poor Man's Country': Living Standards of the 'Lower Sort' in Late Eighteenth-Century Philadelphia," *Working Papers from the Regional Economic History Research Center*, 2 (1979), 1-70; Billy G. Smith, "Struggles of the 'Lower Sort' in Late Eighteenth-Century Phildelphia," ibid., 3 (1980), 1-30. Helpful starting points on artisan conditions and disputes in Europe and Britain before 1800 include Davis, *Society and Culture*, pp. 1-16; Steven Kaplan, "Réflexions sur la police du monde du travail, 1700-1815," *Revue historique*, 261 (1979), 17-77; George Unwin, *Industrial Organization in the 16th and 17th Centuries* (Oxford, 1904).

12. See Laurie, *Working People of Philadelphia*, pp. 3-30. See also Susan E. Hirsch, *Roots of the American Working Class: The Industrialization of Crafts in Newark, 1800-1860* (Philadelphia, 1978), pp. 15-52. For a detailed discussion of the material in this and the next three paragraphs, see Rock, *Artisans in the New Republic*, pp. 237-94; August Baer Gold, "A History of Manufacturing in New York City, 1825-1840" (M.A. thesis, Columbia University, 1932); George Rogers Taylor, *The Transportation Revolution: 1815-1860* (New York, 1951), pp. 215-20, 250-52; Allen Pred, *The Spatial Dynamics of U.S. Urban-Industrial Growth, 1800-1914: Interpretive and Theoretical Essays* (Cambridge, Mass., 1966), pp. 155-59; Robert Sean Wilentz, "Class Conflict and the Rights of Man: Artisans and the Rise of Labor Radicalism in New York City" (Ph.D. dissertation, Yale University, 1980), pp. 14-68, 124-92. For background on how metropolitan industrialization affected residential patterns, housing, and artisan life outside the workshops, see Betsy Blackmar, "Re-walking the 'Walking City': Housing and Property Relations in New York City, 1780-1840," *Radical History Review*, 21 (1979), 131-48; and Wilentz, *Chants Democratic*, chs. 1 and 3.

13. George Foster, *New York Naked* (New York, n.d. [185?]), p. 137. See also William M. Bobo, *Glimpses of New-York City, by a South Carolinian* (Charleston, 1852), p. 109. On the similarities between industrialization in New York and in major European commercial port cities, see the account here and those in Gareth Stedman Jones, *Outcast London: A Study of the Relationships between Social Classes in Victorian Society* (Oxford, 1971), pp. 19-32 and passim; Sally Alexander, "Women's Work in Nineteenth-Century London: A Study of the Years 1820-1850," in Juliet Mitchell and Ann Oakley, eds., *The Rights and Wrongs of Women* (Harmondsworth, Eng., 1976), pp. 59-111; Christopher H. Johnson, "Economic Change and Artisan Discontent: The Tailors' History, 1800-1848," in Roger Price, *Revolution and Reaction: 1848 and the Second French Republic* (London, 1977), pp. 87-114; Lynn Lees, "Metropolitan Types," in H. J. Dyos and Michael Wolff, eds., *The Victorian City: Images and Realities* (London, 1973), I, 413-28. For contrasting interpretations of the place of contracting and put-out work in the larger history of

industrialization see Franklin P. Mendels, "Protoindustrialization: The First Phase of the Industrialization Process," *Journal of Economic History*, 32 (1972), 241-61; and Raphael Samuel, "The Workshop of the World: Steam Power and Hand Technology in Mid-Victorian Britain," *History Workshop Journal*, 3 (1977), 6-72. My own interpretation is closer to Samuels's. See also Sewell, *Work and Revolution in France*, pp. 154-61. On shipbuilding and butchering, see Wilentz, "Class Conflict and the Rights of Man," pp. 177-90; on cigarmaking, see Dorothee Schneider's forthcoming dissertation on German workers in New York after the Civil War (City University of New York) along with the early chapters of Samuel Gompers's autobiography, *Seventy Years of Life and Labor* (New York, 1925). Of course, a few major New York trades—most notably printing and certain branches of the clothing trades—did shift to a mechanized, factory regime, at least in part; nevertheless, even most of these trades suffered from the problems of subcontracting, dilution of the work force, and "sweating." See Wilentz, *Chants Democratic*, ch. 3. On the late-nineteenth-century New York economy, see Moses Rischin, *The Promised City: New York's Jews, 1870-1914* (Cambridge, Mass., 1966), pp. 51-75; and David Hammack, *Power and Society in Greater New York, 1886-1903* (forthcoming, New York, 1982), ch. 2.

14. For a recent restatement of this theme, see Dawley, *Class and Community*, pp. 42-72.

15. See Thomas Earle and Charles Congdon, *Annals of the General Society of Mechanics and Tradesmen in the City of New York, 1785-1880* (New York, 1882), pp. 65-130, 398-415; Wilentz, "Class Conflict and the Rights of Man," ch. 3. To be sure, master mechanics and manufacturers remained a tiny minority of New York's aristocracy of wealth in the mid-nineteenth century, a point amply demonstrated in Edward Pessen, *Riches, Class, and Power before the Civil War* (Lexington, Mass., 1973), pp. 46-75 and passim. The point here is simply that some trade employers—either from established families like the Phyfes or newer arrivals in the city—prospered as New York industrialized. For other impressions of successful craft employers, from the 1830s through the 1850s, see Dun and Bradstreet Collection, Baker Library, Harvard University, especially vol. 449; New-York Trade Agency Reports, 1842, New-York Historical Society, mss; Elizabeth Ingerman, ed., "Personal Experiences of an Old New York Cabinetmaker," *Antiques*, 84 (1963), 576-80; Nancy Vincent McClelland, *Duncan Phyfe and the English Regency* (New York, 1939), pp. 91-137; and (with caution) Moses Y. Beach, *Wealth and Biography of New-York* (New York, 6th ed., 1845, 10th ed., 1855).

16. Foster, *New York Naked*, pp. 141-42; Ingerman, "Personal Experiences"; Diary and Recollections of John Burke, 1839-1892, New-York Historical Society, mss, passim; *Daily Tribune* [New York], Sept. 5, Nov. 15, 1845.

17. On women, see Mary Christine Stansell, "Women of the Laboring Poor in New York City, 1820-1860" (Ph.D. dissertation, Yale University, 1979), pp. 57-136; on immigrants, see Robert Ernst, *Immigrant Life in New York City, 1825-1863* (New York, 1949), pp. 73-111. For further sources and a fuller discussion, see Wilentz, "Class Conflict and the Rights of Man," pp. 132-34, 143-48.

18. Wilentz, "Class Conflict and the Rights of Man," ch. 3. See Carl Neumann Degler, "Labor in the Economy and Politics of New York City, 1850-1860" (Ph.D. dissertation, Columbia University, 1952), pp. 1-17. There are several reasons why historians have depicted New York's industrialization as part of a national shift toward a factory system. First, certain branches of production in

many leading New York trades (especially clothing) did, indeed, turn increasingly to factory work with sewing machines after 1850. It should be noted,
however, that these branches (e.g., hoop-skirt-making, collarmaking, some
shirtmaking) hardly composed the majority of the trade; furthermore, these
changes only appeared in the 1850s. Second, historians have been misled by the
categories of the state and federal censuses of industry. Unfortunately, the
census-takers did not distinguish between in-shop workers and outworkers in
any firm; hence, many firms appear from the census to have been large
factories, hiring 100 or more workers under one roof. If the breakdown between
in- and outworkers is taken into account, the New York scene looks quite
different. The case of the clothing trade is most instructive; contemporary
investigations suggest that up to 60 percent of all clothing trade employees
were outworkers or sweatshop hands. Moreover, many of the sewing machines
(the harbinger of mechanization) eventually used in New York were not in-
stalled in factories but leased to outworkers by contractors, an adaptation of the
outwork system that added to the contractors' profits. See *Hunt's Merchant
Magazine*, 20 (1849), 346; *Daily Tribune*, Aug. 20, 1853; *Herald*, June 11, 1853,
Oct. 27, 1857.

19. *Daily Tribune*, Sept. 5, 9, Nov. 12, 15, 1845; *Herald*, June 15, 1853; *Hunt's
Merchant Magazine*, 20 (1849), 116, 346; Horace Greeley, *Art and Industry*
(New York, 1853), p. 110.

20. *Daily Tribune*, Sept. 5, 9, 11, 15, Nov. 12, 15, 1845, May 22, 1850. For a
clear explication of urban contracting in other cities, see Edwin T. Freedly,
*Philadelphia and Its Manufactures* (Philadelphia, 1867), p. 78; Jones, *Outcast
London*, pp. 19-32; Henriette Vanier, *Les Modes et les Metiers: Frivolités et
Luttes des Classes, 1830-1870* (Paris, 1960).

21. See Wilentz, "Class Conflict and the Rights of Man," pp. 124-92.

22. Alfred F. Young, *The Democratic Republicans of New York: The Origins,
1763-1797* (Chapel Hill, N.C., 1966), pp. 77, 100-103, 157, 201-2, 405-7, 449-52.

23. Alfred F. Young, "The Mechanics and the Jeffersonians: New York, 1783-
1801," *Labor History*, 5 (1964), 247-76; Mohl, *Poverty in New York*, pp. 228-34;
Rock, *Artisans in the New Republic*, pp. 45-122.

24. Jerome Mushkat, *Tammany: The Evolution of a Party Machine, 1789-
1865* (Syracuse, 1972), pp. 75-127. See also Michael Wallace, "Changing Concepts of Party in the United States: New York, 1815-1828," *American Historical
Review*, 74 (1968), 453-91, on the effects of party development on various
strands of republican thought. On artisan politics in the late 1820s, see Wilentz,
*Chants Democratic*, ch. 5.

25. In addition to the works by Morris and Rock already cited, see John R.
Commons et al., *History of Labour in the United States* (New York, 1916), I,
232-33, 459-62; Arthur M. Schlesinger, Jr., *The Age of Jackson* (Boston, 1945),
pp. 192-98; Walter Hugins, *Jacksonian Democracy and the Working Class: A
Study of the New York Workingmen's Movement, 1829-1837* (Stanford, Calif.,
1960); Edward Pessen, *Most Uncommon Jacksonian: Radical Leaders of the
Early Labor Movement* (Albany, 1967); David Harris, *Socialist Origins in the
United States: American Forerunners of Marx, 1817-1832* (Assen, The Nether-
lands, 1967); John Barkley Jentz, "Artisans, Evangelicals, and the City: A
Social History of the Abolition and Reform Movements in Jacksonian New
York" (Ph.D. dissertation, City University of New York, 1977). See Wilentz,
"Class Conflict and the Rights of Man," pp. 194-380.

26. On the American Institute, see Charles Patrick Daly, *Origin and History*

*of Institutions for the Promotion of the Useful Arts* (Albany, 1864), p. 28; John W. Chambers, *A Condensed History of the American Institute* (New York, 1892); Samuel P. Rezneck, "The Rise and Early Development of Industrial Consciousness in the United States, 1760-1830," *Journal of Economic and Business History*, Supplement, 4 (1932), 784-811.

27. Wilentz, "Class Conflict and the Rights of Man," pp. 391-506. See Laurie, *Working People of Philadelphia*, pp. 107-87.

28. John Pintard, *Letters from John Pintard to His Daughter* (New York, 1941), II, 138. On the lack of continuity between old-world artisan culture and the colonial New York crafts, see Samuel McKee, *Labor in Colonial New York, 1660-1776* (New York, 1938), pp. 21-22, 60-62, and passim.

29. Cadwallader D. Colden, *Memoir Prepared at the Request of a Committee of the Common Council of the City of New York* (New York, 1825), pp. 213-36, 250-55, 261-62; William L. Stone, *Narrative of the Festivities Observed in Honor of the Completion of the Grand Erie Canal* (New York, 1825), pp. 319-28; General Society of Mechanics and Tradesmen, Minute Book, 1785-1832, General Society of Mechanics and Tradesmen, New York, mss, Jan. 6, 1789, June 7, 1797, Mar. 7, June 6, 1798, Jan. 1, 1800, June 17, 1801, Dec. 4, 1804, July 4, 1807, Mar. 8, 1808, Jan. 9, 1821, Jan. 19, 1823; Society of Shipwrights and Caulkers, Minute Book, New York Public Library, mss, May 29, June 5, 8, 19, 30, Sept. 14, Oct. 12, 1815, Jan. 22, 1816, Feb. 12, 1818; Union of Shipwrights and Caulkers, Bank Book, New York Public Library, mss, Dec. 8, 1825; *New York Journal*, July 4, 5, 1794; *New York Weekly Chronicle*, July 9, 1795; Edwin P. Kilroe, *St. Tammany and the Origin of the Society of Tammany, or Columbian Order, in the City of New York* (New York, 1913), pp. 177-83. See Howard B. Rock, "The American Revolution and the Mechanics of New York City: One Generation Later," *New York History*, 57 (1976), 367-416. On Fourth of July celebrations in early-nineteenth-century America, see Michael Kammen, *A Season of Youth: The American Revolution and the Historical Imagination* (New York, 1978), pp. 26-58.

30. Robert Withington, *English Pageantry* (Cambridge, Mass., 1918-20), II, 67.

31. E. P. Thompson, *The Making of the English Working Class* (Harmondsworth, Eng., 1968), p. 594; William Hone, *Ancient Mysteries Described* (London, 1823), p. 255. See also Hone, *The Every-Day Book* (London, 1825-26), I, 1387, 1397-1402, 1439-53, II, 470-71, 627-29, 669-76; John Brand, *Observations on Popular Antiquities* (London, 1823), I, 356-67, 408-10; Fredrick W. Fairholt, *Lord Mayors' Pageants* (London, 1843-44); George Unwin, *The Gilds and Companies of London* (London, 1909), pp. 93-109, 176-200, 267-92; P. H. J. H. Gosden, *The Friendly Societies in England* (Manchester, 1961), pp. 2-12; Thompson, *Making of the English Working Class*, pp. 456-69; Robert W. Malcolmson, *Popular Recreations in English Society, 1700-1850* (Cambridge, 1973), pp. 51-52. On late medieval and early modern pageants, in addition to E. K. Chambers's classic works, see Alan H. Nelson, "Some Configurations of Staging in Medieval English Drama," in Jerome Taylor and Alan H. Nelson, eds., *Medieval English Drama: Essays Critical and Contextual* (Chicago, 1972), pp. 116-47. For a very different view of craft ceremony, see Jacques Heer, "Les metiers et les fêtes médiévales en France et en Angleterre," *Revue du Nord*, 55 (1973), 193-202. On craft pride and solidarity, see E. P. Thompson, "Eighteenth-Century English Society: Class Struggle without Class?" *Social History*, 3 (1978), 144-46.

32. See Alfred F. Young, "English Plebeian Culture and Eighteenth-Century American Political Movements" (paper delivered to the International Conference on the Origins of Anglo-American Radicalism, New York, Oct. 1980), Part III. On those survivals of craft that were evident in pre-Revolutionary America, see Morris, *Government and Labor*, pp. 139-56, 198-99.

33. *New York Packet*, July 8, 11, 22, 1788; *Independent Journal*, July 23, 1788; John Bromley and Heather Child, *The Armorial Bearings of the Guilds of London* (London, 1960), pp. 15, 22, 79, 86, 262. See also Alfred F. Young, "'By Hammer and Hand All Arts Do Stand': The Mechanic and Laboring Classes and the Shaping of the Nation" (paper delivered to the annual meeting of the Organization of American Historians, San Francisco, Apr. 1980).

34. Thomas Hamilton, *Men and Manners in America* (London, 1833), I, 59. On the Fourth of July, see also Gabriel Furman, "How New York City Used to Celebrate Independence Day," *New-York Historical Society Quarterly*, 21 (1937), 93-96; Society of Shipwrights and Caulkers, Minute Book, Oct. 12, 1815, Jan. 23, 1816.

35. Colden, *Memoir*, pp. 228-30; Stone, *Narrative*, p. 330.

36. Mercein, *Address*, p. 3. It should be emphasized that labeling some of the features of these celebrations as "pre-capitalist" does not mean that the artisans did not work in a capitalist market or share concepts the twentieth century has called "rational." Rather, the point is that through the early nineteenth century it was still possible for the artisans—and others—to fuse "pre-capitalist" and "capitalist" ethics. For a clear-headed discussion of this problem, in a different context, see Elizabeth Fox-Genovese, "Poor Richard at Work in the Cotton Fields: A Critique of the Psychological and Ideological Suppositions of *Time on the Cross*," *Review of Radical Political Economics*, 7 (1975), 71.

37. George I. Eacker, *An Oration Delivered at the Bequest of the Officers of the Brigade of the City and County of New-York and of the County of Richmond and the Mechanic, Tammany, and Coopers' Societies on the Fourth of July, 1801* (New York, 1801), p. 3; Samuel Berrian, *An Oration Delivered before the Tammany Society, or Columbian Order, Tailors', Coopers', Hibernian Provident, Shipwrights', Columbian, Manhattan, and Cordwainers' Societies in the City of New-York on the Fourth of July, 1811* (New York, 1811), pp. 3-4; Noah, *Address*, p. 5; Samuel B. Romaine, *An Oration Delivered before the Tammany Society, or Columbian Order, Tailors', Hibernian Provident, Shipwrights', Columbian, Manhattan, and Cordwainers' Societies in the City of New-York on the Fourth of July, 1812* (New York, 1812), pp. 3-4; Dr. George Cuming, *An Oration Delivered in the Presbyterian Church in East Rutgers Street before the Tammany, Tailors', Hatters', Hibernian Provident, Masons', Shipwrights', Carpenters', and Columbian Societies* (New York, 1810), pp. 7-8.

38. Samuel Miller, *A Sermon Delivered in the New Presbyterian Church New-York, July the Fourth, 1795, Being the Nineteenth Anniversary of the Independence of America, at the Bequest of and before the Mechanic, Tammany, and Democratic Societies, and the Military Officers* (New York, 1795), pp. 13, 26; George James Warner, *Means for the Preservation of Liberty. An Oration Delivered in the New Dutch Church on the Fourth of July, 1797* (New York, 1797), pp. 4, 12-14; P[eter] H. Wendover, *National Deliverence. An Oration Delivered in the New Dutch Church on the Fourth of July, 1806, Being the Thirtieth Anniversary of American Independence, before the General Society of Mechanics and Tradesmen, Tammany, Coopers', Taylors', Hatters', Masons', Shipwrights', and Hibernian Provident Societies* (New York, 1806), pp. 11-14.

39. John T. Irving, *An Oration Delivered on the Fourth of July, 1809, before the Tammany Society, or Columbian Order, Tailors', Coopers', Hatters', Hibernian Provident, Masons', Shipwrights', House Carpenters', and Columbian Societies* (New York, 1809), pp. 11. On women, work, and the Republic, see Nash, *Urban Crucible*, pp. 194-96; Stansell, "Women of the Laboring Poor," pp. 110-18; Linda K. Kerber, *Women of the Republic: Intellect and Ideology in Revolutionary America* (Chapel Hill, N.C., 1980).

40. Warner, *Means*, pp. 13-14; Mercein, *Address*, pp. 12-13. George Cuming recited verse to make the same point:

> For he who soars to an unwonted height,
> Oppressive dazzels, with excess of light,
> The arts beneath him; yet when dead shall prove,
> An object worthy of esteem and love?

Cuming, *Oration*, p. 7.

41. On this point, see Kelley, *Cultural Patterns of American Politics*, pp. 50-60, 75-93, 137, 271-75, 404-43; Sean Wilentz, "Whigs and Bankers," *Reviews in American History*, 8 (1980), 344-50.

42. John Rodman, *An Oration Delivered before the Tammany Society, or Columbian Order, Sailors', Hibernian Provident, Columbian, Cordwainers', and George Clinton Societies in the City of New-York, on the Fourth Day of July, 1813* (New York, 1813), p. 9; Berrian, *Oration*, pp. 27-28. For a complementary analysis, see Rex Burns, *Success in America: The Yeoman Dream and the Industrial Revolution* (Amherst, Mass., 1976).

43. Alfred F. Young will offer a different elaboration of artisan republicanism—one fully compatible with that outlined here—in his forthcoming study of artisans in the early republic.

44. On Davis and Noah, see Mushkat, *Tammany*, pp. 22-36, 38-41, 43-45, 58-60, 95-96; Matthew L. Davis, *An Oration Delivered in St. Paul's Church on the Fourth of July, 1800* (New York, 1800); Noah, *Address*.

45. Eacker, *Oration*, pp. 14-15.

46. *Independent Mechanic*, June 2, 1811; *National Advocate* [New York], Mar. 8, 1813; Society of Shipwrights and Caulkers, Minute Book, Oct. 12, 1815; Colden, *Memoir*, pp. 212-62.

47. John R. Commons et al., *Documentary History of American Industrial Society* (Cleveland, 1910-11), III, 251-385; Adoniram Chandler, *An Address Delivered before the New-York Typographical Society, July 14, 1816, on Their Seventh Anniversary* (New York, 1816), p. 9; Mercein, *Address*, p. 8. See also General Society of Mechanics and Tradesmen, "To the Public," broadside (1820), New-York Historical Society.

48. Myer Moses, *Full Account of the Celebration of the Revolution in France in the City of New-York on the 25th November, 1830* (New York, 1830), pp. 6-7; Hamilton, *Men and Manners*, p. 59. The previous Fourth of July, the Working Man's party held its own Independence Day celebration, at which a new "workingman's" Declaration of Independence was read, *Daily Sentinel* [New York], July 12, 1830. On this and other early labor celebrations of Independence Day, see the documents collected in Philip Foner, *We, the Other People* (Urbana, Ill., 1976), pp. 46-83.

49. Moses, *Full Account*, pp. 7-21; Hamilton, *Men and Manners*, p. 60. Among the few radical newcomers were the Owenite Ebenezer Ford and the Skidmoreite Alexander Ming, Jr.; among the rest were Gulian Verplanck, Philip Hone, shipbuilder Henry Eckford, Gideon Lee, and Duncan Phyfe. On

the radicals' misgivings about the upcoming event, see *Working Man's Advocate* [New York], Nov. 27, 1830.

50. Unfortunately for the marchers, bad weather on the morning of the 25th forced cancellation of the parade until the following week. Various trades and spokesmen nevertheless mentioned the significance of Evacuation Day during the celebration, Moses, *Full Account*, pp. 48-49.

51. Moses, *Full Account*, pp. 56-71.

52. Hamilton, *Men and Manners*, pp. 69-70.

53. Hamilton, *Men and Manners*, pp. 67-68. See also Allan Nevins, ed., *The Diary of Philip Hone, 1828-1851* (New York, 1936), pp. 30-32.

54. Moses, *Full Account*, pp. 99-119, 128-30, 136-46; *Working Man's Advocate*, Dec. 18, 1830. Although the link would be fascinating, there appears to be no special significance to the Working Man's Committee's use of Masonic Hall for their dinner; many groups used the facility for public meetings and exhibitions, including the American Institute in 1828.

55. Moses, *Full Account*, pp. 103, 118. "Country" or classical republicanism refers to that form of political thought expressed by the so-called Country party in eighteenth-century Britain, concerned most directly with patronage and commercial institutions (especially central banks) as engines of political dependence and corruption. For background, see Pocock, *Machiavellian Moment*; and on the strange career of "country" ideology in America, see Murrin, "Great Inversion." For a fine discussion and exposition of "country" themes in the New York Working Men's party press, see David Jaffee's "Web of Deceit" (honors thesis, Harvard University). I am grateful to Mr. Jaffee for bringing this work to my attention and sending me a copy.

56. Moses, *Full Account*, p. 114.

57. On the fairs, see American Institute, *Reports of the American Institute of the City of New-York on the Subject of Fairs* (New York, 1829); Thomas Mc Elrath, "Sketch of the Rise and Progress of the American Institute," *Transactions of the American Institute*, 1 (1860), 86-87; John Doggett, Jr., *The Great Metropolis; or Guide to New York in 1846* (New York, 1846), p. 84.

58. Nevins, *Diary of Philip Hone*, p. 28.

59. Tristram Burges, *Address of the Hon. Tristram Burges Delivered at the Third Annual Fair of the American Institute of the City of New-York* (New York, 1830), p. 17 and passim.

60. Cyrus Mason, *The Oration on the Thirteenth Anniversary of the American Institute at the Broadway Tabernacle* (New York, 1840), p. 5.

61. *Working Man's Advocate*, Nov. 30, Dec. 6, 21, 1833, Nov. 28, 1834, Sept. 19, 1835; *The Man* [New York], June 25, 26, 27, 1834, Feb. 7, June 17, July 6, 1835; *Evening Star* [New York], Dec. 7, 1833; *The Union* [New York], July 2, 1836; Robert Walker, *Oration Delivered at Clinton Hall to the Journeymen Stone Cutters' Association on the Fifty-Seventh Anniversary of American Independence, July 4, 1833* (New York, 1833); John Finch, *Rise and Progress of the General Trades' Union of the City of New York and Its Vicinity* (New York, 1833), pp. 14-17; Ely Moore, *An Address Delivered before the General Trades' Union in the City of New York* (New York, 1833); *New York Transcript*, Aug. 29, 1834.

62. *New York Transcript*, Aug. 29, 1834; *National Trades' Union* [New York], Sept. 27, 1834; *Working Man's Advocate*, Nov. 30, 1833; Walker, *Oration*, p. 14; Finch, *Rise and Progress*, p. 13; *Man*, June 27, 1834. Harriet Martineau, an astute observer of America despite her blander assumptions about human

nature, was impressed by one GTU parade's trappings to the point of missing the marchers' point; for her, the procession of such enthusiastic "dandy mechanics" confirmed that basic harmony reigned in New York's workshops. See her *Society in America* (London, 1837), II, 62-63. Martineau's observations had been anticipated, in a more pointed way, by "Eckford" (Henry Eckford?), who claimed of one newspaper report about the march in 1833 that "the compliments you bestow upon their appearance indicate anything else than that they are a class of persons in danger of having any part of their daily earnings taken from them by a combination of employers." The speciousness of the remark was evident to "Unionist," who replied, "Is it sufficient for him ["Eckford"] to know that they are able, with all their means, to make a respectable appearance, on a public occasion, *once a year*, to come to the conclusion that the producers of most of the wealth are adequately remunerated for their labor?" See *Evening Star*, Dec. 7, 1833; *Working Man's Advocate*, Dec. 21, 1833. On women, see Stansell, "Women of the Laboring Poor," pp. 118-28.

63. *Working Man's Advocate*, Sept. 19, 1835; *The Union*, Apr. 28, May 20, 1836.

64. *Journal of the American Institute*, 1 (1836), 526-31, 2 (1837), 554, 579-86, 3 (1838), 113-17; Commons et al., *Documentary History*, V, 209-11, 314-15.

65. Burges, *Address*, p. 15. Colton's more celebrated remarks appeared later in "Labor and Capital," *Junius Tracts, Number VII* (New York, 1844), p. 15.

66. *Working Man's Advocate*, Feb. 20, 1830; New-York City Temperance Society, *First Annual Report* (New York, 1830); American Institute, *Report of a Special Committee of the American Institute on the Subject of Cash Duries, the Auction System, etc.* (New York, 1829); American Institute, *Memorial of the American Institute Praying for Certain Regulations of the Banking Capital of This State, March 14, 1829* (New York, 1829); *Journal of the American Institute*, I (1835), 3-5; T. B. Wakeman, *An Introductory Lecture Delivered for the American Institute of the City of New-York* (New York, 1835); Wilentz, "Class Conflict and the Rights of Man," pp. 195-212, 367-85; Jentz, "Artisans, Evangelicals, and the City," pp. 84-95. See Paul E. Johnson, *A Shopkeepers' Millennium: Society and Revivals in Rochester, New York, 1815-1837* (New York, 1978).

67. For discussions of these charges, see *Man*, Apr. 5, 1834; *The Union*, June 7, 10, July 2, 1836. Other anti-unionists also blamed immigrants, but considered them the dupes of a few unscrupulous natives. See Nevins, *Diary of Philip Hone*, p. 199.

68. *The Union*, July 13, 14, 15, 1836; Commons et al., *Documentary History*, V, 317.

69. Thomas De Voe, *The Market Book* (New York, 1862), pp. 347, 438-39, 506-7; Alvin Harlow, *Old Bowery Days* (New York, 1931), pp. 150-51; Charles H. Haswell, *Reminiscences of an Octogenarian of the City of New-York* (New York, 1897), p. 60; Stansell, "Women of the Laboring Poor," pp. 124-25; Wilentz, "Class Conflict and the Rights of Man," pp. 294-95, 349-67; Charles King, *A Full Description of the Celebration Held in Honor of the Opening of the Croton Reservoir* (New York, 1842).

70. See Alan Dawley and Paul Faler, "Working-Class Culture and Politics in the Industrial Revolution: Sources of Loyalism and Rebellion," *Journal of Social History*, 9 (1976), 466-80. For a discussion of this point in different contexts, see Christopher Hill, *Change and Continuity in Seventeenth-Century England* (Cambridge, Mass., 1978); and Gareth Stedman Jones, "Class Expression Versus Social Control," *History Workshop Journal*, 4 (1977), 163-70.

71. Compare Carl Bridenbaugh, *The Colonial Craftsman* (Chicago, 1950), esp. pp. 65-72; Rock, *Artisans in the New Republic*, pp. 151-82. The recent revival of interest in Sombart's simplified sociologisms has also raised this point, appearing to equate America's lack of a communal feudal past with the lack of any artisan cultures or traditions of "the Trade." See, for example, Jerome Karabel, "The Failure of American Socialism Reconsidered," in Ralph Miliband and John Saville, eds., *The Socialist Register 1979: A Survey of Movements and Ideas* (London, 1979). Mike Davis's more recent synoptic review of American labor history at least allows that "artisanal" culture took root in the seaboard cities, but Davis remains vague about what that culture was and ill informed about its more radical expressions in the late 1820s and 1830s. See Mike Davis, "Why the U.S. Working Class Is Different," *New Left Review*, 123 (1980), 23-25 and passim.

72. See Dawley, *Class and Community*, pp. 1-3, 9-10, 58, 60, 65-67, and passim.

73. Sewell, *Work and Revolution in France*, pp. 281-84 and passim.

74. Such searches for ideal types and the roots of false consciousness are hardly restricted to orthodox Marxist scholarship; indeed, far more work like this has been done by historians working in the Sombart tradition or with the methods and questions posed by twentieth-century American sociologists. See, for example, Karabel, "Failure," and several of the essays included in John H. M. Laslett and Seymour M. Lipset, eds., *Failure of a Dream? Essays in the History of American Socialism* (Garden City, N.Y., 1974). The point here is not that class analysis should be abandoned—quite the contrary—but only that the study of class consciousness in America should not be subjected to questions that presume that American workers have not lived up to some ideal Marxist categories or to standards gleaned from a hasty reading of European labor history. Put another way, the question posed by Sombart two generations ago should be turned on its head; rather than ask why there is no socialism in America, or no class consciousness in America, historians should find out more about the class perceptions that did exist. For a provocative assault on some of these problems (from a somewhat different perspective from the one offered here), see Lee Benson, "Marx's General and Middle-Range Theories of Social Conflict," in Robert K. Merton, James S. Coleman, Peter H. Rossi, eds., *Qualitative and Quantitative Social Research: Papers in Honor of Paul F. Lazarsfeld* (New York, 1979), pp. 189-209. See also the introductory section in Davis, "Why the U.S. Working Class Is Different," pp. 6-9.

75. On the uprising of 1850, see Wilentz, "Class Conflict and the Rights of Man," pp. 450-96. On later events, I have profited from Degler, "Labor in the Economy and Politics of New York," pp. 157-97; William Garfinkel, "Guarding the Liberty Tree: New York City and the Panic of 1857" (senior thesis, Yale University, 1977); Basil Leo Lee, *Discontent in New York City, 1861-1865* (Washington, D.C., 1943), pp. 195-228; *New York Times*, June 12, 1872.

76. *New York Tribune*, Sept. 6, 1882.

77. Georgeism, and especially the election of 1886, require a fresh and full-length evaluation, but see Michael Gordon, "The Labor Boycott in New York City, 1880-1886," *Labor History*, 16 (1975), 184-229; Bart Steinfeld, "'The Masses against the Classes': Henry George, the Labor Movement, and the Election of 1886" (senior thesis, Yale University, 1977); Eric Foner, *Politics and Ideology*, pp. 184-99 passim.

78. Walt Whitman, "After All, Not to Create Only," *Daily Tribune*, Sept. 8,

1871. The poem eventually appeared in *Leaves of Grass* as "Song of the Exposition," in Francis Murphy, ed., *Walt Whitman: The Complete Poems* (Harmondsworth, Eng., 1975), pp. 225-35. See also Gay Wilson Allen, *The Solitary Singer: A Critical Biography of Walt Whitman* (New York, 1955), pp. 432-33.

79. See, for example, Carnegie's work collected as Andrew Carnegie, *The Gospel of Wealth and Other Timely Essays*, ed. Edward C. Kirkland (Cambridge, Mass., 1961), especially the title essay; and the essays on labor and capital in Allan Nevins, ed., *Selected Writings of Abram Hewitt* (New York, 1936). For some important observations on this and related points, see Daniel T. Rodgers, *The Work Ethic in Industrial America, 1850-1920* (Chicago, 1978).

80. In addition to Laurie, *Working People of Philadelphia*, and Saxton, *Indispensable Enemy*, see Brian J. Greenberg, "Worker and Community: The Social Structure of a Nineteenth-Century American City, Albany, New York, 1850-1884" (Ph.D. dissertation, Princeton University, 1980); Steven J. Ross, "Workers on the Edge: Work, Leisure, and Politics in Industrializing Cincinnati, 1830-1890" (Ph.D. dissertation, Princeton University, 1980).

81. *Journal of the American Institute*, 1 (1836), 555.

82. *Working Man's Advocate*, Sept. 19, 1835.

# The Origins of the Sweatshop:
# Women and Early Industrialization
# in New York City

## CHRISTINE STANSELL

Between 1820 and 1860, New York City became the foremost manufacturing center of America, a rise to eminence which, as in all industrializing situations, entailed massive disruptions for the city's working people. Antebellum New Yorkers were well aware of the poverty and suffering of their own laboring classes, but contemporaries agreed that of those pulled into the new wage-labor relations, women workers were the most precariously situated of all. In 1830, for instance, labor reformer Matthew Carey called women's wages and working conditions "harrowing truths."[1] Carey was referring to the outside workers, those women who worked for wages in their own households, "outside" a shop or factory. Thirty years later, exploitation had become more deeply entrenched; indeed, the ladies of one women's charity declared with uncharacteristic vehemence that the outworker's wage *"does not decently support life."*[2] By mid-century, low wages, underemployment, and overwork were the rule for outside workers, and outside work had become the prevalent form of women's employment in America's leading industrial city.

The development of the outside system as the dominant form of female wage-labor affected the segmentation of the work force, the segregation of the labor movement, and the formation of class and gender consciousness in one of America's most radical cities. Through the outside system, metropolitan industry turned to its own uses the ties of poor women to their families and households. The core of its labor force was comprised of female heads of households who did not leave their homes because of responsibilities to kin—although as the system expanded, it also incorporated young single women more independent of domestic duties. Instead of pulling these women out of their households, as did, for example, the factories of rural New England, urban manufacturing converted their tenement homes into workshops. On the one hand, this allowed women to do their part as wives, mothers, and daughters, the domestic labor that deteriorating conditions of life in these years made all the more important. On the other, it made them vulnerable to the most severe exploitation as workers and limited their means of redress through collective organizing. Homework had a double edge: the very woman who stayed home, "keeping a house together," as one woman put it,[3] placed herself in the way of the worst abuses of the New York labor market. Through the outside system, the requirements of industrial capitalism meshed with the needs of the working-class family and thus incorporated gender roles into an expanding system of economic exploitation.

To understand the importance of women to "metropolitan industrialization," as Sean Wilentz has termed it,[4] we must first rethink older conceptions of the role of outwork. Historians and economists have usually viewed outwork as a transition, a precursor to the prototypical industrial form of the factory. Eric Hobsbawm, for instance, in 1965 spoke of domestic manufactures as transitional devices which employers utilized to overcome the great social obstacles to industrialization.[5] The dispersed work force and handicraft technology intrinsic to outwork made the system too cumbersome to allow capital accumulation, so the argument goes; as soon as technological innovation occurred and it became possible to centralize the labor force, such wasteful and irrational forms of production disappeared. It is important to understand, however, that although outwork was only a precursor to factories in some settings, it remained at the heart of the industrializing process in many of the great cities. In New York, the outside system flourished through the nineteenth century and into the twentieth: the infamous sweatshops of turn-of-the-century New York were variants on the antebellum form. A similar process occurred in London, Paris, and other metropolitan manufacturing centers in Europe. In late-nineteenth-century Holland, outwork actually superseded factory production: employers shifted industrial wagework from the factory into the home.[6]

In New York City, material conditions did not favor the rise of factories, but in other ways conditions for manufacturing were propitious. Of great advantage to employers were the city's proximity to the port and, most important, the enormous pool of cheap labor which existed from the first wave of immigration following the end of the War of 1812. By expanding their markets and tapping this labor pool, employers transformed the handicraft system from within. In many trades, manufactures developed without the benefit of any new mechanization.[7] In the clothing trade, for instance, until the advent of the sewing machine in the 1850s, clothing was sewn in the same way it had been made in private households and tailors' shops. The outside system was crucial to this kind of labor-intensive industrialization: it gave employers the capacity to expand production outside their shop walls in much the same way as machinery allowed factory owners to increase production inside theirs.

In the commercial port setting of New York, then, the kind of cumbersome enterprise which utilized outwork was at the forefront of industrialization for the first half of the century. We must adjust our notions of class formation accordingly. The female workers of the outside system were not marginal to the industrial proletariat, an auxiliary of wives and daughters, as historians have often believed. Despite the fact that they remained in their households, they found themselves in new relations which were at the center of industrialization and class development. Analogously, the outside system had great significance for the development of new gender relations within the working class: the creation of new modes of wifehood, motherhood, and daughterhood. If employers in some settings utilized outwork only until they overcame the barriers to women working outside the home, New York employers capitalized upon and profited from those very obstacles. Through the outside system, the immobility and apparent marginality of women workers became institutionalized and formalized in urban industrial capitalism.

I

The outside system replicated the gender divisions of the household in the new setting of metropolitan industry. A sexual division of labor developed between branches of New York manufactures, based primarily on outwork; trades like clothing that relied on put-out work became women's trades, while those that did not mostly remained closed to women. The consequence was a segmentation of industry that limited women in the city to a few trades; by 1860, three or four dozen industries employed over 90 percent of the city's workwomen. In the manufactures of paper boxes, hoopskirts, shirts and collars, millinery, artificial flowers, and ladies' cloaks, over 85 percent of the employees were female.[8] The crowding of women into a few industries increased competition for work and thereby made them more vulnerable than men to wage-cutting, overwork, and casualization.

Before 1820, women's wagework had been marginal to the New York economy. Poor women worked mostly in the customary female employments of domestic service and street selling. Commodity production, still centered in artisan shops, had not developed to the point where it could incorporate large numbers of women. Shipping and commerce employed men of the laboring poor as seamen, dock laborers, and road-builders, and there was seasonal work for them on farms in New Jersey, Connecticut, and New York State. But this kind of heavy labor was mostly closed to women. When Mayor Edward Livingston proposed a scheme of employment for the poor in 1803, he suggested work programs for men in street construction, farm labor, and public works, but he could prescribe nothing more concrete for women than a large workroom where they might work at unspecified tasks "suited to their strength."[9]

Some women found work at the turn of the eighteenth century in the putting-out system, the progenitor of outside work. In the period after the Revolution, city merchants and village storekeepers along the northeastern seaboard began "putting out" raw materials to women to work up at home into ready-made goods. Wage payments were given for flax- and wool-spinning, straw-braiding, weaving, glove-making, stocking-knitting, and shoe-binding: all crafts which women also practiced in their own domestic work.[10] Although putting-out appears to have flourished mostly in rural New England, it also provided some opportunities for New York women: work at shoe-binding was available from a number of cordwainers in the early years of the century, and spinning was one of the handful of remunerative employments the Society for the Relief of Poor Widows could encourage among its almoners.[11] Between 1814 and 1819, several hundred poor women found work in given-out crafts at the House of Industry, a charity founded to alleviate destitution among the honest female poor. The House gave out flax and wool to spin, stockings to knit, and gloves and a few fine linen shirts to sew. Although its managers modified putting-out by centralizing some of the work on the premises, the ties of wagework to domestic activity and family life were still evident. One mother brought her youngest children with her, a young widow spun with her baby on her lap, and old women knit stockings, much as they would have done in households where they lived as dependent grandmothers and great-aunts.[12]

In the next decade, manufacturing on both sides of the Atlantic would take over the production of given-out crafts: women like the Widow Hammel, who applied to a charity in 1817 for money to repair her spinning wheel, would have a hard time finding work.[13] Because of the advent of the textile mills, spinning, the staple of the putting-out system, would disappear as handiwork by 1820, although traces of it appeared in the city well into the antebellum years; as late as 1839, the managers of an asylum for old women voted to give one resident a flax wheel to spin sewing thread for the others; "it seems quite necessary for her comfort that she should be employed, and it is the only thing she can do."[14] In New England, spinning mills provided the means for capitalists to utilize female labor beyond the given-out system, but since mills were impracticable in Manhattan, employers there as yet had no way to capitalize systematically on the poverty of women like those who had spun for the House of Industry. Even the stern gentlemen of the Society for the Prevention of Pauperism, ever vigilant against an idle poor, granted in 1821 that "there is often a defect of profitable employment for women and children of indigent families."[15]

It was the outside system which opened up this labor market for profitable employment. After the War of 1812, conditions for other manufacturing besides textiles were beneficial. Because of the thriving port economy, the city was already a major center of capital, and its merchants were seeking new investments for their profits from the war years. The advent of regular trans-Atlantic and coastal shipping lines put New York producers in a favored position over competitors elsewhere to buy raw materials and sell finished goods, and the federal tariff of 1816 gave domestic industry much-needed protection from British goods. The postwar wave of immigration brought to the city highly skilled British artisans, familiar with the most advanced technology, as well as thousands of unskilled workers who would form the first of New York's many armies of cheap labor.[16]

Master and merchant tailors were the first in these advantageous circumstances to hire large numbers of women; the clothing trade would continue to be the leading employer of female labor in New York throughout the nineteenth century.[17] By 1860, the federal census reported 25,000 women working in manufacturing—one-quarter of the entire labor force; two-thirds of them worked in the clothing trades.[18] Garment manufacture would also prove typical of women's industries in its dependence on outwork. Initially, its employers depended almost entirely on home workers, and even as they began to set up factories in the 1840s, they maintained the outside system in tandem with factory labor, or "inside work" as they called it. The outside system allowed employers to cut costs to the bone. There were minimal expenses for overhead, and they could easily hold down wages by taking on and letting go workers according to their needs of the moment. Thus seasonality and casualization became the hallmarks of outwork. When female employment extended to other industries, employers emulated the successful clothing manufacturers in mixing factory work and homework.

Before 1812, there had been virtually no ready-made clothing in America. Except for the poor, who bought their clothes secondhand, Americans had their garments made by artisans—tailors, tailoresses, and seamstresses—and by wives, daughters, and female servants. There was a rough division of labor between the household and the artisan shop. Women at home did the plain sewing; artisans, the garments that required more skill and fitting. So women made most of their own everyday clothes, their children's, and the simpler men's garments— shirts and everyday "pantaloons," or loose trousers. Dressmakers helped them with fancy dresses; seamstresses, with children's clothes, mending, and particularly artful tasks. Thus an eighteenth-century seamstress advertised her deftness in turning old clothes into new: "she will as usual graft Pieces to knit Jackets and Breeches not to be discerned, also to graft and foot Stockings, and Gentlemen's Gloves, Mittens, or makes Children's Stockings out of Old ones."[19] Where tailors were concerned instead of tailoresses and dressmakers, there was a stricter division of labor. Tailors would not touch most women's work—shirts, dresses, children's clothes, and mending. Their province encompassed those men's garments which were closely fitted, like breeches and vests, and cumbersome to sew, like coats and capes.[20] This eighteenth-century division of labor between women and tailors would have important ramifications in the development of clothing manufacture, since industrialization occurred first in the making of *men's* clothes, which tailors had traditionally monopolized, thus introducing female wageworkers as competition.

The only ready-made clothing in the eighteenth century was for sailors. Crews docking in New York needed to outfit themselves quickly and cheaply for the next voyage. By 1805, "slop-shops" by the waterfront catered to their needs with ready-made pants, shirts, and jackets; "slop-work" was the tailors' term for cheap garments made with little care and no fitting. Army uniforms were the other source of slop-work, since during the Revolution and the War of 1812 there had been a great demand for new uniforms which persisted, although much diminished, into peacetime. Between the two, a small but steady trade in slops was established in New York before 1820. Journeymen tailors turned to it in the winter, the slack season for custom orders, while masters put out some of the plainer slop-work—shirts and pantaloons—to women they employed the year round.[21]

The garment trades prospered in the 1820s, as city merchants captured the lucrative "Southern trade" in slave clothing from the British. The tariff of 1816 and cheap textiles from New England mills allowed New York merchants to undercut British prices.[22] With an assured market for slops, employers began to take on more women to sew the work which journeymen preferred to do only in their slow seasons. By the 1830s, some shops employed as many as 500 women, and coarse "Negro cottons," as they were called, were regular cargo on southern-bound packets.[23] From slave clothing, the trade diversified into a luxury trade in fine linen shirts and vests for southern planters, and firms also began to keep high quality ready-mades in stock for local customers, travelers, and gentlemen visiting the city on business. When the Erie Canal connected the city with midwestern and upstate customers, a "Western trade" developed in dungarees, hickory and flashy figured shirts, and flannel drawers; in 1849, the gold rush gave the impetus for a "California trade" in overalls and calico shirts for the thousands of men who had no women to outfit them.[24] By 1860, two-thirds of the garments made in New York went south and the rest were shipped to a nationwide market. "Scarcely a single individual thinks of having his shirts made at home," averred an observer of fashion.[25] He neglected the farm families who continued to make their own clothes well into the late 1800s, but he was right about city people and towns-folk across the country, whose sense of style in men's clothes was already attuned to New York ready-mades by the 1840s: "Everywhere throughout the country, New-York-made clothing is popular over all others."[26]

The clothing trade was one New York business that did offer work-ingmen and immigrants a path from employment to proprietorship. The market was usually dependable and the profit margin always high—an estimated 500 percent markup in the early 1830s.[27] Most important, a man needed very little money to set up shop, since the outside system allowed him to take advantage of the city's cheap labor while minimizing overhead costs. Rents in the business district of lower Manhattan were too high for any but large proprietors to afford the space for an inside shop, and even they limited their overhead by employing a host of outworkers. In 1860, the renowned Brooks Brothers employed 70 workers inside and 2,000 to 3,000 on the outside, and another of the largest concerns employed 500 and 800 workers on the inside and outside respectively.[28] The smallest proprietors, tailors themselves, did not keep shop at all but contracted out goods from the large shops, cut them at home, and put them out, thus passing along all the costs of space, light, fuel, needles, and thread to their home workers.[29]

If the trade offered the common man an entrée to entrepreneurship, however, it did not necessarily bring him affluence. By mid-century, economic pressures on employers were rigorous. The trade operated on a dense network of credit, and the search to maximize credit was the driving force behind operations at every level. Profits could be high, but they seldom appeared in cash. At its most complex, the trade involved a jobber or merchant, a master tailor, his inside workers, one or even two levels of subcontractors, and their outworkers. The jobber/

merchant bought the cloth and sold the finished merchandise, the master cut the goods and gave them to his workers and subcontractors, and the subcontractors put out the goods to their outside workers. Since profit at every level came from the difference between the fixed payment received and costs paid out for labor and overhead, there was heavy pressure to cut wages. All down the line, too, goods were passed along on credit and payment was postponed until the finished work was returned; credit extended to sales as well, to the planters and country storekeepers who visited Manhattan every spring to buy their stock for the year. As a result, there was little cash on hand at any given moment at any level of the trade, the reason that business depressions were calamitous for employers large and small: in both 1837 and 1857 the trade was the first in the city to go under and the last to recover. Dependence on credit was also the factor that above all others bred what were universally acknowledged to be among the worst abuses of workers in the North. As one historian has written, by the 1850s, "hardly a period known for its sentimentality in business," the hardest-boiled contemporaries acknowledged the sewing trade to be unscrupulous.[30]

The economic pressures on small shop-owners at mid-century were one factor which explains the plethora of complaints then about wage-cutting, rate-busting, underpayment, and withholding wages. "The worst features," maintained Horace Greeley, "are its hopelessness and its constant tendency from bad to worse."[31] Women living with a man's support were not so adversely affected, but single women and their dependents could suffer terribly. In the 1855 census report for two neighborhoods on the Lower East Side, nearly 60 percent of 600 workingwomen sampled had no adult male in the household.[32] In their case—that of the majority of New York's female wageworkers, if this sample is indicative—there can be no doubt that Victorian sentimentalizations of the starving seamstress reflected a real situation. Two stories make the point, both from 1855, a depression year. "When flour was so high last winter as to place it beyond the reach of the provident poor," the secretary of the Society for the Relief of Poor Widows related, "One of the Managers visited a respectable Widow, who had maintained herself and her three little girls by sewing." The eldest had just died from what the ladies delicately termed "disease aggravated by improper food," and the second child was also sick with the same malady. When the visitor inquired about the family's needs, the woman asked for flour: "'But you have thought before that meal would answer,' said the Manager, 'and you know we hardly think it right to give flour at its present price.' 'Yes,' said the woman, bursting into tears, 'we have lived on meal this winter, but the Doctor says it killed Mary and now Katy is getting in the same way, and I cannot let her die, too.'"[33] The response of a second mother in the same situation—one of her eight children sick with a chest complaint—was less suited to the terms of Victorian pathos. "Perhaps it will please the Lord to take him," she replied matter-of-factly to the manager's solicitude; "if it would please the Lord to take them all, I should be glad, then I'd know they were well off; but how I shall support them all another year in this world I am sure I can't tell."[34] These were not extreme cases: these were the hardships of a *class*—and a particular group within it—not of isolated individuals.

The outworkers' most pressing problem was underpayment. Like employment in many metropolitan trades, seasonal work peaked in October and April, when orders for winter and summer stock were rushed out. The pattern was sufficiently predictable for women to meet the slack seasons with some forethought: farm labor was an alternative for the mobile in the slow summer months, a sojourn in the almshouse an option for the nonrespectable in winter. Some women pieced together a sequence of employment from other trades; a seamstress could combine sewing with straw-sewing, for instance, which peaked in January.[35] Married women and mothers with grown sons could dovetail employment with their men: the busy season for day labor, to give one instance, was the warm weather, when the clothing trades were slow. But there were also fluctuations week to week that were impossible to foresee; to be out of work one or two days every week was common for outside workers. There was no guarantee that when a seamstress returned her sewing to the shop she would get more, and if she did, it was not necessarily a full week's work. This meant that self-supporting women had to shift about from one shop to another for enough work to live on, a feature of the trade which workwomen protested with particular bitterness. For women on their own, labor time was precious, and they keenly felt the waste in spending hours seeking work, waiting for work, and returning work.[36]

"Small as are the earnings of these seamstresses, they constantly tend to diminish," Horace Greeley observed.[37] Small employers were notorious for vicious rate-cutting, especially the German Jews of Chatham Street slop shops, the perennial target of denunciations which were always laced with anti-Semitism. "A class of beings in human form," angry seamstresses called them after a wage cut in 1831, and two decades later a journalist sympathetic to the seamstresses conjured up the stereotype of the avaricious Jew, the "shopkeeping, penny-turning genius."[38] More prosperous businessmen liked to see themselves as superior to the immigrant entrepreneurs in benevolence and moral scruples and were quite content to see issues of ethnicity obscure those of class. In actuality, their firms—respectable concerns like Brooks

Brothers—profited equally from rate-cutting, although its practice was less visible. They kept their hands clean, in a sense, because they did not set the piece rates for their outside workers but left it to the contractors, men who were the worst gougers in the trade.

Because there were so many women competing for work, there was little that needlewomen could do to prevent wage-cutting. "I have heard it said, and even by benevolent men, in justification of this hideous state of things, that these women do not complain," wrote a nettled Matthew Carey in 1830. "True. It would answer no purpose. If the price of shirts were brought down to six cents (as it sometimes is . . .), they would accept it, and thankfully too. Their numbers and their wants are so great, and the competition so urgent, that they are wholly at the mercy of their employers."[39]

Seamstresses were more militant in posing their grievances in the ensuing years: there were turnouts in 1831, 1836, and 1845, as well as strikes in Philadelphia and Boston. But organization never succeeded in securing their wage demands. In this respect, they were much worse off than their closest male counterparts, the day laborers, who earned about twice as much as fully employed needlewomen throughout the period. Day laborers managed to enforce a customary wage of around a dollar a day, sometimes, it seems, through turning out.[40] Outside workers were never able to use the turnout effectively; there were too many women in the city who would undercut them by taking work at any price. In 1839, for instance, an employer "sought up emigrants, or went to the almshouse, to have his work done; if he could find no women in his neighborhood willing to undertake it . . . so that he forced them to come to his own terms."[41] Three decades later, in the first month of the Panic of 1857, women who were turned away from the failing regular shops had no recourse but to take out work at the lowest prices going from Chatham Street, leading a journalist to infer that the numbers of women living from hand to mouth were more than he had supposed.[42]

The most unscrupulous practice of employers in the moral code of mid-century, and the one which outside workers protested most bitterly, was that of withholding wages. It was not uncommon for employers, especially small proprietors and subcontractors, to postpone paying a woman when she returned to work, to require alterations before they paid her, to refuse to pay her at all, and to hold back the deposits that they required for taking out work. A visitor to New York described one of these transactions in 1852: "He takes the bundle, unrolls it, turns up his nose, as if he had smelt a dead rat, and remarks, in the crossest manner possible, 'You have ruined the job,' makes the whole lot up together, and contempuously throws it under the counter. . . . She then asks for her money back, but only receives a threat in return, with a low, muttering grumble, that 'you have damaged us already eight or ten dollars, and we will retain your dollar, as it is all we shall ever get for our goods, which you have spoilt!'"[43]

In 1855, the outworker Margaret Byrnes took her grievances to the mayor's court when she encountered this treatment. She had taken finished shirts back three times to Davis & Company, suppliers to the western and southern trades; on each occasion the proprietors demanded more alterations, refused to pay for the shirts they did accept, held back her deposit, and finally tried to coerce her into paying them for the sewing they rejected. Soon after Byrnes went to court, Mary Gilroy of Five Points joined the fray with her own charges against the Davises, who had also refused to settle with her and had fleeced her out of a deposit. Clearly not a woman to take foul play sitting down, Gilroy had retaliated by taking out a dozen Davis shirts to hold for ransom. Neither woman, it should be said, seems to have secured much satisfaction in the end despite favorable publicity and testimony from the Davises that could hardly have been more damning; Margaret Byrnes won back her deposit but not her wages, and Mary Gilroy, as far as the record shows, must have taken her hostage shirts to the grave.[44] While the trial shows that the nonpayment of women's wages was an open scandal, the practice would not be systematically challenged until after the Civil War, with the formation of the Workingwoman's Protection Union.[45] Meanwhile, the party who reaped the most benefits from this particular confrontation was Tammany mayor Fernando Wood, whom the press showered with praise for "redressing the wrongs of the unfriended toiler."[46]

Proprietors like the Davises provided the material out of which middle-class investigators sympathetic to the seamstresses fashioned the figure of the villainous employer, a stock figure in so many Victorian renderings of the outside system. "There sat the proprietor in his shirt-sleeves, a vulgar-looking creature, smoking a cigar." "He can browbeat, and haggel with, and impose upon a poor, weak, sickly, industrious work-girl to more purpose, and more to his own advantage than any body else."[47] These images of iniquity so dominate the historical evidence that it is difficult to look at the situation analytically: why, we can ask, should these employers have been so particularly abusive and dishonest? The Victorian accounts certainly do not falsify the situation, although they do obliterate its complexities: as unsentimental an observer as the southerner William Bobo described the typical clothing employer as "a sour, crabbed, ill-grained foreigner, or blue-skinned Yankee, (just as bad,) that has no more feeling of kindness towards his fellow-creatures than a savage."[48] But from the small employer's point of view, what seemed villainy to others was a way to cope with the cutthroat economics in which he operated. "The clothing makers for the southern trade are generally the target of popular hostility on account of low wages, and there can be no doubt that many of them are gripers," the *Tribune* acknowledged. The paper was the self-proclaimed champion of the needlewomen, but its editor Horace Greeley was never a man to get his mind around the imperatives of capitalism, and here his paper pointed out simple economic fact: "If they were all the purest philanthropists, they could not raise the wages of their seamstresses to anything like a living price. Necessity rests as heavily upon them as upon the occupant of the most contracted garret. They can only live by their business so long as they can get garments made here low enough to enable them to pay cost, risk and charges and undersell. . . . If they were compelled to pay living wages for their work, they must stop it altogether."[49]

When proprietors put off paying a workwoman as the Davises did, they were not always lying when they claimed they had no cash on hand. Nor was the issue of flawed work necessarily a sham. For all the extraordinary advantages the outside system gave employers, it was not the most technically efficient and economically rational organization of work, and one of its drawbacks was nonstandardized work—that is, garments sewn too differently from each other to be sold for a unit price.[50]

In the 1850s, employers hard pressed by growing competition took steps to solve the problem of standardization by introducing the sewing machine, which standardized the stitch, and by putting out detail work instead of whole garments. Home workers sewed pieces of the garment—cuffs, buttonholes, sleeves—which were then assembled in an inside shop. In the shop, employers could maximize their supervision of the assemblage, the step in production where the mark of the individual worker was most conspicuous. Hanford & Brothers, reputedly the largest firm in the country, put out shirt wristbands, collars, and bosoms separately; the finished pieces were then sewn together in the factory.[51] New methods of production increased the pressure on small employers, who did not have the resources to shift to such an organization but still had to offer standardized merchandise in order to compete. Consequently, when these men niggled over alterations, they could be genuinely concerned with the quality of their stock as well as covertly engaged in driving down the wage.

For seamstresses, wage-cutting and underemployment bred overwork. When piece rates fell, they could only do more work for the income needed, a principle which Henry Mayhew elucidated in his investigations of London slop-workers.[52] Since work was not always available, they had to work as much as they could when they did find employment. In the 1830s, Matthew Carey had found that seamstresses without male support worked from sunrise to nine or ten at night; in the 1850s, the sewing machine drove piece rates so low that fifteen- to eighteen-hour workdays were not uncommon. "Those who make at the lowest prices appear to have no other mission on earth but to sew up bleached muslin into shirts," maintained Virginia Penny, self-styled Mayhew of New York's working women. "In some instances we have been informed, that where there are two or three or more women or girls engaged in this enterprise of making shirts to enable gentlemen to appear respectable in society, they absolutely divide the night season into watches."[53] To be sure, these stints were intermittent because employment was not steady. But when we consider that the days without work brought mostly anxiety and the search for more employment, it becomes clear that there was little leisure in these women's lives to ease the strain.

To fully comprehend the hardships of outside workers, however, we must understand the nature of the labor itself. Hand-sewing strained the eyes and cramped the back and neck so much that a practiced observer like Virginia Penny could recognize a seamstress on the street by her peculiar stooped carriage: "the neck suddenly bending forward, and the arms being, even in walking, considerably bent forward, or folded more or less upward from the elbows."[54] The curvature came from bending over and sewing in badly lit rooms: most were too dark in the daytime to read without artificial light, and seamstresses had to economize in their use of candles. The tiny backstitch which they used was painstakingly slow; it took about twelve hours to make one shirt. There was, moreover, a multitude of chances to make mistakes. A shirt bosom could be too full, the sleeves too short, and the wristbands too long, and the man who examined the garments—the employer or his "piece master," as the foreman of outside workers was called in large shops—might return the work for alterations on any of these counts. Even a clearheaded woman could easily botch the piecing, but a tired one who had been working for hours was that much more likely to make a mistake that would cost hours to repair, to sew in a sleeve backward or embroider a buttonhole out of line. The doggerel beat of Thomas Hood's "Song of the Shirt," a favorite propaganda piece of seamstresses and their supporters, captures something of the drudgery of the work itself:

> Work-work-work!
> Till the brain begins to swim;
> Work-work-work!
> Till the eyes are heavy and dim!

> Seam, and gusset, and band,
> Band, and gusset, and seam,
> Till over the buttons I fall asleep
> And sew them on in a dream.[55]

The sewing machine, as it was used in the context of nineteenth-century capitalism, did little to lighten the labor. From the perspective of the operatives, machine-sewing was as taxing as hand-sewing; it only shifted the strain from the arms to the lower torso. Women working the machines suffered chronic pain in their hips, nervous disorders from the jarring of the mechanism, and eyestrain from following the long lines of stitching.[56]

In their appeals for help, seamstresses and their supporters stressed the high rate of mortality and disease associated with their trade, what we could call in retrospect the biological experience of class. A doctor in 1860 guessed that a thousand women a year died of causes related to sewing in the outside system.[57] Malnutrition, fatigue, cold, and bad ventilation in the tenements bred pneumonia and consumption, the major killers of nineteenth-century cities. A newspaper investigator in 1853 heard that the hardest-working women could squeeze as much as double the average earnings out of the piece rates, but the extra money usually went to medicines.[58] "Will the men of New-York allow the unfortunate Shirt Sewers to stitch their own shrouds?" one seamstresses' broadside rhetorically inquired.[59]

## II

The outside system of metropolitan industry was grafted onto women's domestic work, and the victimization of women as outside workers was tied to their role as family members and household laborers. Under the pressures of early industrialism, family labor became both the means by which women met their own household needs and the instrument of their exploitation within the work force: to put it another way, it was the source of both respectability and alienation. Outside workers were at the bottom of the city's labor force not only because they were women—the explanation that historians of industrialization have favored; they were there because they were wives, mothers, and daughters with family responsibilities.[60]

By 1860, the outside system had branched out from the clothing trade into other women's industries. The 1840s saw the emergence of a new middle-class market for a panoply of consumer goods: embellishments and adornments to grace the Victorian home and person. Artificial-flower-making, fringe- and tassel-making, embroidery, mantua-making, fancy book-binding, and parasol-making flourished, along with all manner of other fancy worked, burnished, and gilded manufactures. Light and easily transported, most of these goods could be put out; requiring deftness and delicacy in their assemblage, they were considered suitable for female hands. Shoebinding, the female employment that had been second to sewing at the turn of the century, also continued to provide work for women. Although the cordwainers of Lynn, Massachusetts, had captured much of the national market by 1815, New York shoemakers went on making slop shoes for the poor and the military along with luxury slippers for wealthy customers. In all these industries, the organization of outside work was similar to that of the clothing trade.

Throughout the entire system, women turned family labor to the purposes of wagework as well as housework. As they divided up domestic chores with their children, so they divided up homework. Family labor helped them combat the effect of wage-cutting by allowing them to increase the amount of work they could do. In box-making, children helped with the easier parts of cutting and gluing; in matchstick-making, the lowliest of put-out employments, young children dipped the matchheads while mothers and older siblings cut out the sticks. In families of seamstresses, children as young as five could do the simple task of pulling bastings, and at ten years or so, daughters were nimble fingered enough to sew straight seams and attach buttons. Most important, children who knew their way about the streets could save their mothers valuable time by carrying work back and forth from the shop.[61]

In the families of some artisans, an older pattern of outside work persisted in which the entire family worked along with the craftsman. This had been a common practice in the eighteenth century, and it continued—although in a greatly altered context—in the households of fur-sewers, shoemakers, and tailors, in the form of the "family shop."[62] A sample from the 1855 census shows that in one poor working-class neighborhood in the Fourth Ward near the waterfront, 16 percent of seamstresses were living with male kin who worked in the tailoring trade: such households were probably family shops.[63] The men did the most skilled work, negotiated with employers, and integrated the different operations, while women and children worked at the preparatory and subsidiary tasks. In the 1850s, piece rates were too low for journeymen tailors to make a living without family labor: "A tailor is nothing without a wife, and very often a child," went a maxim of German craftsmen.[64]

The family shop was a unit laboring for its own subsistence, dependent on the cooperation of all. From the perspective of our own more fragmented time, such families evoke images of solidarity and mutuality, attachments which we assume such intimate reciprocity would have fostered. Indeed, within the metropolitan economy, family shops did function as cooperative units, but it is important to see that within each group, relations were hierarchical, not egalitarian: men were at the top, children at the bottom. The hierarchical structure may not have been especially important while the family unit was intact, as it was in the eighteenth century, each person working for the common good and sharing more or less equally in the earnings. But it did become significant when each individual earned wages, for then wage differentials developed between men, women, and children, and then it became profitable for adults, especially men, to replicate familial arrangements among non-kin as well as kin. In other words, traditions of family labor became a means of exploitation in the nineteenth century as well as a way for working people to support themselves through cooperation.[65]

In New York, new forms of outside work that replicated the family hierarchy developed out of family labor. Women and girls, for instance, began to work in the 1850s for unmarried journeymen in the same capacities as wives and daughters assisted tailors in their own homes. The journeymen mediated between piece masters and the home shop and took the largest portion of earnings. Poor as these men were, they were still employers and women were their workers: they paid the women fixed wages and took the small profits for themselves.[66] Women also put themselves at the top of this type of arrangement in the "learning" system. Learning was a debased form of apprenticeship which corresponded to the relation of parents and children in family labor. In exchange for the crudest training, girls worked for tailors, seamstresses, dressmakers, and milliners either for their keep or for a few pennies a day. Journeymen also used this system: adults made their profit by taking out work at regular piece rates and paying employees either lower rates or nothing at all to make it up. "Learning" proliferated in the 1850s along with the family shop and its variants as a way for individuals to combat the effects of the sewing machine. Like all child laborers, learners were the humblest of the trade, but since their employers themselves were so poor, the learners' condition was especially lowly. In 1853 a *Herald* reporter found a learners' garret near the waterfront where four teenage girls worked for an Irish seamstress every day except Sunday in exchange for their board; they paid for rent, clothes, and Sunday's food by prostituting themselves to sailors.[67]

All forms of outside work merged with sweating, which spread through the poor districts in the 1850s as trade flourished. There were many levels of sweaters: journeymen tailors, piece masters themselves (who contracted work from their employers), garret masters and mistresses. The journeymen who took out work for their wives were engaged in a kind of sweating, although in the sweating system proper, the contractor invested no labor of his own but took his earnings from the "sweat" of others. So in the case of tailors who contracted out work: "The hands hired by the Journeymen do not generally get more than $3.50 or $4 per week, while the Journeyman receives his $6.25 for every Coat from the employer. . . . Sometimes, also, the same principle is applied in another way: the Journeyman letting out his work by the piece to the lowest bidder and thus making more or less profit on every garment given him by the Cutter—for which, of course, the proprietor of the shop is charged full price."[68]

The use of the sewing machine encouraged sweating, since very few women workers (and few tailors, too) could afford their own but neither could they afford to work without one. Several inventors had taken out patents on sewing machines in the 1840s, but the stitches unraveled too easily and the power came from an unwieldy hand crank. In 1846, Elias Howe devised a lockstitch which imitated the hand-sewers' sturdy backstitch and, in 1850, Issac Singer replaced the crank with a foot treadle and devised other improvements which made the machine practicable for the first time.[69] Employers could push the sewing machine relatively easily upon a system in which small-scale production predominated and workers had been forced to absorb overhead costs for several decades. A German-born New York tailor told the story well. "The bosses said: 'We want you to use the sewing-machine, you have to buy one,'" he recalled. "Many of the tailors had a few dollars in the bank, and they took the money and bought machines. Many others had no money . . . so they brought their stitching . . . to the other tailors who had sewing machines, and paid them a few cents for the stitching. Later, when the money was given out for the work, we found out that we could earn no more than we could without a machine."[70] Since seamstresses were less able to save money than tailors, few could purchase their own machines, and the shift to machine work made it more necessary for them to work for some kind of sweater.

Between 1815 and 1860 the outside system incorporated increasing numbers of male as well as female workers in the city. Nonetheless, there were crucial differences between the experiences of men and women in outwork, differences which would shape the history of labor-organizing in New York. The bonds between male workers were evident in their everyday relations in the outside workplace. In some work situations, masculine associations were immediately felt: there were tailors' and shoemakers' boardinghouses, for instance, where single journeymen worked on goods which the proprietors contracted out to them.[71] But even when a man worked with his family rather than other men, he sustained the bonds of his trade, bonds which were exclusively masculine. His sense of fellowship with other artisans remained alive. He fraternized with other men on the basis of their shared trade, and carried with him a history of work associations with men dating back to his apprenticeship. Trade societies sustained and vivified these associations, and every wave of trade-union militance strengthened the ties; tailors, to take one group of male outworkers, were among the most highly organized artisans in the city.

Women's situation in outwork was less structured by same-sex relations. Most often, women probably worked alone. To be sure, they also worked with other women in garrets, sweatshops, and tenement rooms, and single women sometimes sewed together in units resembling a family shop. Virginia Penny encountered such groups, young seamstresses who rented rooms and worked together in twos and threes.[72] Most commonly, however, these workplace associations were family- rather than gender- or trade-based, as men's were. Rather than female peers, workmates in collective groups could be children and husbands, sisters and mothers;[73] unlike men's, women's network of wage-labor associations did not transcend their domestic world. They did not fraternize with other women on the basis of a shared history in a trade but on the basis of family, neighborliness, and household concerns. A journeyman brought a sense of himself as a man bound to other men to whatever other work relations he had in a sweater's garret or his own home; a woman brought her identity as a mother or daughter, a woman bound to men and children, to her work relations with other women. The psychological associations of the household as well as the actual working relations there made it unlikely that women could develop a sense of a collectivity comprised solely of other women, associated through their common self-interest in the labor market.[74]

The confinement of women workers to their households gave rise to a specific psychology of female subordination in their relations with employers as well as to a particular organization of labor. The outside system masked women's involvement in wage labor; they appeared to be peripheral to industrial production and their identity as workers seemed secondary to their roles as wives and mothers. In actuality, their wagework was not marginal, either in their own lives or in the development of metropolitan industry. But shut away as they were from the primary confrontations of labor and capital, they had little chance to develop a sense of themselves as active in the struggle. In the interstices of the outside system, a plebeian variant of the bourgeois woman's sphere appeared which shut away women from a comprehension of the economy equal to that of the men with whom they lived. In the family shop, after all, it was the man who mediated between the world of the market and the world of the household.

Employers capitalized upon this construction of women as "outside" the economy, lacking acumen about the world outside their doors. "Our employers set up the most frivolous pretexts for reducing our wages," a former seamstress remembered. "Some of them were so transparently false that I wondered how any one could have the impudence to present them." She concluded that they could because they "considered a sewing-woman as either too dull to detect the fallacy, or too timid to expose and resent it."[75] This was a psychology of heterosexuality as well as one of class; likewise, when piece masters used derision in order to drive down a woman's wage: "He pulls at each seam, at each button, from end to end, and over every part of it his keen eye wanders in search of a flaw. Ha! he has found one . . . in a gruff, sharp tone, he asks her: 'Do you call this work?'" "Are they not well done?" replied the timid workwoman in this journalist's sketch. "I'm sure I did my best." "Well done, Woman, well done indeed, why they're blown together." He implied that she had no idea what constituted decent sewing; what she thought was "well done" was in actuality "blown together." With his claim to objective judgment, based on his knowledge of the business, he drove the woman back on the subjective— "I'm sure I did my best"—a meager defense in the world of the marketplace. By revealing her ignorance, he dramatized his own business acumen and effectively undermined any protest she might have made when he lowered her wage: "There, take that," he snapped when he paid her less than the price he promised. "No one shall say I deal hardly with my work people, but I must be just."[76] He had demonstrated his comprehension of value and fair exchange, and in so doing he placed himself above arbitrariness and guile; his claim to meting out justice rested on firm psychological ground. He was a man schooled in the abstract justice of commodity exchange, impatient with a woman who at every turn showed her ignorance of the laws of the marketplace.

Through the outside system, women's domesticity became a practical necessity of industrial capitalism. By the 1850s, employers (should they have been asked) could have agreed with evangelical reformers that the place of women was in the home, the poor not excluded. For the women themselves, outwork reinforced their ties to the domestic world at the same time as the necessities of their lives pushed them more entirely under the rule of the marketplace. As the line between family labor and wage labor was blurred, so was the boundary between their sense of themselves as workers for their families and their sense of themselves as wage laborers. In the long run, this limited their consciousness of themselves as workers: there was little room in the emerging plebeian woman's sphere for women to develop a sense of themselves as individuals bound to like individuals through common self-interest in the workplace. Their loyalties and priorities there were so entangled with children, husbands, and kin: how could the more abstract solidarity of sex replace the felt unity of family? Home workers were literally "outside" the arena of public life where working men were developing the mutual associations which were the basis for a new kind of politicized community in the Victorian city.

## NOTES

1. Matthew Carey, "Essays on the Public Charities of Philadelphia," *Miscellaneous Essays* (Philadelphia: Carey & Hart, 1830), p. 154.

2. Society for the Relief of Poor Widows, Minutes, Nov. 1859, New York Historical Society, New York.

3. New York Children's Aid Society, *Second Annual Report* (New York, 1855), pp. 38-39.

4. See Sean Wilentz's essay in this collection; also his "Class Conflict and the Rights of Man: Artisans and the Rise of Labor Radicalism in New York City" (Ph.D. dissertation, Yale University, 1980).

5. Eric Hobsbawm, "The Formation of the Industrial Working Classes: Some Problems," *3e Conférence Internationale d'Histoire Economique, Congrès et Colloques*, vol. 1 (The Hague, 1965), pp. 176-77. Marx speaks of domestic manufactures as peripheral to the central tendency of industrialization "to conversion to the factory system proper." *Capital*, trans. Samuel Moore and Edward Aveling (Moscow: Progress Publishers, n.d.), vol. 1, p. 445. See also Sidney Pollard, *The Genesis of Modern Management* (Cambridge, Mass.: Harvard University Press, 1965), pp. 34-35.

6. In 1910, Helen L. Sumner noted that the factory system in the clothing trade "has only recently made headway." See her *History of Women in Industry in the United States* in U.S. Congress, Senate, *Report on Condition of Women and Child Wage-Earners in the United States*, S. Doc. 645, 61st Cong., 2d Sess. (Washington, D.C., 1910), vol. 9, p. 116, hereafter cited as Sumner, *History of Women*. On London, see Sally Alexander, "Women's Work in Nineteenth-Century London: A Study of the Years 1820-1850," in *The Rights and Wrongs of Women*, ed. Juliet Mitchell and Ann Oakley (Harmondsworth, Eng.: Penguin Books, 1976), pp. 63, 65; for Paris, Henriette Vanier, *La Mode et Ses Metiers: Frivolités et Luttes des Classes, 1830-1870* (Paris: Armand Colin, 1960); for Holland, Selma Leydesdorff, "Women and Children in Home Industry" (paper presented at the International Conference in Women's History, University of Maryland, Nov. 16, 1977).

7. For a general discussion of the importance of hand technology to industrialization, see Raphael Samuel, "The Workshops of the World: Steam Power and Hand Technology in Mid-Victorian Britain," *History Workshop*, 3 (Spring 1977), 6-72.

8. Carl Degler, "Labor in the Economy and Politics of New York City, 1850-1860: A Study of the Impact of Early Industrialism" (Ph.D. dissertation, Columbia University, 1952), pp. 106, 124.

9. Edward Livingston to James Warner, President of the General Society of Mechanics and Tradesmen, *New York Evening Post*, Feb. 24, 1803. Mary Ryan describes the absence of female employment in the entire Northeast in *Womanhood in America from Colonial Times to the Present* (New York: Franklin Watts, 1975), pp. 100-101.

10. Edith Abbott, *Women in Industry: A Study in American Economic History* (New York: D. Appleton & Company, 1924), pp. 19-20, 42, 70-78; Nancy Cott, *Bonds of Womanhood: "Woman's Sphere" in New England, 1780-1835* (New Haven, Conn.: Yale University Press, 1977), pp. 25, 39-40.

11. Sumner, *History of Women*, p. 167. Sumner also mentions spinning manufactories for poor New York women in the late eighteenth century. Ibid., pp. 53, 124. See also Society for the Relief of Poor Widows, Minutes, Feb. 21, 1803.

12. *Evening Post*, Oct. 27, Nov. 29, 1819.

13. Society for the Relief of Poor Widows, Minutes, Nov. 17, 1817.

14. Association for the Relief of Respectable, Aged and Indigent Females in New York City, Visitors' Book, Feb. 6, 1839, New York Historical Society, New York. For the demise of spinning, see Victor S. Clark, *History of Manufactures in the United States*, 3 vols. (New York: McGraw-Hill Book Company, 1929), vol. 1, p. 531. I should note that the interruption of commerce during the War of 1812 revivified hand-spinning for a short time. Ibid., pp. 563-64.

15. Society for the Prevention of Pauperism in the City of New York, *Fifth Annual Report* (New York, 1821), p. 12.

16. An important component of this pool of cheap labor was the high number of women. See David Montgomery's suggestion that seaport cities in the early nineteenth century had an advantage over other centers of population in America in economic growth because of their surplus of women. "It may be that the westward movement of men created a labor surplus in the East, a surplus of women . . . perhaps . . . one of the major advantages that a city would have had at this time. Women were coming into the labor market in large numbers as widows, as orphans or as single women. You notice that the age bracket in which the women were available, the marrying age, 16 to 25, was where they outnumbered men." In David T. Gilchrist, ed., *The Growth of the Seaport Cities 1790-1825. Proceedings of a Conference Sponsored by the Eleutherian Mills-Hagley Foundation, March 17-18, 1966* (Charlottesville: University of Virginia Press, 1966), pp. 100-101.

In her study of the Sixth Ward, Carol Groneman found a large number of widows with dependents. She attributes this to the high death rate among foreign-born male workers in New York in the prime of life. "'She Earns as a Child—She Pays as a Man': Women Workers in the Mid-Nineteenth-Century New York Community," in *Class, Sex, and the Woman Worker*, ed. Milton Cantor and Bruce Laurie (Westport, Conn.: Greenwood Press, 1977), pp. 93-96.

Among whites in the city, the sex ratio was balanced until 1830, when women began to outnumber men. In 1830, there were 106 women for every 100 men; in 1840, 108; in 1850, 102; in 1860, 125. These calculations are based on population data from Franklin B. Hough, *Statistics on the Population of the City and County of New York* (New York: New York Printing Company, 1866).

17. Indeed clothing manufacture was the leading employer of women in the

city well into the twentieth century. I have traced it in the U.S. census for manufactures as far as 1940, when it still far outstripped any other industry in this regard.

18. *Manufactures of the United States in 1860; Compiled from the Original Returns of the Eighth Census* (Washington, D.C., 1865); calculated from returns for New York County, pp. 380-85.

Precisely because of the prevalence of outwork among women wageworkers, we can only take these census statistics as rough estimates of the number of women in the labor force. Any discussion of female labor-force participation in industrializing countries must take account of this serious problem of under-enumeration. For the same point about women's wagework in England and Holland, respectively, see Alexander, "Women's Work in Nineteenth-Century London," pp. 59, 111, and Leydesdorff, "Women and Children in Home Industry."

19. Quoted in Alexander C. Flick, gen. ed., *History of the State of New York*, 10 vols. (New York: Columbia University Press, 1933-37), vol. 3, *Whig and Tory*, pp. 297-98.

20. Abbott, *Women in Industry*, p. 217; Egal Feldman, *Fit for Men: A Study of New York's Clothing Trade* (Washington, D.C.: Public Affairs Press, 1960), pp. 1-2.

21. For sailors' slops, see Feldman, *Fit for Men*, pp. 1-2; Edwin T. Freedley, ed., *Leading Pursuits and Leading Men* (Philadelphia: Edward Young, 1856), p. 89. For uniforms, see Flick, *History of the State of New York*, vol. 3, *Whig and Tory*, p. 315. In 1819 the ladies of the House of Industry acquired a contract for navy blankets and uniforms to avert insolvency. *Evening Post*, Nov. 29, 1819. For journeymen sewing slops, see Feldman, *Fit for Men*, pp. 77-78; Jesse Eliphalet Pope, *The Clothing Industry in New York* (Columbia: University of Missouri Press, 1905), p. 11. For mentions of women sewing slops, see Ezra Stiles Ely, *Visits of Mercy; Being the Journal of the Stated Preacher to the Hospital and Almshouse in the City of New York, 1811* (New York: Whiting & Watson, 1812), p. 32; Society for the Relief of Poor Widows, Minutes, 1798, Jan. 10, 1803, Apr. 8, 1807.

22. Feldman, *Fit for Men*, p. 3; Sumner, *History of Women*, p. 122.

23. Freedley, *Leading Pursuits*, p. 89.

24. Chauncey M. Depew, *One Hundred Years of American Commerce* (New York: D. O. Haynes & Company, 1895), p. 565; *New York Herald*, Oct. 25, 1857.

25. *Herald*, Oct. 25, 1857. See John C. Gobright, *The Union Sketch-Book: A Reliable Guide . . . of the Leading Mercantile and Manufacturing Firms of New York* (New York: Rudd & Carleton, 1861), pp. 40-41, for the national market.

26. Gobright, *Union Sketch-Book*, p. 40.

27. Sumner, *History of Women*, p. 138.

28. Virginia Penny, *The Employments of Women: A Encyclopaedia of Women's Work* (Boston: Walker, Wise, & Co., 1863), p. 113.

29. For the attractions of the clothing trade for immigrants, see Robert Ernst, *Immigrant Life in New York City 1825-1863* (New York: Columbia University Press, 1949), p. 93. After 1835, when the commercial district was rebuilt after the great fire of that year, rents soared in lower Manhattan. For the expansion of homework in London under similar pressures of high rents, see Gareth Stedman Jones, *Outcast London: A Study in the Relationship between Classes in Victorian Society* (London: Oxford University Press, 1971), p. 23.

Sidney Pollard stresses the importance of subcontracting in early industrial capitalist enterprises in England. The large entrepreneur could thereby reduce his supervisory activities and to some degree stabilize his cost structure by paying the subcontractor a fixed price. *Genesis of Modern Management,* pp. 38-39.

30. Degler, "Labor in the Economy and Politics of New York City," p. 111. See also Freedley, *Leading Pursuits,* pp. 126-27, for the difficulties of small manufacturers. I am indebted to Sean Wilentz for discussions which have elucidated the structure of the clothing trade.

31. Quoted in Sumner, *History of Women,* p. 136.

32. New York State Census, 1855, Population Schedules, Ward 4, Electoral District 2, and Ward 17, Electoral District 3, mss at County Clerk's Office, New York City. I selected these two neighborhoods for sampling because they represented two strata of the laboring classes: the Seventeenth Ward was a new neighborhood for recent arrivals, while the Fourth Ward was an old, extremely poor neighborhood of day laborers and sailors.

33. Society for the Relief of Poor Widows, Minutes, Nov. 15, 1855.

34. Ibid.

35. *Herald,* June 7, 1853.

36. For the importance of dovetailing employment in a casualized labor market, see Jones, *Outcast London,* pp. 39-41. For mentions of both weekly and seasonal unemployment, see Carey, "Report on Female Wages," *Miscellaneous Essays,* p. 267; Shirt Sewers' Cooperative, "Circular of the Shirt Sewers' Association," Broadsides Collection, New York Historical Society, New York; *Daily Tribune,* June 8, 1853; Society for the Relief of Poor Widows, Minutes, Nov. 16, 1854; Penny, *Employments of Women,* pp. 114-15.

37. Quoted in Sumner, *History of Women,* p. 136.

38. *Working Man's Advocate* (New York), Sept. 6, 1831; George G. Foster, *New York in Slices: By an Experienced Carver* (New York: William H. Graham, 1849), p. 13.

39. Carey, "Report on Female Wages," *Miscellaneous Essays,* p. 280.

40. Little is known about day laborers in New York except their wages, which are alluded to throughout the reform and charity literature. I have garnered my impressions about turnouts from examining the cases of the New York County Court of General Sessions, New York County Courthouse.

41. *Working Man's Advocate,* Sept. 11, 1830.

42. *Herald,* Oct. 21, 1857.

43. William M. Bobo, *Glimpses of New York City, by a South Carolinian* (Charleston: J. J. McCarter, 1852), p. 109; see also pp. 107-10. Other references can be found in the *Herald,* June 7, 1853, Oct. 25, 1857; *Daily Tribune,* Aug. 7, 1849, June 8, 1853; *Working Man's Advocate,* Apr. 6, 1844; William W. Sanger, *The History of Prostitution* (New York: Harper & Brothers, 1859), p. 527; *Jonathan's Whittlings of War,* Apr. 22, 1854, pp. 102-3.

44. *New York Daily Times,* Feb. 24, 27, Mar. 1, 1855. A third seamstress sued her employer in court on Mar. 1.

45. The union was founded in 1863, apparently by middle-class men, who comprised its board of directors in the 1870s. Among them, interestingly enough, was police chief George Matsell. Workingwomen's Protective Union, *Twelfth Annual Report* (New York, 1876).

46. *Daily Times,* Mar. 1, 1855.

47. "Needle and Garden. The Story of a Seamstress Who Laid Down Her

Needle and Became a Strawberry Girl," *Atlantic Monthly*, 15 (1865), 170; *Jonathan's Whittlings*, Apr. 22, 1854, p. 102.

48. Bobo, *Glimpses of New York City*, p. 109.

49. *Daily Tribune*, Mar. 7, 1845.

50. Penny, *Employments of Women*, pp. 111, 114, 356. See also Pollard, *Genesis of Modern Management*, pp. 33-34. The inefficiency of putting-out is also discussed in Ivy Pinchbeck, *Women Workers and the Industrial Revolution 1750-1850* (1930; reprint ed., New York: Augustus M. Kelley Publishers, 1969), p. 137.

The other drawback of the outside system was the opportunity it gave workers to embezzle goods. Stephen Marglin has argued that embezzlement was widely practiced by English cottage workers in the eighteenth and early nineteenth centuries. He believes that embezzlement was the most serious of many problems of labor discipline which led capitalists to factory organization: not because factories were initially technologically superior to outwork but because such refractory practices could be better controlled by direct supervision. "What Do Bosses Do? The Origins and Functions of Hierarchy in Capitalist Production," *Review of Radical Political Economics*, 6 (Summer 1974), 33-35.

There is some evidence of embezzlement among New York workers. One employer told Penny that he had taken serious losses from nonreturned work: "On inquiry at the place where the women said they lived, they would find they had never been there." Another mentioned a blacklist of women who did not return their work, and a third corroborated the existence of a blacklist but claimed that he himself had never had any problems with embezzlement: "If they [the women] should keep them, they would soon be known at the different establishments, and have no place to go for work." Penny, *Employments of Women*, pp. 112, 115, 352. There were arrests of tailors for embezzlement during the tailors' strike of 1850, and one employer raised it as a general problem. See *Daily Tribune*, July 26, Aug. 14, 1850. There was an extensive network of illicit trade in New York, comprised of secondhand and pawnshops. If women did not embezzle goods, it would be interesting to know why, given the accessibility of that network and the frequency with which they went to pawnshops.

51. *Herald*, June 11, 1853; Freedley, *Leading Pursuits*, p. 130.

52. Letter subtitled "Over-work makes under-pay" and "Under-pay makes over-work," in Eileen Yeo and E. P. Thompson, *The Unknown Mayhew* (New York: Pantheon Books, 1971), pp. 384-88.

53. Penny, *Employments of Women*, pp. 350-51; evidence on the length of the workday is in Carey, "Essays on the Public Charities of Philadelphia," *Miscellaneous Essays*, p. 167; "Address of the Shirt Sewers' Cooperative," Broadsides Collection, New York Historical Society, New York; Penny, *Employments of Women*, p. 356.

54. Penny, *Employments of Women*, p. 310.

55. Reprinted in "Circular of the Shirt Sewers' Association"; a more accessible reprinting is in Alan Bold, ed., *The Penguin Book of Socialist Verse* (Harmondsworth, Eng.: Penguin Books, 1970), pp. 66-68.

56. Penny, *Employments of Women*, p. 311.

57. Ibid., p. 356.

58. *Herald*, June 7, 1853.

59. "Circular of the Shirt Sewers' Association."

60. In the 1855 sample from the Fourth and Seventeenth Wards, 200 (69.9

percent) of the 286 women who appeared to work "outside" were residing with husbands, parents, children, or kin. New York State Census, 1855, Population Schedules, Ward 4, Electoral District 2; Ward 17, Electoral District 3.

61. There are allusions to family labor in waged employment throughout the case histories of the New York House of Refuge Papers, Case Histories 1825-1860, New York State Library, Albany, and the published reports of the Children's Aid Society. For other references see "Needle and Garden," p. 91; *Daily Tribune*, Aug. 28, 1845; *The New-York Cries in Rhyme* (New York: Mahlon Day, 1832), p. 18; *Herald*, June 11, 1853.

62. Abbott, *Women in Industry*, pp. 2211-22. For contemporary references see Penny, *Employments of Women*, pp. 114, 310-11, 312-14, 355; Freedley, *Leading Pursuits*, p. 129; *Daily Tribune*, Sept. 5, 9, 1845; *Working Man's Advocate*, July 27, 1844.

63. New York State Census, 1855, Population Schedules, Ward 4, Electoral District 2. The sample includes all women ($N = 142$) enumerated as seamstresses in this electoral district. Carol Groneman reached a similar conclusion with her data from the Sixth Ward. "'She Earns as a Child,'" p. 93.

64. Conrad Carl, a New York tailor, testifying before a Senate investigatory committee, cited this proverb. U.S. Congress, Senate, Committee on Education and Labor, *Testimony as to the Relations between Labor and Capital*, 48th Cong., 1885, p. 414.

65. Pinchbeck, *Women Workers and the Industrial Revolution*, p. 2, makes this point about the effect on women of the breakup of the family unit of employment, although she does not extend it to the development of new forms of exploitation and an entire system of wage differentials.

66. *Working Man's Advocate*, July 27, 1844; Penny, *Employments of Women*, pp. 113-14.

67. Penny refers to the learning system throughout *Employments of Women*. See also *Herald*, Oct. 21, 1857. For the Irish garret-mistress, see *Herald*, June 8, 1853.

68. *Daily Tribune*, Nov. 12, 1845. References to the many different kinds of sweaters can be found in the following: *Daily Tribune*, Nov. 15, 1845; Penny, *Employments of Women*, pp. 112, 312, 342-43, 356, 452. In *Hunt's Merchant Magazine*, Jan. 1849, is the very interesting piece of information that piece masters in the large establishments of New York made anywhere from $25 to $150 a week, an indication that they were engaged in quite lucrative subcontracting. George C. Foster mentions sweaters and under-sweaters in *New York Naked* (New York: R. M. DeWitt [185?]), pp. 137-38.

69. Depew, *One Hundred Years of American Commerce*, p. 525; Feldman, *Fit for Men*, pp. 106-7; most important, see the fascinating account of the invention of the sewing machine in Ruth Brandon, *A Capitalist Romance: Singer and the Sewing Machine* (Philadelphia: J. B. Lippincott Company, 1977), pp. 42-89.

70. U.S. Congress, Senate, Committee on Education and Labor, *Relations between Labor and Capital*, pp. 413-14. A machine in the early 1850s was quite expensive ($100-$150) but by 1858 the price had dropped to $50 and there was a substantial secondhand trade. Feldman, *Fit for Men*, pp. 108-9. For another account (from Philadelphia) of how the machine encouraged sweating, see "Needle and Garden," pp. 173-75.

71. Carol Groneman Pernicone found forty tailors' and shoemakers' boardinghouses in the Sixth Ward in the 1850s. "The 'Bloudy Ould Sixth': A Social

Analysis of a New York City Working-Class Community in the Mid-Nineteenth Century" (Ph.D. dissertation, University of Rochester, 1973), p. 105.

72. Penny, *Employments of Women*, p. 112.

73. In the 1855 sample, I located forty-five households containing what appeared to be all-female work groups. Eighty percent of these were based on kin relations. New York State Census, 1855, Population Schedules, Ward 4, Electoral District 2, and Ward 17, Electoral District 3.

74. I was helped in my reasoning on this point by Heidi Hartmann's speculations about the reasons for men's "superior organizational ability" in the transition to industrial capitalism in "Capitalism, Patriarchy, and Job Segregation by Sex," in *Capitalist Patriarchy and the Case for Socialist Feminism*, ed. Zillah R. Eisenstein (New York: Monthly Review Press, 1979), pp. 216-17. See also Alexander, "Women's Work in Nineteenth-Century London," for a picture of the mingling of waged and domestic labor in a similar metropolitan economy. Mary McDougall, writing on industrialization in Europe, makes a point similar to mine about a particular vulnerability of women to sweating: "While the overall number of domestic workers declined in the process of industrialization, mainly men gave it up, leaving behind a preponderance of women." "Working Class Women during the Industrial Revolution, 1780-1914," in *Becoming Visible: Women in European History*, ed. Renate Bridenthal and Claudia Koonz (Boston: Houghton Mifflin Company, 1977), p. 266.

75. "Needle and Garden," p. 173.

76. *Jonathan's Whittlings*, Apr. 22, 1854, p. 102.

# The Uses of Political Power:
## Toward a Theory of the Labor Movement in the Era of the Knights of Labor

### LEON FINK

Perhaps in no other respect does the nineteenth-century American labor movement appear more alien to us than in its attitudes toward politics. Workers' independent political efforts from the workingmen's parties of the Jacksonian era through Populism seem to have gone nowhere and resulted in no lasting accomplishments, while participation in the two-party system, if sometimes more fruitful, sowed the seeds of middle-class ideological assimilation and organizational fragmentation. Almost universally among labor historians, labor politics (at least until the CIO) is associated with illusion, weakness, and/or sellout within the working-class movement.[1] One might almost think that American workers would have been better off without the tempting apple of the suffrage, which they alone in the western world "enjoyed" throughout the century. But while historians have been quick to judge the effects of labor's political forays, they have largely ignored the reasons why and the manner in which the labor movement returned time and time again to the fray.

Modern understanding of the Knights of Labor has especially been affected by this political embarrassment. The critical gaze of Selig Perlman and Gerald Grob, for example, fixes the Knights' political activity in a social reform stream characterized by a "lack of mature class consciousness," meddling by politicians and professional reformers, and petit bourgeois dreams of reestablishing "the relationships of an earlier era." On the other hand, Norman Ware, in his admiring history of the order as "a study in democracy," does his best to distance the Knights from ready identification as a political movement. Defining democracy as "a popular movement" (i.e., without necessary relation to "political" institutions), Ware associates (and embraces) the Knights as an example of a broad-gauged "reformism," equidistant from both "pure-and-simple trade unionism" and "politics," defined as "the outgrowth of reform or engrafted upon the movement by the farmers or the radical fringe of socialists and communists of one stripe or another." In this analysis the Knights "fall" into politics in 1886-87, then abdicate fully in 1890-94 as part and parcel of the paralysis of labor's national leadership and the natural inclinations of its now dominant agrarian or "western" sections.[2]

While these studies touch some important bases, there are serious internal problems with both the Perlman-Grob and Ware approaches to the subject. Simply put, they largely missed a tide of electoral initiatives during the 1880s which represented the most important dimension of Knights of Labor politics. The Knights' political activity may be encapsulated in three phases. The first was a national lobbying effort directed from the top and aimed at specific state and federal legislative action. This effort gathered strength from 1884 to 1886 and was crowned by the passage of a national contract labor law, state anti-convict-labor legislation, and funding of the U.S. Bureau of Labor. The second—and most significant—phase was a grassroots entry into local politics by hundreds of district and local assemblies roughly from 1885 to 1888. Finally, the Knights moved into active association with a national third-party movement led by the farmers from 1890 to 1894.

Discussion of Gilded Age labor politics by both Grob and Ware centered on the first and last of these phases which, while more convenient to analyze, inevitably created distortions. In both phases one and three, political demands were explicitly spelled out, the protagonists neatly aligned, and the results rather easily measurable. It is from the Knights' national initiatives and later alliance with the farmers' movement that Grob drew his argument regarding the reform tradition from which the Knights derived. Similarly, the same record underscored to Ware the very hesitancy of the Knights regarding political action and, once in action, the weak-sister role that the Knights played to Populism. Even the conclusions drawn from such evidence are subject to some questions. On what grounds, for instance, can one separate the attitudes of the middle-class reform-minded leadership from those of the rank-and-file worker? In what sense can politics, as Ware maintains, flow directly from the basic energizing reform vision of the order and yet at the same time, or alternatively, be seen as engrafted upon them from the outside?

More significantly, this national focus presents us from the outset with a circumscribed view of the relation of politics to the life of local assemblies, the heart and soul of the Knights' organization. In the national lobbying phase, for the most part, we are dealing with the front office of what was in fact a sprawling, decentralized operation.

And in the later alliance with Populism, we are addressing a movement already bereft of its dynamic core, namely the interaction of skilled trade unionists with previously unorganized urban industrial workers.

The second phase of the Knights' activities, when we finally uncover it, simply does not fit our present ways of understanding labor politics. For one, the Knights in this period did not always enter politics with a specific reform program in mind. Secondly, the local assemblies showed a marked disinclination to coordinate their political activities with any larger "political" (as opposed to "trade union") strategy or third-party movement beyond the local community. Thirdly, the Knights' political efforts of 1886-88 show little inheritance from agrarian political insurgency, as they generally preceded it. Finally, politics, even when it became a major and sometimes successful endeavor, never during the prime of the organization appeared to any Knights' faction as a solution to the movement's problems, whether defined as immediate organizational health or long-term strategy, such as abolition of the wage system. Theirs was an attitude toward politics not so much contravened as totally unexplained by both the Grob and Ware presuppositions. We have, then, no adequate framework for understanding Knights of Labor political attitudes and behavior. Unfortunately, it is not simply that Ware, Grob, and Perlman did not go far enough with their researches. The problem, I think, lies in a wider lacuna in our understanding of the relation of workers to the state and politics in the nineteenth-century. It may help, first, to reformulate the terms of discussion: within what general framework might we best approach the relation of radical social movements in the nineteenth century toward politics and the uses of the state?

I

American writings on the subject, notwithstanding their internal diversity, have tended to assume the peculiarity of U.S. developments. Probably the most helpful formulation on the record remains David Montgomery's *Beyond Equality*. Unlike both Grob and Ware on the Knights, Montgomery recognizes that the nineteenth-century movements did not opt for political strategies instead of trade unionist ones; rather along with workplace organization workingmen's leaders turned "instinctively to political activity for reform." Politics, in short, was part and parcel of the nineteenth-century labor movement, which often exerted "a significant influence on both the economic and legislative fronts." Yet, as Montgomery argues in dissecting the thought of labor reformer Ira Steward, the problem of labor politics is that while pressing for political power and legislative changes, labor maintained a minimal role for the state: "Steward, like all his contemporaries in the American labor movement, had no conception of an active role for the machinery of state. The sole function they attributed to government was that of enacting just and general laws applying impartially to all citizens. Within the framework of these laws, social development would take care of itself." From this perspective it is the political culture of American radicalism, in common with the dominant liberal tradition, that apparently sets up the likely failures of the continual political efforts. As if to underscore the ideological blind spot in the American approach to government, Montgomery contrasts Steward (and by implication American labor radicalism) with Marx, for whom "the ultimate objective of the workers' movement was to seize state power and wield it against the capitalists."[3]

While illuminating the travails of American labor politics, Montgomery implicitly deflects the problem to the cultural realm of American exceptionalism, i.e., to the "immaturity" of American class consciousness and ideology, even though he offers a different vision of "maturity" than Grob. Still, at the end of *Beyond Equality* we are left puzzled by the political commitment combined with self-limitation which defined the political philosophy of the labor movement. It is an uneasiness laid to rest only if we are able to accept as definitive the peculiarity of American radical thought, separating the workers' movement from alternative, apparently more clear-sighted, political agendas.

The exceptionalism of the American mentality remains the core assumption for David DeLeon's recent overview, *The American as Anarchist, Reflections on Indigenous Radicalism*. DeLeon argues that an antistatist, antiauthoritarian libertarianism, innately suspicious and thoroughly cynical about government and the political process, runs through radical American attitudes from the Garrisonians to the Wobblies, from Paine to Paul Goodman: "The black flag has been the most appropriate banner of the American insurgent." Statist radicalism—"traditional social democracy, communism, and other relatively authoritarian movements that rely upon coercive centers of state power (that is, on involuntary collectivism) rather than on cooperative association," according to DeLeon—has not had a chance in a country living with libertarian dreams.[4] Despite its suggestiveness this argument fails to come to grips with the American radical's faith in republicanism (the word is not even listed in the index), which has brought American movements, again and again, to address the state as the source of both grievance and rectification. It is a conceptual problem which rebounds to labor historians as well: how can American social movements be antipolitical and doomed by politics at the same time?

We can resolve the paradox only by shifting the intellectual context. In particular we might better understand the Knights' ambivalence toward politics as part of a halting reorientation of attitudes affecting western radical political thought as a whole in the nineteenth and early twentieth centuries. Ironically, the worker's relation to politics, which has long served as an important explanation of why class consciousness failed to develop here, might better be addressed by reassimilating American political culture into an international framework.

With a compelling analytical sweep, the Swedish political theorist Daniel Tarschys has outlined four consecutive but overlapping visions of "political utopia" which engaged Karl Marx and other nineteenth-century European radicals: the state, the democratic state, the association, and the commune. The last three of these visions, I think, also had considerable influence on American radicals and offer a useful starting point for reevaluating the ideology of the Knights of Labor. Veneration of the democratic state (following the Hegelian infatuation with the state *tout court*) accompanied the optimistic revolutionary rationalism of the late eighteenth and early nineteenth centuries. Nineteenth-century socialists, although increasingly critical and pessimistic, thus never "turned against democracy." For example, Marx and Engels, who by the 1840s saw the democratic breakthrough as "no longer the end" but "the beginning" of the struggle, still (unlike their Leninist progeny) "anticipated the social transformation to begin immediately on the conquest of a democratic constitution."[5]

For the radical political forces, by the mid-nineteenth century, a combination of setbacks (most notably the 1848 revolutions) and disillusioning victories (most notably the northern triumph in the American Civil War) prompted an important strategic revision. Democratic hopes henceforth adhered less to any form of the state than to the association, the liberation of civil society through economic self-organization. In their essential inspiration I think we may subsume here many of the goals of both the trade-union and cooperative movements of the nineteenth century, with their emphasis not only on the self-organization of workers but, through this activity, on the more or less gradual creation of an ethically superior "higher social order." The writings of Blanqui, Fourier, and Lassalle, as well as Marx, which themselves reflected the changing dimensions of the workers' movements, articulated a vision of the movement as community. Within this framework, a humane social order would emerge less by direct intervention of the democratic state (although, to be sure, the priority placed on state support remained a key dispute among radicals, e.g., Marxists versus Lassalleans) than by voluntary cooperation among workers themselves.[6]

The last great political vision of the century was represented by the Paris Commune, which we might envisage as the reappropriation of the state by society. The commune, at least in the eyes of Marxist interpreters and critics, represented the ultimate reunification of the workers' movement with the state and institutional centers of political-economic power. The "withering away" or "blowing up" of the state, the ultimate dream of so many nineteenth-century revolutionaries, meant (except to some very hard-core anarchists) not "blowing up society" but eliminating the "bureaucratic apparatus" which aided the social power of one class over another; even the revolutionary initiative of the commune (and later, at least in their idealized form, of the soviets) aimed primarily to allow rational self-government (the association redefined) to go forward. How extensive a role in coordination the residual central governmental authority should occupy were questions which divided European theorists (especially Marx and the anarchists) but did not contradict an essentially common vision of the desired and possible future: "If not interfered with by the authorities, the classical economic man would use all his faculties to promote his own welfare and thereby the public good. Marx's producer, released from the old social system, would just as certainly follow the precepts of his own reason and join together with his fellow men to organize a planned economy."[7]

Simultaneous commitment to politics as active citizenship and to subordination or minimalization of political (i.e., state-related) society as opposed to civil society thus defined important currents of late-nineteenth-century radicalism. We might broadly attribute the first pillar of this faith to the democratic revolutionary spirit of the late eighteenth century and the second to the relative immaturity of monopolistic and bureaucratic concentration, for there does seem to be a rather sharp break in radical and socialist thought, roughly coincident with the rise of monopoly capitalism, around the turn of the century. Henceforth the state was now more often viewed as either the primary obstacle to or the major source of change. Responding quite differently, anarcho-syndicalists (as well as conservative trade unionists) tried, in principle, to avoid entrapment in the state apparatus, whereas social revolutionaries (as well as social democrats) made the seizure and use of state power the immediate focus of their activity.

## II

It is against this European background, one of contending and changing strategies for the working-class movement, that we return to the assumptions and practices of the North American labor movement. On reexamination, American labor radicals and the Knights of Labor in particular do not seem far removed from the major currents of thought affecting their European contemporaries. Rooted in revolutionary democratic enthusiasm (Paineite republicanism), American radicalism by the era of the Knights had evolved into ambivalence regarding the role of the state and the proper political strategy for the labor movement. The evolving reconsideration of basic strategy in European working-class thought is equally apparent in the Knights' own Declaration of Principles:

> This preamble well says, that "the alarming development and aggressiveness of great capitalists and corporations, unless checked, will inevitably lead to the pauperization and hopeless degradation of the toiling masses. . . ." The method of checking and remedying this evil is, first, the organization of all laborers into one great solidarity, and the direction of their united efforts toward the measures that shall, by peaceful processes, evolve the working classes out of their present condition in the wage-system into a co-operative system. This organization does not profess to be a political party, nor does it propose to organize a political party but, nevertheless, it proposes to exercise the right of suffrage in the direction of obtaining such legislation as shall assist the natural law of development. It is true that the demands are revolutionary, as it is the purpose of the Order to establish a new and true standard of individual and national greatness.[8]

In this statement, diagnosis of the threat and identification of the source of salvation as well as ambivalence toward the exact means of redress all place the Knights within a larger western radical tradition. It is worth noting that even the avowal of peaceful means, by which the Knights hoped to allay fears of a European-style insurrection, was not a point upon which Marx himself necessarily disagreed.[9] For the Knights this intellectual juncture did indeed spawn rather conflicting attitudes toward the American political inheritance. Worshipping political nationhood, they displayed a mixture of fear and loathing for the prevailing uses of state power. As a result no contemporary organization celebrated the symbols of the Republic—the flag, the ballot box, the Fourth of July—with more enthusiasm than the Knights while more steadfastly avoiding commitment to a state-oriented program or strategy.

To acknowledge trans-Atlantic conceptual similarities, of course, is not necessarily to imply an explicit borrowing of ideas one way or the other. It is perhaps more likely that the specific and unique issues which radicals encountered within each national culture inevitably involved larger problems affecting working-class movements in all more or less liberal capitalist societies. Subjectively, it is clear, Gilded

Age labor radicals attributed their political attitudes to a combination of pragmatic analysis and what they thought was good American common sense. The halting reorientation of the Knights' political stance in the 1880s is a case in point. High principle commingled constantly with immediate tactical decisions as new situations continually presented themselves. Initial aversion to electoral initiatives, for example, rested in part on the overwhelming failure of the Greenback-Labor Party in the late 1870s. The difficulty and cost of such efforts, in which many labor leaders had been involved (Powderly, for instance, had served six years as mayor of Scranton), had left a sour taste about the possibilities of "high politics" in the United States. Exclusion of lawyers, the technicians of American politics, from membership in the Knights of Labor in part reflected a desired distance from the contaminated machinery of the state. Again, from a practical point of view the very process of organizing a new political party risked further inflaming the partisan rivalries already undermining the unity of the producing classes. Beginning in 1880, therefore, the Knights had proscribed any official electoral activity by their assemblies, and Powderly quickly branded grassroots agitation for labor tickets in the mid-1880s as diversionary pipe dreams. Finally, the American embrace of an associationalist idealism tended to discourage political mobilization. The social and moral regeneration of the "commonwealth of toil" claimed highest priority with Powderly and many contemporaries. Their very dedication to the order as a community and the exertions necessary to ennoble its internal life made irrelevant, if not pernicious, any protracted contact with the seamier sides of American politics. In support of this line a California district master workman reported to Powderly in 1883 that his assemblies were "growing slowly and recovering from an overdose of politics in the shape of Greenbackism, Prohibition and City Charter" and were "commencing to get back to first principles."[10]

Their resulting nonalignment policy placed the Knights in the anomalous position of advocating workers' political rights without offering a way to take advantage of those rights. Since 1879 the Knights' platform had included several planks directly addressed to legislative action. Internal education campaigns urged the worker to make use of "the high and sacred privilege of the ballot," but to beware of "machine hacks, scheming politicians, and money and land thieves." The conscientious Knight at one moment was advised to "let political parties and political clubs, of whatever name, severely alone"; the next moment he was told to "organize, co-operate, educate till the stars and stripes wave over a contented and happy people." It was very well for the official Knights of Labor organ, the *Journal of United Labor*, to chastise Americans for voting away, like the French, "the freedom of a Republic" to "our Napoleon—the monopolists, corporations, and bosses." But how was the labor voter to make "a wise, independent, and individual ballot," when he could decide only between the representatives of two "cash-cursed" parties? A Newark machinist believed he had found the only consistent solution—"when I think there is no use of my voting as the monopoly ring will succeed anyhow; but my duty as a citizen demands my vote . . . I vote a clean blank ticket." One Thomas B. McGuire, a truck driver who had once owned an express company which failed for lack of capital, voiced this same politically ambivalent strain of folk republicanism before the Senate Committee on Labor and Capital in 1883:

> McGuire. You [politicians] have got the power to see that every man gets what the Constitution guarantees to him—an opportunity to enjoy life, liberty, and the pursuit of happiness.
> Q. Do you understand it to be a fact that we have that power?
> A. Yes, the Constitution reads that way.
> Q. Is that all there is in the Constitution?
> A. This is about as far as I want to go.
> Q. That is in the Declaration of Independence, is it not?
> A. Well, have it the Declaration. When I was 13 years old I was in the Army of the United States, so I have had but little opportunity for education or study. . . .
> Q. Why do not the horny-handed sons of labor send men of their own choosing to make laws for them?
> A. Simply because the entire system from top to bottom is a system of bribery and corruption.[11]

The circumstances of the Great Upheaval of labor conflict from 1884 to 1886 nevertheless led many Knights of Labor to reconsider the political option. Explosive growth in 1885-86 lent the labor movement greater potential than ever before.[12] With large fractions of whole communities aligned with the order, the very numbers promised to carry substantial political weight if once united in a common direction. Bruising strike defeats suffered in the unprecedented industrial conflicts of these years also resurrected the weapon of the ballot, if only as a last resort. Disorderly withdrawal from the Southwest strike and the reverberations of Haymarket left Knights' assemblies across the country not only confused and demoralized but open to serious retaliation by employers unless some new show of strength could be mustered. Indeed, widespread resort to the judicial and military arms of the state in putting down the Great Upheaval reinvigorated for many labor partisans an older radical greenback message. As labor editor John Swinton wrote bitterly in mid-May 1886: "The country drifts from its ancient moorings. The constitutional method of remedying public grievances is disregarded. An anti-democratic Money Power is enthroned over the people."[13]

This juncture of resolve and circumstance fired what may still stand as the American worker's single greatest push for political power. Beginning with the early spring municipal elections and symbolically sanctioned by the special General Assembly in June 1886, the Knights flexed their political muscle virtually everywhere they were established. The secondary literature and the contemporary national labor press refer to labor tickets—called variously "Union Labor," "United Labor," "Knights of Labor," "Workingmen," and "Independents"—in 189 towns and cities in 34 (out of 38) states and 4 territories. Close investigation by state or region, particularly if one included relevant two-party contests, would doubtlessly turn up scores of other cases where local elections were waged on the basis of allegiance or opposition to the aims of the labor movement. Areas affected ranged from Eureka, California, to Gardiner, Maine; from Red Wing, Minnesota, to Fort Worth, Texas. The activity encompassed tiny rural hamlets as well as major metropolitan areas, frontier settlements as well as old New England towns, marketing centers as well as manufacturing and mining communities. The movement linked old immigrant farmers with new immigrant industrial workers, skilled white artisans with unskilled black laborers. Nationally, the biggest spotlight fell on Henry George's narrow and protested loss of the New York City mayoralty to Democrat Abram Hewitt (while trouncing GOP candidate Theodore Roosevelt) and on the Chicago United Labor party, which elected seven assemblymen and five judges while falling only sixty-eight votes shy of electing a congressman. In less-celebrated contests a common wave of labor feeling brought a black miner to the mayor's office in Rendville, Ohio; replaced a prominent attorney with a bank janitor as mayor of Waterloo, Iowa; and secured several constables from the ranks of Peabody, Massachusetts, leather workers. Avoiding the continuing official ban on direct political activity by forming shadow "Progressive" committees or political clubs, Knights of Labor locals across the country marshaled their forces at the polls. A Leroy, New York, partisan celebrated in song the workers' turn to politics:

> The ballot box, the ballot box!
> There comrades, you will find the rocks
> To hurl against the tyrant's head;
> Nor iron, dynamite or lead
> Can match the ever-potent knocks
> Shot from our Yankee ballot box.
> The ballot box, the ballot box!

> No merely warlike weapon shocks
> With such effect the would-be boss;
> It closes his accounts with loss.
> Ho! rally to the polls in flocks
> Right's standard is the ballot box.[14]

For a brief period labor reform leaders held high hopes of building a national independent political movement. In addition to numerous inroads at the municipal level, in November 1886 the Knights claimed to have elected a dozen congressmen (usually in fusion with one of the major parties). Envisioning "a Parnell party" in a partisanly split House, the order's Washington lobbyist, Ralph Beaumont, was jubilant: "God has answered our prayers and the Knights hold the balance of power in the organization of the 50th Congress." With the Knights and the burgeoning National Farmers' Alliance as a base, advocates of independent political action foresaw a powerful new party bringing together greenbackers, socialists, single-taxers, and antimonopolists. John Swinton threw his support behind just such a coalition of "new political forces" slated to convene in Cincinnati in late February 1887. Following a symbolic endorsement of the Knights of Labor platform, the meeting chartered the National Union Labor party and set its sights on the 1888 federal elections. Readers following the crescendo of political success recorded in *John Swinton's Paper* could well believe by the spring of 1887 that "there will soon be but two parties in the field, one composed of honest workingmen, lovers of justice and equality; the other . . . composed of kid-gloved, silk-stockinged, aristocratic capitalists and their contemptible toadies."[15]

But Swinton's senses as well as his sympathies had been carried away by the political fever. Efforts to create a national workingmen's party were hamstrung from the start by internecine strife. Powderly's order to "let political parties alone," together with general skepticism on the part of trade unions, significantly reduced labor's involvement in the political project. Within the Farmers' Alliance as well, antipolitical tendencies still dominated outside of Kansas, Arkansas, and Texas. In New York squabbling between socialists and single-taxers destroyed George's Clarendon Hall coalition by the end of 1886; both, in turn, refused to work under the banner of the western-oriented Union Labor people. George's United Labor party even made certain to hold a separate convention in Cincinnati simultaneous with the Union Labor conclave. Transformed by the defections into primarily an agrarian and western instrument, the Union Labor party emerged as a weak forerunner to Populism. Within the Knights the battle to impose a coherent political strategy was won too late: the order began to connect with the agrarian third-party movement in 1890 and completed the process with the deposition of Powderly in 1893; but by that time the Knights, having suffered mass defections to the trade unions as well as to the iron hand of employers, had dwindled to relative insignificance among American workers.[16]

## III

The content of labor's political vision in these years is best discerned in the multiple experimentations at the local level in 1886 and in the year or two thereafter, when heady expectations were accompanied by real achievements. At least four uses of political power were articulated— sometimes separately, sometimes in tandem—in these locally diverse efforts. First, there was politics as a spillover effect. Organization of the local working-class population into Knights of Labor assemblies tended in and of itself to undermine the legitimacy of the commercial-industrial elite as community leaders. Now that the community was voluntarily divided by differing conceptions of common need, the mere assertion of citizenship rights led in some places almost inexorably in the direction of a labor ticket. In many cases, the Knights did not set out to do anything dramatically unconventional with political power. Rather, with new pride, solidarity, and power, workers determined to show not only that they could do what had previously been done for them but that they could do it better. Thus, after Rochester, New Hampshire, Knights took over town meeting in March 1886, one of their number boasted that whereas two days was "the usual time required to do the town business . . . on this occasion only three hours were consumed in adjusting affairs with everything done decently and in order." That the Knights-in-office were celebrating a social-political transformation accomplished primarily by mobilization and organization in civil society was apparent in an act of the 1887 Rutland town meeting. In a gesture more symbolic than substantive, the workingmen voted to place an American flag in every schoolroom.[17]

There were other ways as well in which the social reorganization of a community around the Knights produced an almost inevitable political spillover or partisan realignment. In Richmond, Virginia, for example, the Knights gave voice to an evolving coalition of interests between white skilled workers and black factory operatives and unskilled laborers. Since the two prevailing southern parties of the 1880s not only reflected but sustained a world divided along race lines, the Knights had either to extend biracial cooperation into politics or, sooner or later, to abandon it altogether. Such underlying logic, I think, accounts for the several southern workingmen's tickets which arose in 1886-87.[18]

The second use of politics—again essentially unrelated to positive exercise of state power—derived from the need to curtail state repression of and interference with the life of the social movement. Most clearly in the wake of major strike defeats or massive counterthrusts to worker mobilization by the business classes, politics here emerged as at least one remaining way to "punish your enemies." Following the suppression of Milwaukee's eight-hour movement in the Bay View massacre and the subsequent conspiracy trials, for example, Wisconsin Knights' leader Robert Schilling in June 1886 announced his intention to "gain revenge—by the ballot." Response to antilabor use of the police and courts would similarly inspire Chicago workingmen's efforts in the aftermath of Haymarket. In Kansas City, Kansas, too, control of the police power would emerge as a major political issue following the collapse of the Great Southwest strike.[19]

Specific class-related legislation was the third use of local labor politics. Particularly where public bodies had assumed a direct administrative role in the economy, political conflict was assured. The fact that the municipality was also an employer, for example, led to a variety of political demands. In addition to establishment of an eight-hour day for city workers and an end to municipal subcontracting, Richmond Knights, with many members in nearby quarries, insisted on the use of Virginia granite in the new city hall. Under similar labor pressures, in 1887 the Quincy, Massachusetts, town meeting adopted a nine-hour statute and a $2 minimum wage and promised to employ only town residents.[20]

Expansion of the public sector emerged only slowly as a political issue in the era of the Knights of Labor. The nation's new intra-urban transit systems, around which bitter strikes would swirl by the turn of the century, from the beginning evoked conflict between public and private interests. When Kansas City, Kansas, labor mayor Tom Hannan insisted on a series of reforms in the street-railway ordinance of 1887, for example, the local board of trade (appealing to the jurisdiction of the courts over the city council) actually enjoined the city's major public improvements bond issue. The urban transit controversy might in an abstract sense be likened to the contemporary fight of the farmers over railroad rates and, ultimately, railroad ownership. William Appleman Williams, most notably, has stressed the limited ideological reach of such political demands focusing on "commercial arteries" of the marketplace (railroads, telegraphs, telephones, etc.), while leaving the system of private enterprise untouched. An alternative, perhaps more convincing, explanation for the centrality of transit and communication systems to the radical demands of the period lies in the fact that it was here that public authority appeared most baldly not only to have sanctioned but to have colluded with private "monopoly."[21]

Within this third category of positive uses of state power, a few other tendencies of local Knights of Labor regimes are worth noting. Depression in the 1890s did trigger demands for government to serve as the employer of last resort. While the business classes encouraged private charity—provision of clothing and soap to needy youngsters, voluntary expansion of domestic service—Rutland labor representatives in 1894 pushed for short-term public projects like street-grading and landscaping to relieve widespread distress. Even so, demands for public welfare in the nineties seem not to have advanced beyond the terms which Herbert Gutman has documented for the depression of the 1870s. Again, without necessarily breaking new ground, the Knights did act as a force for expansion of public services and expenditures. In 1886 the first labor-dominated town meeting in Rochester, New Hampshire, for example, increased appropriations for street lights, poor relief, and education by 20 percent over the preceding year. In various ways the Knights also addressed the question of tax equity. Following the doctrine of Henry George, Rutland workingmen clamped a punitive tax on unoccupied land. Nevertheless, even allowing for the brevity of their tenure in office or hopes for office, the workingmen's substantive political experience did not yield an identifiable "labor" political agenda. For them local politics was generally not an arena for imaginative effort or experimentation; rather it was primarily a means of consolidation and preservation of gains largely achieved elsewhere.[22]

A fourth use of politics surfaced in only the most tentative form until the rise of the People's party in the 1890s. This was the path of the movement as politics, to make political agitation and organization the focus of a national labor strategy. Particularly as the industrial campaigns of the Great Upheaval fell, one by one, into defeat, the attempt to revive the movement through politics did gain credence in certain quarters. The United Labor party of Henry George, the 1887 agrarian-based coalition of "new political forces" in Cincinnati which led to the Union Labor party, and the Socialist Labor party all gave voice to this reaction. But by 1888 support for any third-party candidate beyond the local level was negligible even where the Knights still exercised considerable influence.

Among the obstacles which third-party advocates faced and could not overcome was one of the Knights' own making. While becoming political, the Knights convinced themselves that they were doing the opposite, that they were really rescuing society from the depredations of politics. Thus at the local level they preferred to identify themselves as independent or nonpartisan; politics and parties in their minds were associated with social parasitism, "ring rule," and "baneful" central authority. To commit themselves to a political party was to align

themselves with a political strategy, an acceptance of necessary dependence on the state for their identity as a movement which they denied
from the outset. Unless absolutely necessary, such a commitment was
unlikely in an organization which could extol a candidate for the
Vermont state legislature simply on grounds that he "has not been a
politician because he was too honest to have anything to do with their
dirty contemptible little tricks." The only way the Knights could
cleanse the political process was to remain outside it, acting from
political strength rooted in a moral order of their own making.[23]

Here it is worth considering an important difference between the
paths of the Knights and the Farmers' Alliance. The alliance, after all,
while rooted like the Knights in associational strength and sharing
many of their ideological presuppositions, did, unlike the Knights,
manage to shift effectively to a political strategy. Because the farmers
found much of their oppression linked to institutions of circulation and
credit (in which, through control of the money supply, the government
was already involved), they could jump to a political demand (a sub-
treasury) to redefine their problems in a nationally coherent way. But
the workers', and therefore the Knights', problems did not converge
nearly so neatly on the public domain. Not the coordination of finance
or transportation, after all, but the consolidation of corporate control
over private production sent them into battle. To be sure, government
and the political parties had everywhere made it more difficult for "the
people to rescue the heritage which we received from our fathers from
the grip of gold and greed." But, aside from sending men "untrammeled" and "closely identified with the struggling masses" into
office to clean things up, no common or acceptable political solution
could have saved the workers' movement. Indeed, precisely when politics became primary in the order, the Knights could effectively count
themselves dead.[24]

## IV

We may thus put forward some general propositions regarding the
relation of the American labor movement to the international currents
of political radicalism circulating in the mid to late nineteenth century.
Essentially, the events of the Great Upheaval period led the Knights of
Labor to a repoliticized associationalism, a vision they shared with
others even if it was for them (as undoubtedly elsewhere as well)
defined by particular national political circumstances. Thus, in the
United States the contemporary industrial conflict threw a labor movement which would have preferred to go its own autonomous way back
into contact and confrontation with state-organized power. To the

extent that the state had become an appendage of the money power, the Knights believed, it had to be liberated before rational self-government, as organized by the people in civil society, might flourish. Reappropriation of the state by society, the political vision symbolized by the Paris Commune of 1871, in American translation became "recapturing government for the people." That the task here involved no insurrectionary mobilization does not necessarily imply that American workers were less radical but perhaps only that their circumstances were different. In a country which still waved its republican banner, a post-millenarian confidence dictated use of the ballot rather than apocalyptic appeal to rifle and cannon as means of redress.[25]

We might compare the Knights' attempts to control community political levers with the evolving contemporary search for control at the workplace. Just as the late-nineteenth-century "workers' control" impulse (to use Montgomery's phrase) tended to represent an extension of traditional craft autonomy into a changing and threatening work environment, so these local political efforts grew out of the adaptation, particularly on the part of skilled workers and small producers, to a demeaning of citizenship. While workers sought initially to defend themselves and their communities, the movement in politics, as on the shop floor, began to take unprecedented initiatives and even to envision a structurally altered environment.[26]

From a defense of their stake in civil society, the Knights took on the state to dispel its opposition and to identify its institutions with the interests of a well-organized body of producers. How things might have turned out had that body remained strong is a separate question which will not detain us here. But such a perspective, I think, explains why the Knights could jump into politics enthusiastically without much of a political program. It also explains why, at the height of what appeared to middle-class Rutland as political insurrection, a regional labor leader could sincerely declare, "We stand as the conservators of society."[27] The Knights of Labor looked to self-organized society—not to the individual and not to the state—as the redeemer of their American dream. Neither ultimate antagonist nor source of salvation, the state represented to them a mediator in the conflict between the civil forces of democracy and its enemies. A source perhaps of both the order's strategic strength and its weakness, the Knights' perspective, not ours, ought to be the initial point of departure for evaluation of their actions.

Despite the passage of time and perspective, the Knights may nevertheless share more with their progeny than we would like to admit. The dilemma that they faced in trying to harness state power to democratic ends has continued to bedevil the American working-class movement (not to mention others). A comparatively modest scale of production, a feeble public administrative apparatus, and a rich nexus of local community ties all combined in the late nineteenth century to minimize radical demands on and expectations of the state. The problem for a powerful social movement seemed to be one of eliminating governmental roadblocks and perhaps of assimilating by political control certain limited state services to the needs of the movement. Essentially, however, the Knights made no imaginative leap with regard to the future relation of state and civil society. If anything, as labor radicals began to realize too late, it was their corporate antagonists who learned far earlier than they new uses of politics and state power.

Beginning in the 1890s the state took on more and more the role of coordinator of the socioeconomic order. The banking system and the money supply, the tariffs, the courts, and ultimately the enhanced regulatory role of government came to serve in crucial ways to stabilize a decreasingly democratic society. Faced with a practically irrevocable leviathan, radicals were forced into new but no less difficult choices. Telescoping many levels of activity over many years, we might suggest that the craft unions, sensing the odds, abandoned a political strategy in favor of the immediate economic struggle. The Wobblies cloaked this same political retreat in more ambitious syndicalist terms. Socialists, labor progressives, and ultimately Communists, on the other hand, hoped to capture the state to overhaul society and in the meantime to squeeze from it at least a social welfare role. Neither approach, it must be concluded, proved very satisfactory. If to abandon politics meant to risk being hemmed in by leaving the state's powers in the hands of labors' enemies, to pursue the state-oriented strategy meant to risk the assimilation and taming of the movement which had launched it. The respective fates of the IWW and the CIO reflect the alternate potential polarities. The pervasive bureaucratic state, in short, has not only hampered efforts to implement radical change but has stifled even the vision of democratic alternatives. No longer able by their own efforts to create oppositional forms of production or to convey an oppositional culture, labor unions and radicals alike have turned to the reformative power of government (e.g., the civil-rights movement, labor-law reform, the war on poverty) as a partner in progress. But whether the political path can, indeed, be used at once to achieve practical ends and to invigorate a social movement still remains to be seen. That the Knights of Labor did not provide a definitive solution to the strategic dilemma of the relation of a democratic movement to the state should not, in retrospect, surprise us. Even in their failure, they were clearly grappling with one of the more important questions of modern times.

NOTES

An earlier draft of this paper was presented at the Knights of Labor Centennial Symposium, Newberry Library, Chicago, May 17-19, 1979. I am grateful to Susan Levine and Joan Wallach Scott for helpful comments on the text and to editors Frisch and Walkowitz for helping to clarify my thinking at several crucial points. The political experience of the Knights will be discussed at greater length in *Workingmen's Democracy: The Knights of Labor and American Politics* (University of Illinois Press, forthcoming 1982).

1. For the most recent elaboration of these themes, see Alan Dawley, *Class and Community: The Industrial Revolution in Lynn* (Cambridge, Mass., 1976), pp. 214-19; and Daniel J. Walkowitz, *Worker City, Company Town: Iron and Cotton-Worker Protest in Troy and Cohoes, New York, 1855-1884* (Urbana, Ill., 1978), esp. pp. 253-57. Also see David Montgomery, *Beyond Equality: Labor and the Radical Republicans, 1862-1872* (New York, 1967), p. 215.

2. Gerald N. Grob, *Workers and Utopia, a Study of Ideological Conflict in the American Labor Movement, 1865-1900* (Chicago, 1961), pp. 34-59, esp. p. 58, and pp. 79-80; Norman J. Ware, *The Labor Movement in the United States, 1860-1895, a Study in Democracy* (New York, 1929), pp. xi-xiii, 350-70; Selig Perlman, *A Theory of the Labor Movement* (New York, 1970), pp. 182-200.

3. Montgomery, *Beyond Equality*, pp. 195-96, 249-60, esp. pp. 259-60.

4. David DeLeon, *The American as Anarchist, Reflections on Indigenous Radicalism* (Baltimore, 1978), esp. pp. 102-14, quotations from pp. 102, 114.

5. Daniel Tarschys, *Beyond the State, the Future Polity in Classical and Soviet Marxism*, Swedish Studies in International Relations (Stockholm, 1971), pp. 47-86, quotation from p. 65.

6. Ibid., p. 77.

7. Ibid., p. 86.

8. George MacNeill, *The Labor Movement, the Problem of Today* (Boston, 1887), p. 485.

9. See William R. Schonfeld, "The Classical Conception of Liberal Democracy," *Review of Politics*, 33 (July 1971), 260-76.

10. On associationalism within American labor ideology see Brian Greenberg, "Free Labor & Industrial Society: The Idea of a Cooperative Commonwealth in Mid-Nineteenth Century America" (paper delivered to annual meeting of the Organization of American Historians, Apr. 12, 1979); *Journal of United Labor*, Apr. 1883.

11. *Journal of United Labor*, Jan. 15, 1887; Dec. 1882; Dec. 24, 1887; *John Swinton's Paper* (hereafter *JSP*), Jan. 23, 1887; John A. Garraty, *Labor and Capital in the Gilded Age* (Boston, 1968), p. 152.

12. The Knights grew from 19,000 members in 1881 to 111,000 in 1885 to a reported 800,000 in 1886 before falling back to 100,000 by 1888.

13. *JSP*, May 16, 1886.

14. Ibid., Nov. 1, 1886.

15. Ibid., Nov. 7, 1886; Ralph Beaumont to Powderly, Nov. 5, 1886, Terence V. Powderly Papers (Catholic University, Washington, D.C.); *JSP*, Apr. 17, 1887.

16. Ware, *Labor Movement*, p. 363.

17. *JSP*, Mar. 21, 1886.

18. For elaboration see Leon Fink, "'Irrespective of Party, Color or Social Standing': The Knights of Labor and Opposition Politics in Richmond, Virginia," *Labor History*, 19 (1978), 325-49.

19. Milwaukee *Journal*, Oct. 4, 1886. The general point here was perfectly encapsulated by a resolution of the Workingmen's Convention which gave rise to the Chicago United Labor party in 1886: "As the economic encroachments of aggregated wealth have caused the defensive organization of the producers into trade unions, Knights of Labor, and grangers, so must the political encroachments of the same aggregated wealth (which are still more dangerous to the liberty and existence of the people) inevitably force the people into defensive political organizations as distinct and antagonistic to capitalist political parties as the trade union is to the club, cabal, or clique of the monopolist" (*JSP*, Nov. 10, 1886).

20. Quincy *Patriot*, Mar. 5, Apr. 2, 1887.

21. William Appleman Williams, *The Contours of American History* (Cleveland, 1961), pp. 334-38.

22. Herbert Gutman, "The Failure of the Movement by the Unemployed for Public Works in 1873," *Political Science Quarterly*, 80 (June 1965), 254-76; Rochester *Anti-Monopolist*, Dec. 12, 1885; Mar. 13, 1886; Mar. 11, 1887; Rochester *Courier*, Mar. 12, 1886; Mar. 11, 1887. The protective role of local working-class politics in another context has recently been noted by Joan Wallach Scott, "Social History and the History of Socialism: French Socialist Municipalities in the 1890's" (paper presented to the First Annual North-American Labor History Conference, Wayne State University, Oct. 18-20, 1979).

23. Rutland *Herald*, Oct. 6, 1886.

24. See Lawrence Goodwyn, *Democratic Promise, the Populist Movement in America* (New York, 1976) for the general interpretation of populism offered here; Kansas *Cyclone*, July 9, 1887; Rutland *Herald*, Oct. 6, 1886.

25. Frank M. Pixley, editor of the nativist San Francisco *Argonaut*, returned from Paris in 1871 praising the "order and organization" of the commune and had this to say regarding the reception of Americans by the communards: "Americans had a universal pass in the city [along] with soldiers of the Commune. I treated a regiment of Vilette to half a cask of red wine. It was cheap, and I was paid in having them cheer the toast I gave them in very bad French—'The Republic of France and the Grand Republic of America. I shall live to see its realization'" (*American Non-Conformist*, Apr. 7, 1887, reprinted from *Argonaut*).

26. See David Montgomery, "Workers' Control of Machine Production in the 19th Century," *Labor History*, 17 (1976), 475-509.

27. Rutland *Herald*, July 25, 1887. From a diametrically opposite perspective the Chicago *Tribune*, even in its hostility, also understood that labor in politics primarily was aiming to buttress its role in civil society: "They [the United Labor Party] want to control the police force so that they can throw bombs with impunity, the fire department so that they can ravage and burn without having their work of anarchy arrested, the machinery of taxation so that they can confiscate property by form of law and throw the revenues of honest enterprises into a common pool for plunder" (quoted in *JSP*, Mar. 27, 1887).

# The Triumph of Commerce:
## Class Culture and Mass Culture
## in Pittsburgh

### FRANCIS G. COUVARES

I

In the last decades of the nineteenth century, leisure became a "problem" in Pittsburgh. Businessmen and middle-class reformers found the subordinate classes increasingly alien and their leisure habits increasingly disturbing. This growing cultural distance between the classes reflected an intensification of conflict in the iron and steel industry and the arrival of great numbers of southeastern European immigrants in the late 1880s and 1890s. It also marked a decisive shift in class power in favor of the business and professional classes, who imagined for the first time that they could shape the values and habits of the masses. But class power could not simply be cashed in the coin of culture. Although Pittsburgh's plebeian culture underwent change, neither its defenders nor its detractors predicted or determined the character of cultural reorientation in the early twentieth century.

Concerning elite efforts to reform popular culture in early modern Europe, Peter Burke has made a few observations which apply nearly as well to the case of Pittsburgh at the turn of the century. He notes, first, that "changes do not always take place because someone wants them." "In fact," he goes on, "European popular culture altered in ways which no one intended, ways which no contemporary could have foreseen." Furthermore, although Burke describes the "Triumph of Lent" over traditional, semipagan culture, he locates the major cause of cultural change in the "commercial revolution" which permanently transformed communications, markets, and consumption.[1]

It is the intent of this essay to argue that similarly in Pittsburgh—and by implication in much of nineteenth-century urban America—commerce overmatched reform and generated unpredictable cultural consequences. The very "merchants of leisure"[2] who had emerged from and invigorated local plebeian culture ultimately subverted it by forging the links of a nationwide, centralized mass culture industry. Neither "captains of consciousness" in the army of capital nor simple servants of democratic choice, leisure entrepreneurs rushed ahead of businessmen, reformers, and even audiences in defining and discovering ways to satisfy collective desires.[3]

As in Europe earlier, no one could have predicted the shape, intensity, or direction of those desires. From P. T. Barnum, Barney Dreyfuss, and the vaudeville syndicates, the road to Walt Disney, George Steinbrenner, and the television networks is less than direct or obvious. What is clear is that in America at the turn of the century, despite the growth of prohibitionism, Comstockery, and other repressive movements, mass commercial entertainments were winning large and loyal popular audiences. Indeed, as the case of Pittsburgh amply demonstrates, militant leisure reformers merely accelerated the rush of working people (and many of their betters) into the arms of the merchants of leisure. They thereby helped to mobilize audiences for baseball, movies, and amusement parks rather than for churches, settlements, or libraries. The triumph of commercial leisure can be read clearly in the fact that, by the early twentieth century, the means of satisfying desires—mass entertainments, sports, and media—had themselves become the objects of contention. The question had become not "whether" but "whither" mass culture.[4]

## II

From mid-century to the 1880s, Pittsburgh had been a plebeian city. Autonomous craftsmen regulated production and labor in the iron mills and built one of the strongest unions in late-nineteenth-century America. Loose and shifting political coalitions gave workingmen real influence—sometimes effective control—over city council and city hall. And, along with shopkeepers and small businessmen, craftsmen and other workers supported a constellation of theatrical and sporting pastimes that were highly responsive to local plebeian tastes and interests.[5]

By the turn of the century, the plebeian city had been overwhelmed. Having crushed or neutralized the craft unions, a technologically revolutionized steel industry employed immigrant labor for proletarianized work. In politics, power-brokers like "Boss" Magee organized patronage machines and restricted access to an expanding local government. Moreover, having first withdrawn to newly developed suburbs, the business and white-collar classes turned their attention back upon the city and presumed to assert over the working class a moral and political authority that had eluded them in the past.[6] It was in this context that plebeian culture declined, leisure reform intensified, and mass culture took root in Pittsburgh.

That popular leisure had become a new and more serious problem registered first in the local temperance movement in 1885. Although they had always aimed to reform popular drinking habits, local temperance advocates emphasized voluntarism more than prohibition or other coercive methods of reform. Their approach was exemplified by the genial and uncensorious Francis Murphy, who founded his nationwide Gospel Temperance society on the basis of an immensely successful crusade in Pittsburgh in 1876-77. Among Murphy's warmest admirers were skilled unionists who welcomed calls to "manliness" and worker self-discipline. Many union leaders saw in the blandishments of saloonkeepers and "festive ward bummers" serious threats to labor organization and working-class solidarity. Well into the 1880s, they gave at least verbal support to temperance as an antidote to the indiscipline of life in the streets and saloons of an industrializing city.[7]

But the Law and Order movement put an end to interclass cooperation and to moderation in the temperance cause.[8] In May 1885, a group of church people in Pittsburgh's eleventh ward hired a lawyer to prosecute the proprietor of a new roller coaster which had begun operating on Sunday. Winning a quick conviction, they proceeded to bring suits, most of them successful, against thirty-two saloonkeepers and vendors who defied the Sunday closing laws. From the start their intention was not to help or redeem the lawbreakers or the citizenry at large, but to assert control over their neighborhood. If in doing so they alienated the craftsmen and shopkeepers with whom they had hitherto cooperated, the new enforcers seem to have cared little. Appalled by the flood of aliens and the rise of conflict in the nearby mills, the Law and Order activists forsook persuasion and compromise in favor of immediate, rigorous enforcement of the laws.

In the next two years similar organizations arose in other mixed residential wards on the fringes of the central business district. After the passage of the new state high license law in May 1887, the Pittsburgh Law and Order League was founded to coordinate their activities. Well funded by city churches, the league asserted "the absolute necessity of regularly employed and reliable agents." Moreover, it soon began a campaign against prostitution based on the same principles that had made its earlier efforts against saloonkeepers and Sunday vendors so effective. The league "never proposed to reform anyone, but solely to *enforce the law* and leave the reformation of the inmates to those societies whose particular province it may be." It mocked the notion that prostitutes were just poor girls gone wrong and in need of loving care. Drawn from "the very lowest dregs of society, they entered upon their life of shame simply to escape from honest work, and . . . they laugh deep and long at the sentimental gush that is periodically indulged in at their expense."

Despite middle-class, Protestant support, however, the league won no cooperation from city officials. Police Chief Nate Brokaw (formerly an officer in the Amalgamated Association of Iron and Steel Workers) wrote a letter urging an alderman to "fix" cases brought by the Law and Order League against ten bawdy houses in his ward. The letter was discovered and published, but Mayor McCallin ignored the incident. Though the leaguers condemned city officials, however, they expected little from them, relying instead on the ability of their own lawyers and investigators to win cases before the county courts. Indeed, the league ventured actively into electoral politics only to support tough county judges. Thus, J. W. F. White won the strong support of the league in his race for a judgeship by vowing a "terrific cleaning out" of saloons in Allegheny County, especially in the vicinity of steel mills. True to his word, Judge White deferred to the league's judgment in most license hearings, reducing in two years the number of licensed establishments in the county from 3,500 to 389 and in the city from 1,500 to 223.[9]

Even more than had an earlier campaign for state prohibition, the activities of the Law and Order League decisively alienated most workingmen from the cause of temperance. What infuriated them most was the league's petty cruelty. Its agents swooped down upon crippled cigar vendors and seventy-year-old candy sellers with a cool self-righteousness that working people accurately attributed to class bias. The courts reinforced that impression. In 1888 and 1889, the state Supreme Court upheld the convictions of two Allegheny County men—one a milk dealer, the other a baker—for selling on Sunday. At about the same time, however, it reversed the convictions of two Pennsylvania Railroad employees, ruling their Sunday labor a "necessity." These were landmark cases which overturned the precedent set in 1853 in *Johnston* v. *Commonwealth of Pennsylvania*. In that case the court had ruled that neither competition nor public convenience was sufficient grounds for permitting a bus driver to work on the Sabbath. Twenty-five years later it was clear that what was merely convenience for the plebs had become necessity for the Pennsylvania Railroad.[10]

Given free rein, the new enforcers precipitated a kind of guerilla warfare in Pittsburgh between 1887 and 1890. They pitted middle-class Protestants against working-class Catholics. Moreover, at trials and license hearings they used tactics which provoked nasty exchanges between neighbors called upon to testify against one another. Against this "star chamber business" popular reaction was strong. In September of 1887, William A. Herron, the old and distinguished figurehead president of the Pittsburgh Law and Order League, resigned from the organization in protest. The league tried to ascribe Herron's departure to ill-health, but the old man had confided his real reasons to former labor leader John Jarrett, who promptly made them public: "He is opposed to this system of persecutions, and told me that he would not be a party to it."[11]

The *National Labor Tribune* kept up a drumbeat of criticism of the league. It asked why the organization's chief agent "does not turn his attention to industrial establishments that run their works on Sunday." The followers of Francis Murphy joined prominent Episcopalians and German Lutherans in denouncing the leaguers' hard-hearted pietism. The Personal Liberty League, organized by retail liquor dealers to fight the Law and Order crusade, was blessed by Lutheran pastors who rose to defend "the German Sunday" from attack. Democrats took full advantage of these events, cultivating the antipietist backlash and nearly electing to the Common Pleas Court John Bailey, whom critics labeled "the candidate of the Liquor League." Bailey lost by only 400 votes in that 1887 race (carrying the normally Republican city of Pittsburgh by 1,500). Moreover, his victorious opponent was no temperance man but rather a stalwart machine Republican, unfriendly to the Law and Order cause.[12]

Thus, though the Law and Order movement disrupted hundreds of lives, it accomplished none of its long-term aims. By 1890 it had lost its bite. Law enforcement remained weak and the popular desire to evade the law strong.[13] Moreover, the league proved in the end nothing more than a rear guard covering the retreat of the very people most interested in disciplining the chaotic city. Middle-class Pittsburghers were succumbing to the lure of the streetcar suburb.[14] Having failed to hold the line, they redrew it around the pastures of the east end. There they found escape not only from the vicious, however, but also from the confines of their own narrow virtue. To understand the progress of leisure reform, it is therefore useful to explore the experiences which transformed the reformers.

## III

New transportation technology certainly provided the means of bourgeois escape to the suburbs for, until the development of cable and electric cars in the late 1880s and 1890s, mass transit made no sense in hilly Pittsburgh. But new wealth and cultural ambition were the true vehicles of the suburbanizing middle class. In the east end, a new generation rebelled against "the worst mid-Victorian taste" and "the whole Presbyterian repression."[15] Abandoning the dour and provincial standards of the Iron City, it prepared itself for leadership in the more cosmopolitan and progressive Age of Steel.

Once lodged in their suburban homes, bourgeois Pittsburghers seemed suddenly to have heard and absorbed the "Gospel of Relaxation." The demand for fine music, cuisine, art, and other entertainments created a small boom in the luxury and service trades in the 1890s. By the turn of the century, the "Classic East End" contained not only beautiful homes but a whole range of exclusive services, including fine retail shops, a market, a theater, a dancing school, the city's only auto club, and two preparatory schools. It spawned the *Index*, a paper which claimed to mirror "the spirit of the socially elite, in society, in literature, in the fine arts and in politics." It boasted the city's only luxury high rise, advertised as the last word in comfort, privacy, and security ("Each dwelling has a forged steel wall safe, while watchmen patrol the building day and night.").

Though some imagined that the "magic circle" of suburban life offered an Edenic retreat from the "devilish" city and its inhabitants, however, the dominant mood among bourgeois Pittsburghers was not escapist but expansive and confident. They aspired in the long run to make Pittsburgh respected by their peers in other cities and to assert their right to dominate their city on the basis of superior access to and acquaintance with the wider world of commerce and culture. Thus, the Duquesne and Pittsburgh Clubs began to organize local elite culture and to connect it with that of Philadelphia and New York. Middle-class women demanded and patronized fancy new department stores which linked them to a network of fashion and consumption based in the East. Convinced that "the theatre should be commensurate with the importance of Pittsburgh as he saw it," Henry W. Oliver joined other businessmen in sponsoring a theatrical building wave in the 1890s. They gave Pittsburgh's aspiring middle class what it wanted and what local plebeian theaters had long denied them: "rococco" surroundings, ticket prices that excluded the plebs, and a steady diet of "New York theatre" and syndicated stars.

Along with this growing spirit of cosmopolitanism, a new emphasis on energetic and assertive living arrived to correct tendencies toward suburban retreat. Indeed, Pittsburgh's middle and upper classes responded to the impulse to "the strenuous life" that John Higham has identified as one of the ruling passions of the age.[16] Suburban Pittsburghers succumbed to "a delightful epidemic" of tennis, golf, archery, swimming, gymnastics, bicycling, and other sports. Moreover, in the late 1880s team sports began to flourish at Pittsburgh's private academies, at Central High School (which taught the children of the east end and which fancied itself "one of the best preparatory schools outside New England"), and at Western University (later the University of Pittsburgh). College graduates carried "the old-time enthusiasm" into local amateur athletics, where the East End Athletic Club and the Allegheny Athletic Club organized clerks, professionals, and businessmen into highly competitive track, baseball, and football teams. Responding to the new mood, the University of Pittsburgh greatly increased its athletic budget and in 1907 hired as head coach the estimable Glen S. ("Pop") Warner, who succeeded in bringing champion-caliber football to the city for a decade. By 1900 it had become clear that *"esprit de corps . . .* intensified by the discipline of wholesome athletics," was the sine qua non of middle-class student life.[17]

Though seemingly unrelated to developments in elite consumption or to the evolution of more cosmopolitan tastes and values, the rise of middle-class sport promoted the same growth in class consciousness to which the *Index* and the Duquesne Club gave more obvious testimony. It certainly fortified those who rejected the counsel of retreat in favor of activism and self-assertion, but who nonetheless renounced the austere and obsessive style of the Law and Order League. They could, it seemed, realize the suburban ideal and at the same time venture into the hurly-burly, compete for the attention of the masses, and put their stamp on the life of the city.

Thus, even in withdrawal to the suburbs, middle-class culture evolved in counterpoint to developments below. Pastoralism, cosmopolitanism, and strenuousity represented different modes of a continuing interaction with those variously described as dangerous, parochial, and debauched. However earnestly suburbanites sought not to be of the metropolis, they could not escape the fact that they lived in it. Since the first campaign of William C. McCarthy and his plebeian coalition of the 1860s, the issue of suburban improvements lay at the heart of Pittsburgh politics. Tax rates, zoning regulations, streetcar franchises, sewers, and all the other services which made the suburbs possible, depended on the Pittsburgh city council.[18]

Moreover, even if suburbanites wanted simply to avoid contact with the city and its alien masses, they could not have done so, for the city had already begun to come out to them. When the wind was right, even the east end, which was surrounded by industrial zones, suffered from the smoke and smell of steelmaking. In East Liberty, poolrooms, taverns, a popular theater, and the city's only amusement parks disturbed the calm of suburban life. Perhaps most telling, the Pittsburgh

Free Dispensary found it necessary before the turn of the century to open an east end branch.

Clearly, elite residential communities were themselves enclaves in the great industrial metropolis. In the twentieth century true escape was vouchsafed only to the Mellons, Fricks, Carnegies, and their peers. The bulk of Pittsburgh's professional and business families could not doubt that the fate of the few was bound to that of the many.

Indeed, most of their cultural efforts revealed both a recognition of and an ambivalence toward that social interdependence. As great parks, museums, and libraries rose in the 1890s, the burghers of the Steel City showed that they could not simply remake themselves without also setting out again to remake the working class.

## IV

In the year 1895, a signal event marked a turning point in the cultural history of Pittsburgh: the erection of that complex of structures—music hall, library, museum, and art institute—that bore the name Carnegie. For the children of the iron barons, the phrase "before the Carnegie Institute" signified a past sunk in provinciality and repression.[19] Immense and imperial, the Carnegie complex offered suburbanites the grand entertainments hitherto lacking in Pittsburgh and confirmed their right to think of themselves as members of a leisure class with cosmopolitan tastes and connections. Equally important, however, was the fact that, unlike private clubs or commercial theaters, the Carnegie complex was a public institution with an explicit social agenda: to define, create, and disseminate "the highest culture" and thereby to civilize the inhabitants of the industrial city.

An early expression of this cultural mission was the inauguration in 1896 of free Sunday organ recitals at the music hall. The recitals reportedly attracted "the people for whose benefit they have been established—viz., the wage workers." Organist and music director Frederic Archer planned Saturday programs for students and Sunday programs for the general public. Of the latter he explained: "In order to develop the musical instincts of the people *en masse*, the adoption of a *repertoire* of diverse character is absolutely necessary, for by such means alone can universal interest be aroused and catholicity of taste promoted. My Sunday programmes are therefore constructed on this plan, although all music of low or vulgar character is excluded."

It is difficult to determine the identity of those who attended Archer's recitals, and it may be doubted that workers who could barely afford the necessities of life expended precious time and money on a trip to Oakland. Nonetheless, up to his death in 1901, Archer reported an average attendance of one thousand. In its first five years the series drew an astonishing 381,000.[20] Whatever their impact, the organ recitals represented only the first in a series of "outreach" efforts directed from the new center in Oakland.

Indeed, as important as the erection of the Carnegie complex was its location. Poised midway between downtown and the east end, Oakland served as the pivot for a middle class trying to balance pastoral vision and social ambition. It was a kind of frontier of east-end culture, at once a buffer against encroachment and a staging ground for forays into alien terrain. Already the site of the relocated campus of the University of Pittsburgh (soon to be joined by the Carnegie Technical Schools), of the Bellefield and Athletic Clubs, and of the exclusive new Schenley Hotel, Oakland was also the locus of Schenley Park, the jewel of the emerging metropolitan park system. Earlier and more clearly than the erection of the Carnegie center, the development of Schenley Park reflected middle-class desires both for a gracious style of life and for social order.

Although elite Pittsburghers had for decades lamented their city's lack of "public park, fountain, or garden," all park proposals met defeat at the hands of a plebeian electorate unwilling to finance "a public pleasure ground" or other suburban improvements. Despite increased demand for industrial and residential property in the 1870s, residents of the old city still had easy access by foot or by short train or boat ride to numerous sites for swimming, sledding, fishing, pigeon-trapping, picnicking, and other forms of informal play. Thus the plebeian majority—and most tax-conscious businessmen—generally ignored advocates of romantic park development.[21]

Increasingly in the 1880s, however, park promoters joined utilitarian to aesthetic arguments. Parks, they argued, could uplift base temperaments or at least provide a safety valve to vent the frustrations of urban industrial life. Whether park promoters believed it or merely employed it to convince reluctant burghers, the idea that a Schenley Park could serve as a substitute for saloons and rowdy pastimes and thereby create civic harmony weighed heavily in subsequent debates.

Moreover, massive industrial and demographic change in the late 1880s made utilitarian arguments more and more convincing to all Pittsburghers. In 1889 Edward Bigelow, the city's aggressive new chief of public works, convinced the council to accept from Mary Schenley a gift of 300 acres and an option to buy 100 more for $125,000. In promoting his program, Bigelow appealed both to the suburbanizing middle class, which sought a pastoral preserve, and to the masses from whom the suburbanites were escaping. He recognized sooner than his contemporaries that popular opposition to park development was disappearing along with old neighborhoods and informal recreational sites and that, increasingly, the scarred and vanishing natural landscape made its own case.

Almost simultaneously with the Schenley deal, Bigelow announced plans to develop the Highland Reservoir site. Residents of the elite area were disconcerted by the news. They saw in Bigelow's proposal not simply a plan to preserve beautiful landscapes—they had already accomplished that privately—but a direct threat to their golf course, their country club, and their pastoral way of life. No less than the poor south-siders who fought the creation of McKinley Park in 1898—and no more successfully—the Highlanders couched their resistance to planned development as a defense of nature and of received patterns of leisure. By the 1890s, however, the argument for "democratic planning" had won the day.

Despite that victory, Bigelow's park plans remained relatively modest. Though pressure for more interventionist strategies steadily mounted, Bigelow's parks emerged less as social engineering than as grand rhetoric. Like the nearby Carnegie complex, Schenley Park extended to the urban masses in whose name it was built a welcome that was at best tacit. And like Highland, which one progressive critic complained "does some social work although far from the desired amount," Schenley was "typically . . . the East End's park, adapted fairly well to its neighborhood, but not at all serving the democratic needs of Greater Pittsburgh."[22]

Neither the Carnegie center nor Schenley Park was fitted to perform "social work." Organ recitals, picture galleries, and stacks of books were, like park lawns and trees, simply made available to the public. For middle-class Pittsburghers concerned to ameliorate social disorder and decay, mere availability was not enough. Because they doubted that the distant cathedrals of Nature and Culture could do the necessary missionary work, reformers turned to more direct and active methods of influencing working-class leisure. These included expanding the functions of parks, building neighborhood playgrounds, and launching a library extension service. In all cases, reform became at once more intrusive and more subtle than that practiced by the Law and Order crusaders. Intended to restructure space and to reeducate those who occupied it, "social work" comported better with the new middle-class notion of itself as a worthy and cultured elite. Furthermore, it promised to compete better with the merchants of leisure for the time and attention of the working class.

Bigelow's most obvious attempt to practice such reform involved redesigning the celebration of the Fourth of July. By the late 1880s the plebeian Fourth[23]—in which craftsmen, shopkeepers, and fire companies had played so prominent a part—had succumbed both to demographic change and to pressure for a reformed celebration. That pressure came especially from the forces of Christian piety and from the labor movement. In their different ways, both pietists and unionists anticipated elements of Bigelow's more organized and centralized Fourth of July pageant of the 1890s.

Appalled by what Frederick Law Olmsted referred to as "grotesque performances by montebanks [*sic*] with fireworks and music," and by the drunken fights and fire company brawls that often marred the holiday, pietists tried for years after the Civil War to promote Memorial Day as a sober substitute for the plebeian Fourth. By the 1880s, however, they admitted failure. Not only had Memorial Day failed to win mass support, but even the loose integrity of the Fourth had given way to scattered observances and private pleasures. Ethnic, fraternal, religious, and other groups went their different ways—to commercial amusements, sporting events, and private parties. Picnics and excursions drew more people to more distant sites as railroads, boat companies, and agents devised travel plans with special holiday rates. Moreover, in the face of the rise of the Knights of Labor, increased strike activity in the steel industry, and rapidly changing patterns of immigration, pietists in the late 1880s rediscovered the virtues of "the old-time Fourth of July," finding it preferable to Memorial Day because the latter recalled rebellion and civil war at a time when people needed a message of unity.[24]

Ironically, the antilabor *Christian Advocate* found itself echoing the *National Labor Tribune* when in 1887 it asserted, "It lies with labor organizations to revive old-time celebration of the Fourth of July . . . the one particular holiday of the year which wage-workers should mark with patriotic ardor."[25] What pietist and unionist had in common was a desire to focus the celebration, to impose serious, thematic content upon a holiday that had always been more carnival than somber ceremony. Thus, in 1887, after Terence Powderly called on workingmen to turn the Fourth into an expression of labor unity and patriotism, local Knights began organizing modified versions of the plebeian Fourth of July. While they filled the day with the usual games and events, they also made temperance the order of the day and strove explicitly to associate the cause of labor with the republican heritage. Though the effort to put labor at the head of a movement to revive the old Fourth succeeded in many smaller towns in Western Pennsylvania, it made little impact in Pittsburgh. In a city of such size, where hostile and powerful forces competed for control of patriotic symbols, the Knights were in no position to dominate celebrations.[26]

The year 1887 also witnessed a very different attempt to organize the holiday: leading politicians and businessmen tried to develop a decentralized celebration in keeping with the more fragmented and dispersed character of life in the Steel City.[27] In at least a dozen sections of the expanded city, prominent men financed and organized fireworks displays and other festivities. Boss Magee spent $500 on downtown pyrotechnics, and other area patrons, such as Henry C. Frick in the east end, may have spent as much. On the other hand, the efforts of the butcher and boilermaker who took charge of one of the south-side celebrations were doubtless more modest. In any case, this experiment in neo-feudalism was not repeated. For, even as it was being carried out, Edward Bigelow (whose brother Thomas had sponsored the 1887 celebration in the Hill district) was formulating his plans for Pittsburgh's modern park system, one part of which was the mobilization of massive Fourth of July festivals in Schenley Park.

Bigelow took the Fourth of July seriously. Unlike pietists, however, he sought not to spurn the plebeian Fourth but to absorb it. To the park he invited vaudeville performers, ethnic dancers, balloonists, pyrotechnicians, horse and mule racers, and a myriad of other plebeian entertainers. On the other hand, unlike the sponsors of decentralized festivities, Bigelow contained the celebration within Schenley Park, thus standardizing the observance and detaching it from plebeian associations in the old city. He then reinforced that detachment by allowing only licensed vendors in the park, by banning liquor and peddling, and by deploying large police contingents to maintain order. Finally, unlike the Knights, Bigelow had no intention of associating patriotism with the cause of labor. Instead, he mounted elaborate ceremonies in which businessmen and politicians took center stage and which featured pageants asserting a new social ideal, at once cooperative and hierarchical, for the Steel City. Extolled in poems and speeches, enacted in dramatic tableaux, and chanted in choral anthems, patriotism became a kind of service, a doing one's part for the larger, progressive purpose.

Though ambitious and well financed by business contributions, however, Bigelow's patriotic extravaganzas may not have had their desired effect. Their intended message could be variously interpreted, taken lightly, or ignored. Moreover, the official veneer could simply break down, as it did dramatically on July 4, 1892. Then "eloquent old Tom Marshall" cried the one word which no one on the platform wanted to hear: Homestead. An old Mugwump, founding member of the Republican party, former local and state official, and labor arbitrator, Marshall was universally respected and had a reputation for fiery oratory. More to the point, perhaps, he was too old to imbibe fashionable progressivism and too cranky to acquiesce in a charade intended to celebrate unity even as, a few miles away, the social tinder of the Steel District was about to explode. His bitter excoriation of monopoly capitalism and his endorsement of labor's crusade to "assert the manhood of man" fell "like a bombshell" on the audience. But it was a fugitive dissent from an otherwise smooth performance, and it was never repeated.[28]

More persistent threats to Bigelow's plans were public indifference and the danger that, in his effort to appeal to the masses, the medium might overwhelm the message. Thus the *Gazette,* one of the city's more straitlaced newspapers, saw in the 1892 celebration little more than a vulgar "country fair" run for the benefit of the political machine and the "street-railway combine" which Boss Magee owned. Oblivious to any intended preachments about social order—which it would have applauded—the *Gazette* noticed nothing but "money-making schemes." "'Everything goes' was the order of the day. . . . Organ grinders, peddlars and fakirs of all classes took hold early . . . while many merchants and others took advantage of the supposed solemn and patriotic occasion to advertise their respective concerns to the fullest extent."[29] Indeed, promoters could only be certain that the very attractions they had hoped would draw crowds—picnic grounds, ball games, and the ever-reliable "montebanks with fireworks and music"—had done just that.

The *Gazette*'s obliviousness suggests that Bigelow's success lay not in indoctrination but, as the fate of another holiday suggests, in his ability to define public space. For a time in the 1880s, Labor Day inspired a working-class version of what pietists had hoped for Memorial Day, i.e., the mobilization of huge crowds in a sober and serious affirmation of citizenship. However staid those demonstrations—in 1887 workers marched under the banner of "Unity, Stability, Conservatism"—they were at least implicitly class-conscious expressions of the same social context which was producing an extraordinary number of strikes and other labor disturbances. Even more important, however, they were vestiges of a passing era. The Labor Day parade customarily wound its way through the old wards of downtown, south side, and Allegheny, claiming, as it were, the working city for the workingman. Along the route, neighborhood merchants and other middle-class residents joined in the sort of plebeian festivities that their suburbanized peers had left behind. For workingmen, the celebration of Labor Day demonstrated just that distinction between capitalist enemies at work and middle-class friends in the community which the passing of the plebeian city was making anachronistic. Indeed, by Labor Day of 1892 the city had so changed that labor leaders contemplating ways to mark the day could think of no better place to demonstrate than Schenley

Park.[30] In effect, as Frick was directly and brutally snatching from iron and steel workers their claim to "workers' control" within the factory, so Bigelow—less directly and less consciously, perhaps—had begun to redefine the space beyond the factory gate.

V

As Edward Bigelow redefined public space, other reformers increasingly delved into inner space. Seeing an opportunity to shape values and habits in a way that neither public works nor Law and Order could, they explored more manipulative forms of leisure reform which promised more continuous and effective supervision of lower-class values and habits. In the Pittsburgh area, librarians and playground workers were especially active in that exploration. They were also especially encouraged in their efforts by the ideas and actions of Andrew Carnegie.

"How a man spends his time at work may be taken for granted," announced Carnegie in 1898 at the dedication of his library in Homestead, "but how he spends his hours of recreation is really the key to his progress in all the virtues."[31] This announcement is striking for the disclaimer with which it opens ("How a man spends his time at work" was one thing Carnegie never took for granted), but even more for the portent with which it closes. That the "key to progress" in human relations lay in control of "hours of recreation" was an insight increasingly shared by many of Carnegie's reform-minded contemporaries. But in Homestead Carnegie discerned a unique opportunity. Unlike Pittsburgh, where all efforts to influence the behavior of employees had to be mediated through a complex of cultural and political institutions and conventions, where, in brief, history intervened between people and those aspiring to shape or master them, Homestead had only recently and suddenly risen around Carnegie's mill. In such a virgin context, Carnegie hoped to develop the "three natures in the make-up of every human being," that is, "the mental, moral and physical." He believed that, through wise intervention in the cultural environment, great capitalists might complete the process already begun in the mill. Having remade the world of work, they could now turn to the larger world of leisure.

Homestead's library thus operated according to its master's plan. Mill officers dominated the library board and the professional staff seemed to know its duty: "If it is proper for the library to furnish books for the people, it is right that they should be good books. If the library has the right to control the character of the reading, it has a right to direct the reader to the desired information."

Even in Pittsburgh, where things operated a little less smoothly than in Homestead, extension librarians clearly revealed paternalistic assumptions. The chief of the library's children's department, for example, understood her main task to be social control through literacy. Books were an "important socializing factor" through which she was able "indirectly to instill lessons of courtesy, cleanliness, care of public property, respect for the rights of others and many other valuable lessons."[32]

She and her extension staff were systematic and energetic in pursuing those ends. Organized "like a business house into departments," the library did not wait upon its public. "To reach the working men, the foreigners and their children in their homes," the library created seven branches and 177 distribution stations. In one twelve-month period alone, more than 31,500 foreign-language books circulated from the Carnegie Library of Pittsburgh. Although 13,000 of these were written in German and thus reached few of the newer immigrants, the rest represented the languages of those recently arrived southern and eastern Europeans.

The library set up extension stations in factories, department stores, churches, YMCA buildings, fire houses, public and private schools, Sunday schools, settlements, bath houses, vacation schools, playgrounds, and juvenile detention facilities. It even allowed children to establish "home libraries" for the use of friends and neighbors, and it sent librarians to lead weekly "library hours" in those homes. Inspired by Jacob Riis's call to fight "the gang" with "its own weapon—the weapon of organization," librarians did special work among boys' gangs. It may be doubted that such outreach activities affected working people precisely as intended, but there can be no doubt about the seriousness of the effort.

While extension workers tried to reform behavior by means of literacy and the cultivation of sensibility, playground workers looked instead to the strenuous life and, in particular, to team sports. "Play is a social inheritance," announced Beulah Kennard, the moving force behind Pittsburgh's playground movement. Unlike romantic park planners who envisioned the tired worker reviving his spirit in verdant and tranquil solitude, Kennard insisted that play "has almost no existence away from group life."[33]

Linked closely to public schools and settlements, the campaign for playgrounds tapped the optimistic and strenuous strain in middle-class culture. Good progressives all, the playground workers talked incessantly of hygiene, organization, and "morals efficiency." They believed that the disorder of urban life followed from society's failure to socialize children and that playgrounds would teach isolated and stunted children the satisfaction and creative power of collectivity. The "play spirit" was the spirit of civilization itself. Only by harnessing the instincts through strenuous team play could social health be restored.

Thus attuned to instinctual demands and convinced of organizational solutions, playground workers promoted the healthy release of energy through a myriad of group activities. To achieve "positive educational results," they created playgrounds and programmed activities in working-class neighborhoods wherever they could find space— schools, settlements, church yards, factory grounds, and empty lots. They also took to politics, sponsoring bond proposals and competing for park development funds, arguing always that "schools of play" were more effective agents of socialization than were schools of Nature. What they wanted for their charges was not "breathing space" but ceaseless, directed activity. Playgrounds had to be close at hand, easy of access, and supervised so that no child would be left with hands or thoughts unengaged. Imagining herself free of romantic illusions about natural morality, the new activist was in fact obsessed with "the whole hygenic aspect of life among the working people." Unable to trust her charges to God, to Nature, or to themselves, however, the playground worker eventually found her "persistent attention" inadequate to the task of "comprehensive social formation."

In fact, most playground workers probably never realized the neopuritan expectations raised by their rhetoric. Experience with working-class children and their families taught most playground workers that, beyond the simple provision of service and the spontaneous demonstration of kindness, their ministrations were coolly received. When they became censors or moral instructors, their clients retreated. If they chose to serve the working class, they would have to do so on terms dictated by a clientele which recognized with acute discrimination the difference between service and domination.

Moreover, it may be that playground workers came to pay no more than lip service to their own professional uplift jargon. Despite talk of turning every playground into "the headquarters of a kind of neighborhood guild" wherein would grow an "invaluable village . . . loyalty," playground workers were compelled to settle for more modest, yet real, achievements. They created safe places for children who were crowded into mill neighborhoods; they supplied equipment and some instruction in sports, arts, and crafts. Despite the pronouncements about socialization, in practice they endeavored "to keep the activities spontaneous, childlike, and joyous, without strain and without self-consciousness."

Similarly, even when extension librarians intended to instill values and habits in their charges, they gave as much emphasis to the need "to think independently" as to the wisdom of decorum and submission to authority. In claiming that they purveyed only "suitable stories illustrating ethical subjects," librarians may have been broadcasting what trustees and superiors wanted to hear. Whatever they intended, moreover, they often did little more than read stories and fairy tales to children. Like their colleagues in the playgrounds, librarians avoided the hard sell: "The methods of the children's librarians are those of informal teaching. The children come and go as they wish, there being no compulsion in their attendance at the library."[34] To working-class parents, the library was probably just a pleasant place staffed by pleasant people into whose hands children could safely be deposited for a few hours on weekends.

Finally, library staffs were often too busy providing services to keep clearly in mind the ultimate aims of profession or institution. This was especially true when, as in Homestead, the staff included recreation workers, music directors, and teachers, who were expected to organize and maintain most of the town's athletic and cultural activities, from basketball, gymnastics, and bowling teams to bands, choruses, and instrumental clubs. Thus, to whatever extent it intended to "Americanize" its clientele, the library staff could be certain only that it provided welcome diversion, especially for youngsters. However serious its efforts to bend play to ulterior social ends, the staff had eventually to treat play as an end in itself.[35]

Though they may have been valuable to working-class children, however, the playground and the library extension mattered little to their parents. As playground workers had no luck with "neighborhood guilds," so librarians found extension work among mill men frankly discouraging. "The library and the lecture course are fine things for business men, women and children," but not for himself, one steelworker told John Fitch. His indifference reflected motives mixed but not unrelated. In addition to competition from bars and pool halls, "Conditions at the mill, overtime work, and the fact that the men were not readers, or distrusted the company's motives" were cited for the failure of extension stations in factories. Similarly, Fitch noted that, while the twelve-hour day made self-improvement of any kind practically impossible, there also existed "a great deal of prejudice against the gift of Mr. Carnegie on account of the several labor conflicts that have occurred in the mills." The conservative glassblowers union scorned Carnegie's alleged magnanimity, finding only irony in the claim that his library was "Free to the People." On the contrary, the taxpayers would forever sustain Carnegie's monument to himself and to the money sweated from the workers at Homestead. His self-glorification, like his use of Pinkertons, was "a challenge to the manhood of free American laborers."[36]

Indeed, working people viewed Carnegie's philanthropies as forms of company public relations and as attempts to appease and distract them. Whereas in the 1880s the *Labor Tribune* and other labor spokesmen had been in the habit of praising Carnegie for his enlightened labor policies and philanthropies,[37] after Homestead their attitude cooled considerably. Even earlier, they had begun questioning the wisdom and morality of such gestures. In 1890, for example, workingmen and their representatives in Allegheny raised serious questions about who would control the library which Carnegie had offered the city. Carnegie and other upper-class citizens naturally assumed that a blue-ribbon board of trustees should administer the institution, but the *Labor Tribune* and, as it turned out, a majority of the city council disagreed: "A committee of [city council] would represent the people; a special committee of unofficial citizens might be composed of snobs who would make the Library anything but popular."[38]

Though the issues were often very different, questions of power and authority lay behind all working-class criticism of welfare capitalism. It is therefore not surprising that some of the earliest and most comprehensive programs of welfare capitalism were first attempted by companies which, like the famous Lowell mill, hired predominantly female labor forces. Management might exercise a paternalistic authority over women that would have provoked resistance if applied to men.[39]

The best example of such paternalism in late-nineteenth-century Pittsburgh was the "German Welfare System" applied to its 600 women employees by the H. J. Heinz Company.[40] Besides providing scrupulously clean surroundings, uniforms, and equipment, Heinz gave each "girl" a weekly manicure and supplied free treatment from company physicians and dentists. Several times every summer, each worker had the chance "to climb into a horse-drawn wagonette with eight other girls and spend a morning or afternoon, at no loss of pay, being driven through the park and downtown areas." On the Fourth of July she could board the company paddle-wheeler for the slow trip to Beaver County, where the lavish annual picnic took place. She could use the company roof garden, the pool, the washroom, and the lunchroom, where one penny bought coffee, milk, and sugar and where she was serenaded by piano music. Even more impressive was the great auditorium: "It had a musical director, 1500 opera-type seats, a gallery with two proscenium boxes, 2000 incandescent bulbs, a pipe organ, a Pianola, a Steinway Concert Grand Piano, an Edison Stereo-Projecting Kinetoscope, and a splendid large dome with artistically designed stained glass . . . on which appeared the motto, 'The World Our Field.'" The auditorium featured professional shows as well as employees' theatrical, choral, and instrumental productions, an annual dance, and a Christmas party.

Owned and managed by Germans, staffed largely by German and Bohemian workers supervised by matrons, the Heinz plant may for a time in the 1880s and 1890s have operated according to its founder's grand paternal design. By the turn of the century, however, when Elizabeth Butler investigated the firm for the Pittsburgh Survey, most of the workers were Slavs, and the veneer of paternalistic benevolence had worn thin. Though there was little open rebellion, Butler sensed resentment against that cheerful and sterile regime under which women might, like "girls," be "summoned to the auditorium at noon to hear an address by some visitor or to sing." She also recognized the brute hardship under which the women labored: "A girl who cuts onions at $.75 a day cares very little for the polished piano in the lunch room, or for the roof garden." To exceptionally noxious and unrewarding work at very high speeds, Heinz's welfare measures added only indignity. "When high wages are paid, even if fewer gifts are given, women employees have the precious opportunity to work out their own lives."

Corporate paternalism evoked in the working class a proletarian version of laissez-faire,[41] an instinctive demand simply to be let alone. That instinct was revealed in the similarly dubious reception that working people gave to nearly all varieties of public and private welfare work. They refused to be patronized, whether by employers or by reformers who were deeply critical of those very employers. They especially resisted the efforts of those who proffered service in return for good behavior, usually defined in middle-class Protestant terms.

Thus, the Playground Association failed to attract to its Lawrence-ville field house the very Polish and black working women of the Strip and lower Hill areas for whom it had been built in 1907. Instead, only German, Irish, and "American" women—nearly all clerks, stenographers, and other white-collar employees—took advantage of the classes, concerts, and athletic facilities. Settlement houses had similar experiences. Though the Kingsley and Columbian settlements in the Hill district attracted immigrant boys to their basketball courts, they and others made little impact on blacks or on the Slavic majority. Similarly, in Lawrenceville and on the south side, the YWCA failed to attract working women to its lunchrooms or to its evening programs, with their evangelical bias and their emphasis on "Character building." With extreme understatement, John R. Commons noted in the survey that the YWCA "has yet to reach the rank and file of girl wage-earners, especially factory employees." Like the Carnegie Library extension, the YWCA put the best face on its failure and anticipated a more fruitful field for service in "the army of clerks [and] stenographers . . . who daily traverse the thoroughfares" downtown.[42]

It is clear that what working people most wanted from the middle class were allies against Big Steel, not teachers or therapists. It is also clear that, to the working class, "Progressive Recreation" meant supervision, constraint, and blandness. In their pursuit of excitement they gave it only passing attention, turning instead to a new set of free and easy mass entertainments which transfigured or displaced those rooted in the plebeian city.

The 1880s and 1890s witnessed the remaking of working-class culture in Pittsburgh. Important centers of plebeian recreation and sociability declined or disappeared in those years. But in each case they were replaced by new commercial amusements, not by hygienic substitutes fashioned by reformers.

Local theaters had been central to the plebeian culture of the Iron City.[43] They catered to a working-class audience and specialized in comedies and melodramas based on local themes and events. For example, within a year of the railroad riots of 1877, a play based on the events was written by a local author and produced at the Fifth Avenue Lyceum. Wholly sympathetic to the workers, the show employed "veteran rioters" as extras and was a great popular success. But it was also one of the last, for by the 1880s two major developments spelled doom for the plebeian theater.

First, newly class-conscious bourgeois patrons began demanding "New York theatre" at the same time as immigrants unfamiliar with stage conventions began looking for entertainment. Managers of the old houses tried to straddle the social cleavage pulling their audience apart, but they failed to match the new Nixon and Alvin theaters in grandeur or in ability to attract the best syndicated acts. They also failed to attract the immigrant customers of the "ten-cent houses" which, for the price of a drink, offered a comedy act or a little song and dance.[44]

Well before the flood of immigration in the late 1880s, moreover, nationwide changes in the theatrical business had begun to affect local houses. In 1879, the last stock company in Pittsburgh disbanded. In a few years, John Ellsler, who had referred to the company as his "acting school," left the city. Genteel critics who had bitterly lambasted his effort to provide mixed programs for mixed audiences much preferred the impressive touring shows of the New York and Philadelphia syndicates. The new system turned local managers into booking agents for legitimate, vaudeville, and burlesque syndicates. Those who could not afford syndicated shows relied on liquor and on free-lance acts of a decidedly inferior stripe.[45]

Though vaudeville tried to repackage the variety show into a more respectable product for the white-collar lower middle class, burlesque appealed to less respectable audiences.[46] Anti-elitist and contemptuous of snobs and do-gooders, burlesque made up for the loss of local reference and topical interest with a libertine demeanor and a frenetic pace. Still, in the first decade of the twentieth century, burlesque too began losing its audience—now to nickelodeons and movies. Produced and distributed by small-time operators, many of them Jewish immigrants, the new medium was undemanding and militantly escapist. John P. Harris, whose "Museum" had been the most successful ten-cent house in Pittsburgh, quickly sensed the trend and built "the first all-motion picture theater" in America. In 1905, the *Post* began a series explaining to an intensely interested public the process of filmmaking. And in 1915 the *National Labor Tribune* celebrated Charlie Chaplin as a "national hero, whose funny hat, walk, cane, and mustache are now better known than the prayer book."[47]

Regarding the nickelodeon in Homestead, Margaret Byington exclaimed: "The part these shows play in the life of the community is really surprising." That children were "always begging for five cents to go to the nickelodeon" she found less noteworthy than that men on their way from work, women out shopping, and, on Saturday nights, whole families regularly sought "a glimpse of the other side of life." Similarly, Elizabeth Butler noted the working girls lined up outside downtown picture shows on Saturday evening, "hot and tired and irritable, but willing to wait" and "determined to be amused."[48] Out of such determination was created the audience for Chaplin's *The Tramp*, *The Immigrant*, etc. With their fugitive assertions of freedom and their images of unconquerable dignity amid the wreckage of urban industrial society, such films demonstrated that the new medium could offer more than mere escape. On the other hand, almost any kind of one-reeler could draw an audience from a population so desperately in need of consolation and escape.

Though they could not rival the popularity of the movies, Pittsburgh's three amusement parks, all of which were built in the first decade of the twentieth century, drew large working-class crowds. To a certain extent, they replaced the old Exposition, which had been transformed by the Chamber of Commerce from a plebeian fair into a slick advertisement for the city's industrial concerns. The larger of the two east-end parks, Dream City, opened on Memorial Day, 1906, to a crowd of 37,000. Operated by a national amusement corporation, it offered "pavilions, theatres, 'shoot the chutes,' . . . pony tracks, miniature railroad, and similar attractions." It also featured dance halls and skating rinks, two varieties of entertainment that were especially popular with young people because they permitted physical contact between the sexes. The amusement parks also offered hundreds of acres of wooded grounds and picnic sites, thus competing successfully with the public parks for the holiday crowds (including union workers celebrating Labor Day.)[49] Amusement parks appealed to that wide cross section of the urban citizenry in search of excitement that was relatively inexpensive, always exciting, and unreformed.

Comparable changes were occurring in the realm of sport. The last boat race on the Allegheny River took place in 1887, marking the passing of the plebeian boat clubs.[50] Dominated by skilled workers and closely associated with factories and neighborhoods, these clubs had offered celebrity and sociability to participants as well as spectacle to the citizenry at large. Their disappearance was a result both of the growing demand for riverfront property and of the declining fortunes of skilled workers. Furthermore, sporting audiences had begun to change. As the college-educated middle class turned to amateur sports, especially football and British-style sculls and crews, the working class was won over in ever-greater numbers to another traditional sport that had undergone transformation.

Boxing emerged as a mass spectacle at the turn of the century. It was still illegal, and police occasionally raided local slug-fests run by small operators. But more highly skilled professionals increasingly drew bigger crowds and purses. Public attention turned to nationally reported contests between symbols of ethnic identity such as John L. Sullivan, Harry Greb, and Jack Johnson. Moreover, newspapers and athletic clubs became the sport's leading sponsors, and their influence made boxing respectable in spite of persistent condemnation from church and reform groups. Indeed, the consolidation of athletic club sponsorship of boxing represents the first example of elite patrons successfully dominating lower-class sport in Pittsburgh.[51]

In the twentieth century, the typical prize fight featured immigrant-stock fighters in the ring and a combination of immigrant workers and "prominent businessmen" in the seats. Though club oversight and Queensbury rules made the sport more respectable, the significance of the new arrangement had little to do with what went on in the ring. More important was the fact that each fight became, in a sense, an enactment of a new set of social relations. Workingmen might still enjoy their leisure, but it was now controlled by patrons who supplied a professionalized, nationally distributed product for mass consumption.

No spectator sport won a following as large or as devout as that of baseball. The game, however, was markedly different from that brought home by Civil War veterans. After shedding the gamblers and sharpers who had made notorious the old "Beer and Whiskey League," the National League gained respectability and a broader financial base in the 1890s. It professionalized, tightened its organization, codified its rules, and raised its ticket prices. It also weathered the defection of many of its stars to the Baseball Brotherhood and turned back a loosely organized campaign to lower ticket prices (both of which won the support of Pittsburgh's Knights of Labor).

But the game never became too respectable. Instead, it quickened its pace and began successfully to exploit its natural market, the urban working class. Pittsburgh's team president, William C. Temple, exemplified the new breed of market-oriented baseball man. Originally an iron worker with a zest for sports, Temple became an enthusiastic inventor of baseball promotions, the most enduring of which was the National League All-Star game. Most important, he and his successors hired first-rate managers and players whose success on the field brought success at the box office.[52]

Thus, far more than did boxing, baseball gained respectability as a result of popular success and not vice versa. Important people took respectful note of it because they wanted customers or votes, and the change in attitude was striking. In 1887 Judge J. W. F. White (of Law and Order fame) administered to the defendant in a larceny case a severe lecture about the dangers of baseball: "You should never go to a ball game. A majority of the persons connected with baseball bet on the result of the games, and all betting is gambling. Baseball is one of the evils of the day."

Such a lecture would have been inconceivable in 1910, when the stolid William H. Taft became the first president to throw out the pitch that opened the baseball season. In that same year, John K. Tener sat in the governor's chair in Harrisburg and prepared to accept the presidency of the National League. Earlier in his career, before rising from bank clerk to bank officer, Tener had been a professional baseball player. Indeed, in 1887, only a few days after Judge White's admonition and only a few miles from the courthouse, Tener had pitched an exhibition game in Pittsburgh.[53]

Thus, after Barney Dreyfuss's Pirates won their first World Series in 1909, the city's finest toasted the manager at a fancy reception in the Fort Pitt Hotel. After the party, Mayor William A. Magee, accompanied by National Guard units and political clubs, led a parade of thousands to Forbes Field, the new arena in Oakland. There Congressman J. F. Burke introduced each player to the crowd. And there is in fact an ironic sense in which the players needed introduction. Pirate heroes (with the exception of the great Honus Wagner who came from nearby Mansfield) were nationally recruited professionals, not locals. Though amateur teams continued to flourish in Pittsburgh, they did so under the new dispensation in which the line between amateur and professional was sharply drawn. Thus, while neighborhood and factory teams continued to offer exercise and sociability, little remained of their audience or their public function. The heroes of the diamond now played in Forbes Field.[54]

By the onset of World War I, the outlines of a new popular culture had taken shape in Pittsburgh as elsewhere in America. Some features of that new pattern emerge clearly, e.g., the triumph of commerce and professionalism, the rise of elite patronage, and the integration of local audiences into national ones. The persistence of working-class resistance to leisure reform hardly requires restatement. What should be emphasized, however, is the extent to which class and cultural conflict, though they interacted, often proceeded along different lines. In particular, the contest between neo-puritan pietists and the champions of mass culture was neither superficial nor directly traceable to class conflict. It represented a fundamental dispute over how to live in a society that was at once capitalistic and democratic, increasingly organized, and ethnically diverse. Thus, in Pittsburgh, the immigrants' strongest allies against nativism and prohibition were, on the one hand, high-church people, elite cosmopolitans, and sportsmen and, on the other, machine politicians who preferred neither to make enemies nor to jeopardize the profits associated with licensing and regulation.

Moreover, the intensity with which the working class embraced and defended its leisure could not be ignored. Perhaps subordination at work and indignation over cultural censorship contributed repressed energy to the cause of leisure. It is clear, in any case, that, until the New Deal, organized labor in Pennsylvania fought as long and as hard against Prohibition and for Sunday baseball as it did for almost any other campaign.[55] Politicians such as state senator John P. Harris, the burlesque and movie king, and machine reformers such as William Magee and the Bigelow brothers lost no time in responding to the popular demand for leisure or in associating themselves with popular tastes. Thus, even as Prohibition was about to triumph in America, an "urban liberal" alternative was emerging in direct opposition to it.[56] Whatever its deficiencies, that alternative, with its tolerance of new styles and its acceptance of ethnic diversity, represented a positive advance for a working class subjected to recrudescent Anglo-Saxon pietism as well as to new, more "scientific" reform efforts.

And yet, however valuable were such allies and such enlightened views, working people expressed their preferences most clearly in those small moments of cultural assertion which seldom won the recognition of observers. A striking example of such a moment of recognition occurred when Leroy Scott, an investigator for the Pittsburgh Survey, discovered "Little Jim Park," a tiny plot of U.S. Steel property on Pittsburgh's south side. Opened with children's choir, skits, and other flourishes on Decoration Day, 1909, Little Jim was built by neighborhood men—"when any of us was laid off at the mill"—from remnants of the church that had last occupied the site. The park sported brick flower beds, benches, iron gate, arch, canopy, and flagpole topped by the American flag. When asked, "Who gave the park?" one man answered, "We took it."[57]

Almost lost within the bulk of the survey, Scott's brief description casts a withering light on the professional uplift rhetoric informing the reports which surround it. At once heroic and pathetic, the building of Little Jim may be taken as emblematic of the wider struggle of the working class for cultural space. In progressive Pittsburgh, working people had to settle for available space, to choose within narrow limits. Their stubborn cultural victories were distinctly partial—snatched, as it were, from defeat at the workplace and within the industrial city.

Nevertheless, perhaps because it was so partial and so infrequent, victory was precious. The immigrants and their children developed an intense loyalty to baseball, movies, and other commercial amusements precisely because, like Little Jim Park, they offered freedom from regimentation and reform. And, though sold frankly as commodities for general consumption, those commercial amusements could be mined for and invested with greater meaning. The terse aggressiveness of a Honus Wagner and the subversive autonomy of a Charlie Chaplin meant something special to their working-class audiences, though interpreting that meaning is difficult. Offering oblique challenges to the existing order, cultivating a realm of spontaneity and drama within a framework of subordination and tedium, suggesting that that framework was indeed temporary, commercial amusements won mass audiences before they won the compliment of elite criticism. That the latter has so regularly followed upon the former may explain the persistence of working-class loyalty to the changing forms of mass culture in the twentieth century.

## NOTES

This essay is based on my Ph.D. dissertation, "Work, Leisure, and Reform in Pittsburgh: The Transformation of an Urban Culture, 1860-1920" (University of Michigan, 1980), a revised version of which is forthcoming from the State University of New York Press. The reader is directed there for fuller treatment and annotation of the subjects discussed here. I would like to thank Michael Frisch and Daniel Walkowitz for serving not simply as compilers but as editors. In my case, at least, they are responsible for whatever clarity this essay manages to rescue from the slough of academic monography. For its failures, however, I remain responsible.

1. Peter Burke, *Popular Culture in Early Modern Europe* (New York, 1978), p. 244.

2. This expression is used by Gareth Stedman Jones in "Class Expression versus Social Control? A Critique of Recent Trends in the Social History of 'Leisure,'" *History Workshop*, 4 (Autumn 1977), 163.

3. Stuart Ewen, *Captains of Consciousness: Advertising and the Social Roots of the Consumer Culture* (New York, 1976). Russel Nye, *The Unembarrassed Muse* (New York, 1970), offers the healthy-minded view of popular culture as the people's choice, as does Herbert J. Gans in a more abstract way in *Popular Culture and High Culture* (New York, 1975). On the evolution of urban cultures in the nineteenth and twentieth centuries, see Neil Harris, "Four Stages of Cultural Growth: The American City," *Indiana Historical Society Lectures, 1971-1972: History and the Role of the City in American Life* (Indianapolis, 1972). An excellent synthesis is Asa Briggs, *Mass Entertainments: The Origins of a Modern Industry* (Adelaide, 1960).

4. A key assumption of this study is that the pursuit of fun, excitement, escape, and other kinds of dramatic release from ordinary reality is normal and not evidence of a pathology in need of diagnosis. Therefore, I will not ask why the working people of Pittsburgh sought entertainment, though I will ask why they chose specific entertainments. What follows is therefore a chronicle of their choices and especially an investigation of the context in which they chose, not an essay on the origins of "false consciousness." I will not argue that mass culture is the opiate of the people. I will argue that those changes in work and social relations which undermined an older plebeian culture also generated vast new audiences for mass culture in the twentieth century; that in shaping those audiences the merchants of leisure had far more power than the reformers of leisure; and that the success of the former rested in part in their responsiveness to suppressed desires for freedom among the urban working class. In my efforts to develop a way of thinking about popular culture that is neither excessively debunking nor celebratory, I have found most useful the dramaturgical approach employed by Joseph R. Gusfield in "The Sociological Reality of America: An Essay on Mass Culture," in Herbert J. Gans et al., eds., *On the Making of Americans: Essays in Honor of David Riesman* (Philadelphia, 1979), pp. 41-62.

5. See Couvares, "Work, Leisure, and Reform," chs. 1 and 2.

6. Ibid., ch. 4. On the steel industry, David Brody's *Steelworkers in America: The Nonunion Era* (Cambridge, Mass., 1960) is invaluable.

7. Couvares, "Work, Leisure, and Reform," ch. 3. On Murphy, see W. H. Daniels, ed., *Temperance Reform and Its Great Reformers* (Chicago, 1879), pp. 435-510; Earl C. Kaylor, "The Prohibition Movement in Pennsylvania, 1865-1920" (Ph.D. dissertation, Pennsylvania State University, 1963), pp. 221-55. See also the *National Labor Tribune* (hereafter *NLT*), Nov. 24, 1876, and Feb. 3, 1877.

8. The history of the Law and Order movement is well narrated in Kaylor, "Prohibition Movement," ch. 9. See also Pittsburgh Law and Order League, *Report* (Pittsburgh, 1888).

9. *Pittsburgh Post*, Nov. 7, Nov. 11, 1887; Kaylor, "Prohibition Movement," pp. 298-301; Law and Order League, *Report*, pp. 11, 18, 21-24, 27-28, 34-36, 48-49.

10. Phyllis L. Ayers, "The History of Pennsylvania Sunday Blue Laws" (M.A. thesis, University of Pittsburgh, 1952), pp. 20-22, 26-27, 30-31, 44-45; Law and Order League, *Report*, pp. 43-44; *NLT*, Jan. 4, 1890, Aug. 31 and Sept. 3, 1887.

11. *Post*, Aug. 31, Sept. 3, Sept. 8, Sept. 9, 1887; see also *Commercial Gazette*, July 6, 1892; Law and Order League, *Report*, p. 29.

12. *Post*, Aug. 31, Sept. 3, Sept. 5, Sept. 15, Oct. 21, Nov. 7, Nov. 15, 1887; *Commercial Gazette*, Aug. 8, 1887; *NLT*, Jan. 4, 1890; Kaylor, "Prohibition Movement," pp. 300-301; Law and Order League, *Report*, pp. 21-28.

13. See, in George Korson, ed., *Pennsylvania Songs and Legends* (Philadelphia, Pa., 1949), pp. 432-33, a popular song inspired by the Pittsburgh Law and Order campaign and containing the following defiant refrain:"And the new license plan, it ain't worth a damn, In Soho on Saturday night." Evasion of the blue laws and of prohibition became a western Pennsylvania specialty and a point of honor among workingmen. See *NLT*, June 13, 1891; John W. Bennett, "Iron Workers in Woods Run and Johnstown: The Union Era 1865-1895" (Ph.D. dissertation, University of Pittsburgh, 1977), p. 132; Paul U. Kellogg, ed., *Wage-Earning Pittsburgh* (New York, 1914), pp. 310ff; Kellogg, ed., *Pittsburgh District Civic Frontage* (New York, 1914), pp. 10-11; "Prohibition in Pennsylvania," *Survey*, May 14, 1921, pp. 198-99.

14. Joel A. Tarr, *Transportation Innovation and Changing Spatial Patterns: Pittsburgh, 1850-1910* (Pittsburgh, 1972), pp. 17-27; Robert J. Jucha, "Anatomy of a Streetcar Suburb: A Development History of Shadyside, 1852-1916," *Western Pennsylvania Historical Magazine* (hereafter *WPHM*), 62 (Oct. 1979), 301-20.

15. Elizabeth Moorhead, *Whirling Spindle: The Story of a Pittsburgh Family* (Pittsburgh, 1942), pp. 233, 256. On the evolution of bourgeois culture in Pittsburgh, see Couvares, "Work, Leisure, and Reform," ch. 5. See also John N. Ingham, "The American Urban Upper Class: Cosmopolitans or Locals?" *Journal of Urban History*, 2 (Nov. 1975), 70-75.

16. John Higham, "The Reorientation of American Culture in the 1890s," in his *Writing American History* (Bloomington, Ind., 1970), pp. 73-102; see also Guy Lewis, "The Muscular Christianity Movement," *Journal of Health, Physical Education and Recreation*, 37 (May 1966), 28, 42; John A. Lucas, "Prelude to the Rise of Sport: Ante-Bellum America, 1850-1860," *Quest*, Dec. 1968, pp. 50-57; John R. Betts, *America's Sporting Heritage: 1850-1950* (Reading, Mass., 1974), pp. 91-92; Richard Harmond, "Progress and Flight: An Interpretation of the American Cycle Craze of the 1890s," *Journal of Social History*, 5 (Winter 1971-72), 235-57.

17. On school spirit, see Pittsburgh Central High School, *Class Book of 1880* (Pittsburgh, 1906), pp. 8-9, 107-10. On the cult of strenuosity among college men in the late nineteenth century, see Joseph F. Kett, *Rites of Passage: Adolescence in America 1790 to the Present* (New York, 1977), esp. ch. 7. See also Thomas Jable, "The Birth of Professional Football: Pittsburgh Athletic Clubs Ring in Professionals in 1892," *WPHM*, 62 (Apr. 1979), 131-47.

18. See Couvares, "Work, Leisure, and Reform," chs. 1 and 3; and Samuel P. Hays, "The Development of Pittsburgh as a Social Order," *WPHM*, 57 (Oct. 1974), 431-48.

19. Moorhead, *Whirling Spindle*, pp. 268, 270.

20. Carnegie Library of Pittsburgh, *First Annual Report* (Pittsburgh, 1897), p. 33; *Fifth Annual Report* (Pittsburgh, 1901), p. 73-74; *Sixth Annual Report* (Pittsburgh, 1902), pp. 69-70. See also Margaret Byington, *Homestead: The*

*Households of a Mill Town* (New York, 1910), pp. 258-60, on organ recitals at the Homestead library.

21. On the development of Pittsburgh's parks, see Howard B. Stewart, ed., *Historical Data: Pittsburgh Public Parks* (Pittsburgh, 1943); Barbara Judd, "Edward Bigelow: Creator of Pittsburgh's Arcadian Parks," *WPHM*, 58 (Jan. 1975), 53-68; see also Roy Lubove, *Twentieth-Century Pittsburgh: Government, Business, and Environmental Change* (New York, 1969), pp. 51ff. On the ideology of the park movement, see Robert Lewis, "Frontier and Civilization in the Thought of Frederick Law Olmsted," *American Quarterly*, 29 (Fall 1977), 385-403; see also Roy Rosenzweig, "Middle-Class Parks and Working-Class Play: The Struggle over Recreational Space in Worcester, Massachusetts, 1870-1910," *Radical History Review*, 21 (Fall 1979), 31-48.

22. Charles M. Robinson, "Civic Improvement Possibilities of Pittsburgh," *Charities and the Commons*, Feb. 6, 1909, pp. 823-24. See also Lawrence A. Finfer, "Leisure as Social Work in the Urban Community: The Progressive Recreation Movement, 1890-1920" (Ph.D. dissertation, Michigan State University, 1974), for an enlightening discussion of this entire subject.

23. See Couvares, "Work, Leisure, and Reform," ch. 2, esp. pp. 90-92.

24. Robert Lewis, "Frontier and Civilization," p. 403. On late-nineteenth-century Fourth of July celebrations in America, see Willard Glazier, *Peculiarities of American Cities* (Philadelphia, 1886), pp. 332-47; J. E. H. Skinner, *After the Store; or Jonathan and His Neighbors in 1865-6* (London, 1866), I, 1-13; Edward H. Rogers, *Reasons for Believing that the People Will Use Leisure Wisely* (Boston, 1866), p. 4. For Pittsburgh, see especially *Christian Advocate*, June 3, 1871, July 6, 1882, June 30, 1887; *Gazette*, July 6, 1867, May 31, 1892.

25. *Christian Advocate*, June 30, 1887; *NLT*, July 1, 1876.

26. *Commercial Gazette*, July 5, 1887; *NLT*, July 5, 1887; *NLT*, July 9 and July 16, 1887; Knights of Labor, District Assembly 3, *Proceedings of Second Quarterly Meeting* (Pittsburgh, 1888), p. 24.

27. *Commercial Gazette*, July 5, 1887.

28. Ibid., July 5, 1892.

29. Ibid., July 5, 1892.

30. Ibid., Sept. 5, 1887, Sept. 1, Sept. 2, Sept. 15, 1892; *NLT*, July 23, Sept. 3, Sept. 5, Sept. 10, 1887; *Post*, Sept. 3, 1887; Shelton Stromquist, "Working Class Organization and Industrial Change in Pittsburgh, 1860-1890" (seminar paper, University of Pittsburgh, 1973), pp. 19-22.

31. Byington, *Homestead*, pp. 255ff.

32. Frances J. Olcott, *The Public Library a Social Force in Pittsburgh* (Pittsburgh, 1910). Olcott's study for the survey was also published in Kellogg, ed., *Civic Frontage*, pp. 325-36.

33. On the playground movement in Pittsburgh, see Beulah Kennard, "The Playgrounds of Pittsburgh," in Kellogg, ed., *Civic Frontage*, pp. 306-24; see also Robinson, "Civic Improvement Possibilities," pp. 816, 824; Byington, *Homestead*, pp. 120-21; Lubove, *Twentieth-Century Pittsburgh*, pp. 50ff. For the national context, see Finfer, "Leisure as Social Work," ch. 3.

34. Olcott, *Public Library*, pp. 13, 15, 18.

35. On the nature of play and its social functions, classic explorations are Johan Huizinga, *Homo Ludens: A Study of the Play Element in Culture* (Boston, 1950), and Josef Pieper, *Leisure, the Basis of Culture* (New York, 1963).

36. Olcott, *Public Library*, p. 12; John A. Fitch, *The Steel Workers* (New York, 1910), pp. 203-4; Window Glass Workers Association, LA 300, Knights of

Labor, *Report of Sixth Convention* (Pittsburgh, 1892), p. 19; the pastor of Sts. Peter and Paul Catholic Church in Pittsburgh condemned Carnegie's philanthropy in terms almost identical to those of the glassworkers: Theodore P. Sturm, "The Social Gospel in the Methodist Churches of Pittsburgh, 1865-1920" (Ph.D. dissertation, West Virginia University, 1971), p. 246.

37. *NLT*, Jan. 12, 1884, July 9, 1887, Jan. 11, Jan. 25, Feb. 15, 1890; Harold C. Livesay, *Andrew Carnegie and the Rise of Big Business* (Boston, 1975), pp. 131ff.

38. Carnegie Free Library of Allegheny, *Annual Report* (Pittsburgh, 1891); *NLT*, Jan. 11, 1890.

39. On welfare capitalism, see Daniel Nelson, *Managers and Workers: Origins of the New Factory System in the United States, 1880-1920* (Madison, Wis., 1975), ch. 6; Brody, *Steelworkers in America*, ch. 8; Fitch, *Steel Workers*, pp. 211ff. For provocative discussions of the nature of authority and control in the industrial milieu, see Richard Sennett, *Authority* (New York, 1980); David Montgomery, *Workers' Control in America: Studies in the History of Work, Technology and Labor Struggles* (New York, 1979). On Lowell, see Thomas Dublin, *Women at Work: The Transformation of Work and Community in Lowell, Massachusetts, 1826-1860* (New York, 1979), and Thomas Bender, *Toward an Urban Vision: Ideas and Institutions in Nineteenth-Century America* (Lexington, Ky., 1975).

40. Robert C. Alberts, *The Good Provider: H. J. Heinz and His 57 Varieties* (New York, 1973), esp. ch. 10; Elizabeth B. Butler, *Women and the Trades, Pittsburgh 1907-1908* (New York, 1909), pp. 314-15; Kellogg, ed., *Wage-Earning Pittsburgh*, pp. 219, 224, 229, 231, 236, 250, 255, 258-59.

41. See, for example, Pennsylvania Bureau of Industrial Statistics, *Annual Report*, 15 (Harrisburg, 1887), 7B. For a brilliant discussion of a "popular form of *laissez faire*" in a different context, see Brian Harrison, "Religion and Recreation in Nineteenth-Century England," *Past and Present*, 38 (Dec. 1967), 98-125.

42. Butler, *Women and Trades*, pp. 316-30; Kellogg, ed., *Civic Frontage*, pp. 36-37; Kellogg, ed., *Wage-Earning Pittsburgh*, pp. 453-54; Carnegie Library of Pittsburgh, *Seventh Annual Report* (Pittsburgh, 1903), p. 21; Chet Smith, *Pittsburgh and Western Pennsylvania Sports Hall of Fame* (Pittsburgh, 1969), p. 51.

43. On theater in Pittsburgh, see Couvares, "Work, Leisure, and Reform," chs. 2 and 5.

44. James A. Lowrie, "A History of the Pittsburgh Stage, 1861-1891" (Ph.D. dissertation, University of Pittsburgh, 1943), pp. 155ff; John A. Ellsler, *The Stage Memories of John A. Ellsler* (Cleveland, 1950), pp. 106-7.

45. "The Great Theatrical Syndicate," *Leslie's Monthly Magazine*, Oct. 1904, pp. 581-92, and Nov. 1904, pp. 31-42.

46. Harris, "Four Stages of Cultural Growth," pp. 40-41; Nye, *Unembarrassed Muse*, pp. 170ff.

47. *NLT*, Nov. 11, 1915; *Post*, Dec. 24, 1905; Lowrie, "Pittsburgh Stage," pp. 170-74; George T. Fleming, *History of Pittsburgh and Environs* (Pittsburgh, 1922), II, 636-37; Margaret C. Golden, "Directory of Theater Buildings in Use in Pittsburgh, Pennsylvania since Earliest Times" (M.A. thesis, Carnegie Institute of Technology, 1953), p. 4; on the early history of film, see Robert Sklar, *Movie-Made America: A Cultural History of American Movies* (New York, 1975), chs. 1 and 2.

48. Butler, *Women and Trades*, pp. 333, 324; Byington, *Homestead*, pp. 110-11. Briggs, *Mass Entertainments*, p. 18, notes that "the cinema did not so much divert an older audience from other kinds of entertainment as create an enormous new one."

49. Pittsburgh Board of Trade, *The East End* (Pittsburgh, 1907), unpaginated; Byington, *Homestead*, pp. 30-31, 110-15; Butler, *Women and Trades*, p. 333; Fitch, *Steel Workers*, p. 177.

50. On rowing in Pittsburgh, see Couvares, "Work, Leisure, and Reform," ch. 2; see also Samuel Crowther and Arthur Ruhl, *Rowing and Track Athletics* (New York, 1905), pp. 160, 199-202; Robert F. Kelley, *American Rowing* (New York, 1932), pp. 25, 267-71; Dale A. Somers, *The Rise of Sports in New Orleans 1850-1900* (Baton Rouge, 1972), pp. 140, 151-58.

51. Thomas M. Croak, "The Professionalization of Prizefighting: Pittsburgh at the Turn of the Century," *WPHM*, 62 (Oct. 1979), 333-43; see also Nye, *Unembarrassed Muse*, pp. 154ff; Betts, *Sporting Heritage*, pp. 166ff.

52. *The Commoner and Glassworker*, Nov. 6, 1887, Mar. 10 and May 5, 1888; Chet Smith, *Sports Hall of Fame*, pp. 14-24; William E. Benswanger, "Professional Baseball in Pittsburgh," *WPHM*, 30 (Mar.-June 1947), 11-13; Frederick G. Lieb, *The Pittsburgh Pirates* (New York, 1948), pp. 26-50. For a provocative answer to the question "Why was baseball our national game?" see Allen Guttmann, *From Ritual to Record: The Nature of Modern Sports* (New York, 1977), ch. 4.

53. *Commercial Gazette*, Oct. 8, Oct. 14, and Oct. 15, 1887; Lieb, *Pittsburgh Pirates*, pp. 17-18; Betts, *Sporting Heritage*, pp. 121-23.

54. *Post*, Oct. 9, Oct. 18, Oct. 19, 1909; Betts, *Sporting Heritage*, p. 119; Chet Smith, *Sports Hall of Fame*, p. 24. A cartoon in *NLT*, Oct. 21, 1915, suggested that Pittsburghers were far more interested in "World Series Scores" than in European "War Scores."

55. J. Thomas Jable, "Sport, Amusement, and Pennsylvania Blue Laws, 1682-1973" (Ph.D. dissertation, Pennsylvania State University, 1974) chs. 4-6; Ayers, "History of Pennsylvania Sunday Blue Laws," pp. 32, 47, 50ff; "Prohibition in Pennsylvania," pp. 198-99; see also *Journal of United Labor*, Sept. 12, Sept. 19, Nov. 14, 1889.

56. See John D. Buenker, *Urban Liberalism and Progressive Reform* (New York, 1937); Eugene M. Tobin, "Direct Action and Conscience: The 1913 Paterson Strike as Example of the Relationship between Labor Radicals and Liberals," *Labor History*, 20 (1979), 73-88; see also David A. Hollinger, "Ethnic Diversity, Cosmopolitanism, and the Emergence of the American Liberal Intelligentsia," *American Quarterly*, 28 (Summer 1975), 133-51.

57. Leroy Scott, "Little Jim Park," *Charities and the Commons*, Feb. 6, 1909, pp. 911-12. Along with the rest of Painter's Row, the park was demolished by the U.S. Steel Corporation even before the survey was completed. Scott's report was not published with the summary volumes.

# Trade-Union Evangelism:
# Religion and the AFL in the
# Labor Forward Movement, 1912-16

ELIZABETH AND KENNETH FONES-WOLF

Beginning in 1912 scores of city central labor unions, with AFL backing, initiated trade union "revivals" as part of a campaign known as the Labor Forward movement. In these revivals the local craft-union leadership adapted the methods of evangelism and the ideals of the Social Gospel to revitalize and blend with trade-union traditions. AFL president Samuel Gompers, seizing upon the movement's relationship to both trade-union and broader American cultural patterns, urged using zealous labor evangelists to build union membership, to organize new unions, to educate the community about trade-union principles, and to "serve a 'revival' function by arousing the members to renewed and increased activity and zeal."[1]

Labor Forward resists easy categorization as a historical movement. Not only was it quite diverse in its various manifestations in cities across the country, but even within one locality there were contradictions. It combined elements of genuine religious enthusiasm with calculated manipulation of religious forms for organized labor's ends. It had deep roots in working-class traditions and values, yet it often sought to distance itself from the industrial working class and from general critiques of the culture of industrial capitalism. Despite all its paradoxes, however, and in fact largely because of them, it offers an excellent vantage for examining the changing relationship between a traditional working-class culture and the realities of labor struggle in early-twentieth-century American society. And beyond the light that study of the movement throws on this particular historical phase, it shows as well a broader historical dilemma, one currently quite alive historiographically: how we are to understand the relation of religious forms and experiences to the development of the working class in general and to organized labor in particular.

Elie Halevy claimed that the spread of Methodist revivalism in England blunted a potential revolution in the first half of the nineteenth century. More recent studies have disputed that finding, arguing that, on the contrary, Protestant evangelicalism's growth paralleled that of trade unions, and that the labor tradition of dissent derived both form and substance from Methodism.[2] In the United States Paul Faler and Herbert Gutman have demonstrated that Protestant revivalism informed labor culture, sanctioned worker protest, and undergirded trade-union ideology in the antebellum period and the Gilded Age. A perceptive recent study by Paul Johnson, however, shows a Finney revival in 1830 to be the tool of budding Rochester capitalists trying to convert workers to docile respectability. Other works have characterized Protestantism's conservative influence in the late nineteenth century through its gospel of wealth, focusing on such popular evangelists as Dwight Moody. And, in fact, several authors have suggested that Catholic and Protestant leaders helped prevent the rise of a Socialist labor movement.[3] While these diverse researches have hardly produced any consensus about the exact role of religion, they have shown how central a place it has occupied in working-class life. Consideration of the Labor Forward movement can offer some historical focus and precision, while also providing a new perspective on labor history in the years before World War I, a crucial period whose religious dimension has generally been overlooked and underappreciated.

Labor Forward illustrates how religion could enclose labor within the norms of the larger society while at the same time helping it to challenge those aspects of industrial society that contradicted its professed values. We will argue here that to understand exactly what this meant in the early twentieth century, one must understand how deeply the evangelical dimension of the Labor Forward movement was rooted in the particular culture and ideology of craft unionism, and why it is significant that the movement emerged at just the time when craft unionism was under enormous pressure from both above and below.

This essay begins by providing a chronological and demographic overview of the campaign, describing its origins and assessing its attraction for both AFL and local union leaders. Then, we will explore the social and cultural milieu of labor's camp meetings, inquiring particularly into their link to craft-union traditions and the sources of Labor Forward's broader appeal to other groups. This will lead to a closer examination of the content of evangelism's complex message, seen as an amalgam of trade-union ideology and elements of American religious culture. At a time of rapid change, organized labor reacted in many ways to the varied challenges of monopoly capitalism, radicalism, immigration, and urbanization. Labor Forward enables us to

see how religion influenced and informed the responses of craft unionism to these new dilemmas. The paper will conclude by examining
local influences upon the success or failure of Labor Forward by
looking at several cities in greater detail. This vantage will give a sense
of the various ways in which the movement and the forces surrounding
it could interact. Even more, for all the vitality of this evangelical
movement, it suggests something of the contradictions facing craft
unionism in the early twentieth century.

I

The Labor Forward movement had its roots in the Social-Gospel-
inspired Men and Religion Movement of 1911-12. This campaign, in
turn, followed in the tradition of the evangelical reform movements of
the 1830s. By the 1860s and 1870s, with the surge of industrial capitalism, the acquisitive gospel of wealth overshadowed earlier Christian
reform impulses. Protestant denominations joined in defending rapid
economic growth and reinforcing through their Calvinist doctrines the
idea that poverty and failure was equivalent to sin. But many Chris-
tians could not remain indifferent to the great extremes of poverty and
wealth that accompanied this economic growth and the consequent
social unrest of the late nineteenth century. By the 1880s the older
social concerns had revived in the form of what came to be called the
Social Gospel. Christian reform reached its peak in the first decade of
the twentienth century. Leaders like Washington Gladden, Walter
Rauschenbusch, and John Ryan preached for social and economic
justice in both Protestant and Catholic churches.[4]

The "Labor Question" had been a central concern of the Social
Gospel from its earliest days, though rarely in systematic or sustained
programmatic form. Accordingly, at the turn of the century a machin-
ist-turned-minister named Charles Stelzle sought to institutionalize the
connection between the church and organized labor and thereby solid-
ify trade-union support behind the clergy's ideas on social justice. In
1903 he formed and headed a Workingmen's Department within the
Presbyterian church and a year later arranged for an exchange of delegates between the Ministerial Association and the Central Labor Council of Minneapolis. By 1910 Stelzle had become a frequent delegate to
AFL conventions, a contributor to trade-union journals, and had
helped begin the observance of Labor Sunday. His concern, however,
was more with religion than with the worker. In 1908 Stelzle founded
the ecumenical Federal Council of Churches which three years later
began the Men and Religion Forward movement, a broadly targeted
revival campaign that, in the estimate of Walter Rauschenbusch,

perhaps did more than "any single agency to lodge the social gospel in the common mind of the church."[5]

The Men and Religion drive blended mass-appeal evangelism and Progressive reform spirit. Led during its 1911-12 lifespan by such diverse social crusaders as Stelzle, Booker T. Washington, and Jane Addams, the movement reached more than 1500 communities. It developed methods emphasizing maximum community and media attention through eight-day campaigns featuring nationally prominent teams of organizers. Evangelists moved through a given city's neighborhoods organizing parades and mass meetings to attract public attention and used smaller meetings and even individual canvassing to draw in special interest groups and individuals. The campaigns integrated mass publicity with church, neighborhood, and interest-group support to encourage personal involvement.[6]

This personal involvement aimed at a wide variety of economic, social, and moral issues. These issues reflected a concern for the poor, but also an underlying assumption that the answers rested in an elite-controlled campaign of moral suasion and appeals to public opinion. In Chicago, Men and Religion leaders sent a delegation to study municipal lodging houses and the Cedar Rapids campaign organized a Social Service Council to relieve suffering and poverty. In other cities the campaign turned to problems of morals, vice, and social purity. The Philadelphia program resulted in a "civic righteousness" movement; and Hartford, Connecticut, achieved its most noted success when the Federation of Churches, the Equal Suffrage League, and the Central Labor Union joined together to shut down every brothel in the city.[7]

Stelzle, more than other Men and Religion leaders, realized that the campaign would have to do more for workers if it hoped to obtain assistance from organized labor. He recalled that at Men and Religion meetings held for workingmen "considerable enthusiasm was aroused by the presentation of the ethical and moral values of trade unionism and the relation of the church to these questions, a plea being made for 'a square deal' for the workers as well as for the church." But the Men and Religion square deal stopped with collective bargaining, fair wages and hours, and legislation for women and children achieved through appeals to fair play. No major change in the system of production was suggested, and such traditional union tactics as strikes and boycotts were discouraged.[8]

The possibility of a stronger tie to labor was occurring to trade unionists as well. Labor leaders like United Mine Workers' president John Mitchell and AFL organizer Peter Brady viewed the reform emphasis of Men and Religion, as well as the broad tactical possibilities for using revivalism to reach the working class and the middle class, as a way of revitalizing organized labor. Mitchell and Brady had participated in the Social-Gospel revivals, and they encouraged labor to employ this method to educate both consumers and workers about the union label or the deleterious effects of prison and child labor. Brady, in fact, suggested that New York City unions sponsor a campaign utilizing movies and church halls to present labor's gospel.[9] That Brady and Mitchell, both Catholics, responded so quickly to a Protestant-based movement, however, suggests that there was an element of manipulation in their motives. Both leaders preferred the middle-class progressivism of the Men and Religion movement to more radical alternatives.

Men and Religion's appeal for social harmony fit a particular need for organized labor in 1912. At that time, trade unions were intent upon improving their public image and offering a vibrant alternative to the challenge of radicalism within the labor movement. AFL membership, which had risen dramatically until 1904, had leveled off at just under two million. A militant open-shop campaign led by the National Association of Manufacturers had branded labor unions as un-American institutions, and the indictment of the McNamara brothers for dynamiting the *Los Angeles Times* building had severely tarnished the AFL's reputation. In many factories, new technology and organization of production deskilled jobs and broke craft-union control over the work process. Within the labor movement the Industrial Workers of the World's flamboyant success in organizing the immigrants and the unskilled, groups that craft unions had proved unwilling to reach, threatened AFL dominance. In addition, the Socialist party, pressing for industrial unionism, ousted the heads of the Machinists' and Tailors' unions and posed strong opposition in several others. Many craft unionists believed that the appeal of the Socialists and the IWW among both immigrant and native workers originated in the emotional methods and idealistic goals these groups offered. To counter, many began to urge unionists to reach into their own traditions for principles that workers might use in their struggle for a voice in running industry.[10]

A Minneapolis labor editor, Tom Hamlin, was the first to propose a Labor Forward movement based on evangelism and craft-union culture. Impressed with the appeal of the city's Men and Religion drive, in October 1911 Hamlin suggested that the local Trades and Labor Assembly put a revival spirit to work in organized labor's interest. The assembly appointed a committee of fifteen which eventually rose to over two hundred, representing every Minneapolis labor union, and set aside a two-week period beginning April 21, 1912, for the drive. The committee invited all international unions to send organizers to Minneapolis for the campaign, but intended it to be educational rather than organizational or political. Indeed, a basic theme of this revival was that labor was not a menace to society but an "instrument for social uplift." The Minneapolis *Labor Review* claimed the campaign would be the "greatest propaganda movement" ever promoted by organized labor. It would cement ties with churches and reach those outside the ranks of unions to explain the ideals of brotherhood and communal benefits of unions, and involve the general public in the movement for better working conditions, shorter hours, higher wages, and the union label.[11]

The Minneapolis Federation of Men's Church Clubs, a group of business and professional leaders, agreed to serve as an intermediary with clergymen for the Trades and Labor Assembly, believing that such cooperation reflected the spirit of brotherhood between the church and workers. The federation urged Minneapolis ministers to preach sermons dealing with industrial welfare on the opening day of the campaign or to open their pulpits to labor spokesmen. It also pressed ministers to invite trade unionists to prayer and church club meetings and to let workers use their auditoriums for evening gatherings. By March 1912 more than twenty-five ministers, representing Baptist, Methodist, Congregational, Presbyterian, and Unitarian churches, had announced that organized labor would be welcome in their meeting-houses during the labor revival.[12]

Like the Men and Religion campaigns, the Minneapolis Labor Forward movement began on a Sunday. On opening day, April 21, labor spokesmen occupied twenty-two pulpits. Forty international unions sent representatives to preach the "true doctrine of trades unionism," and Labor Forward leaders divided the city into districts so that neighborhood meetings could be held simultaneously. Some were mass meetings aimed at the general public, while others targeted single trades. Five to ten meetings were held daily in different parts of the city, in public halls, churches, the YMCA building, the courthouse, schools, and trade-union headquarters.[13]

Minneapolis Labor Forward speakers preached a complex message aimed at different audiences. Drawing on the city's strong Social-Gospel traditions, many spoke to middle-class concerns, stressing the moral value of trade unionism, the efficiency and quality of union labor, the need for female- and child-labor reforms, and the desirability of the AFL over the IWW or the Socialists. Union evangelists also attempted to instill a renewed commitment to the principles of craft unionism among the working class. They exhorted workers to push for higher wages through collective bargaining, to buy union-made products, and to exhibit renewed vigor for the union cause by attending meetings and recruiting new members.[14]

In this first campaign in Minneapolis, Labor Forward proved an effective mechanism for promoting trade unionism. Local labor leaders declared themselves "highly gratified with the way the people of the city . . . responded to the invitation to listen to organized labor's explanation of its reason for existence." The Westminister Presbyterian Men's Club, made up of business and professional men, endorsed unions, arbitration, high wages, short hours, and good working conditions.[15] Furthermore, the heightened consciousness Labor Forward awakened among workers led directly to the organization of six new unions in Minneapolis. AFL organizer John Chubbuck also reported that many craft unions added significantly to their membership rolls. Cigarmakers' organizer W. S. Best concluded that Labor Forward equaled the power of religious revivalism, noting its successful appeal to both "repentants and sinners."[16]

Over the next six months trade unionists who participated in the Minneapolis revival laid the groundwork for the spread of the campaign. Almost immediately after the initial movement, Duluth and St. Paul labor leaders invited the organizers to remain in the state and conduct revivals in their cities.[17] As the labor evangelists moved to other cities in the region they carried the form and content of Labor Forward. In their letters to the international union journals, they praised the revitalizing power that an enthusiastic return to traditional craft-union mechanisms exerted when blended with evangelical rhetoric and a camp-meeting atmosphere. Such reports encouraged central labor unions in Topeka, Kansas; Logansport, Indiana; and Grand Rapids, Michigan, to start Labor Forward movements. Logansport trade unionists held "[o]pen meetings, social and educational campaigns for the purpose of spreading the gospel of trade unionism." Carpenters' leader William Hutcheson urged holding a revival "at frequent intervals" because of its success in boosting Grand Rapids craft organizations.[18] Testimonies of organizing successes and support from the local middle class also attracted the attention of labor leaders. Finally the trade union evangelists sought to ensure the continuation of Labor Forward by soliciting AFL support.

Shortly after the campaigns in Minnesota, state labor federation president E. G. Hall reported to Samuel Gompers at length on his state's efforts. Other Labor Forward evangelists wrote to AFL officials for organizing help. The Federation Executive Council discussed the revivals at its May and August meetings and developed an extensive plan for a Labor Forward campaign.[19] Gompers at once saw its instrumental possibilities, feeling that revivalism could be used as an effective organizing technique, particularly at a time when the AFL needed a new surge of energy. Sensitive to the open-shop movement, IWW victories among textile workers, and the capture of several AFL unions by Socialists, Gompers could see that workers wanted vibrant, active organizations with which to fight manufacturers. In Labor Forward, the AFL president saw a way to use the ethical principles associated with religion to reassert the federation's leadership, reinforcing its ideals and hopes for a better life within the capitalist wage system.

To be sure, Gompers was not at all religious. He emphasized the need to link trade unionism to broader religious and moral ideals if the AFL was to compete with Wobblies and Socialists for the unorganized, but his notion of the labor struggle focused squarely on the skilled craft fight for and the legitimizing of the worker's Christian dignity. Thus, Gompers's plan, published in the October 1912 *American Federationist*, urged local leaders to utilize the social spirit aroused by a common meeting of all workers to further the progress of trade unionism. Religion for him was a means to a labor end. Given how well Labor Forward techniques meshed with the heritage and culture of craft unionists, Gompers felt the campaign could "give a tremendous impetus to the organization . . . of workers. The sweep and the scope of a work movement would carry an incalculable chain of influences and results—both psychic and material."[20]

Gompers detailed specific proposals for the Labor Forward campaign that included trade-union control and cooperation with middle-class organizations. He urged international unions and the AFL to supply a team of organizers for each region and to recruit speakers from sympathetic organizations, such as the National Child Labor Committee. The plan also advised the formation of state teams, consisting of labor officials, factory inspectors, education experts, and doctors who could discuss social hygiene, disease prevention, and the effect of work on child development. City central labor unions, however, would assume the bulk of the responsibility. The AFL president advised local organizing committees to build up anticipation through intense publicity, observing that a "certain mass psychological value is obtained by community of interest and conversation—centering attention and thought on one common interest—a mass psychology little understood but of great power."[21]

For all Gompers's cooperation with middle-class community groups, however, and for all his emphasis on widely shared community ideals, his central purposes remained steadfastly and narrowly trade unionist:

the need for organizing was the major stimulus for Labor Forward, and concrete organization was its major goal. Concerned about the challenge of rising militance in the labor movement, Gompers hoped that labor revivalism would redirect workers back toward conservative trade-union principles. Borrowing from evangelist Billy Sunday's technique of handing out decision cards which the converted signed at revival meetings, he urged that blank cards be circulated among the audience, requesting the unorganized to fill in their names, trades, and addresses. Similarly he urged labor organizers to request nonunion men and women to remain after the Forward meetings, adapting the practice of Dwight Moody's inquiry rooms which guided "sinners" to conversion. Such mass-appeal techniques with ideals born of common beliefs, Gompers felt, could present an AFL alternative to IWW and Socialist organizing.[22]

Trade unionists responded enthusiastically to Gompers's editorial. S. S. Geitel of the Printers urged the AFL head to "try to get through a resolution" at the upcoming Rochester AFL convention. "Make it strong as you can" so that "the various trades, affiliated with the A.F. of L. will send organizers through the country districts." He agreed that the revival technique was a "mine of wealth." George Perkins, president of the Cigarmakers, also felt that Labor Forward was of great importance, but cautioned that if the movement was to succeed it needed systematic planning. Perkins suggested that a "corps of organizers . . . sweep across the country" and pressed Gompers to make definite plans in Rochester. At the convention, even the predominantly Catholic trade-union leaders lent their support to the Protestant-inspired movement.[23]

Official AFL endorsement of Labor Forward provided a strong impetus to the movement's expansion. During the next three years Labor Forward revivalism reached thousands of workers throughout the country. Syracuse, Pittsburgh, Erie, and twenty other cities had campaigns in 1913, the major push being made in eastern Pennsylvania, including Philadelphia's two-year Labor Forward campaign. Among other cities affected in 1913 were Los Angeles; Dallas; Wheeling; St. Joseph, Missouri; and Herrin, Illinois. In 1914 the movement still centered primarily in the mid-Atlantic states and the Midwest: Detroit; Canton, Massillon, and Bellaire, Ohio; and Mount Vernon, Illinois, having campaigns. But the movement rapidly spread to include Seattle and Spokane in the Northwest; Port Arthur, Texas, in the Southwest; and Charleston and Birmingham in the South. By 1915 Labor Forward, truly national in scope, encompassed twenty-nine cities in all regions. Among others holding campaigns were: Galveston, Texas; Tacoma, Washington; Dubuque, Iowa; Omaha, Nebraska; Meriden, Connecticut;

Roanoke, Virginia; New Orleans, Louisiana; and the Arkansas Federation of Labor. Trade-union revivalism peaked in 1916 with thirty city campaigns and four statewide drives. In all, trade unionists in some 150 cities conducted drives.[24]

Clearly, activity on this scale cannot be attributed solely to Gompers's leadership and his interest in undercutting radicalism. In fact, in most cities the impetus for Labor Forward came not from the national level down, but from local leaders and regional organizers intimately familiar with the power and depth of the camp meetings. This was true not only of Labor Forward but of other organizers as well, such as the southwestern Socialists, who relied on these traditional forms for building grassroots support.[25] All this suggests that it will not do to see Labor Forward as simply a tactical improvisation. Rather, if we are to understand its sudden growth and its enormous appeal, we must understand it on its own terms. This requires us to understand the deeper harmony between the evangelical techniques of Labor Forward revivalism and the values of traditional craft-union culture.

## II

In the face of the industrial-capitalist transformation of the early twentieth century, craft unionists found in the labor revival a particularly effective method of reinforcing their own social and cultural traditions. Such customary activities as parades and mass meetings demonstrated trade-union strength. Other activities like union-sponsored dances, smokers, and picnics heightened feelings of interdependence and class solidarity. During Labor Forward, craft unionists combined these traditional mechanisms with the intensity of a camp-meeting atmosphere familiar to them in their own religious experience, utilizing evangelical tactics such as door-to-door canvassing and the conversion experience. Each of these activities was part of a "vast accumulation of past devices" which craft unionists adapted to their particular organizing goals.[26]

Labor evangelists found that several tactics used by religious revivalists could also spread the message of trade unionism to all types of workers. Perhaps the most intensive method adapted from the Christian missionaries was the door-to-door canvass. During the Columbus, Ohio, campaign, local machinists appointed a committee of sixty "to bring home the bacon" by visiting every nonunion machinist in the city. Los Angeles and Kansas City trade unionists were even more ambitious. They listed the names of every working man and woman in the city directory according to occupation and then divided the city into wards. Each ward had a captain with lieutenants for each precinct.

The unionists eventually formed a canvassing force of one thousand "to get in touch with those outside the fold and teach them what the movement for common uplift means."[27]

Similarly, unionists attempted to relate the mass psychology of the conversion experience learned from evangelism to a labor culture. International Typographical Union president James M. Lynch noted that "old-time religious revivals" exerted a continuing cultural impact. A recent revival, he stated, "brought to the 'mourners' bench some 10,000 converts." Trade-union evangelists also hoped to change the hearts of individuals through a shared emotional experience. In Syracuse the sermons and hymn-singing of Carpenters' organizer Charles Kimball added "many converts" to the "trade union fold."[28] A Tacoma, Washington, union preacher recognized that "man is made in such a way that he requires frequent stimulation in order that he fulfill his duty to himself and his fellow man. Being a social animal he is subject to the influence of his fellows . . . and moved to action by the enthusiasm of the orator." Just as the churches used this for conversion, the Tacoma evangelist hoped that the Labor Forward "missionary movement" could obtain the same type of commitment for unionism.[29]

Music, which provided an atmosphere of excitement, gaiety, and entertainment during religious revivals, served a similar purpose for Labor Forward. The Eighth Ward Orchestra and Carter Brothers' banjoists played for the Lancaster, Pennsylvania, union revival. Atlanta planned its revival so as to intersperse music provided by the Musicians' Union with speeches on trade unionism. In 1915 the AFL Executive Council encouraged the continued use of music, asserting that labor could not afford to abandon emotion, and that "one of the most common and primitive means of expression of sentiment is through music."[30]

Other Labor Forward mechanisms relied more heavily on craft-union traditions. In particular, Minneapolis unionists used the intensity of the movement and the strength of craft organizations to plan many revival activities. They sponsored a craft ball which drew hundreds to "the most unique social event" in the history of organized labor in Minneapolis. People came dressed in the working uniform of their craft, an obvious exhibition of labor solidarity and craft pride. Minneapolis unionists also raised funds through such activities as selling buttons and providing an athletic entertainment featuring wrestling matches, weightlifters, and dancers.[31] The craft-union orientation of the Minneapolis campaign was perhaps most evident in the smaller social events such as "woodcraft night," where speakers urged cabinetmakers, carpenters, millwrights, and parquet-floor layers to unite for better wages, hours, and mutual assistance.[32]

In other cities, Labor Forward leaders returned to such customary craft-union activities as parades, picnics, and smokers to arouse interest in the campaign. Jamestown, New York, unionists, for example, kicked off their campaign with a march that included the Thirteenth Separate Company Band, a coronet band, and a drum corps, besides the various delegations of the crafts. A picnic brought together craft unionists from Pittsfield, Springfield, and Westfield, Massachusetts, to hear the labor gospel.[33] Similarly smokers, like the one held by Syracuse Carpenters' Local No. 1211, proved an effective organizing technique. The open smoker reminded one observer "of a camp meeting; there was preaching, also singing and music; there was an orchestra of three pieces," and Hugh Robinson, a tailor, concluded with a "typical Irish stump speech which caused much merriment."[34]

These traditional and revival activities stemmed from a craft-union culture that encouraged both individual commitment and group solidarity. Their seeming distance from the struggle of organized labor belies their value in providing a continuity to craft-union experience and consciousness. For example, Spokane label trades workers constructed a permanent building to exhibit union cards and labels. Likewise a trade bazaar planned by Richmond workers alerted many people to the quality of union-made goods.[35] Sisters Nina Marquart and Emma Krumm demonstrated their commitment to unionism by together selling the most tickets to a union fund-raising stage show. In Wheeling, West Virginia, hundreds of workers pledged twenty-five cents each to back their Labor Forward, and many unions made it easier to recruit new members by lowering initiation fees.[36]

As a national phenomenon, Labor Forward's diversity met the needs of local unionism; each community drew upon particular aspects of craft-union culture and evangelical traditions. In Dallas, labor revivalism took the form of Sunday morning meetings devoted to education on legislation for women, children, and worker safety. Those in attendance heard speeches, poems, and piano solos, sang songs, and participated in the "Question Box." Others assumed a more intense guise, especially the canvasses of Kansas City and Los Angeles trade unionists.[37] Even the length of the camp meetings varied according to local needs. While most lasted two to four weeks, several, including the campaign in Brooklyn, consisted of only a Labor Sunday. Grand Rapids and Duluth trade unionists held several separate short drives. At the other extreme was Philadelphia's, by far the longest movement, lasting well over two years with a good deal of AFL support.[38]

The parades, craft balls, and smokers, all suggest how much Labor Forward drew on and spoke to the traditional culture of craft unionism.

Its successful use of the tools of religious revivalism shows how well craft unionists understood the place of evangelicalism in that culture. And yet for all their depth in this ground, the roots of Labor Forward did not spread out very widely; the movement was essentially focused on the organization of craft workers in the kind of unions with which they were most familiar. This is not to rule out appeals to industrial workers; indeed, Labor Forward frequently designed parades, socials, and musical events with the intention of bringing these workers into its fold. Nevertheless, the leaders of Labor Forward, and most of those involved in it, were self-consciously facing the dual challenge of industrial capitalism and industrial unionism and struggling to distinguish themselves from the new, largely immigrant, industrial working class. The place of Labor Forward in this struggle makes it important to explore the political and ideological content beneath the movement's social forms and evangelical techniques.

### III

To the extent Labor Forward embodied a certain combination of craft-union culture and evangelical religion, it was also an expression, at a particular historical moment, of a somewhat ambivalent ideology that had linked Christianity to the labor movement through much of the nineteenth century. Central to this ideology was the tension between stressing harmony and social unity or conflict and class struggle as the values which were to inform analysis, rhetoric, and organizing strategy.[39] On the one hand, labor's theology rested in socially conservative doctrines such as sobriety, the virtue of hard work, and the idea that the "best class of workers" should share in the growth and prosperity of Christian society. Trade-union evangelists promoted all of these ideas as part of their heritage, asking the middle class, the clergy, and even employers to recognize the stabilizing influence of responsible collective action by workers. On the other hand, Protestant ideals of brotherhood sanctioned labor protest by providing a standard of morals and values against which expectant wage earners might measure the progress of society, especially that of the industrial capitalists. Employers who exploited innocent women and children or refused to pay a fair wage for a fair day's work were breaking their sacred trust with God, who commanded that all righteous people share in society's wealth. Labor Forward organizers preached that the trade union's mission was to force, through strikes or boycotts if necessary, recalcitrant manufacturers to live up to Christian ideals.[40] These two diverse strands of labor theology merged in the Progressive Era labor compact, the collective-bargaining agreement.[41] Here the trade unions could prove their respectability to the middle class and at the same time offer workers real gains in wages and hours, combining stability and collective action.

The craft-union ideology contained much that appealed directly to the middle class. In Minneapolis, for example, Labor Forward speakers contended that unions helped integrate workers into the mainstream of American society and make them responsible citizens. Electrical Workers' organizer James Noonan explained to Riverside Baptists that the "laboring man wanted time to spend with his family, to cultivate his mind, to think of something besides work, to interest himself in religion and to study political conditions." In fact, organized tailors were the first to demand public education for children, claimed cigarmaker W. S. Best. Another Labor Forward meeting discussed the damaging results to society of child labor in mines and factories by displaying slides that showed its "stunting and stupefying" effects; aside from improving conditions for workers and their children, unions also provided social stability. N. C. O'Connor, secretary of the Minneapolis printers, listed the beneficial features of trade unions, including health insurance and old-age pensions. Bakers' organizer Herman Ross further argued that effective organizations "would obviate the need of striking" by gaining the employer's recognition, thereby saving the social expense of the strike. Trade unionists also advised businessmen to accept labor's demand for a voice in the control of industry or suffer the consequences. "Already the working class is flirting with that working class party," warned T. E. Latimer of the Western Federation of Miners.[42]

In this spirit, trade-union evangelists encouraged cross-class coalitions for labor objectives. Syracuse printer Thomas Gafney demanded better pay for women, claiming that "the low wage paid girls who must work is responsible in no small part for the wave of immorality that threatens the whole moral fabric of the nation." Rochester speakers promised the campaign was not intended to start strikes but to teach the middle class its Christian duty to promote reforms and to buy union-label products. Duluth held meetings for employers on the problems of convict labor, and Dallas evangelists urged nine-hour legislation for women.[43] Atlanta revivalists hoped its union revival would "arouse the men of labor" in the city "to deeds of patriotism" resulting in immediate reform and ultimate prosperity without disturbing existing conditions. Many other campaigns adopted the hopes of cigarmaker E. E. Greenawalt, who felt that Labor Forward was "designed to hurry the day when men can live in peace and enjoy tranquility on terms which mean prosperity to the whole of society."[44]

These socially conservative doctrines enabled Labor Forward to attract religious leaders to its union revivals. In fact the degree to which labor actively sought out the church was perhaps unprecedented. In Duluth state federation of labor president E. G. Hall secured promises from many churches that their pulpits would be open to national labor organizers. Ministerial Association delegates in Herrin, Illinois, joined the city central labor union in the hope of furthering industrial peace. Organizers recognized the propagandistic value of this cooperation. The *Journeyman Barber* contended that, with the aid of the church, labor was in a "position to show to the general public what our movement stands for and what we are doing, not only for the organizations, but for the entire population."[45]

Indeed clergymen agreed that craft unions and the church shared many goals and values. Charles Stelzle, who wrote labor sermonettes for over 250 union journals, asserted that the church had been "organized by a company of workingmen" and that "it was received most cordially by the workingmen who formed the great labour guilds of the day—the labour unions we would now call them." He felt that so much of the social spirit of the church lay embedded in trade unionism that "it will some day become a question of whether the church will capture the labor movement or the labor movement will capture the church."[46] Labor Sundays effectively exploited the clergy's support. On June 2, 1916, Richmond, Virginia, ministers gave sermons dealing with "the workingmen and the church" and "Christ and labor." In Brooklyn trade unionists combined media with clerical support, persuading a local newspaper to fill several pages with Labor Sunday sermons. W. B. Wallace, a local Baptist minister, used the occasion to emphasize the concern of Jesus for workingmen, noting that "He himself had been a carpenter. He called workingmen to follow Him. . . . So the Church ought always to feel interested in the laboring man." A Brooklyn rabbi desired "to see a John Mitchell church and a Samuel Gompers synagogue," and a Methodist preacher claimed that the "church holds the secret of industrial success. It is announced in the Golden Rule."[47]

Beyond being accepted as valid by organized religion, the ideals expressed in Labor Forward also proved generally acceptable to the business and professional communities in many cities. Judge J. W. Kintzinger addressed the Dubuque revival on the stabilizing effects of a workmen's compensation law. In Syracuse an Onondaga Historical Society gathering praised trade unionism as the "father of invention." Dallas trade unionists received commendations on successive Sundays from a lawyer, a college professor, and a high school principal. Even some employers were sympathetic to the Labor Forward spirit of labor-capital harmony, making craft unions reluctant to give up notions of community consensus. In Birmingham, for example, several manufacturers believed that unionism stood for "the highest type of citizenship," and Duluth businessmen helped the local Central Labor Union fight against convict labor.[48]

It is important to understand that Labor Forward's courting of business cooperation, and its general stress on reestablishing a harmonious social order, was itself a traditionally grounded aspect of both craft and evangelical ideology. Yet it was far from the whole, and the equally traditional orientation around class-based conflict and evangelically inspired opposition to the ethics of capitalism also found consistent expression in the Labor Forward movement. Religious appeals and values were regularly invoked to unite workers not in a middle-class mainstream but rather in a Christian condemnation of capitalists who would deny wage-earners a decent living. A Lancaster, Pennsylvania, speaker found it "strange that any man would ask for a just God's assistance in wringing bread from the sweat of other men's faces." The Canton, Ohio, *Union Reporter* called attention to "souls that are famished for want of proper nourishment," and claimed that this nonunion city had "the semblance of the coat of Joseph." Even Gompers invoked religious sanctions when he criticized employers for demanding a seven-day work week. Other trade unionists confronted church leaders who preached principally to wealthier segments of the population. United Mine Workers' organizer Robert Harlin argued that workers "need a revival that promises a relief from want rather than spiritual relief."[49]

Many labor evangelists emphasized biblical truths that imposed upon craft unions a religious mission to secure fair wages and hours for workers. That they attempted to make trade unions the base of a religious impulse was not unusual. West Virginia coal miners had earlier focused their religious enthusiasm through the United Mine Workers and Massachusetts shoe-workers had parlayed moral principles into an early industrial union, the Knights of St. Crispin. Twentieth-century labor evangelists shared a similar desire to smooth the roughest edges of industrial capitalism by uniting around scriptural sanctions. "Unions should practice the golden rule, think of others, and do to them as they would be done by," declared one union organizer. In Syracuse a labor speaker, citing the Bible, admonished, "whatever you find to do, do it with all your might," in summoning support for labor activity. Another speaker recommended inviting organizers so that "the gospel of unionism may fall in fertile fields and bring forth a least a hundred fold."[50]

In Labor Forward, craft unionists found a contemporary means of expressing and acting on an older traditional link between the ideal of

Christian brotherhood and the concept of worker solidarity. Cigar-makers' organizer W. S. Best likened the movement to a revival "where repentants and sinners alike were welcomed into the outstretched arms of labor and given the trade union hand of fellowship." Speaking at the Springfield, Massachusetts, Labor Forward movement, Gompers warned that unless "we lift the burden from the shoulders of our brothers it is a certainty that we shall be crushed under it." The Duluth *Labor World* likewise cautioned that no "political or industrial Moses will be able to free the laborer alone. He must have behind him the great fighting force of organized labor." In Atlanta a trade unionist, alert to the worker's need for idealism and fellowship, commended unionists for leading "the flock" as the ministers led, "without hope or expectation of reward."[51]

Generally, Labor Forward, despite its frequent conservative appeals, focused its zeal upon a vision of society perfected through trade union-ism. Craft workers envisioned a version of the "workers' paradise" based on Scripture and the existing trade-union structure rather than ideological tracts and radical organizations. Garment Workers' orga-nizer Abe Gordon praised the Labor Forward movement for showing "the good work it is doing in uplifting the workingman and his family and contributing to the advancement of the state toward a more perfect civilization." Machinist Thomas Wilson assured an Auburn, New York, labor revival gathering that God would not answer a worker's prayers until he belonged to a trade union. The *Amalgamated Sheet Metal Workers' Journal* expected some day to witness a "band of preacher-labor leaders" who would not be "bound by narrow creeds, but . . . will teach the intensely human Gospel which Christ Himself preached."[52]

The life of Jesus provided trade unionists with a model and a justification for organized labor. "Go ye hence and preach the gospel" stated the Canton, Ohio, *Union Reporter*, "thus quoting from the greatest and grandest tradesman and human organizer that ever trod this earth, who by his every act and word portrayed the true unionism." Indeed, the historical figure of Jesus himself became linked to union-ism. He was, for workingmen, a carpenter and a union leader. Or-ganized labor, like Christ, intended to "lift up the downtrodden" and sought to "save souls." J. E. Paxton added that unionism "was not a selfish movement but an unselfish and democratic movement for the uplift of humanity, and the betterment of society in every way."[53] Supporting trade unionism in achieving these goals was thus a sacred cause. For instance, the *Garment Worker* proclaimed: "The union label is a religious emblem. It is a religious act to buy goods to which this label [is] attached, an act blessed on earth and honored in heaven."[54]

By invoking religious imagery, biblical passages, and divine sanction, the trade unionists of Labor Forward not only legitimized their battle, they also drew on the ideological support and inspiration offered by a vital and accessible religious tradition, one which was consistent with a vision of the necessity for labor's organized struggle. It would not be accurate to call this a class-conscious vision, since Labor Forward sought, as part of the craft-union tradition, to enable workers to take the lead in a more socially inclusive battle for a better life. But, in contrast to the vision of class harmony discussed earlier, this aspect of the movement did presume that conflict was a natural correlate of industrialism, and it emphasized a value system that justified resistance in the form of organization and struggle.

Since harmony and struggle had always been linked in an uneasy tandem in traditional craft-union culture and ideology, this heritage could hardly be resolved in Labor Forward. The chance for harmonizing these themes rested on the emergence of a complex, negotiated collective-bargaining agreement as a central feature of employer-worker relations in the Progressive Era. This focus well suited the stabilizing, practical, responsible, yet militant vision the AFL sought to project in union revivalism. Cigarmakers' organizer E. E. Greenawalt, for example, extolled the superiority of collective bargaining over "the antiquated methods of bygone days when it was everybody for himself and the Devil take the hindmost." The bargaining agreement also meshed well with AFL voluntarism, a doctrine that advocated collective self-reliance and self-help rather than relying on legislation or governmental change. Garment worker Abe Gordon's claim that the "hope for the abolition of sweatshop labor lay not in legislation so much as in the buying of goods bearing the union label" exemplified the craft-union adherence to this creed. Voluntarism and collective bargaining were especially crucial in Labor Forward's appeal to both the middle class and the workers because they differed so much from the ideology of the Socialists and the IWW. The Dubuque, Iowa, trade-union revival thus attained the pinnacle of success when it helped create an Adjustment Agreement Plan to foster collective bargaining and end labor-capital disputes.[55]

All of this was fine for workers securely rooted in the craft tradition. But the ideology of labor revivalism did not speak to the largely unorganized, industrial working class in a period of enormous stress and change. Immigrants whose skills and stature were being constantly undermined had little use for traditional notions of community harmony and little apparent stake in the struggle of established unions.[56] These workers were moved instead by the battle for industrial unionism, by the Socialists and other radical parties, and by the IWW. The battle against this challenge had always been one of the central concerns of Gompers and the Labor Forward leadership: labor evangelicalism was explicit in aiming to counter the appeal of the various radical ideologies, organizations, and programs, and the underlying social vision and critique they tended to share in general terms. Yet these challenges were an unresolvable problem for Labor Forward, in that it sought to reaffirm craft leadership in organized labor while simultaneously distancing itself from precisely those workers who would have to be part of any broadly based modern labor movement.

Nor was this its only problem. Many modern industrialists also proved relatively indifferent to the community harmony appeal of labor evangelists. Giant monopolistic enterprises like U.S. Steel or International Harvester were indifferent to Labor Forward's message of cooperation, rooted as it was in obsolete artisanship and in what to them seemed the almost equally obsolete mutuality of the local community.[57]

For all its timeliness then, Labor Forward was speaking from a relatively narrow base to an ultimately narrow conception of the problem. In any final assessment of what Labor Forward has to teach about the labor movement in the early twentieth century, it is crucial to appreciate the relationship between its genuine working-class vitality and these limiting contradictions. Perhaps the best way to do this is to conclude by examining some specific situations that illustrate both sides of this tension.

## IV

The difficulties of Labor Forward campaigns in Syracuse and Auburn, New York, and in Pittsburgh and Erie, Pennsylvania, exemplify the limitations of the revival movement and, in many ways, of craft unionism itself. In New York and Pennsylvania, AFL affiliates faced challenges both from new monopolistic industries and from radical industrial unionists. In addition, large numbers of South and East European immigrants populated all four of these cities and made up a significant percentage of the workers in the new industries. Local labor leaders promoted craft-union traditions and revivalism's methods to halt the growing tensions created by the radicals' struggle against industrial capitalism and to attract immigrants into the more stable trade organizations. These traditions, however, exerted a limited control over the immigrants. Instead of achieving moderation, Labor Forward's millennial rhetoric and organizing success encouraged increased militance among the immigrant industrial workers. Nor did the craft unions' stress on social harmony ease the anti-union sentiments of industrial capitalists, who launched aggressive counterattacks to insure their continued control of the factory. Beset on both sides, in some areas craft unionism's culture and ideology appeared weak and contradictory even amid the labor revivals.

In January 1913, Syracuse labor began its two-month revival with a grand march of all trade unionists to City Hall. The campaign stressed organizing but also sought to educate the middle class to the virtues of interclass collaboration. As in such craft-union centers as Minneapolis, organizers secured the cooperation of churches, schools, and public halls, and the organizing committee visited all the local unions to drum up support. The city trades assembly assessed each union member five cents to cover the expenses of the movement and organizers placed a wagon emblazoned with signs on the street. Unionists also posted newspaper clippings about the movement on bulletin boards in many shops. The trade-union revivals quickly spread to other cities, including Auburn, Utica, and Watertown. Labor editor Edward Wood warned that if the campaign "proves to be a failure it will cast a gloom over the trade union horizon that will take many years to erase." But if a success, it would "build a monument to the memory of everyone of the 10,000 wageworkers of the city that never will be forgotten."[58]

Local craft-union leaders and national organizers utilized the sympathy of the clergy and professional groups to mount a successful Labor Forward organizing drive, very much on the ideological and programmatic lines discussed above. The rapidly changing social and economic bases of Syracuse and Auburn, however, tested the effectiveness of the craft unions' appeal and illustrate the ambiguous, complex role revivalism could play for the working class. Steel manufacturers, the textile industry, and monopoly enterprises like International Harvester had established factories surrounding the cities. These corporations attempted to take advantage of the area's resources, transportation system, and, more important, the flood of South and East European immigrants who provided an abundance of cheap, surplus labor. The manufacturers solidified their position through the support of the local businessmen and professionals who prospered because of the new industries.[59]

Syracuse and Auburn labor leaders recognized the potential danger to the craft-union movement posed by less-skilled Polish and Italian immigrant workers. Local employers were already pitting semiskilled Poles against native Americans to lower the wages of the skilled iron molders. In Syracuse, Socialists nearly captured the leadership of the Trades Assembly in 1912. Near Auburn, the IWW conducted a successful strike among Little Falls, New York, immigrant textile workers, circumventing AFL organizer Charles Miles. The entire upstate New

York area was aglow with radicalism.[60] AFL "pure and simple" unionists countered with the revival argument that workers did not require
"a new method of bettering their conditions, but rather patience and
enthusiasm sufficient to assure the thorough application of the trade
union principles."[61] They pitched their appeal to immigrants and
industrial workers in the enthusiasm of the camp-meeting atmosphere
and the solidarity of the craft-union culture of control. They employed
Polish and Italian organizers and also used immigrant halls for their
smokers, mass meetings, and socials. For example, over 500 rope-
makers crammed a courthouse meeting in Auburn addressed by Joseph
Mnichewski and Joseph Graci. The revival in the two cities numbered
over 6000 "converts" to trade unionism, including many Italian laborers and Polish steel and foundry workers recruited in Garbinski's Hall,
a favorite immigrant center.[62] And the movement produced not only
recruits but a solidarity that is itself somewhat surprising, given the
conservative craft ideology. Indeed, skilled American molders joined
semiskilled and unskilled Poles in a strike against the Pierce, Butler,
and Pierce foundry until the company met the Poles' demands.[63]

Labor Forward's success in attracting immigrants to craft unionism,
however, intensified employer opposition and led to contradictions
with which the skilled workers proved incapable of coping. Two large
Auburn manufacturers, International Harvester and the Columbian
Rope Company, planted spies at revival gatherings and began firing
participants. This precipitated a strike of Polish and Italian factory
workers led by Charles Miles, fresh from his battle with the IWW at
Little Falls. Shortly after, Syracuse building contractors declined to
deal with the largely Italian Laborers' Union there, and the Crucible
Steel Company refused to recognize a union formed by Polish and
Slavic steelworkers, also causing strikes. The walkouts in both Auburn
and Syracuse became violent after International Harvester and Crucible
Steel hired strikebreakers and threatened to take their plants elsewhere.
City leaders in Syracuse and Auburn, fearing the loss of major employers, called out the militia to suppress the strikes. Meanwhile, many
craft unionists, sensing the growing public fear of losing industries,
reverted to a more familiar hostility toward immigrant strikers. Attempting to portray unionism as respectable and peaceful, many skilled
workers argued that these immigrant industrial workers lacked the
patience and dedication necessary to make unionism work in American
society. Furthermore, craft unionists proved unwilling to risk their
hard-won gains, especially middle-class sympathy and the collective-
bargaining agreements, to assist immigrants and unskilled industrial
workers toward those same achievements. The unity of business and
government leaders and the breakup of labor solidarity forced the

immigrants to accept company-dictated settlements in each of the disputes.[64]

If Labor Forward proved unequal to overcoming the power of employers determined to break unions, from the AFL point of view it was more successful as a craft-union ally against the IWW and the Socialists. At the peak of the revival in Syracuse, the reinvigorated local labor leadership handily defeated the Socialists in an election for control of the Trades' Assembly.[65] In Auburn, Charles Miles had the rope-workers enlisted in the AFL, at least temporarily. The emotion and enthusiasm of labor revivalism appealed to the immigrants and unskilled industrial workers even if the skilled native workers ultimately proved less than willing to provide the needed solidarity.

In January 1913, AFL leaders decided to use the Labor Forward organizing techniques to launch a campaign directed against anti-union metal trades manufacturers, especially in Pittsburgh and Erie, Pennsylvania. Trade unions had failed in single-union attempts to organize these workers, and they hoped that a "virile and aggressive" federation effort could succeed in overcoming the obstacles to organizing. In the metal trades, conglomerates like U.S. Steel had reduced the number of skilled workers in the industry and broken the craft-union hold on production. Employing immigrants to perform many of the unskilled jobs, metal trades manufacturers adeptly resisted all attempts to unite their employees by constructing a diverse work force that often did not understand a common language.[66] The only organizing effort that had made any headway against steel manufacturers was the strike conducted by the IWW at McKees Rocks in 1909. This, in conjunction with some Socialist successes in toppling metal-trades-union leaders, pressed the AFL to conduct "an energetic and persistent campaign of organization, with special efforts directed toward interesting [workers] speaking the foreign tongues."[67]

James O'Connell, recently deposed by the Socialists from his position as head of the Machinists, and John L. Lewis led the AFL metal trades campaign. Although Pittsburgh and Erie Labor Forwards shared the moderate reform goals of these trade unionists, O'Connell and Lewis imposed the movement from outside the community, ignoring church and middle-class support. Generally, they met staunch resistance from all but the metal trades workers. Lewis had difficulty obtaining meeting halls in Pittsburgh and eventually had to hold the meetings without prior notice to reduce the number of company spies who reported on workers attending union revival gatherings. In Erie, the Manufacturers' Association endeavored to keep workers from talking to AFL organizers and it took out full-page advertisements in local papers claiming its members would not run a union shop or deal with union negotiators. The Pittsburgh *Iron City Trades Journal* reported that manufacturers hired forty former state troopers to disrupt Labor Forward meetings.[68]

Still, union evangelists in Pittsburgh and Erie reached many workers by borrowing the technique, if not the content, of Labor Forward. While failing to use millennial Christian rhetoric or to capitalize on what middle-class support might have existed, Lewis ably promoted class solidarity through fiery speeches, vigorous organizing, and a camp-meeting atmosphere. He employed immigrant organizers and circulated pamphlets in a dozen different languages comparing the wages of union and nonunion workers. Over 1,000 workers at the American Locomotive Works attended one noonday assembly, and during the first week of the campaign organizers signed up several hundred workers in the Pressed Steel Car works. Iron Molders' organizer D. M. Shalkop organized a strike of some 500 molders, over 75 percent of whom were foreign born.[69]

The Pittsburgh and Erie Labor Forward campaigns, however, proved incapable of solidifying their early gains, largely because of the inherent limitations of craft organizations when facing both industrial unionism and corporate capitalism. While workers received some immediate wage hikes, the AFL leaders downplayed the previous IWW efforts to organize along industrial lines. It planned to accustom the immigrants "to being union men" and then "distribute them among the various crafts to which they belong." This scheme did not fit the realities of the situation: steel manufacturers could easily break isolated craft unions, especially where little skill was involved, while immigrants simply deserted craft unions that charged high dues. After limiting the initial successes of Labor Forward through a combination of increased wages, suppression, and propaganda, steel producers broke immigrant attachment to craft unions when the revival enthusiasm dissipated. American labor traditions of craft-union control did not correspond to the experiences of South and East European immigrants. Ironically, however, one group of workers benefited in the Pittsburgh and Erie campaigns. Crafts that used labels for their products felt that purchases of union-made products had increased, and they perceived the movement as extremely beneficial.[70]

## V

After 1916 the AFL discontinued its support of the Labor Forward movement. Trade-union revivalism gave way to labor patriotism as the federation sought to maximize its growth and its respectability by helping the United States prepare for war. Prowar fervor replaced religious zeal as an organizing principle. While it lasted, however, for the educational value and emotional enthusiasm which the revivals generated, many labor leaders believed Labor Forward had no equal. The *Journeyman Barber* perhaps best expressed labor's gratitude to revivalism: "The labor forward movements . . . are very essential to stimulate the various organizations and to aid in organizing the unorganized." Several cities felt that Labor Forward was valuable enough to return to in the postwar period. For example, Milwaukee called in the union evangelists in 1918 and Superior, Wisconsin, held a campaign as late as 1922.[71]

A measure of the success or failure of Labor Forward is shrouded in the complex and often contradictory directions the movement took in different cities. Labor Forward strengthened, solidified, and extended the trade-union movement in many places. Baltimore alone counted an increase of 13,738 members. In Philadelphia unions such as the Asbestos Workers and the Lace Workers announced "100% union organization," and the Carpenters and Bartenders doubled their numbers.[72] In other cities union leaders attested to the ability of revivalism to create harmony within the ranks of labor. In Camden, New Jersey, and Birmingham, Alabama, evangelists closed the "gap in the defences of labor" by resolving factional fights frequently exploited by manufacturers.[73] Similarly, the revivalists in several cities sought to enlist wage earners often thought to be unorganizable. Kansas City labor formed unions of waitresses and laundry workers and Richmond "perfected" a union of municipal street cleaners.[74] Nevertheless a look at several cities might suggest that the movement failed. For example, St. Louis and Brooklyn workers canceled their campaigns because of high unemployment, and in Des Moines, Barbers' organizer G. M. Feider reported that "the officers of the forward movement seemed to put forth every effort to make it a success, [but] the rank and file was apathetic."[75] Even in cities where revivalism spurred the working class, manufacturer counteroffensives and lukewarm middle-class support dampened Labor Forward's impact. At its core the conservative craft unionists mobilized Labor Forward as a wedge against IWW and Socialist insurgency, but, in fact, AFL membership remained relatively stagnant.

Ultimately, the success or failure of Labor Forward would be less interesting—were it measurable—than the view the movement provides of the complex role of religion in the history of the American working class. These craft-union revivals took remarkably different directions in different social contexts. One important factor in the reception of union revivals was the degree of industrial development.[76] Workers in cities dominated by large monopolistic industries, such as the steel industry in Pittsburgh, showed the least interest in craft-union culture, the trade organization, or the patient gains made through the collective-bargaining process. Minneapolis skilled workers, largely free from industrial employers like U.S. Steel or International Harvester, exerted a controlling influence in local labor concerns and the craft unions expanded and solidified. In Syracuse, the labor movement was in transition. The traditions and culture of the skilled workers still dominated the labor movement, but the unions faltered when attempting to draw in the new industrial workers.

The homogeneity of the community and the attitudes of the local employers added to the tensions of the industrial development. While local employers in Minneapolis chose to bargain with the predominately skilled native craft workers, the monopoly industries in Pittsburgh and Syracuse resisted union growth and used their clout to pressure the local business and government leaders for help in suppressing union activities. The high percentage of South and East European immigrants that worked at unskilled jobs in these industries added to the difficulty of labor leaders attempting to unite craft-union support behind these wage earners. Furthermore, Labor Forward's appeal to the social, political, and religious values that skilled workers shared with the middle-class Protestant culture held out little hope for the low-paid, Catholic, unskilled immigrant workers.[77]

The attitude of the religious leaders also shaped the response to craft-union revivalism in many cities. Indeed, the content of Social-Gospel religion, as discussed earlier, sanctioned worker activity and informed trade-union culture. In Minneapolis, the revival campaign grew tremendously with the help of a local clergy that had a long history of concerns for social and economic justice. Labor Forward also spread quickly in New York's "burned-over" district. The Syracuse revival appeared headed for tremendous success until the counteroffensive of Crucible Steel and International Harvester. In Pittsburgh, on the other hand, the local ministers had brought in the socially conservative evangelist Billy Sunday shortly before the city's union revival, an indication of their political inclinations. Again, these religious factors intertwined with local social and economic conditions. Even generous support from local Protestant ministers could do little to attract immigrants who did not share the same cultural traditions as the craft workers, who thrived on a particular American version of Christian morality and millennial Protestantism.

From a look at Labor Forward in Syracuse, Pittsburgh, and Minneapolis, it thus becomes apparent that union revivals had their greatest impact when part of a strong, dominating, and homogeneous craft-union movement. Under unfavorable circumstances, Labor Forward exposed the weakness of AFL-style trade unionism when grappling with the rapidly changing forces of urban-industrial society. In fact, craft unionism's ambiguous ideology and weakening culture (even if temporarily revived), remained vulnerable to the far stronger historical developments of industrial unionism and corporate capitalism. This is not to say that the movement was a mere tactic that suited skilled workers fighting employer incursions on the one hand and radical threats to labor leadership on the other. Nor should this imply that the AFL was uninterested in organizing unskilled and immigrant workers; many campaigns specifically targeted these groups. It is more important to see Labor Forward as emblematic of attempts to respond to new social and political conditions within a creative and deeply rooted craft-union culture. Religious principles and camp-meeting traditions strengthened that culture, but in no way solved the basic contradictions facing the craft unionists.

## NOTES

The authors would like to acknowledge the helpful and probing comments of friends and colleagues who read earlier drafts of this paper: Patty Cooper, Jim Gilbert, David Grimsted, Dolores Janiewski, Stuart Kaufman, Joe Reidy, and Leslie Rowland. Michael Frisch and Daniel Walkowitz significantly improved both the style and the content.

1. Samuel Gompers, "Labor Forward Movement," *American Federationist*, Oct. 1912, p. 828.

2. For religion's ability to blunt revolutionary consciousness in Britain, see Elie Halevy, *A History of the English People* (New York: Harcourt, Brace, 1924), I, 371-74. E. J. Hobsbawm, in *Primitive Rebels: Studies in Archaic Forms of Social Movement in the 19th and 20th Centuries* (New York: Norton, 1959), pp. 128-29, and in *Labouring Men: Studies in the History of Labour* (New York: Basic Books, 1965), pp. 23-33, argues the latter interpretation. The fullest description of the complex relationship between Methodism and the labor movements is found in E. P. Thompson, *The Making of the English Working Class* (New York: Vintage Books, 1966), pp. 375-400, and in Robert Wearmouth's books. Thompson claims that Methodism and labor did not necessarily grow together but were spiritual and political thrusts of a general social unrest. Methodism, however, provided many leaders to labor's political movements.

3. Paul Faler, "Workingmen, Mechanics and Social Change: Lynn, Massachusetts, 1800-1860" (Ph.D. dissertation, University of Wisconsin, Madison, 1973), p. 275; Herbert Gutman, *Work, Culture, and Society in Industrializing America: Essays in American Working-Class and Social History* (New York: Knopf, 1976), ch. 2; Paul E. Johnson, *A Shopkeeper's Millennium: Society and Revivals in Rochester, New York, 1815-1837* (New York: Hill and Wang, 1978); James Findlay, *Dwight L. Moody: American Evangelist* (Chicago: University of Chicago Press, 1969); William G. McLoughlin, *Revivals, Awakenings, and Reform: An Essay on Religion and Social Change in America, 1607-1977* (Chicago: University of Chicago Press, 1978), pp. 141-50; Marc Karson, *American*

*Labor Unions and Politics 1900-1918* (Boston: Beacon Press, 1965), pp. 212-84; David Montgomery, *Workers' Control in America: Studies in the History of Work, Technology and Labor Struggles* (Cambridge: Cambridge University Press, 1979), pp. 74-83.

4. Timothy L. Smith, *Revivalism and Social Reform* (New York: Harper, 1957); Ronald C. White, Jr., and C. Howard Hopkins, *The Social Gospel: Religion and Reform in Changing America* (Philadelphia: Temple University Press, 1976); Henry F. May, *Protestant Churches and Industrial America* (New York: Harper, 1949).

5. George H. Nash, "Charles Stelzle: Apostle to Labor," *Labor History*, 11 (1970), 151-74; Sidney Mead, *The Lively Experiment: The Shaping of Christianity in America* (New York: Harper and Row, 1963), p. 121.

6. "Campaigning with the Men and Religion Teams," *Survey*, Dec. 23, 1911, p. 1393; "Social Forces," *Survey*, Oct. 14, 1911, p. 989; "What the Men and Religion Forward Movement Actually Accomplished," *Current Literature*, June 1913, p. 673; "The New Evangelism as Contrasted with the Old," *Current Literature*, Nov. 1911, p. 530.

7. "What the . . . Forward Movement Accomplished," pp. 673-75; "Campaigning with a Men and Religion Forward Team," *Survey*, Feb. 3, 1912, p. 1678; John Aiken and James McDonnell, "Walter Rauschenbusch and Labor Reform: A Social Gospeller's Approach," *Labor History*, 11 (1970), 131-50.

8. Harry G. Lefever, "The Involvement of the Men and Religion Forward Movement in the Cause of Labor Justice, Atlanta, Georgia, 1912-1916," *Labor History*, 14 (1973), 522; "Men and Religion in the South," *Survey*, Apr. 6, 1912, p. 12; "Campaigning with the Men and Religion Teams," p. 1395.

9. Fred B. Smith to John Mitchell, Jan. 25, 1912; Charles Stelzle to Mitchell, Jan. 15, 1912; Peter J. Brady to Mitchell, Apr. 2, Apr. 6, 1912, all in John Mitchell Papers, Catholic University of America, Washington, D.C.

10. Leo Wolman, *The Growth of American Trade Unionism, 1880-1923* (New York: National Bureau of Economic Research, 1924), pp. 29-66; Joseph G. Rayback, *A History of American Labor* (New York: Macmillan, 1959), pp. 207-26; Melvyn Dubofsky, *Industrialism and the American Worker, 1865-1920* (New York: Crowell, 1975), pp. 101-6; William M. Dick, *Labor and Socialism in America: The Gompers Era* (Port Washington, N.Y.: Kennikat Press, 1972), pp. 97-108; Bernard Mandel, *Samuel Gompers: A Biography* (Yellow Springs, Ohio: Antioch Press, 1963), pp. 310-21; Graham Adams, Jr., *Age of Industrial Violence, 1910-1915: The Activities and Findings of the United States Commission on Industrial Relations* (New York: Columbia Univ. Press, 1966), pp. 1-24, 75-100; David Montgomery, *Workers' Control in America*, pp. 48-108.

11. *American Federationist*, Oct. 1912, p. 828; Minneapolis *Labor Review*, Apr. 12, 19, 26, May 3, 1912; St. Paul *Minnesota Union Advocate*, May 10, 1912; *Weekly Bulletin of the Clothing Trades*, May 10, 1912; *Cigar Makers' Official Journal*, May 1912, p. 27.

12. John D. Chubbuck to AFL Executive Council, Feb. 29, 1912, Mitchell Papers; Minneapolis *Labor Review*, Apr. 5, May 3, Mar. 8, 1912.

13. Minneapolis *Labor Review*, Apr. 19, 26, May 3, 1912; *Cigar Makers' Official Journal*, May 1912, p. 27; *American Federationist*, Oct. 1912, pp. 828-29.

14. Minneapolis *Labor Review*, Apr. 26, May 3, 1912; *Weekly Bulletin of the Clothing Trades*, May 10, 1912; American Federation of Labor, Executive Council Minutes, Aug. 12-17, 1912, in AFL-CIO Headquarters, Washington,

D.C. (hereafter AFL EC Minutes). White and Hopkins, *Social Gospel*, p. 150, notes the tradition begun in Minneapolis by George D. Herron's publication, *The Kingdom*; the city was also the scene of the first Men and Religion drive.

15. *Minneapolis Journal*, Apr. 22, 1912; Minneapolis *Labor Review*, May 3, 1912.

16. John D. Chubbuck, "Synopsis of Organizing Work Accomplished," Apr., May 1912, Mitchell Papers; *Cigar Makers' Official Journal*, May 1912, p. 27.

17. St. Paul *Minnesota Union Advocate*, May 3, 10, 1912; Duluth *Labor World*, May 11, 18, 25, June 1, 8, 1912.

18. Mitchell to Frank Morrison, July 1, 1912, Mitchell Papers; Youngstown *Labor Record*, Aug. 1, 1912; *American Federationist*, Feb. 1913, p. 332; *Carpenter*, June 1913, p. 24. See also *Mixer and Server*, Apr. 15, 1913, p. 41; *Garment Worker*, Dec. 20, 1912, p. 6; *AFL Weekly News Letter*, Nov. 2, 1912, p. 1, for other evidence of the spread of Labor Forward through craft-union mediums. Lawrence Goodwyn, *The Populist Moment: A Short History of the Agrarian Revolt in America* (Oxford: Oxford University Press, 1978), describes an earlier "movement culture" that spread in this region through a local grassroots enthusiasm.

19. AFL EC Minutes, May 9-11, 13-17, Aug. 12-17, 19, 1912.

20. *American Federationist*, Oct. 1912, pp. 828-31; Bernard Mandel, *Samuel Gompers*, pp. 9-12.

21. *American Federationist*, Oct. 1912, pp. 828-31.

22. Ibid.; William G. McLoughlin, Jr., *Billy Sunday Was His Real Name* (Chicago: University of Chicago Press, 1955), pp. 12-15; Findlay, *Dwight L. Moody*, p. 266.

23. G. W. Perkins to Gompers, Nov. 6, 1912; S. S. Geitel to Gompers, Nov. 11, 1912, in AFL Microfilm Convention File, 1912 Convention, reel 2, AFL-CIO Headquarters, Washington, D.C., (hereafter AFL CF); American Federation of Labor, *Proceedings*, 1912, pp. 385-86, 391. Karson, *American Labor Unions and Politics*, suggested that union leaders' connection with Catholicism played a strong anti-Socialist role in the AFL; he made no mention of Protestantism's important part in fighting radicalism.

24. To identify cities conducting campaigns (150 were located), the authors consulted the AFL *Proceedings*, the *AFL Weekly News Letter*, the AFL convention files, the *American Federationist*, and organizers' reports in trade-union journals.

25. James R. Green, *Grass-Roots Socialism: Radical Movements in the Southwest, 1895-1943* (Baton Rouge: Louisiana State University, 1978), esp. pp. 151-62.

26. This section of the paper benefited greatly from a similar analysis of craft-union culture in Bryan D. Palmer's *A Culture in Conflict: Skilled Workers and Industrial Capitalism in Hamilton, Ontario, 1860-1914* (Montreal: McGill-Queen's University, 1979) esp. chs. 2 and 3; from E. J. Hobsbawm's *Labouring Men*, esp. "Labour Traditions"; and from the work of several students of worker culture, Patty Cooper, Dolores Janiewski, and David Corbin.

27. On Columbus, *Machinists' Monthly Journal*, May 1915, p. 446; for Kansas City and Los Angeles, Kansas City (Mo.) *Labor Herald*, Apr. 3, 10, 1914; Charles F. Stockhahn to Gompers, Feb. 28, 1914, AFL CF, 1913 conv., reel 2; *AFL Weekly News Letter*, Jan. 10, 1914.

28. Syracuse *Post-Standard*, Jan. 16, 1913; Syracuse *Industrial Weekly*, Jan. 24, 1913.

29. *Tacoma Labor Advocate*, June 4, 1915. The evangelist who made this remark in 1915, Carpenters' organizer Jay Fox, participated in the very first Labor Forwards.

30. Lancaster (Pa.) *Labor Leader*, May 3, 1913; Atlanta *Journal of Labor*, Mar. 12, 1915; AFL, *Proceedings*, 1915, p. 66.

31. Minneapolis *Labor Review*, Mar. 29, Apr. 12, 19, 1912.

32. Ibid., Apr. 26, May 3, 1912; *Weekly Bulletin of the Clothing Trades*, May 10, 1912.

33. Jamestown (N.Y.) *Union Labor Advocate*, Aug. 26, 1915; *Machinists' Monthly Journal*, June 1916, p. 593.

34. Syracuse *Industrial Weekly*, Feb. 14, 1913; Syracuse *Post-Standard*, Feb. 5, 1913.

35. Charles Perry Taylor to Gompers, Sept. 26, 1914, AFL CF, 1913 conv., reel 2; Richmond *Square Deal*, Mar. 24, 1916.

36. *Omaha Unionist*, Jan. 15, 1916; *American Federationist*, Sept. 1913, p. 774; *Garment Worker*, Aug. 8, 1913; Richmond *Square Deal*, Apr. 7, 1916.

37. Dallas *Laborer*, July 26, Aug. 16, Sept. 20, 1913; Kansas City (Mo.) *Labor Herald*, Apr. 3, 10, 1914; *AFL Weekly News Letter*, Jan. 10, 1914.

38. *Brooklyn Eagle*, Feb. 9, 1914; Duluth *Labor World*, Feb. 5, 1916, Apr. 27, 1912; *American Federationist*, Mar. 1916, p. 208.

39. One of the central themes of labor history in the twentieth century is this continuing tension between cooperation or conflict with industrial capitalism. James Weinstein, *The Corporate Ideal in the Liberal State, 1900-1918* (Boston: Beacon Press, 1968), citing Gompers's role in the National Civic Federation, contends that the AFL opted for cooperation. David Montgomery, in *Workers' Control*, offers a much more insightful picture, discussing both the elements of accommodation and conflict that resided in the craft unions as well as in the labor movement more generally.

40. Among the best works analyzing the complexity of religion's social conservatism and the "transforming power of the cross" in labor protest are E. P. Thompson, *Making of the English Working Class*, pp. 375-400; Alan Dawley and Paul Faler, "Working-Class Culture and Politics in the Industrial Revolution: Sources of Loyalism and Rebellion," *Journal of Social History*, 9 (Winter 1976), 466-80; Paul Faler, "Cultural Aspects of the Industrial Revolution: Lynn, Massachusetts, Shoemakers and Industrial Morality, 1826-1860," *Labor History*, 15 (1974), 367-94; Herbert Gutman, *Work, Culture and Society*, ch.2; Bruce Laurie, "'Nothing on Impulse': Life Styles of Philadelphia Artisans, 1820-1850," *Labor History*, 15 (1974), 337-66; E. J. Hobsbawm, *Primitive Rebels*; and especially useful was David Alan Corbin's excellent study, *Life, Work, and Rebellion in the Coal Fields: The Southern West Virginia Miners, 1880-1922* (Urbana: University of Illinois Press, 1981), ch. 6.

41. The importance of collective bargaining to Progressive Era labor solutions is discussed in Bruno Ramirez, *When Workers Fight: The Politics of Industrial Relations in the Progressive Era, 1898-1916* (Westport, Conn.: Greenwood, 1978).

42. All quotes from "What the Speakers Said at the Labor Forward Meetings," Minneapolis *Labor Review*, Apr. 26, 1912.

43. Syracuse *Post-Standard*, Mar. 17, 1913, p. 7; *Garment Worker*, Mar. 3, 1916; Duluth *Labor World*, May 6, 1916.

44. Atlanta *Journal of Labor*, Mar. 5, 1915; Lancaster (Pa.) *Labor Leader*, May 24, 1913.

45. E. G. Hall to Gompers, Feb. 27, 1916, AFL CF, 1915 conv., reel 3;

*American Federationist*, May 1913, p. 405; *Journeyman Barber*, June 1916, p. 198.

46. *International Molders' Journal*, June 1913, p. 475, May 1913, p. 377; White and Hopkins, *Social Gospel*, pp. 66-68; Youngstown *Labor Record*, Dec. 20, 1912.

47. Richmond *Square Deal*, June 2, 1916; *Brooklyn Eagle*, Feb. 9, 1914; *Weekly Bulletin of the Clothing Trades*, May 3, 1912.

48. Dubuque *Labor Leader*, Feb. 13, 1915; Syracuse *Post-Standard*, Feb. 15, 1913; Dallas *Laborer*, Sept. 6, 13, 1913; Birmingham *Labor Advocate*, Feb. 5, 1915; Duluth *Labor World*, May 6, 1916.

49. Lancaster (Pa.) *Labor Leader*, May 31, 1913; Canton (Ohio) *Union Reporter*, Dec. 1913; *American Federationist*, Oct. 1912, p. 830; *Tacoma Labor Advocate*, Apr. 16, 1915.

50. Corbin, *Life, Work, and Rebellion*, ch. 6; Dawley and Faler, "Working-Class Culture," p. 472; Lancaster (Pa.) *Labor Leader*, Apr. 26, 1913; Syracuse *Industrial Weekly*, Jan. 3, 1913; St. Paul *Minnesota Union Advocate*, May 3, 1913.

51. *Cigar Makers' Official Journal*, May 1912, p. 27; *Garment Worker*, July 9, 1915; Duluth *Labor World*, Apr. 8, 1916; Atlanta *Journal of Labor*, Mar. 5, 1916.

52. Thompson, *Making of the English Working Class*, p. 34; *Weekly Bulletin of the Clothing Trades*, May 10, 1912; Auburn (N.Y.) *Daily Advertiser*, Jan. 31, 1913; *Amalgamated Sheet Metal Workers' Journal*, Apr. 15, 1912, p. 136.

53. Canton (Ohio) *Union Reporter*, Dec. 1913; Lancaster (Pa.) *Labor Leader*, July 5, 1913. See also Gutman, *Work, Culture and Society*, p. 95.

54. *Garment Worker*, Feb. 27, 1914.

55. Lancaster (Pa.) *Labor Leader*, May 31, 1913; Minneapolis *Labor Review*, Apr. 26, 1913; Dubuque *Labor Leader*, Jan. 2, 9, 1915.

56. See, in particular, David Montgomery, *Workers' Control*, for more on the native skilled workers.

57. Herbert Gutman, "Workers' Search for Power: Labor in the Gilded Age," in H. Wayne Morgan, ed., *The Gilded Age* (Syracuse: Syracuse University, 1970), pp. 38-68, discusses the lack of concern that industrial capitalists expressed for community sanctions or opinions; Richard Edwards, *Contested Terrain: The Transformation of the Workplace in the Twentieth Century* (New York: Basic Books, 1979), ch. 3, also offers an excellent overview of the concerns of monopolistic enterprises for this period.

58. Syracuse *Industrial Weekly*, Dec. 20, 27, 1912, Jan. 3, 1913; *Machinists' Monthly Journal*, Mar. 1913, p. 263.

59. See in particular Robert Ozanne, *A Century of Labor Management Relations at McCormick and International Harvester* (Madison: University of Wisconsin, 1967), pp. 96-103; and information on the local metal trades industries in Charles Yates to Samuel Gompers, Jan. 6, 1913, in AFL CF, 1912 conv., reel 2.

60. Syracuse *Post-Standard*, Mar. 3, 1913; Syracuse *Industrial Weekly*, Nov. 22, 1912; Robert E. Snyder, "Women, Wobblies and Workers' Rights: The 1912 Textile Strike in Little Falls, New York," *New York History*, 60 (Jan. 1979), 29-57.

61. See the letters from "Pure and Simple" of Syracuse in *Machinists' Monthly Journal*, Feb. 1913, p. 167, Mar. 1913, p. 286.

62. Syracuse *Post-Standard*, Mar. 11, 1913; Auburn (N.Y.) *Daily Advertiser*, Feb. 20, 25, 1913. Although there is no evidence of Catholic immigrants attending a gathering in a Protestant church, the campaign was successful in this largely Catholic area. Indeed Catholics also had a revivalist tradition and Labor Forward organizers utilized an evangelical atmosphere in religiously neutral meeting places to attract immigrants. For Catholic and immigrant revivalist tendencies, see Jay P. Dolan, *Catholic Revivalism: The American Experience 1830-1900* (Notre Dame, Ind.: University of Notre Dame, 1978); and Timothy Smith, "Lay Initiative in the Religious Life of American Immigrants, 1880-1950," in *Anonymous Americans: Explorations in Nineteenth-Century Social History*, ed. Tamara Hareven (Englewood Cliffs, N.J.: Prentice-Hall, 1971), pp. 214-43.

63. Syracuse *Industrial Weekly*, Feb. 21, 1913.

64. This account is gleaned from the *Post-Standard*, the *Industrial Weekly*, and the Auburn *Daily Advertiser*. An additional overview of the Auburn situation with the attitude of International Harvester is in Robert Ozanne, *Century of Labor Management Relations*, pp. 96-103.

65. Syracuse *Post-Standard*, Mar. 21, 1913.

66. For a discussion of the steel and metal trades situations, see David Brody, *Steelworkers in America: The Nonunion Era* (New York: Harper, 1970), esp. pp. 125-46, which concludes with one of the few secondary mentions we encountered of a Labor Forward campaign; Ramirez, *When Workers Fight*, ch. 6; and Montgomery, *Workers' Control*, chs. 3 and 4.

67. *AFL Weekly News Letter*, Apr. 5, 1913.

68. Pittsburgh *Iron City Trades Journal*, Apr. 18, 25, May 2, 1913; Erie *Union Labor Journal*, Feb. 28, 1913.

69. Pittsburgh *Iron City Trades Journal*, Apr. 11, 18, 1913; *International Molders' Journal*, Mar. 1913, pp. 223-24.

70. *Iron City Trades Journal*, Apr. 11, 1913. See Brody, *Steelworkers in America*, pp. 141-46, on the reasons for the short impact of the movement. On the label trades' perception of its success, see Minutes of the International Executive Board, July 14, 1913, Series I, Box 91, p. 125, Tobacco Workers' International Union Papers, McKeldin Library, University of Maryland, College Park.

71. *Journeyman Barber*, Feb. 1916, p. 18; Thomas W. Gavett, *Development of the Labor Movement in Milwaukee* (Madison: University of Wisconsin, 1965), p. 133; *AFL Weekly News Letter*, Feb. 4, 1922.

72. Henry Eichelberger to Gompers, Oct. 12, 1916, AFL CF, 1916 conv., reel 4; "Bulletin: [Phildelphia] Labor Forward Movement," ca. Sept. 1914, AFL CF, 1913 conv., reel 2.

73. Birmingham *Labor Advocate*, Jan. 29, 1915; *Machinists' Monthly Journal*, Oct. 1915, pp. 913-14; *Amalgamated Sheet Metal Workers' Journal*, Feb. 15, 1916, p. 43.

74. John T. Smith to Gompers, Sept. 23, 1914, AFL CF, 1913 conv., reel 2; J. C. Duke to Gompers, Apr. 29, Sept. 9, 1916, AFL CF, 1915 conv., reel 4.

75. *St. Louis Labor*, Apr. 6, 1915; Hugh Frayne to Gompers, Sept. 29, 1914, AFL CF, 1913 conv., reel 2; *Journeyman Barber*, June 1916, p. 198.

76. Much of the following discussion comes from census publications. Included are: *Thirteenth (1910) Census of the United States* (Washington, D.C.: GPO, 1913), vols. 2, 3, and 9 (Population and Manufactures); *Fourteenth (1920)*

Census of the United States (Washington, D.C.: GPO, 1923), vols. 3, 4, and 10 (Population and Manufactures); and *Religious Bodies, 1916* (Washington, D.C.: GPO, 1919).

77. Minneapolis had a high concentration of immigrants, but they were predominately Northern European Protestants who came from an already industrialized society.

# "The Customers Ain't God":
# The Work Culture of Department-Store
# Saleswomen, 1890-1940

Observers of workers' conduct on the shop floor have long recognized that customs and unwritten rules compete with employers' prescriptions for day-to-day life on the job. Building on the insights of contemporary observers such as Stanley Mathewson, Frances Donovan, and Elton Mayo, labor historians have recently begun to write the history of these shop-floor practices and of the ideology and social organization that support them. Frequently focusing on a single industry or workplace, detailed studies are beginning to recapture the complex history of the social relations of the workplace as they developed through daily contact among and between workers and managers.[1] When a third element—the patient in a hospital, for example, or the customer in a department store—enters into the equation, the possibilities for workers to manipulate the situation become yet more various and complicated. A labor history written from this point of view focuses on daily interactions within the workplace, rather than on formal union organization and dramatic events such as strikes. Like women's historians and social historians, writers in this vein share an interest in the quotidian rather than the exceptional, an awareness of the importance of culture, and a sensitivity to the double potential of constraint and possibility in a given situation.

The concept of work culture—the ideology and practice with which workers stake out a relatively autonomous sphere of action on the job—is a useful tool for analyzing shop-floor interactions. A realm of informal, customary values and rules mediates the formal authority structure of the workplace and distances workers from its impact. Work culture is created as workers confront the limitations and exploit the possibilities of their jobs. It is transmitted and enforced by oral tradition and social sanctions within the work group. Generated partly in response to specific working conditions, work culture includes both adaptation to and resistance to these structural constraints. But more than being simply reactive, work culture also embodies workers' own definition of a good day's work, their own sense of satisfying and useful labor. While condemning oppressive aspects of the job, it also celebrates the skill it demands and the rewards it brings. Work culture is very much an in-between ground: it is neither a rubber-stamp version of management policy nor is it a direct outcome of the personal—class, sex, race, ethnicity, age—characteristics of the workers. It is the product of these forces as they interact in the workplace and result in collectively formed assumptions and behavior.[2]

The study of work culture opens the way to a fuller understanding of the consciousness of women workers, a matter often ignored or obscured in both labor and women's history. On the one hand, historians have frequently equated workers' consciousness with craft consciousness, in effect excluding women by definition because of their notable underrepresentation in the skilled trades.[3] On the other, writers have maintained that home and family were the primary determinants of women's consciousness and that their experience as unskilled or semiskilled workers has had a minimal effect on their outlook. Leslie Woodcock Tentler has offered the most eloquent and well-developed arguments for this position, asserting that an interest in romance, marriage, and rebellion against parental constraints dominated the outlook and interactions of women wage earners.[4] While she quite correctly emphasizes the intense sociability of women at work, she attributes it almost solely to the age and sex homogeneity of the work force. These factors were, of course, important, but Tentler curiously undervalues the role of the shared experience of the work itself and of the authority relations it entailed. Moreover, she criticizes women workers for resorting only to short-term protests about working conditions and for neglecting union organization, overlooking that such "spontaneous, disorganized" protests were important features of the work life of men and women alike, both inside and outside labor unions.[5] And, most important of all, she fails to examine these actions for evidence of the consciousness that underlay them.

My discussion of the work culture of department store saleswomen differs from the tenets of these writers in regard to the roles of both skill and family. First, I assume that skill is not an objective category but rather a function of social and economic imperatives. It has, for example, become a commonplace that jobs performed by men tend to be labeled as more skilled than those performed by women, even when the tasks involved are quite similar. In fact, all workers, whatever the level of skill attributed to their jobs, shape their workplace experience in ways that revise and expand managers' notions of the job, using the special "working knowledge" they develop.[6] Second, I assume that the family consciousness/work consciousness dichotomy distorts and over-simplifies the complex process by which forces both within and outside the workplace shape the consciousness of male and female workers alike. Department-store saleswomen's work culture reflected a consciousness of themselves as workers, as women, and as consumers, and its complexity mirrored the complexities and contradictions of their lives.

The historian faces a serious problem in writing about work culture: traditional historical sources focus on the written and the formal, and the very essence of work culture is that it is oral and informal. The most useful sources are those based on firsthand observation of people at work. Saleswomen appear in a variety of such accounts, including social investigations, theses in retailing, and human relations studies.[7] Another perspective on daily life in a department store comes from the *Echo*, the newspaper of the Filene Co-Operative Association, one of the foremost American experiments in industrial democracy.[8] Trade periodicals provide less direct evidence: department-store managers complained with gusto and candor about the failings of their employees, and careful analysis of their complaints can reveal a great deal about the actual behavior of saleswomen.[9]

In seeking to understand the complex dialectics of the shop floor, historians have learned a great deal both conceptually and methodologically from anthropologists, who have contributed the useful notion of social network and a sensitivity to informal structure and influence in social situations.[10] Equally important have been the vivid evocations of workplace atmosphere in participant observation studies.[11] Intrigued by the notable ability of these studies to portray the complexities of the workplace as a system of social relations, historians have begun a kind of historical anthropology. Since we cannot observe our subjects on the job but can only at best question them about past experiences, we cannot study a single workplace with anthropological intensity. Instead, our work can outline the range of attitudes and behavior that arises out of a given industrial or occupational setting rather than the specific form that work culture takes in one workplace.

The period from 1890 to 1940 might be called the golden age of the American department store, the era during which large urban stores played a key role in forming and satisfying the consumption desires of millions of Americans. A lively work culture flourished among the legions of women who sold the merchandise in these great emporiums, created and sustained by the interaction of at least four general factors common to most stores and their workers: the meaning of department-store selling as a job; the policies of the department-store industry toward saleswomen; the class base of selling; and its gender base. The combination of ideological and material influences in each of these areas provided the context and raw material for saleswomen's work culture.

The women who joined the selling staffs of American department stores brought with them an elaborate and sometimes conflicting set of assumptions about the meaning of department-store work. First, and perhaps most important, saleswomen shared with millions of American workers an ethic of independence: they would work, but they would not serve. David Montgomery has spoken of an ethic of "manliness" that informed craftsmen's bearing and behavior toward their bosses and toward one another; while the term is obviously inappropriate to women workers, women's thoughts and actions were in some ways quite similar.[12] The vocabulary of early labor reformers and organizers was available for women workers to describe their experience, but they used it with different points of reference in mind.[13]

In the late nineteenth and early twentieth centuries, women workers most often expressed their ideal of independence as a condemnation of domestic service. For the half-century under consideration, domestic service was the single largest women's occupation. Social investigations revealed that women workers regarded being a maid as a "final degra-dation," not because of an aversion to the work itself but because of the class position of the domestic servant.[14] Typically, women condemned domestic service as lacking in freedom and independence, objected to being "bossed around" at any hour of the day or night, and termed the servant's position one of "slavery."[15] This rejection of paid household work seems to have been particularly strong among saleswomen. In an 1898 survey almost half of the shop workers but just over a third of the factory workers mentioned the social stigma as a negative feature of domestic service.[16] Store managers noticed the same aversion: Edward Filene flatly stated that he had "never known of a salesgirl becoming a servant."[17] The decision to be a clerk instead of a maid, however, was problematic, since selling involved many of the troublesome aspects of domestic service. A persistent theme in saleswomen's work culture was the effort to reject those elements of the selling job which implied or recalled servile status.

In fact, one of the definite attractions of department-store selling was that a saleswoman commanded more respect from her superiors than most blue-collar workers; if nothing else, the presence of a customer imposed a decorum not necessary behind factory walls. As one early-twentieth-century editor put it, "Maggie" in the factory became "Miss" in the store.[18] Selling was more accessible than other white-collar occupations such as clerical work, which required far more training. Although saleswomen in general worked longer hours for lower pay than other women white-collar workers, selling offered remarkable opportunities for a few women, particularly in comparison to other occupations open at the time.[19] Most observers agreed that, although men continued to occupy the highest store positions, women's salaries and chances for advancement to middle management level were more nearly equal than in other fields. For a fortunate few, department-store selling offered more than a shabby white collar; it held out the slim but definite chance of real economic independence.[20]

At its best, selling provided genuine job fulfillment. The work offered variety, changing rhythms, a wide range of social interaction, and the chance to exercise initiative and experience autonomy. The women of the infants' department at Filene's were enthusiastic about suggestive selling, maintaining that it was "a study and not a hardship. It is a better type of selling than the old dull grind of selling just one article to a customer. It also means a wonderful knowledge of merchandise in other stocks."[21] One saleswoman developed her skills to the point that women entrusted her with the selection of whole wardrobes; she learned not just "the pleasure of selling" but "the pleasure of creating."[22] Few factory or office jobs included such opportunities. What woman working in the most modern factory or in the most glamourous office could say, as Leah Cramer said of her days selling gloves in the tawdriest of department stores, "I was the person who connected them with their dreams, their special saleslady.... [The merchandise] was the bottom of the line, imitation *schlock*, that's all, pure and simple. They knew it, I knew it, but if you don't keep the dreams alive, people themselves don't want to be alive."[23] Despite the undeniable toil of department-store selling, it could be a source of personal satisfaction.

Department-store life had other attractions; the saleswoman found there the distilled glamour, excitement, and material bounty that were part of the promise of the American city. The stores themselves were more dazzling, luxurious, and eventful than the factory or the home. Observers frequently remarked on the contagiousness of this spirit, noting clerks' vivacity and stylishness—Prairie Parisiennes, as a Chicago writer termed them.[24] Basking in the reflected prestige of the goods over which she presided, taking her place at the center of action of a culture in which personal and public fulfillment were increasingly defined by material goods, the saleswoman could become a minor priestess of consumption. Her sense of her pivotal role in the palace of consumption emboldened her and constituted the wiry backbone of her work culture.

Department-store managers' efforts to rationalize the selling floor created in many ways the ideal conditions for the flourishing of sales-women's work culture. Like their compatriots in manufacturing, in the early twentieth century they were obsessed with productivity, efficiency, and control. In fact, however, department stores as a whole were less bureaucratically managed than factories of comparable size. Managers' conceptions of the store as a whole and of the role of saleswomen produced an extremely plastic environment in which saleswomen had broad discretion, in marked contrast to the experience of men and women who worked in factories.

The key feature of a department store was its departmental organization. In breaking up stores into small units, managers hoped to achieve economies through specialization, but their actions had unintended results. Departmentization, as the trade journals termed it, did result in financial and accounting efficiencies, but it undermined at least as much as it increased selling efficiency. While clerks became more expert in dealing with their section's merchandise, they also became more isolated from the other departments' wares and hence much less likely to encourage customers to purchase items outside their purview. Departmental groups also tended to have limited social interaction with clerks in other sections. The result, as a Milwaukee store executive put it in 1939, was that people became "department-minded rather than store-minded."[25]

Staffing policies broadened the gaps between departments by placing different, supposedly appropriate, types in each: motherly women for the children's department, young attractive women for the first floor, and mature women for the high-priced departments.[26] As a result, the staff within a department was relatively homogeneous, a characteristic which fostered divisiveness between departments although it did not guarantee solidarity within them.

Moreover, the cohesiveness of departmental groups was not paralleled by a coherent system of authority. The development of a functionally organized staff fractionalized responsibility for the sales force. Members of the buying, operations, advertising, personnel, accounting, and sales promotion staffs all had some degree of authority over salespeople. In theory, this meant more thorough supervision, but in practice it meant that authority was hopelessly divided and frequently inconsistent; saleswomen's work culture both exploited this weakness and mediated the contradictions in the situation.[27]

Management's definition of the work process was also an unintentional prop to the formation of saleswomen's work culture. The key to department-store productivity was the encouragement of more and larger sales per customer. Until well after World War II retailing executives pursued this goal by shunning self-service schemes and

emphasizing persuasive "personal" sales efforts.[28] This basic managerial decision gave salespeople a central role in the store's profit
picture: if clumsy, indifferent, or offensive, they would thwart sales,
while if resourceful, eager, and engaging, they could vastly increase
them. There was a powerful double potential contained in this policy;
the skilled saleswoman might be able to manipulate customers, but she
could use the same skill at social interaction to manipulate her relationship with her bosses as well as to forge solid ties with her co-
workers. Ironically, the most valued employee could be the most subversive.

On the selling floor, the issues of class and sex were crucial. The
department-store counter was not just a barrier between salesperson
and customer but also a barrier between classes, with predominantly
working-class women doing the selling and predominantly middle-
class women doing the buying. Managers were intensely conscious of
the fact that any but the most perfunctory sales transaction depended
upon the salesperson's ability to deal effectively with a client of another
class. A standard feature of training programs for saleswomen was the
effort to give the clerks a veneer of middle-class or elite culture. Selling
classes sought to erase telltale signs of working-class origins in saleswomen's dress, language, and demeanor, while trying to acquaint
clerks with middle-class styles of life so that they might better sell the
appropriate material accompaniments.[29] Department-store selling offered women workers the opportunity to behave like and associate with
members of the middle and upper classes, albeit in a subordinate
position and at the price of turning their backs on patterns they had
grown up with. The prospect appealed to some and repelled others, but
in any event management's persistent and explicit concern with the
issue of class reinforced saleswomen's sense of difference from bosses
and customers alike.

Selling skill was also sex-specific. Definitions of women both as
workers and as consumers made the department store's selling floors
overwhelmingly a female preserve. A journalist described the department store in 1910:

> Buying and selling, serving and being served—women. On every
> floor, in every aisle, at every counter, women. . . . Behind most of
> the counters on all the floors, . . . women. At every cashier's desk, at
> the wrappers' desks, running back and forth with parcels and
> change, short-skirted women. Filling the aisles, passing and re-
> passing, a constantly arriving and departing throng of shoppers,
> women. Simply a moving, seeking, hurrying, mass of femininity,
> in the midst of which the occasional man shopper, man clerk, and
> man supervisor, looks lost and out of place.[30]

The qualities which managers most desired in saleswomen were exactly those which were the props of nineteenth-century women's culture: adeptness at manipulating people, sympathetic ways of responding to the needs of others, and a familiarity with domestic things—qualities which would enable the saleswomen to convince the woman across the counter to part with her money. In so defining selling skill, bosses in effect gave exchange value to women's culture, encouraging women to transfer skills and behavior from the home into the store, to treat their customers as "guests" in a store so designed as to make it "a supplement to the home."[31] In purchasing this commoditized sisterhood, managers again grasped a double-edged sword. The clerk's womanly rapport with her sisters on both sides of the counter could as easily be used against his interests as for them.

The selling floor was rich with possibilities for the development of saleswomen's work culture. On the one hand, selling as work offered more autonomy than most factory or office jobs. A confused authority structure and a job definition that emphasized worker initiative combined with managers' inability to control the pace of work, creating an atmosphere highly congenial to workers' attempts to impose their own ideas about the proper way to run a department. On the other hand, selling as a social situation was fraught with contradictions that at once inspired and were manipulated by saleswomen's work culture. The social relations of department-store selling involved a complicated triangle of saleswomen, managers, and customers, overlaid with the vexed issues of class and sex. Differentiated from bosses and customers alike on the basis of class, saleswomen asserted themselves as workers. Linked to their customers and to one another by a common gender experience, and particularly by their shared role as consumers in the developing economic order, saleswomen asserted themselves as women. In the process, they created a complex work culture which gave to the selling floor a tone and a structure sharply at variance with managers' plans.

Saleswomen's work culture reflected the contradictions within and between managers' and workers' conceptions of the job. One important theme in it was saleswomen's resistance to the built-in class system in the store—the set of rules that underscored their subordinate position, cast them in servant-like roles, and subjected them to the same sort of control as factory employees faced. Clerks resented rules that confined them to segregated store facilities and clearly conveyed that resentment to management. They objected to separate employee entrances, particularly when they were tucked into dingy back streets and contrasted too obviously with the ceremonial portals designed for customers.[32]

They were even unhappier when there was a time-clock inside the employees' entrance. Dorothy Foster, a saleswoman at Rich's of Atlanta, expressed her delight that her store did not have one, for time-clocks made "one feel more like a member of a goat herd than a human being."[33] A number of enlightened stores responded to employee pressure and removed their time-clocks during the 1920s.[34] Saleswomen also loathed the systems stores used to control or inspect employees' packages; one manager testified that no single measure earned him more of his employees' good will than his store's abolition of the parcel-checking system.[35] At Filene's, saleswomen cavalierly disobeyed rules restricting them to certain elevators and underlined their rebellion with boisterous behavior in the face of customers.[36] On the one hand, the two-class system of store facilities smacked of the upstairs-downstairs division of the servant's life; on the other, it echoed the regimentation and anonymity of the factory. Servants and factory workers doubtless resented these rules and tokens of rank as much as saleswomen did; but only saleswomen could use their bosses' own pronouncements as an ideological foundation for their rebellion. When managers reminded salespeople that they were the store's emissaries to the public, when they told them that selling was a dignified profession, they were setting the stage for saleswomen to insist that they be treated like first-class citizens.

Saleswomen similarly scorned other store rules and practices that emphasized their subordination to the customer. Generations of clerks chafed under John Wanamaker's pronouncement that the customer was always right; although few stores enforced it literally, the maxim still affected store atmosphere in a general way by prescribing servile and unquestioning demeanor for the saleswoman. One feisty woman framed the clerk's response to Wanamaker: "The customers ain't God!"[37] The head of Lord & Taylor showed that he understood this sentiment when he told a trade association that his store had explicitly given up the idea of the customer's infallibility in favor of "policies . . . that any person we employ can loyally support without any sacrifice of self-respect."[38]

Certain features of the selling routine also awakened saleswomen's unwillingness to behave like a servant to the customer. Many, for example, objected to helping customers to try on clothing since it involved the servile intimacy associated with being a maid.[39] But no single issue so inflamed saleswomen at Filene's as the question of dress. At least until World War II, the industry's usual dress standard for saleswomen mandated black or another dark color in the winter and white in the summer. During the twenties and thirties there was a slow trend toward more flexible rules about color and style, but most stores continued to demand conformity despite pressure for liberalization from saleswomen.

At Filene's, dress was a highly charged issue which crystallized the curious doubleness of saleswomen's consciousness: it reflected both their firm sense of their independence as workers and their developing vision of their role in a consumer society. Saleswomen questioned by the *Echo* in 1902, while resigned to wearing black, were emphatic that management should neither prescribe the style of their dress nor provide them with uniforms. Their answers left no question that they viewed uniform dress as "a badge of service," in the words of Miss Wickerson of the suit department. Others complained in the same vein that uniforms would make them look, variously, like orphans, prisoners, charity patients, paupers, and waitresses. Similarly, they felt that having the store buy their clothing would undermine their dignity as workers; another woman from the suit department stated that "it gives one more reliance, independence, to furnish your own [clothing]."[40]

In 1913, four-fifths of Filene's saleswomen voted to demand the right to wear either black or white garments the year round, on the grounds that "the management owed us the right to dress as we pleased."[41] By 1930, when saleswomen voted twenty to one in favor of a proposed rule stating only that their clothing be in "business-like styles and neutral shades," the argument integrated their rights as consumers with their rights as workers. The women of one department warned management that they could not sell effectively if they didn't feel that they were "dressed well and look[ed] smart."[42] Women working in other stores suggested other objections to dress regulations. A saleswoman who did not want to wear the regulation black or black-and-white garb all the time had to go to extra expense to buy separate clothing for social occasions, clothing that could not later be used for work. Moreover, a saleswoman who simply could not affort a dual wardrobe found that her employer was in effect dictating what she wore off the job as well as on it.[43] Dress rules underlined the saleswoman's subordinate status in the store and her inability to consume freely outside the store.

Storewide unity on such issues as the dress standard was the exception rather than the rule in department stores; the primary locus of saleswomen's work culture was the department. The complex social situation on the selling floor provided a rich array of possibilities which saleswomen could manipulate to their advantage, and saleswomen made it clear to both managers and customers that the selling floor was their turf. The rest of my discussion will focus on the implications of clerks' work culture for their relations with managers.

Building on the structural foundation of management's policy of treating departments as quite distinct units, saleswomen formed strong intradepartmental ties. This departmental solidarity can be expressed quantitatively. A survey of one store's employees showed that virtually all liked the members of their own departments, while only one out of five wanted a promotion if it meant leaving their departments.[44] In another store, women placed departmental matters highest on their list of morale factors; men, significantly, placed this factor eleventh.[45] But the cohesiveness of some departments cannot be adequately captured in figures: a waist department at Filene's, for example, had an informal alumnae association which held reunions of past and present members of the department.[46]

Departmental solidarity included a definition of the department's distinctiveness from other sections of the store, frequently expressed in ways that reflected an elaborate hierarchy of class within the store. At Filene's, an *Echo* editorial bemoaned the widespread "social stratification—otherwise known as class feeling. This shows itself in the form of snobbishness on the part of those who feel themselves a bit superior to somebody else."[47] But the ranking varied throughout the store: while the clerk in an upstairs department might look down on basement saleswomen, the members of the basement staff had an equally firm conviction of their superiority to upstairs departments.[48] The one placed a primary value on the prestige of higher-priced goods, while the other emphasized the lively atmosphere of the basement; the world of the department store was varied enough to validate many different hierarchies.

Tensions between departments reinforced saleswomen's tendency to associate almost exclusively with members of their own sections. Management's standard metaphor in deploring this situation was that the clerks built "a stone wall" around their departments.[49] Exclusivity easily led to outright hostility. Salespeople might willingly allow a customer to leave the store rather than recommend another department's merchandise to her, and they were frequently heard to criticize other departments' service and merchandise to customers.[50] A more direct form of aggression was to treat a saleswoman from another department insultingly by refusing to sell her choice merchandise or to make adjustments in her purchases.[51]

Cohesiveness within departments was as impressive as enmity between them. Solidarity grew out of the intense social interaction which co-workers shared; huddling, or gathering together and talking, was the most universally remarked feature of saleswomen's work culture. An assistant buyer at Filene's despaired of squelching saleswomen's gregariousness: "Call-downs don't work here. They quiet down for the day, but it only seems to give the jawbone a rest which improves its speed and stamina. The next day they are at it, again."[52] A shop-floor vocabulary furthered the sociability of the huddles. A crepe-hanger, for instance, was a saleswoman who ruined a sale by talking a customer out of something she had resolved to buy; a clerk who called "Oh, Henrietta," while waiting on a customer was alerting her co-workers to the fact that the customer was a hen, a difficult type.[53]

Although some accounts note a certain level of tension within a department, all observers remarked the way in which the work groups submerged internal antagonisms in collective action when it was called for. In one department, women contributed to the support of Aggie, a particularly destitute co-worker; they paid her insurance and sick benefit premiums, brought extra food for her lunch, and helped her to stretch her meager clothing budget. But their actions went beyond self-help within the department; they also confronted management on Aggie's behalf. When a manager halted their yearly collection to send Aggie on vacation and made them return the money, they ostentatiously collected it again outside the door after work. They knew, however, that the only real solution to Aggie's problems was a higher salary, and their most impressive victory was in backing her up when she asked for and got a raise.[54] Other observers related the impressive ability of departments to rally for mutual support even in the face of the brutal Christmas rush season.[55]

Saleswomen, in confronting management, shared with skilled male craftsmen many of the forms of their work culture, but adapted them to their own needs and to the constraints of their situation. Clerks had genuine pride in their selling skill. Departments at Filene's praised their collective selling skill in doggerel in the *Echo*; typical was a coat department's vision of itself: "as a team they're hard to beat, . . . / and they're lightning on their feet. . . . / just to watch them at their work is quite a treat."[56] Different departments emphasized the special little skills necessary to sell their merchandise, and some salespeople's talents were notable. Apparel saleswomen, for example, learned to guess a woman's size and the cost of the outfit she wore at a glance.[57]

Saleswomen developed shop-floor wisdom about their merchandise as well. Their instincts for what would sell were legendary; as the manager of Filene's put it, they could "spot a lemon quicker than a Mediterranean fruit fly."[58] Buyers disregarded saleswomen's judgment at their peril; merchandise that clerks considered below the level of the department was doomed to grow dusty and await eventual markdowns. In one toy department, for example, saleswomen refused to sell sleazy stuffed toys that they labeled "drug-store Easter bunnies."[59] Saleswomen sometimes enhanced the salability and attractiveness of their goods by concocting elaborate displays; the clerks in one ribbon department festooned its counters with fancy ornaments made from their merchandise. The observer reporting this practice clearly understood the connection between women's culture and selling skills, praising them for their "domestic, homely ability."[60]

Selling skill and departmental solidarity were inseparable, for selling skill was in large part collectively developed and transmitted. Saleswomen keenly observed one another in dealing with customers, both learning from and criticizing their sisters' performances. Frances Donovan, a sociologist who worked in department stores in preparation for her book *The Saleslady*, joined the other clerks of the Mabelle frock department in the game of "Playing Customer": two among them acted out a sale, impersonating familiar types from both sides of the counter. The game was a ritual, reemphasizing the women's group solidarity against the customer and establishing the saleswomen as the masters in a complicated social situation. It was also a conduit for oral tradition, passing along and elaborating selling skill. Finally, it was a form of initiation and apprenticing: Donovan knew she was accepted into the group the first time her selling style was caricatured in a skit. She fully understood that "Playing Customer" was no frivolous diversion: "I was always amazed at the seriousness with which they invariably regarded it. They applauded, not with their hands, but with the attitude of their bodies, the expression in their eyes. This bit of make-believe drama enabled them to see themselves, not as saleswomen, tired with a daily routine of monotonous drudgery, but as actresses in the play of life—their part not small to them but of the utmost significance."[61]

Not all departments had such an elaborate ritual for conveying skill and socializing group members, but selling skill was in important ways a group phenomenon. Like craft workers, saleswomen collectively protected their knowledge from the boss and restricted its application on the job. The saleswomen's notion that they had the right to control the use of their own time died hard, and they repeatedly thwarted management's efforts to fill up with other tasks the significant proportion of their time that was not claimed by customers. One Filene's saleswoman directly confronted the issue when she challenged management's right to subtract the price of a returned item from her sales total; her justification was that "as she had given her time, she was entitled to the credit of the sale."[62] Her suggestion provoked a store executive to argue in the *Echo* that the firm bought full control of the saleswoman's time when it paid her wages.

By far the most impressive instance of saleswomen's collective action was their enforcement of the stint. Saleswomen had a clear concept of the amount of sales—a "good book"—that constituted a good day's work. The amount varied from department to department according to the price level of the merchandise and the difficulty of selling it. A saleswoman deviated from the stint at her own peril: sales totals too far below it would bring management down on her head, while sales too far above it would alienate her peers. Saleswomen's careful conformity to the stint was particularly impressive in view of the uncontrollable fluctuations to which their trade was subject. Within a given day, they tapered off their selling efforts as they approached the informal quota, sometimes calling other clerks with lower "books," or sales tallies, to take customers. They balanced out the number of sales they made to compensate for the size of the purchase; if they made a few large sales early in the day they might retire to do stock work. When customers were few and far between during bad weather or in the summer doldrums, saleswomen tried more aggressively to sell than during the busy season, when they could attain their quotas and still ignore some of the customers. The worst sin the saleswoman could commit was to be a grabber: to ignore the stint and to compete too energetically for customers. As an Arkansas saleswoman delicately put it, "While it is well to have an eye open for prospective buyers, undue pushing ahead of another creates an unpopularity that makes those about you unpleasant and reacts on your disposition."[63]

Saleswomen had a range of methods for enforcing the stint and the social rules of the department. Penalties for violation included messing up the offender's assigned section of stock, bumping into her, banging her shins with drawers, ridiculing or humiliating her in front of peers, bosses, or customers, and, in the final extremity, complete ostracism.[64] At Filene's, saleswomen used the department-gossip column of the *Echo* to warn those who deviated from group norms. Typical offenses were: refusing to reveal to co-workers the amount of one's book, habitually coming to work late, associating too exclusively with only one member of the department, never giving a customer to another clerk, and socializing with members of the prestigious French department rather than with one's own department members.[65]

The work group devoted special attention to new clerks, for department discipline would have collapsed if they were not properly socialized. There was a shift in the treatment of newcomers during the period which I am considering, but the level of concern about their subversive potential remained high. In the earlier decades, when stores' training programs were rudimentary and casual, departments seem to have welcomed new saleswomen with sisterly support and friendliness.[66] The early initiation process took the form of a kind of apprenticeship, as the department taught the newcomer the ropes. Later, however, as training departments sought more energetically to socialize new employees in the art of selling and to limit the role of departmental work culture, the reception of the neophyte more frequently took the form of a trial by fire. Suspicious that she might have been successfully indoctrinated into management's dangerous ideas about a good day's work, the departments made it clear to the newcomer that she had to prove herself before she would be accepted.[67] The life of a new, part-time, or temporary clerk could be made miserable indeed as old-timers exiled them to dull corners of the selling floor, kept them from making sales, and saddled them with the most distasteful stock work.[68]

On occasion, the initiation process could include a message to management as well as to the newcomer. In one children's wear section, the executives made the mistake of firing a popular though unproductive saleswoman, and compounded the offense by immediately replacing her with another clerk. The newcomer, experienced in the ways of saleswomen's work culture and sensible of the hazards of her position, tried eagerly to learn how the department defined a good book. Her co-workers, bent on revenge and willing to sacrifice her to group solidarity, ostracized her, refused to tell her what the informal sales quota was, and effectively crippled her performance in the department.[69]

Like a skilled craft, however, selling countered the emphasis on solidarity with an appreciation of individual aptitude and accomplishment. Saleswomen's work groups provided for temperament or personal quirks by allowing a certain degree of specialization within departments. One department elaborately allocated the turf by consensus, despite bosses' persistent efforts to change the arrangement. The group functioned peacefully because everyone knew her place and kept to it.[70] Individual saleswomen also specialized in certain types of customers—some delighted in fitting stout women, others enjoyed the challenge of convincing resolute "lookers" to buy.[71]

Saleswomen had a respectful admiration for each individual's particular tricks, and their lore emphasized the need for each to develop her personal style of selling and to tailor her conduct to the wide variety of situations she faced. Mary Ellen Riley wrote to the *Echo* describing a sale which she thoroughly bungled by repeating, parrot-like, phrases which she had heard other clerks in her department use. She pointed the moral clearly: "the next time I was careful not to use borrowed thunder."[72] Saleswomen guarded their own transactions jealously; one of the truly serious offenses a saleswoman could commit against a sister behind the counter was to interfere in her sale and impugn her judgment. Only the rawest new clerk would call in another saleswoman to help save a losing sale.[73]

The work culture of the selling floor thus maintained solidarity in part by providing space for individual saleswomen to exercise their talents and eccentricities. Individual feats of selling were objects of admiration, but only when they did not involve unacceptable competition with other department members. Two illustrations make clear the permissible types of selling coups. One was the marathon variety, in which a saleswoman assigned alone to a special lot of goods outdid herself. A case in point was Charlotte Broad of Filene's, who sold 1503 boxes of hairnets in a single day, for a total of $902—over 200 boxes per hour.[74] Another type was the stroke of genius—a single sale stupendous in its size or ingenuity. Pauline Leyman of Strawbridge and Clothier's glove department dazzled her fellow employees by selling a dozen pairs of gloves because she had remembered for a full year the exact size and shape of the hands of a woman she had observed only briefly.[75] That such exercises of skill boosted profits helps to explain why many managers tolerated and tacitly encouraged the aspects of work culture which supported such efforts.

Tolerant as they were of work culture's appreciation of individual skill, managers persistently attacked its collective aspects. They tried to take over saleswomen's shop-floor wisdom and to break the power of their work groups, and saleswomen just as determinedly opposed their efforts. Managers devised a variety of training programs to teach new saleswomen the "right" way to sell. Saleswomen picked and chose among these programs, responding to those that increased their knowledge about their merchandise and grumbling at those that mindlessly encouraged courtesy or tried to drill working-class behavior out of them.[76] Saleswomen in fact showed an eagerness for information about their wares that was not limited to training programs. When Empress Eugenie hats became the rage, for instance, Filene's saleswomen flocked to the store library to bone up on the appropriate historical background.[77] But learning about one's merchandise did not imply a willingness to use the knowledge at the bidding of one's employer.

In addition to sending information from the top down, managers also tried to co-opt saleswomen's collectively devised selling secrets. Their tactics included suggestion contests and demands that the clerks fill out "call slips" whenever a customer asked for something that was not in stock. Salespeople were massively uncooperative, simply refusing to submit suggestions or call slips. One of their most important pawns in the battle with management was their contact with customers' desires, and they were not about to surrender it lightly.[78]

Above and beyond training, managers mounted repeated offensives against the subversive aspects of saleswomen's work culture. By their own accounts, they had little success. Beginning around 1910, they introduced a bewildering variety of complicated commission, commission-plus-salary, and quota-bonus payment schemes in an attempt to use money incentives to break worker solidarity around the stint. Saleswomen, like skilled craftsmen and less-skilled factory operatives, resisted these tactics. The definitive industry study of these incentive plans concluded that no pay scheme could be depended upon to increase sales output, but that sales levels were linked to the overall atmosphere of the workplace.[79] Saleswomen, clearly, exercised their skill to the utmost only when they were treated with the respect they felt they deserved.

As universally as managers complained about the power of saleswomen's work culture, nowhere did a boss testify to the successful elimination of its practices, even in the most insecure days of the depression. Two stories typify saleswomen's small, quiet, collective victories against management. In 1915, a desperate floorwalker mounted a major campaign against an obstreperous and temperamental department. He succeeded in subduing them temporarily and in whipping them on to higher levels of sales, but his success was short-lived. The store manager, faced with imminent insurrection among the saleswomen, finally had to transfer him to another floor.[80] In 1933, a University of Pittsburgh retailing student reported on her field work in an extremely solidaristic women's shoe department. The saleswomen not only enforced the stint rigorously, but they also violated the dress code by wearing large hoop earrings, unilaterally extended their lunch hour from forty-five minutes to an hour, and resolutely ignored all storewide activities. Not even the pressure of high levels of unemployment deterred them.[81]

Just as male craftsmen bolstered their control of the shop floor with aspects of men's culture such as sports, so saleswomen used women's culture to defend their turf as skilled workers and to assert their presence as women. The "clerking sisterhood" integrated into the life of the selling floor the rituals of women's culture; employee newspapers reported scores of showers and parties to commemorate engagements, marriages, and births. In Boston, some of the rituals had a special twist: co-workers showered women who were about to be married with confetti.[82] Moreover, saleswomen made a place in the store for domestic skills as well as for job skills. They traded back and forth the household methods which enabled them to juggle home and job responsibilities more easily.[83] On a more prosaic note, they often brought in home-cooked food to share with co-workers and sometimes developed friendly rivalries over cooking skill.[84]

The store, like other women's workplaces, was indeed a place where women traded information about their beaux and learned the rituals of courtship and dating, as Leslie Woodcock Tentler has pointed out. Women met, dated, and married men from the store force, male relatives of their co-workers, and men whom they met across the counter; tales of romance were one of the staples of the *Echo*'s gossip columns. But saleswomen's work culture also supported and encouraged varieties of feminism. As Barbara Melosh has noted in regard to nurses, sex segregation on the job has a subversive potential.[85] In the all-female work group, women develop close bonds of solidarity and mutual respect, as well as an understanding of their skills and competence as workers. Far from being simply a source of victimization, sex segregation can provide a space where self-respect and initiative flourish. Female clerks made it clear to male employees that they were on hostile ground in a women's world; one beleaguered floorwalker got the message when he observed, "These imperious dames seemed to resent even the very presence of a 'mere male' in their sections."[86] Filene saleswomen used the *Echo*'s gossip columns to warn male employees to desist from behavior that we would today call sexual harassment.[87] Woman suffrage was a much discussed topic at Filene's, both in the departments and in the women's club. Apparently a majority of store women were eager for the vote and used store networks to recruit for the cause.[88] Saleswomen's work culture used women's culture in both a traditional and an oppositional way, expressing and sustaining saleswomen's complex lives as workers and women.

Selling skill was useful off the job as well as during working hours. At the same time as she learned to sell, the saleswoman also learned to consume. When she crossed to the other side of the counter, the saleswoman-consumer purchased with care and an insider's knowledge. Managers were well aware of the power of the saleswoman's example within the store and in her community, and eagerly solicited her to buy where she worked, adding the incentive of employee discounts. The canny clerk, however, used her consumer expertise outside the store as independently as she used her selling skills inside the store, withholding the unquestioning loyalty her boss so eagerly solicited.[89]

Consumption, like selling, had important collective aspects. Consumer lore circulated in female networks, with saleswomen as prime sources of advice and information, an expert elite in the world of consumption at the same time that they were the foot soldiers in the department-store army. Frequently, saleswomen used their position to further the interests of their own store. Pages of the *Echo* abound with stories of saleswomen who buttonholed friends on the subway or at social functions and regaled them with tales of the store's wares. One anecdote shows both clerks' impressive ability to improve an opportunity and the way in which their role could give them a sense of mastery in a difficult situation. A Filene saleswoman, languishing in a hospital, asserted her identity as something other than a patient when she noticed a departing fellow patient cramming her belongings into a tiny bag. She successfully persuaded her to go to Filene's to buy a larger one from a special selection the store had just received.[90]

All the same, saleswomen had no hesitation in criticizing the store to their friends; managers repeatedly warned them of the severe damage they did to the store in this way.[91] True to their sense of their skill, saleswomen became unofficial consumer authorities, but, equally true to their sense of independence, they used their authority both to encourage and to subvert their employers' interests. In the process they also became spokeswomen for consumer capitalism. Both sellers and buyers, workers and consumers, they found themselves in a curious in-between position straddling two worlds. Outside the store as well as inside it, saleswomen's selling skill as it was administered by their work culture had a powerful double potential.

The nature of saleswomen's work culture shows their notable ability to exploit a flexible and ambiguous situation. Because successful selling could not be carried on according to a rigid formula, clerks could liberally interpret employers' rules and instructions with relative impunity. For example, managers urged saleswomen to help one another, and they went overboard in forming solidary and subversive work groups. Management emphasized selling skill, and saleswomen made those skills the basis of a resourceful work culture. Management encouraged saleswomen to use their domestic knowledge and women's culture in the store, and they went a step farther in forming "the clerking sisterhood." Management encouraged clerks to become adept at social interaction, and they made huddling a major feature of the selling floor, using their social skills with their peers as well as with their customers. Management emphasized the importance of fashion, and saleswomen used their arguments to justify an insurrection against dress rules. As a study of saleswomen's work culture makes clear, however, clerks' ideas about themselves as women and as workers both expanded and exploited the possibilities offered by their work situation. Work culture is always interactive.

Aspects of saleswomen's work culture that governed their relations with customers are beyond the scope of this study, but they were similar to saleswomen's ways of dealing with their bosses. Class and gender were central dynamics, as saleswomen waited on women of, as a general rule, a higher class. Saleswomen's techniques for disciplining the unruly customer were similar to those used to hedge in bosses. Saleswomen withheld their knowledge about merchandise from customers, and often sullenly withheld the merchandise itself. Clerks had an enormous range of discretion in dealing with customers as well as in dealing with their employers: they could calculatingly fawn over or condescend to them; they could terrorize them or kill them with kindness; they could ignore them or overwhelm them with attention. A writer in the *Echo* neatly phrased the ambiguity—the customer was "our friend the enemy."[92]

In the final analysis, saleswomen's work culture must be seen not only in terms of its vibrant and resourceful control of the selling floor, but also in the longer historical perspective of the development of large-scale retailing in the twentieth century. Since World War II the managers of American department stores have, partly by choice and partly by necessity, worked to eliminate selling skill and to substitute a variety of arresting design and display techniques. The decline of central city shopping districts, mass suburbanization, the rise of discount chain stores, and the resolute unwillingness of saleswomen to perform as their bosses wished all converged to bring about the change. The productivity of the old-style department store fell below acceptable levels, and managers opted for a new method of selling which they had earlier scorned: self-service.

In the last thirty years the substance of a department-store saleswoman's job has been seriously degraded from what it was during the golden age of the department store. In one respect, this long view suggests that perhaps the very strength of clerks' work culture was also its weakness. Based in the department, relying on informal rules and procedures and on willing solidarity, it was not congenial to the formation of labor unions. Its potential to feed into collective action on an industrywide or even a storewide basis was limited, and male-dominated retailing unions in the period before 1940 did not capture saleswomen's imaginations. But this is not to blame the victim; saleswomen could hardly be expected to stand up alone against the massive social and economic forces weighing on the department-store industry and against the legendary resistance of white-collar occupations to unionization.

The study of saleswomen's work culture not only illuminates the lives of those legions of women who were a part of it, but also suggests ways of revising the history of women workers in particular and of life on the shop floor in general. At least one group of women workers, and doubtless others, developed a shop-floor culture that combined a keen sense of themselves as workers and as women. Both elements contained contradictions. As workers, saleswomen developed an appreciation of the skill of selling but an unwillingness to exercise that skill to the utmost. As women, they integrated both a traditional home-and-family outlook and a more critical feminist stance into their work culture. The long-standing assumption that women's consciousness is overwhelmingly the product of domestic imperatives oversimplifies the complicated dynamic of women workers' daily lives.

The tactics of saleswomen's work culture were those long familiar to male skilled workers, but now mobilized to protect interpersonal and consumer skills rather than artisanal or mechanical ones. Perhaps it is time to ask if these tactics are less specific to skilled workers than generalized among workers under conditions of capitalist production. All workers have a knowledge of the work they do that surpasses the prescriptions of their employers. Understanding the modes by which workers protect and expand that knowledge can help to fix the boundary between the struggle and the acquiescence that are part of every worker's life.

Finally, the work culture of saleswomen suggests that the society of mass consumption was not, and is not, a seamless web. The dictates of consumer capitalism had created and defined saleswomen's roles as workers at the same time as their female roles as consumers, but their patterns of independence and resistance made them less than perfect paragons of either role. Saleswomen played both sides of the counter: on the one hand they were the finest flower of a consumers' society, yet on the other hand they were expert at subverting it. As a group, they occupied a peculiar position straddling the realms of production and consumption: just as their image of themselves as workers undermined their absolute allegiance to a life of consumption, so too did their image of themselves as the high priestesses of consumption circumscribe their actions as workers. Perhaps the position of the saleswoman was not in fact unique after all, but rather an extreme case of the dilemma of all workers under consumer capitalism—driven by the social relations of the workplace to see themselves as members of the working class, cajoled by the rewards of mass consumption to see themselves as middle-class. We should not dismiss this as false consciousness, but rather try to understand its contradictions by studying the complex interactions between manager and worker, life on the job and life off the job.

## NOTES

My thanks to Edward Benson, Maurine Greenwald, and Barbara Melosh for helpful and supportive criticism. This study is part of my dissertation in progress at Boston University, "'A Great Theater': Saleswomen, Customers, and Managers in the American Department Store, 1890-1940."

1. See, for example, Barbara Melosh, *The Physician's Hand: Nurses and Nursing in the Twentieth Century*, forthcoming from Temple University Press in 1982; Patricia Cooper, "From Skilled Craft to Mass Production: Work and Work Culture of American Cigar Makers, 1900-1919" (Ph.D. dissertation, University of Maryland, 1981); and Katherine Stone, "The Origins of Job Structures in the Steel Industry," *Review of Radical Political Economics*, 6 (Summer 1974), 113-73.

2. Barbara Melosh and I jointly wrote this paragraph. It grows out of a long collaboration between us.

3. An example of this tendency is Harry Braverman, *Labor and Monopoly Capital: The Degradation of Work in the Twentieth Century* (New York: Monthly Review Press, 1974).

4. *Wage-Earning Women: Industrial Work and Family Life in the United States, 1900-1930* (New York: Oxford University Press, 1979), pp. 60-71.

5. Tentler, *Wage-Earning Women*, p. 78; U.S. Commissioner of Labor, Eleventh Special Report, *Regulation and Restriction of Output* (Washington, D.C.: GPO, 1904); Stanley B. Mathewson, *Restriction of Output among Unorganized Workers* (1931; reprint ed., Carbondale: Southern Illinois University Press, 1969), pp. 20-21.

6. Ken Kusterer ably argues this point in *Know-How on the Job: The Important Working Knowledge of "Unskilled" Workers* (Boulder, Colo.: Westview Press, 1978).

7. The theses were written by graduate students in retailing at Simmons College and the University of Pittsburgh during the 1920s and 1930s. The major human relations study, a rich source indeed, is George F. F. Lombard, *Behavior in a Selling Group: A Case Study of Interpersonal Relations in a Department Store* (Boston: Harvard University Graduate School of Business Administration, 1955). The thesis on which the book is based contains additional detail: Lombard, "Executive Policies and Employee Satisfactions: A Study of a Small Department in a Large Metropolitan Store" (D.C.Sc. thesis, Harvard University, 1941). Both grow out of shop-floor research done in Macy's children's wear department in 1940.

8. On Filene's, see Mary LaDame, *The Filene Store: A Study of Employes' Relation to Management in a Retail Store* (New York: Russell Sage Foundation, 1930).

9. The journals include *Bulletin of the National Retail Dry Goods Association*; *Dry Goods Economist*, and its successor *Department Store Economist*; *Journal of Retailing*; and *System* and its successors, particularly *Business Week*. Trade periodicals are more useful than individual store histories, which tend to be less frank and shamelessly celebratory of the stores' founders. I use the term department store to include both "classic" department stores—which carry home furnishings as well as clothing—and large specialty stores—which focus on clothing and accessories. The narrower definition, that of the Census Bureau, is useful for economic and financial analyses, but the distinction between department and specialty stores disappears when ideology and personnel policies are under discussion. Managers of specialty stores such as Filene's and Lord & Taylor were central figures in department-store management circles, and in general the day-to-day management of such stores proceeded along the same lines as that of department stores.

10. Elizabeth Bott, *Family and Social Network: Roles, Norms, and External Relationships in Ordinary Urban Families*, 2d ed. (New York: Free Press, 1971); Michele Zimbalist Rosaldo and Louise Lamphere, eds., *Woman, Culture, and Society* (Stanford, Calif.: Stanford University Press, 1974).

11. James Spradley and Brenda Mann, *Cocktail Waitress: Women's Work in a Man's World* (New York: John Wiley and Sons, 1975); Ann Bookman, "The Process of Political Socialization among Women and Immigrant Workers: A Case Study of Unionization in the Electronics Industry" (Ph.D. dissertation, Harvard University, 1977); and Nina Shapiro-Perl's dissertation in progress on class and consciousness among women jewelry workers (University of Connecticut).

12. David Montgomery, "Workers' Control of Machine Production in the 19th Century," *Labor History*, 17 (1976), 491-92, reprinted in *Workers' Control in America: Studies in the History of Work, Technology, and Labor Struggles* (Cambridge: Cambridge University Press, 1979).

13. Women imbibed the nineteenth-century idea of the labor theory of value with its assertion of the dignity and worth of labor as the source of value, but were excluded by definition from the traditions of the skilled male crafts and from the republican vision of independent citizenship. For a discussion of the labor theory of value, see Alan Dawley and Paul Faler, "Working-Class Culture and Politics in the Industrial Revolution, 1820-1890," *Journal of Social History*, 9 (Winter 1976), 466-80.

14. Statistics on women's occupations may be found in Rosalyn Baxandall, Linda Gordon, and Susan Reverby, eds., *America's Working Women: A Documentary History—1600 to the Present* (New York: Vintage Books, 1976), pp. 406-7. The quoted phrase comes from Helen Campbell, *Prisoners of Poverty. Women Wage-Workers, Their Trades, and Their Lives* (1887; reprint ed., Westport, Conn.: Greenwood Press, 1970), p. 182.

15. "Social Statistics of Workingwomen," *Massachusetts Labor Bulletin*, 18 (May 1901), 46-48; Mary E. Trueblood, "Housework versus Shop and Factories," *The Independent*, 54 (Nov. 13, 1902), 2691-93.

16. "The Objections to Domestic Service," *Massachusetts Labor Bulletin*, 8 (Oct. 1898), 27-29.

17. Edward A. Filene, "The Betterment of the Conditions of Working Women," *Annals of the American Academy*, 27 (1906), 621.

18. Editor's Note to William Hard and Rheta Childe Dorr, "The Woman's Invasion," *Everybody's Magazine*, 20 (Jan. 1909), 73.

19. I discuss the relation of saleswomen's wages to those of other working women at length in chapter four of my dissertation.

20. "Women in $6,000 to $30,000 Jobs," *American Magazine*, 88 (July 1919), 60-61, 131-32; "They Put Martha in the Kitchenware, and Left Her—So Someone Else Got Her," *Dry Goods Economist*, 74 (Jan. 3, 1920), 19-20. Questionnaires given to women in department stores, mostly in executive positions, by the Bureau for Vocational Information in the early 1920s also confirm this fact. See the completed questionnaires in the papers of the Bureau of Vocational Information at Schlesinger Library, Radcliffe College.

21. *The Echo*, 20 (July 14, 1922).

22. "Mary Used Her Head, All Right; But Jean Used Her Heart," *Dry Goods Economist*, 74 (Aug. 21, 1920), 42.

23. Thomas J. Cottle, *Hidden Survivors: Portraits of Poor Jews in America* (Englewood Cliffs: Prentice-Hall, 1980), p. 174. I am indebted to Sonya Michel for calling my attention to this account.

24. Hard and Dorr, "Woman's Invasion," p. 77; see also Mary Rankin Cranston, "The Girl behind the Counter," *World To-Day*, 10 (1906), 273.

25. Gertrude H. Sykes, "Employment Policy and Practise Which Takes Advantage of Experience Rating," *National Retail Dry Goods Association Management Conference Proceedings . . . May 1939* (New York, 1939), p. 114. See also "Help in Departmentizing," *Dry Goods Economist*, 65 (July 8, 1911), 27-28; *The Echo*, 13 (Mar. 16, 1917). I will hereafter refer to the National Retail Dry Goods Association as the NRDGA.

26. "Mr. Newmaier Speaks His Piece about Making First Floor Departments Pay," *Dry Goods Economist*, 78 (May 10, 1924), 15; Anna May Johnston, "An Analysis of a Linen Department in a Department Store" (M.A. thesis, University of Pittsburgh, 1932), p. 83; Alice Hughes, "A Customer's Idea of Good Store Service," *Bulletin of the NRDGA*, 17 (Feb. 1935), 75, 179; Margaret Durand, "A Study of a Millinery Department (with Special Emphasis on Personnel and Sales Promotion Factors)" (M.Sc. thesis, Simmons College, 1937), p. 16.

27. William E. Davidson, "Department Store Organization . . . History and Trends," *Department Store Economist*, 24 (Jan. 1961), 69. Men as well as women sold in department stores, but women made up a growing majority of sales staffs after about 1900. Salesmen had their work culture as well, and it overlapped with saleswomen's at some points, but it is not my concern here. All of my examples refer to women's attitudes and behavior. I have not fully investigated salesmen's work culture, but my impression is that their work groups were less solidaristic than women's.

28. Typical references to the importance of skilled selling are "The Efficiency Way in a Western Store," *The Survey*, 31 (Oct. 18, 1913), 65-66 and Edward A. Filene, *Next Steps Forward in Retailing* (Boston: Edward A. Filene, 1937), p. 127.

29. *The Echo*, 13 (Dec. 21, 1917); Personnel Group of the NRDGA, *Specialized Training for Salespeople* (New York, 1930), p. 16; *Training Contingents* (New York, 1931), pp. 50-54; and *The World of Fashion* (New York, 1931), I, 9-45; "Expose Employees to Knowledge," *Department Store Economist*, 1 (Aug. 10, 1938), 35.

30. Rheta Childe Dorr, *What Eight Million Women Want* (Boston: Small, Maynard, & Co., 1910), pp. 115-16.

31. "A Creed," *Dry Goods Economist*, 68 (Jan. 31, 1914), 69; G. W. Stoddard, "Giving a Store Home Surroundings," *System*, 15 (June 1909), 666.

32. "Martha in Kitchenware," p. 19.

33. *Rich Bits*, May 1938, p. 6; quoted in Henry Givens Baker, *Rich's of Atlanta: The Story of a Store since 1867* (Atlanta: University of Georgia Press, 1953), p. 310.

34. David Ovens, "Management's Job in Better Selling," *Bulletin of the NRDGA*, 23 (Feb. 1941), 26.

35. NRDGA, Store Management Group, *Mid-Year Convention Proceedings* (New York, 1942), p. 139.

36. *The Echo*, 10 (Dec. 7, 1912, and Apr. 30, 1913), 14 (Jan. 11, 1918), 22 (Feb. 6, 1925), 24 (Feb. 18, 1927).

37. Lauren Gilfillan, "Weary Feet," *Forum*, 90 (1933), 208.

38. NRDGA, Store Managers' Division, *Convention Proceedings* (New York, 1927), p. 115. The speaker was Samuel Reyburn.

39. *The Echo*, 26 (Mar. 30, 1928); Susan Katherine Manning, "An Analysis of a Merchandising Department (Foundation Garments) with Organized Material for a Departmental Training Program: A Study Made in Nine Pittsburgh Stores" (M.A. thesis, University of Pittsburgh, 1930), p. 26.

40. *The Echo*, 1 (Dec. 1902).

41. *The Echo*, 10 (Feb. 26, 1913). See also Jan. 29, Feb. 12, and Feb. 19, 1913.

42. The quoted phrases are from *The Echo*, 29 (June 27 and July 18, 1930); see also July 11, Sept. 26, and Oct. 3, 1930, and Mar. 27, 1931.

43. *Wage-Earning Women in Stores and Factories*, vol. 5 of *Report on Condition of Woman and Child Wage-Earners in the United States* (Washington, D.C.: GPO, 1910), pp. 109, 129.

44. NRDGA, *Joint Management Proceedings, 1940* (New York, 1940), p. 17.

45. "'Clinic' Prescribes Treatment for Ailments of Employee Morale," *Bulletin of the NRDGA*, 21 (Feb. 1939), 41, 122.

46. *The Echo*, 17 (Mar. 11, 1921).

47. *The Echo*, 14 (July 19, 1918).

48. *The Echo*, 13 (Nov. 30, 1917).

49. *The Echo*, 1 (May 1903).

50. *The Echo*, 13 (June 3, 1915), 15 (Sept. 18, 1919).

51. *The Echo*, 9 (Mar. 1912).

52. *The Echo*, 11 (June 26, 1913). References to huddling abound in all varieties of retailing literature. See, for example, "Hints for December," *Dry Goods Economist*, 64 (Dec. 4, 1909), 43; "Harmony Essential," *Dry Goods Economist*, 66 (Aug. 3, 1912), 39; "What It Means to Be a Department-Store Girl—As Told by the Girl Herself," *Ladies' Home Journal*, 30 (June 1913), 8; Rowena Elizabeth Hoisington, "Analysis of a Hosiery Department" (M.Sc. thesis, Simmons College, 1931), p. 107; Florence L. Luman, "An Analysis of the China and Glassware Department in a Department Store" (M.A. thesis, University of Pittsburgh, 1932), p. 84.

53. "What Would *YOU* Do with the Crepe Hanger?" *Dry Goods Economist*, 76 (Mar. 4, 1922), 37; "Here Is the Clam—What Would *YOU* Do?" *Dry Goods Economist*, 76 (Apr. 1, 1922), 119; W. H. Leffingwell, "Sizing up Customers from behind the Counter," *American Magazine*, 94 (July 1922), 150.

54. Mary Alden Hopkins, "The Girls behind the Counter," *Collier's*, 48 (Mar. 16, 1912), 17.

55. Sue Ainslie Clark and Edith Wyatt, *Making Both Ends Meet: The Income and Outlay of New York Working Girls* (New York: Macmillan, 1911), pp. 29-34; Rheta Childe Dorr, "Christmas behind the Counter," *The Independent*, 63 (Dec. 5, 1907), 1346-47.

56. *The Echo*, 15 (Sept. 18, 1919); see also 25 (May 6, 1927).

57. Martha Elliott, "The Buyer's Share in Training," *Bulletin of the NRDGA*, 16 (July 1934), 39.

58. The quotation is from Lawrence Bitner, cited in *Joint Management Proceedings, NRDGA* (New York, 1934), p. 78.

59. Mildred Farquhar, "An Analysis of a Toy Department in a Department Store" (M.A. thesis, University of Pittsburgh, 1933), p. 14.

60. Elizabeth Nickolls, "Inquiry into Departmental Methods of a Department Store for the Purpose of Making Constructive Criticism" (M.Sc. thesis, Simmons College, 1929), pp. 73-74.

61. Frances R. Donovan, *The Saleslady* (Chicago: University of Chicago

Press, 1929), pp. 76-77. The whole discussion of the game is on pp. 74-78.

62. *The Echo*, 1 (July 1903).

63. "Making Good on the Sales Job," *Dry Goods Economist*, 81 (May 7, 1927), 16. See also Edward Mott Woolley, "A Short Cut to Salvation," *McClure's Magazine*, 40 (Dec. 1912), 231; "Study of a Ribbon Department," *Bulletin of the NRDGA*, 9 (Oct. 1927), 524; Donovan, *Saleslady*, p. 48; Anne Bezanson and Miriam Hussey, *Wage Methods and Selling Costs: Compensation of Sales Clerks in Four Major Departments in 31 Stores* (Philadelphia: University of Pennsylvania Press, 1930), passim; Mathewson, *Restriction of Output*, pp. 20-21; Ruth Farquhar, "The Analysis of a Drapery Department in a Department Store" (M.A. thesis, University of Pittsburgh, 1932), p. 87; Charlotte Anne Feazel, "An Analysis of a Women's Shoe Department in a Department Store" (M.A. thesis, University of Pittsburgh, 1933), p. 51; Katherine Barbara Fetterman, "An Analysis of a House Dress Department in a Department Store" (M.A. thesis, University of Pittsburgh, 1933), pp. 55, 60; Georgia Wittich, "Constructive Use of the Shopping Report," *Joint Management Proceedings, NRDGA* (New York, 1934), pp. 14-20; Charlotte Collins, "A Study of the Oxford Shop" (M.Sc. thesis, Simmons College, 1938), p. 73; Lombard, *Behavior in a Selling Group*, pp. 147-67.

64. Lombard, *Behavior in a Selling Group*, pp. 147-67.

65. *The Echo*, 16 (Jan. 16 and Apr. 16, 1920), 20 (May 26, 1922), 24 (Jan. 21 and Feb. 25, 1927).

66. Compare, for example, Annie Marion McLean, "Two Weeks in Department Stores," *American Journal of Sociology*, 4 (May 1899), 721-41, and Leah Morton [Elizabeth Gertrude Stern], *I Am a Woman—And a Jew* (1926; reprint ed., New York: Arno Press, 1969), pp. 152-57, with accounts of later initiations.

67. Lombard, "Executive Policies," pp. 318-28.

68. "Putting a Punch into the Departments," *Dry Goods Economist*, 69 (May 8, 1915), 33; Imogene McIlvain, "Merchandise Training for Contingents" (M.Sc. thesis, Simmons College, 1927), pp. 7-10; Irene Winifred Gallagher, "An Analysis of a China and Glassware Department" (M.Sc. thesis, Simmons College, 1929), p. 75; Alice Paul Fehr, "An Analysis of a Merchandise Department (Electrical Appliances) with Organized Material for a Training Program" (M.A. thesis, University of Pittsburgh, 1931), pp. 17-18; Emma Wilson Smith, "An Analysis of a Sportswear Department in a Department Store" (M.A. thesis, University of Pittsburgh, 1935), p. 48; Helen Johnson, "The Employment and Subsequent Handling of Extra Salespeople" (M.Sc. thesis, Simmons College, 1939), pp. 37-38.

69. Lombard, "Executive Policies," p. 327.

70. This is one of Lombard's central theses.

71. *The Echo*, 24 (July 9, 1926), 25 (May 6, 1927); Julia Campbell, "An Analysis of a Girls' Wear Department in a Department Store" (M.A. thesis, University of Pittsburgh, 1933), p. 53.

72. *The Echo*, 4 (Mar. 1907).

73. *The Echo*, 2 (Apr. and Oct. 1904), 5 (May 1907).

74. *The Echo*, 24 (Apr. 30, 1926). Broad handled the special hairnet sale each year; see 21 (Feb. 15, 1924), 23 (June 12, 1925).

75. "A Valuable Asset," *Dry Goods Economist*, 71 (Oct. 6, 1917), 14.

76. "Vocational Education Survey of Richmond, Virginia, August, 1915," whole number 162, misc. series number 7, *Bulletin of the United States Bureau of Labor Statistics* (Washington, D.C.: GPO, 1916), p. 254; Virginia Gerding, "A Study of a Women's and Misses' Coat and Suit Department (with Special Emphasis on Personnel and Sales Promotion Factors)" (M.Sc. thesis, Simmons College, 1937), p. 47; Annette M. Law, "True-to-Life-Teaching," *Department Store Economist*, 3 (Feb. 25, 1940), 2, 10.

77. *The Echo*, 30 (Aug. 7, 1931).

78. *The Echo*, 13 (Mar. 23, 1917), 15 (Feb. 21 and May 23, 1919).

79. Bezanson and Hussey, *Wage Methods and Selling Costs*, pp. 7-14, 345-49.

80. "Putting a Punch," pp. 33-34; "What Happened to Aggressive Floorman," *Dry Goods Economist*, 69 (May 22, 1915), 31, 34.

81. Feazel, "Women's Shoe Department," pp. 47-57.

82. Notices of these social occasions appear in virtually every issue of *The Echo* as well as in the Jordan Marsh employee newspaper, variously titled *The Fellow Worker, Store Topics*, and *The Tally*. Confetti-throwing is mentioned, for example, in *The Echo*, 6 (Apr. 1909) and 26 (Aug. 12, 1927). The phrase, "the clerking sisterhood," is from Zelie Leigh, "Shopping Round," *Atlantic Monthly*, 138 (Aug. 1926), 205.

83. Morton [Stern], *I Am a Woman*, pp. 156-57.

84. *The Echo*, 15 (Feb. 14, 1919), 26 (Mar. 30, 1928).

85. "Doctors, Patients, and 'Big Nurse': Work and Gender in Post-War Hospitals," forthcoming in an anthology on the history of nursing from Teachers' College Press, 1982.

86. "Putting a Punch," p. 33.

87. *The Echo*, 15 (Oct. 24, 1919).

88. *The Echo*, 1912-19, passim. Some examples of the interest in suffrage: a third-floor department took a suffrage play on tour (11 [June 4, 1913]); a notice urged attendance at a suffrage meeting (12 [Dec. 24, 1914]), a suffrage poem appeared (12 [Jan. 28, 1915]); straw votes in several departments showed a majority favoring suffrage (13 [Oct. 28, 1915]). Perhaps most interesting of all was a suffragist's link of the vote to women's rights within the store; she asserted that women should be allowed to vote just as men did outside the store, and to wear what clothes they pleased just as men could inside the store (14 [Dec. 6, 1918]).

89. *The Echo*, 13 (July 29, 1915), 29 (Jan. 30, 1931); "Employees' Sales," *Dry Goods Economist*, 63 (Dec. 5, 1908), 17; *Joint Management Proceedings, NRDGA* (New York, 1934), pp. 77-80.

90. *The Echo*, 27 (Mar. 22, 1929); see also 24 (Feb. 11, 1927).

91. *The Echo*, 13 (Sept. 21, 1916).

92. *The Echo*, 3 (Feb. 1906).

# Dress Rehearsal for the New Deal: Shop-Floor Insurgents, Political Elites, and Industrial Democracy in the Amalgamated Clothing Workers

STEVE FRASER

## Dress Rehearsal for the New Deal

During the presidential campaign of 1944, the Republican party attempted to discredit its opponent by suggesting the Democratic party had become the political hostage of the CIO. The evidence amounted to a rumor that President Roosevelt had given Sidney Hillman, chairman of the CIO-PAC, veto power over the choice of Roosevelt's vice-presidential running mate when he instructed party leaders to "clear it with Sidney."

The charge, while greatly exaggerated, was not entirely groundless, and highlighted a fundamental change in the social chemistry of the nation's political economy. Over the preceding ten years the growth of mass industrial unionism and the apparatus of the Keynesian welfare state had together recast the institutional structure of American industry and politics. No man was more closely identified with that transformation than Sidney Hillman. Indeed, long before the Great Depression, Hillman, along with the union he founded and led, the ACW (Amalgamated Clothing Workers of America), prefigured the essential ideological assumptions, programmatic reforms, and political realignments characteristic of the New Deal. On the eve of the depression, the Amalgamated was already a leading exponent of social-welfare liberalism, committed to a policy of state-managed capitalism and to the distributive reforms suggested by Keynesian monetary and fiscal theory. Moreover, it had established working relationships with that broader network of liberal businessmen, scientific management technocrats, lawyers, economists, and social workers, and Progressive political reformers which functioned as a kind of shadow government until it actually assumed power during the "second" New Deal. The formative experience of the Amalgamated, lasting from 1910 through the decade of the 1920s, was thus a kind of dress rehearsal for the historic drama of the 1930s. Examining that experience can help illuminate the "crisis of the old order" that gave rise to a new system of industrial labor relations, a system predicated on the restructuring of working-class behavior and culture and on decisively enlarging the terrain of state authority.

The ACW represented one of the earliest successful efforts to organize immigrant workers along quasi-industrial lines. In so doing, it accomplished a major innovation in the structure of collective bargaining by introducing a system of impartial arbitration as a regular and central feature of labor relations in the men's clothing industry. In the arena of social reform its initiatives included a system of unemployment insurance, the construction of low-cost cooperative housing, and successful ventures in labor banking. The ACW managed to use the conventional practices of collective bargaining as a means to achieve broader social goals through political and economic action. It was the best and most durable representative of the "new unionism," frequently singled out by contemporary observers of the labor movement for its sense of industrial and social responsibility and its pathbreaking achievements in the field of social welfare.

What was distinctly new about the new unionism, aside from its specific innovations in the conduct of labor relations and in the arena of social welfare, was the remarkable process of its own creation. It emerged at the dawn of the age of mass consumption and mass production, when the operating assumptions and day-to-day functioning of laissez-faire capitalism had begun to cause serious anxiety, not only among radical intellectuals and social reformers, but among industrial and political elites as well. While nearly every established social and economic relationship was the subject of concern, certain critical issues directly affected the evolution of the new unionism.

The first had to do with the erosion of managerial authority on the shop floor. The second involved a crisis of the free market, as unrestricted competition undermined the conditions of industrial and commercial stability. A third, closely related matter of growing concern was the structural flaws in the economy, in particular its uneven distribution of the national income, which threatened to abort the full flowering of a mass consumption society. Together, these problems of work, industry, and economy inevitably raised a fourth, more strictly political question about the future of liberal democracy: How was it possible to restore managerial authority, regulate the marketplace, and redistribute

wealth while preserving the formal institutional framework of a democratic polity. In a word, it was a crisis of legitimacy, of authority and
consent to authority.

There was no shortage of answers to these questions as the history of
the Progressive and more radical political movements makes clear. The
new unionism was one such answer, a partial one to be sure, but of
broad significance nonetheless. During a period in which, especially
after the war, it became increasingly difficult to exercise reform initiatives on a national scale, the ACW particularly functioned as a laboratory of social experimentation. In that laboratory, union, industrial,
and political elites worked out a concert of interest and ideology which
helped to civilize and modernize an industry notoriously uncivilized
and premodern. In the process of doing so they came to appreciate the
potential advantages for the economy as a whole of industrial planning, of carefully regulated conditions of labor, and of state intervention to insure the first two were carried out. Moreover, they discovered
that to install the new system of commercial and social cooperation,
which they enthusiastically dubbed "industrial democracy," they had
first to reorient the behavior of manufacturers and workers whose
political and cultural inclinations predisposed them to resist the new
order. For their part, immigrant garment workers did more than merely
resist, for on some counts elite innovations reinforced as well as transformed the customary rights and prerogatives of workers on the shop
floor and in other instances industrial democracy proved flexible
enough to incorporate practices not included in the original strategic
blueprints. This essay is meant to sketch this process of reform and
resistance, to interpret the union as its institutionalized expression, and
to suggest its implications for the recasting of the American political
economy under the auspices of the New Deal and the CIO.[1]

## Unionism and the Quest for Stability

Most analysts have emphasized that the men's clothing industry, like
the rest of the needle trades, was a spawning ground for a protean mass
of small businesses, employing primitive technologies and chronically
engaged in mortal competition. Living always on the edge of commercial oblivion, these petty manufacturers naturally resisted the intrusion of a unionism that threatened to eliminate the principal basis
of competitive survival—the exploitation of sweated labor. Honoring
no standards either of production or of labor, these marginal entrepreneurs maintained relations with their workers which were personal
and entirely arbitrary, and which rested on archaic structures of domination and docility.

Accurate as far as it goes, such a description does not go far enough. The industry also contained large modern factories, recognizably of the twentieth century in their technological complexity and in the extent of their division of labor. Some were committed to the principles of scientific management. Their relationship to the mass market and their attitudes toward unionization were often distinctly different from those of the petty manufacturer. Within one industry, two business cultures existed in uneasy symbiosis, mutually dependent and mutually antagonistic. This structural duality was crucial to the shifting balance of power within the industry as elite manufacturers would sometimes collaborate with the union in the interests of disciplining or eliminating their smaller competitive rivals, while petty contractors, incapable of self-organization, were alternately led by better-organized workers or manufacturers but proved to be unreliable allies of either.

Contracting shops, which usually specialized in the making up of pants, coats, and vests that had been designed and cut in "inside shops," were microscopic in size, especially in New York, where at least 78 percent of all firms in 1913 employed five or fewer workers. Two-thirds of all men's clothing workers worked in shops the value of whose annual output amounted to less than $100,000.[2]

The amount of capital required to enter the industry was remarkably low. Ambitious cutters or salesmen could set themselves up in business merely by renting a small loft and cutting table, if necessary hiring a cutter, and shipping out the cut-up garments to contractors whose level of capitalization might be no greater than their own. Such concerns lasted a year or two or as long as their desperate hunger for business did not lead them to sell at prices below the level of mere survival.[3]

While larger manufacturers might resent the competition of these petty producers, they nevertheless depended on the specialized contractors to relieve them from burdensome overhead expenses, unpredictable fluctuations in costs, and the anxieties of supervising a sometimes intractable labor force. Thus the singular advantage of the contracting system was its plasticity, but it was otherwise grossly inefficient. Work was poorly supervised, varied widely in quality, and contractor shops were notoriously unclean, lacked sufficient light and air, and constituted a positive menace to workers and consumers alike.[4]

New York, Philadelphia, and Boston especially were breeding grounds for small-scale manufacturers and for worker-entrepreneurs, precariously established as contractors and subcontractors, who from season to season were as likely to be the employers of others as they were to be working for someone else. Often enough they were proletarians by day, petty capitalists by night. To be sure, there were as well large inside factories in these markets, but they were so overwhelmed by their lilliputian rivals that they could exercise little or at best sporadic control over prices in the labor and commodity markets.[5]

However, the balance of industrial power in the other three major markets, Rochester, Chicago, and Baltimore, was distributed quite differently. There, large inside factories, employing hundreds or even thousands of workers and the most sophisticated technologies in the cutting and pressing departments, produced standardized items for the medium and high-priced end of the market. Average capital investment was greatest in these markets, as was the extent of mechanization, labor segmentation, and the volume of production. These larger producers also enjoyed some semblance of market control through formal or informal ties to mass retailers or by acquiring their own retail outlets.

These modern concerns comprised a tiny elite. But while small in number, they increasingly voiced their concern over the chronic state of chaos and crisis imparted to the industry by the anarchic behavior of the mass of petty producers and worker-entrepreneurs. Elite manufacturers maintained a scale of operations, a level of capital investment, and rationalized systems of management that demanded a continuity and stability in the production process that would permit reasonable cost estimates, advance planning, and some modicum of control over the oscillations of the market. More established manufacturers favored standardizing wages, hours, and working conditions throughout the industry in order to put a floor under competition.

It is too often assumed that stability is synonymous with social inertia, that it precludes change. As often as not, however, stability requires change. Such was the case in the men's clothing industry, where leading enterprises came to see the advantages of union-directed labor stability. Of all the imponderable uncertainties of garment manufacturing, labor costs and supervision were the most unpredictable and disturbing. Only a union, exercising constant surveillance over the industry's labor markets and shop-floor procedures, could curb its natural tendency to mutually destructive competition. Even in the larger plants, direction of the shop floor depended on antiquated systems of personalized control at variance with the more rationalized methods adopted in other phases of the business. Organized around the uncontrolled authority of departmental foremen, life in the shop resembled nothing so much as a state of permanent civil war, with the hostile if intimidated ranks of abused workers massed on one side, the arsenal of the foremen's arbitrary tyrannies on the other. Inside the factory and outside in the market place, pressures accumulated. [6]

Thus it was that in the midst of the great Chicago clothing strike of 1910, the industry's premier firm, Hart, Schaffner, and Marx, decided to seek a settlement that would, at least in part, recognize its workers' grievances and establish procedures for resolving them. Management sensed that its own as well as the industry's future depended on developing a lawful, constitutional framework of labor relations. Although they were initially alone in this position, the HSM perspective was gradually adopted by many elite firms during the ensuing decade.

The profits of HSM shrank in 1911-12 thanks to the strike of the previous year. But the partners never regretted their decision to recognize the union. Testifying before the Commission on Industrial Relations in 1914, Joseph Schaffner reported: "In our own business, employing thousands of persons, some of them newly arrived immigrants, many of them in opposition to the wage system and hostile to employers as a class, we have observed astonishing changes in their attitudes during the four years under the influence of our labor agreement."[7]

This astonishing transformation in attitudes was observed elsewhere. Meyer Jacobstein, labor manager for a large Rochester firm, reported to a Taylor Society conference in 1920 that among the chief advantages of the industry's newly established relations with the ACW was the development of a "social conscience" and "self-imposed discipline" among the workers, which in some cases had converted former radicals to a practical sense of the industry's needs. This union-inspired self-restraint had allowed for the introduction of improved technology, new and better methods of production, mutually agreed upon standards of production, and, most important of all, a drastic reduction in labor turnover and work stoppages. All in all, Jacobstein concluded, this new system of industrial democracy made for greater efficiency in the long run "than that type of Prussian discipline which is purely mechanical and superimposed by officials vested with superior authority."[8]

The principal enterprises in Baltimore and Chicago were equally appreciative of the union's superior ability to generate production. In 1921, the National Industrial Conference Board summed up the experience of all those clothing manufacturers producing under union agreements and concluded that "the decrease in the number of shop strikes . . . has bettered output through reduction in lost time and avoidance of shop disorganization." Since sudden work stoppages, enormous labor turnover, and deliberate production slowdowns were chronic in the pre-union era, the board's assessment indicated no mean accomplishment.[9]

Motivations prompting leading manufacturers to assimilate the union into their own enterprises also encouraged them to seek ways of making it a legitimate institution throughout the industry. As large inside factories grew in importance, regional markets lost their autonomy and became intercompetitive so that wage levels and conditions of labor became matters of national concern. The pressure to regulate labor relations nationally culminated in the 1919 decision by the National Association of Clothiers to establish a separate National Industrial Federation of Clothing Manufacturers whose purpose was "to stabilize wages, hours, and standards of efficiency and all conditions of employment" in conjunction with the ACW. The chaotic New York market continued to undermine all attempts at coordination, however, and the federation died on the vine.

Despite the federation's short life, it had crystalized the elite's sanguine expectations for a national collaboration with the ACW. George Bell, impartial chairman for the New York market, hoped that a conference of labor managers and union officials would lead to "some formal or informal plan for standardizing and stabilizing not only wages but the entire labor question in all the labor markets." Eventually, he hoped to see a "National Joint Council, representing manufacturers and workers . . . created along lines similar to the Whitley Councils in England."[10]

Outside the precincts of the industry itself there were others who shared Bell's historic hopes. For years they nurtured the ACW experiment not only because it promised to civilize the clothing industry, but for what it portended for the future of industrial labor relations and the political economy of post-laissez-faire capitalism.

### *Efficiency and the Ideology of "Consent"*

The internal structural and political dynamics of the industry were insufficient by themselves to generate a durable institutional edifice of collective bargaining. Indeed, the same centrifugal and destabilizing forces that caused some to turn to unionism for relief also made unionizing acutely difficult to accomplish without help from sources outside industry. The development of needle-trades unionism everywhere called for the contributions of interested businessmen, social workers and social engineers, political reformers, and agencies of the state.

To begin with, mass retailers selling large volumes of ready-to-wear men's clothing had an obvious stake in assuring a reliable flow of goods at predictable prices. Time and again they used their considerable influence to convince recalcitrant manufacturers to settle with the ACW. Perhaps the most spectacular instance of this organization *ab extra* was the nearly single-handed unionization of the Rochester market in 1918 by Louis Kirstein. Kirstein managed the Filene retailing empire, headquartered in Boston, and together with the Filene brothers maintained close relations with Sidney Hillman. Drawing upon his substantial commercial clout, Kirstein induced all the major Rochester manufacturers, with one exception, to enter a general agreement with the ACW, and did so at a time when the union had been generally unsuccessful in penetrating the ranks of the city's clothing workers.[11]

It would be shortsighted, however, to assume that manufacturers responded to such pressure, or that men like Filene or Kirstein exerted it to begin with, strictly for reasons of narrowly calculated self-interest. The manufacturing elite, often of German or East European Jewish extraction, was anxious to win the social esteem accorded other established elements of the Jewish community. It was therefore sensitive to the secularized religious aspirations and social conscience of reform Judaism, and to wider currents of Progressive social pleading.

For their part, men like the Filenes developed a pronounced commitment to democratizing the workplace and the economy, at least after a fashion. They were amenable to the idea of planning and open to the emerging ideology of underconsumption and industrial democracy with its multiple objectives of sustained mass purchasing power and expanded and rationalized production under joint union-management auspices. They experimented with methods of redeploying managerial authority, sometimes through coercion but more often through mechanisms of voluntary compliance. Not surprisingly, they were enmeshed in a wider network of relationships which included not only prominent political figures in the Progressive movement, men like Louis Brandeis, Felix Frankfurter, and Newton Baker, but also social liberals from within the more narrowly circumscribed circles of scientific management and industrial labor relations.[12]

The molding of the ACW was part of a more general wartime proliferation of collective bargaining arrangements sanctioned by a government worried about labor shortages, escalating rates of labor turnover, and the rising tide of labor unrest and strikes. This period of government-authorized collective bargaining was the most decisive phase of the ACW's development, as membership increased from 48,000 in 1916 to 138,000 in mid-1919.[13]

To begin with, the war generated an extraordinary demand for military clothing, thereby improving the bargaining leverage of the garment workers. Moreover, lucrative government contracts together with a tight labor market made even the most stubborn manufacturers vulnerable to the proddings of the union. The union's leadership, for its part, was willing to put its own moral authority at risk by disciplining those portions of the membership who sought to take undue advantage by inducing employers to bid against each other for the diminished supply of skilled labor. In the end, however, it was the visible hand of the government that proved decisive.

A series of meetings between Florence Kelley, secretary of the National Consumers League, Hillman, and Walter Lippmann and Felix Frankfurter, then both working for the War Department, and the secretary of war, Newton Baker, defined the parameters of government intervention. Under Baker's authority, the government established a Board of Control of Labor Standards, which announced its intention to eliminate child labor, homework, and unsanitary facilities, and to establish the eight-hour day/forty-eight-hour week as a national standard while recognizing the legitimate status of the union. The ACW quickly made use of the board's investigative and mediating powers to embarrass manufacturers who resisted unionization, and trusted the board's administrators, who were themselves committed to the industrial and social virtues of independent unionism, to withdraw contracts from firms which remained adamant.[14]

Although the union was not officially represented on the board, it was regularly consulted on labor as well as on more general matters of production. Hillman collaborated with board personnel, men like Kirstein, labor-relations expert William Z. Ripley, and ex-socialist N. I. Stone, in an effort to upgrade and standardize conditions throughout the industry and to establish scientifically-arrived-at piece rates. Hillman announced the union's commitment to war production even if it meant temporary suspension of union rules on overtime and Sunday work, and denied charges that the ACW was pacifist or engaging in deliberate slowdowns. When slowdowns or strikes did occur, the leadership went out of its way to discipline offending workers, ordering strikers to return and sometimes fining or firing insubordinate members of the rank and file, while submitting their grievances to the board.[15]

As the war drew to a close, at the initiative of Franklin Roosevelt the government created the War Labor Policies Board, chaired by Felix Frankfurter and designed to "eliminate all those factors . . . reducing the productivity of the workers." Under Frankfurter's leadership, the WLPB established an advisory board for the New York clothing industry which recommended the adoption of a forty-four-hour week nationwide and a system of impartial arbitration. More important, the board evolved a strategic plan for modernizing the New York market which envisioned an alliance of inside manufacturers, Progressive reformers, liberal technocrats, and the ACW, designed to eliminate the archaic contracting system.[16]

In a sense, this Frankfurter-proposed *entente cordiale* among political, industrial, and labor elites was a microcosm of the larger designs for social harmony which wartime experiences with the methods of planning, improved efficiency, and industrial democracy had encouraged. For the Hillman group particularly, the war was a formative experience of the greatest importance. It not only convinced the leadership of the advantages of state intervention, but it acquainted them with the mechanisms of policy-making and the institutional interior of a state apparatus just then undergoing a vast functional and organizational expansion. Moreover, it provided the first serious attempt at revising the antagonistic premises of labor relations while preserving discipline within a framework of democratic negotiation. In so doing, it established a set of working relationships with the urban Progressive wing of the Democratic party, and with independent Progressives like Robert La Follette and Fiorello La Guardia, which endured throughout the 1920s and encapsulated plans to recast the nation's political economy. The ACW was thus becoming an edifying social experiment commanding the attention of all those aware that the old order was in crisis.[17]

Social and industrial engineers were among those sensing the end of an era, and they sought to construct institutions appropriate for the new age of mass production and consumption. High on their agenda of reform was the restructuring of work. The liberal wing of the scientific management movement was committed to achieving shopfloor discipline and efficiency by "consent." In their eyes, this entailed some form of autonomous labor organization as the vehicle through which such voluntarily internalized discipline could be registered and sustained.

Consent was indeed forthcoming from the ACW leadership. Hillman was prepared to embrace scientific management so long as greater efficiency was accompanied and accomplished by mechanisms of democratic (i.e., union) control and substantial economic concessions to the rank and file. The accommodation with Taylorism was struck even before the war and came to fruition after the war through Hillman's close relationship with Morris Cooke. Cooke, future president of the Taylor Society and New Dealer, initially persuaded Hillman of the advantages of objectively adjusted piece rates, and enlisted fellow Taylorites to help the ACW in its efforts to apply uniform production standards through the medium of union democracy. The ACW, as they saw it, was to play a major managerial and administrative role in modernizing the clothing sector. At the same time, Cooke was convinced that the comanagement and workers' participation scheme envisioned for the clothing industry was broadly applicable to the economy at large. It was the best administrative strategy for dealing with problems of legitimacy and discipline. It would, he further theorized, help reorient the attention of workers to matters of consumption and purchasing power which lay at the root of the new capitalism. Finally, he shrewdly noted that such a program was not incompatible with the revolutionary political inclinations of the rank and file, as its rhetoric was not so very far removed from the then current fascination with movements for workers' control.[18]

Social liberals generally were well aware of the ACW's contribution to modern management and its innovations on behalf of industrial democracy. The pages of the *New Republic* and *Survey* were frequently given over to praise of the union's social prescience and responsibility. When attacked by its enemies within and outside industry, the union could invariably count on the legal support of Felix Frankfurter and his prestigious colleagues, the advice and counsel of respected labor relations experts like William Leiserson, and the political assistance of Progressive Senators Borah and La Follette. Robert Bruere, head of the Bureau of Industrial Research, summed up the feelings of many when he wrote to Hillman in 1920 to say, "Many of us have been looking to the fresh developments in the Amalgamated as the most important sign of a new order in the industrial and social world of America that has hitherto appeared."[19]

Men like Bruere were anxious for a success, for some tangible sign that modern industry, despite its taste for the autocratic, could nevertheless be made to cohabit the same social space with a democratic impulse just then at its zenith. They hoped that the system of industrial democracy would ameliorate the class struggle, lubricate the wheels of progress, and preserve democratic institutions. Hopes of this magnitude, however, stood little chance of realization unless the infrastructure of the new order was successfully erected first of all at the level of the shop floor. Despite the best intentions of managerial and union elites, designing and installing the apparatus of industrial democracy at the workplace turned out to be an undertaking of great social and psychological complexity, which initially generated more antagonism than harmony.

The leaders of the new order found that they had to orchestrate an alliance between the informal traditions of workers' control from below and the rationalized bureaucratic procedures of comanagement from above. The former was to be preserved but institutionalized and transformed through the development of a multitiered grievance machinery which gradually transferred authority from shop chairmen to outside business agents and their superiors in the union hierarchy. The new democracy at the workplace furthermore depended on formulating a new language and ideology, including a shared concept of interest and especially of industrial justice and equity. The "rule of law" on the shop floor was case law, painstakingly accumulated, analyzed and reanalyzed until a heavy admixture of formal justice and practicality emerged. Its central tenet was an industrial law of discharge. Once "just cause" for the firing of workers was stipulated—poor quality of production after a fair trial period, deliberate restriction of output, refusal to obey reasonable orders—the broad contours of power and responsibility were established.[20]

Thus the new unionism commanded intensive social surveillance not only because it undertook a major reform in the mechanics of industrial labor relations, but also because it promised to transform the social and psychological dynamics of the workplace. Progressive ideologue Paul Blanshard astutely noted that to endure industrial civility had to sink its roots deep into the social psyche of the garment workers. He reported that the new democracy was "developing trained citizens— trained citizens who are informed, enlightened, and disciplined."[21]

As movements for workers' control blanketed all of Europe after the war, the ideology and practice of industrial democracy was viewed as a kind of political prophylaxis and therapeutic. Hillman warned that if nearsighted opposition to industrial democracy continued, the recent revolutionary doings in Russia would be repeated elsewhere. The *New Republic*, aware that democracy was being subjected to "tests of unprecedented severity throughout the world," concluded that its future "depends . . . upon the capacity of employers and workers to harmonize democratic ideals of freedom with the voluntary self-discipline essential to efficient production." The editors could happily report that "no group in America has a keener appreciation of this fact than the ACWA."[22]

Sidney Hillman agreed emphatically. At the height of domestic and global unrest in late 1919, he boasted: "We have actually worked out the moral sanction behind work." That moral revolution, he believed, would "keep our industry isolated from the general unrest." However, perhaps better than anyone, Hillman also knew that if the new industrial republic had already selected its governing elite, it had not as yet secured its citizenry. Before the "rule of law" could be permanently ensconced in the industry's workshops it first had to be settled whose law was to rule.[23]

### The View from the Shop Floor

Industrial democracy in the garment industry, implemented through the institutions of the new unionism, accorded a decidedly greater share of real power to the sovereign organization of the workers than did the employee representation and welfare plans, company unions, and company-directed arrangements with accommodating AFL and railroad unions that proliferated during the 1920s. Still, premised as it was on the collaborative initiatives of union, managerial, and political elites, it represented a variety of corporatist syndicalism from above.

Moreover, in the interests of establishing a new industrial equilibrium, it deliberately set out to upset the prevailing structural balance of the industry. In the process of doing so, it ignited the resistance of workers whose animus was also syndicalist but not corporatist.[24]

Thus the processes culminating in the creation and consolidation of the ACW were more complicated than is suggested by the concert of interests arrived at by union, business, and political leaders. The union after all was more than a bureaucratic institution of collective bargaining and industrial stability. It was at the same time an ensemble of work groups and ethnocultural clusters which often acted in accordance with older social agendas not always compatible with the one prescribed by the new unionism. Its organizational integrity depended on integrating the molecular activities on the shop floor with the macrohistorical environment in which the union was embedded.

One reason the ACW cast such a long shadow forward into the era of industrial unionism was that it managed to domesticate an industry accustomed to the worst predatory practices of the free market while successfully assimilating its own membership into the procedures of modern labor relations, despite the inclinations of many on the shop floor to cleave to older forms of resistance to industrial exploitation. Neither was accomplished easily and this produced a prolonged period of internal factional turmoil which was not conclusively terminated until the late 1920s.

Long before there was a union there were strikes. Overexertion, endless hours, the personal tyrannies of foremen and contractors, sudden cuts in the rates or unannounced changes in production quotas and work rules produced frequent flash floods of rebellion and ephemeral organization. John Commons noted the enthusiasm and determination of these largely Jewish strikers, but nevertheless concluded that, "when once the strike is settled, either in favor or against the cause . . . that ends the union." By 1900, the Jewish garment workers' strike had become an annual ritual.[25]

Out of this madness grew a tradition if not exactly a method. Grievances were settled on the fly and through the exercise of naked economic power. While the balance of power usually favored the boss, skilled work groups especially had some leverage of their own. This was true both in tiny contractor shops, where artisanal hand skills persisted, and in large inside factories, where archaisms of artisanal solidarity survived among highly skilled cutters, pressers, and others. In general, the industry was characterized not by unskilled but by skilled and semiskilled labor arranged in elaborate hierarchies which provided the basis for chronic guerilla warfare on the shop floor.

What slowly emerged was not a body of law but a set of customs governing the pace, organization, and quantity of work. These customary relations, which persevered only to the extent that power could be mobilized to enforce them, were sovereign not throughout the industry or even in particular markets but only within subregions of the industry's occupational terrain.

This was an incongruous setting in which to implant a system of industrial democracy which presumed a certain self-restraint on the part of both workers and manufacturers. Instead of settling grievances in the heat of battle, the new arrangements demanded patience, deliberation, and a willingness to accept decisions arrived at by men removed from the fray which might provide less than had been expected by the aggrieved party. It depended on the workers' willingness to honor work rules, standards of performance, disciplinary procedures, and new codes of shop-floor behavior which they only indirectly participated in formulating. Most important of all, it depended on work groups relinquishing their right to strike whenever they felt justice or self-interest demanded they exercise it.[26]

The practices of a generation could not be abolished in a day. From the outset, unauthorized work stoppages and other violations of contractual agreements dogged the sober deliberations of grievance boards and boards of arbitration. Within months of the settlement with HSM in 1911, unilateral changes in work rules and rates prompted numerous short strikes among pants-seamers and pants-makers, sometimes led by anarchists whose faith in the newly established trade board was minimal. Instances of insubordination caused the union leadership endless aggravation. Cutters and trimmers, who displayed a remarkable degree of internal cohesion, obeyed management, union, and impartial authorities when it was convenient to do so. The board of arbitration condemned such "unwarranted rebellion" and expressed its dismay that such occurrences took place among "the most highly paid, the most skilled and presumably the most intelligent and advanced group of workers." It reflected badly, the board concluded, on the workers' capacity "for democratic self-government" and suggested the "inability of the local officials to control its members."[27]

The board could express its disappointment and the union leadership do its best to restore discipline, but the cutters remained determined to defend their traditional skills and work rules. Thus, for example, when ordered to cut "lays" of mixed fabrics, a departure from past practice and a threat to jobs and skills, the cutters first stopped work and then engaged in systematic production slowdowns. Even shop stewards, ostensibly committed to the formal grievance procedures, often enough ended up abetting rebellious workers when they believed an older sense of justice was at stake. Initially, the union elite could not even depend on its own most trusted local cadre. Organized in "activities" outside the formal structure of the union and subject to their own internal discipline, the union cadre was sometimes torn between their devotion to the union and the equally compelling principles of shop-floor artisanal solidarity.[28]

Compliance depended on the artful orchestration of psychological, behavioral, and cultural currents not absolutely inimical to management and union objectives. Militancy on the part of local leaders, even when accompanied by a sense of class injustice, was not necessarily a bad thing, as it enhanced the credibility of the union not only among its own membership but also among elements of the industry less inclined to accept the new arrangements without a struggle. But such popular sentiments had to be rechanneled, transformed, and encoded in a new rhetoric of workers' demands and perceptions emphasizing economic self-interest and industrial equity. Success in this process of linguistic socialization was variable. Thus, Meyer Jacobstein reported the case of a former radical who "is struggling constantly to hold in check a strong class-conscious feeling in order to be fair to the employers side." In another case, an Italian leader who had been "the most radical in the group" became a business agent, and "instead of merely delivering keen, sarcastic tirades he had to put things across for his workers consistent with the principles laid down in our agreement." Unable to handle the tension, he resigned.[29]

Most stoppages and instances of deliberate, collective slowdowns occurred among the more skilled workers. Skilled work groups maintained a rigid if informal jurisprudence all their own, and if a member violated a traditional shop-floor practice of importance, by exceeding the output previously agreed upon for example, he was punished without delay or ceremony. Less-skilled workers, finishers for example, tended to rebel less often, more spontaneously, and almost invariably in groups of some size. Mutinies by the less-skilled and newer immigrants tended to be less self-conscious, as it was not uncommon for such workers to be quite genuinely in the dark about the sort of discipline expected of them as citizens of an industrial democracy.[30]

In smaller firms the precipitating incident was often highly personal, abusive language or even physical abuse by a foreman, for example. In larger firms it was often the modernizing or rationalizing initiatives of management which sparked the explosion, even something as apparently simple as introducing a time clock among a group of bushelers accustomed to their own sense of work time.[31]

Impartial arbiters found they had to accommodate artisanal democracy if industrial democracy was to survive. The Chicago board declared that "the motive of group loyalty is to be relied upon to secure the average production" and condemned unilateral efforts to abolish "past practice." Indeed, decisions by boards in various markets were attempts to mediate across a broad range of historical relationships as well as to eliminate the more conventional sources of industrial rancor. Workers at disciplinary hearings faced charges ranging from the rather prematurely modern "failure to meet union obligations" to "refusal to do work as directed" and from there to problems of manners and morals, including "insubordination" and "improper language and conduct."[32] On innumerable occasions bureaucratic rationality had to make its peace with more traditional approaches to work not wedded to the ethos of industrial efficiency.

Throughout the industry, but especially in New York, the period of the war and its aftermath was the high point of shop-floor self-confidence. As much as Hillman might have hoped to quarantine the union against the contagion of wartime and postwar revolutionary upheaval, it was irrepressibly infectious as echoes of the Bolshevik revolution and European movements for workers' control resounded throughout the U.S.

William Z. Ripley reported that with the Bolshevik revolution "anarchy came to prevail to an undreamed of extent in the hundreds of little clothing contractors' shops throughout New York City." Following the armistice, "discipline, production, efficiency, low enough at best, were shot all to pieces." Recollecting his own anxiety, he noted that "in many instances the workers virtually took over the establishments."[33]

It all sounded quite ominous, but fortunately Ripley supplied some homely examples of just what such control meant in the claustrophobic precincts of the city's atomized industry:

M. Katz . . . Told pressers to make the work better and the people went on strike. Katz was fined $25. His people kept on strike until he paid same.

J. Goldstein . . . Operator opened the window. Bushel girls caught a cold and requested that window be closed. Mr. Goldstein closed the window, because there was a draft in the place. The operator opened the window. Mr. Goldstein requested that the window must be closed. The people went on strike and Mr. Goldstein was fined and he paid the people wages for the day they were not working. His people were on strike until he paid.

S. Adelson . . . Worker threw a bundle of work on Mr. Adelson's wife and because Mr. Adelson gave the worker an argument, Mr. Adelson was fined $25 and people were kept on strike until he paid.

The fate of private property in the manufacture of men's clothing was clearly not at issue. The industrial and political perspectives of those who "took over establishments" often extended no farther than the horizon created by their own tiny shops. Moreover, it is important to note that workers' control was sometimes exercised by and on behalf of narrowly self-interested groups. Thus union discipline was not only directed against those defending the rights and traditions of an earlier era, but also restrained the more selfish impulses of skilled cadre to monopolize work, to exploit their inexperienced *landsleit* as apprentices, or to aggrandize their individual incomes and social position at the expense of fellow workers.[34]

Artisanal democracy was thus a complex and ambiguous phenomenon. Anarcho-syndicalist in spirit, it was localist in orientation, decentralized, averse to long-term contractual obligations, accustomed to semispontaneous action in a firm-specific context, rarely conscious of the industry as a whole, and sometimes shared the craft-conscious parochialism it criticized in the AFL. It was demonstrably militant, but its militancy was in large measure conservative, rooted in impulses to defend the work skills and independence still surviving precariously in tiny shops and under factory roofs but mortally threatened by a degrading standardization of tasks.

In the nineteenth century, unionism often grew up on the basis of such defensive insularity. The new unionism, however, was predicated on the process of its disintegration and reabsorption into a new institutional and even characterological structure of behavior. But it is noteworthy in that connection that these same shop-floor oppositionists were also the union's most reliable cadre during its formative years. Again and again, the leadership relied on the stamina and tenacity of these skilled work groups, especially the cutters, who had sustained independent organizations for years under difficult circumstances. They were often the first to respond to union organizing efforts and proved absolutely dependable in strike confrontations.[35]

## The Ethnoculture of Work

The loyal opposition of these shop-floor insurgents thus bore within it all the ambiguity of an artisanal culture undergoing decomposition. It cast its shadow back into the handicraft past as well as forward into the industrial future.

Mainly Jewish in composition, its adherents were usually older first-generation immigrants from the tailoring centers of Byelorussia and Lithuania, where clothing production remained largely unmechanized and had yet to be brought within the confines of the factory. The first

Jewish "proletariat" was very much the residue of a disintegrating and impoverished artisan world whose animosity, in the old country as in the new, was often directed against bosses nearly as impoverished as they—a war of "pauper against pauper."[36]

During the 1890s this pre-industrial proletariat erupted in a series of mass strikes and demonstrations, partly conservative in nature, aimed at preserving what was left, and perhaps recouping some of what had been lost, of their social existence and identity as artisans. Yet these artisan outbursts also looked ahead to the future and "aimed at instituting 'modern' relations between employer and employee, relations based on contract, not on habit and whim." Strike organizations, along with the General Jewish Workers Union in Russia and Poland, better known as the Bund, were the agencies through which revolutionary politics and secular learning first reached large numbers. Most important, these institutions, especially the Bund, which was always strongest among handicraft workers, were incubators of a new morality and character structure that promoted self-restraint, social solidarity, a sense of mission, and individual integrity, and that helped supplant the age-old resignation and apathy of the shtetl.[37]

Contemporary observers and historians of the Jewish labor movement have all remarked that the generation of immigrants fleeing to the U.S. after the 1905 revolution exhibited a capacity for self-organization, a fighting élan, a political sophistication, a general level of literacy and individuation, and an ethos of self-improvement far in advance of earlier arrivals. There is little doubt, moreover, that the first lessons in industrial citizenship were learned in the Old World. The movements against political autocracy, the stigmata of caste and religion, national discrimination, and the economics of the sweatshop created intense interest in the dawning of a new civil order. Such movements expressed, albeit in the language of socialism, the historic aspirations of the third estate—the rights of man and citizen, equality, democracy, and fraternity—which the ideologues of industrial democracy sought to make room for inside factory walls.[38]

Although Jews comprised the main body of artisanal resistance to industrial democracy, other ethno-occupational groups made their presence felt as well. Perhaps the most consistently obstreperous were the Lithuanians. They were by tradition skilled tailors and pressers, and years before other new immigrants showed the same inclination, Lithuanians in the clothing industry were disposed to join trade unions. They tended, in addition, to identify with the most radical-secularist wing of the Lithuanian nationalist movement in America.

Politically articulate Lithuanians in the ACW were, in the main, avowedly syndicalist and initially belonged to the IWW (Industrial

Workers of the World). As "Wobblies" they attacked the ACW, especially in Baltimore, but could also be just as passionate on behalf of the Amalgamated in opposition to its enemies, including conservative AFL craft organizations like the United Garment Workers (UGW), from which the ACW had split in 1914. Thus, like their Jewish artisanal counterparts, the Lithuanians could be counted on to defend unionism militantly while jealously guarding their independence. That independence was an admixture of revolutionary nationalism, which periodically inspired separatist maneuverings against the national leadership, a deep-rooted anti-Semitism, and a penchant to strike or undertake other job actions without regard for the machinery of impartial arbitration and in the face of official union displeasure.[39]

Immigrants from southern Italy, the other major immigrant component of the industry's labor force, presented a different set of historic problems for the new unionism. While artisanal syndicalism flourished among Jews, Lithuanians, and other non-Jewish East Europeans in small contractor shops and in the skilled departments of larger factories, southern Italians, together with second- and third-generation northern and western Europeans, congregated in larger factories in the more centralized, capital-intensive sectors of the industry.

While some Italians arrived with tailoring skills mastered in the old country, most learned the tailoring trades in the U.S. They operated sewing machines and performed a wide variety of semiskilled jobs. The development of the section system with its extensive division of labor made it "possible for a Sicilian peasant that knows nothing at all about tailoring to learn any special operation in a short time."[40]

Cultural taboos prohibited Italian wives from working outside the home. Married Italian women thus became the industry's chief source of homeworkers, performing tedious hand labor for abysmal pay. Even when younger, unmarried Italian women did enter the factory, they continued to perform traditional jobs as fellers and finishers in sections segregated from the male labor force, usually under the supervision of an Italian foreman and in factories located close to Italian neighborhoods. Homeworkers particularly were subject to a pervasive patriarchal pressure only slightly less stupefying than that for women factory operatives. Even in cases where manufacturers actively collaborated with the ACW and the machinery of impartial arbitration in an effort to eliminate the destabilizing influence of homework, Italian women, along with their padrones and employers, clung tenaciously to the old ways. Homework thrived until the advent of the NRA.[41]

A minority of Italian clothing workers demonstrated the same pattern of artisanal resistance to industrial democracy exhibited by other skilled work groups, and supplied the ACW with some of its early Italian organizers. More commonly, however, the mass of Italian operatives behaved more like subjects than like citizens or subversives of an industrial republic. In contrast to the precocious political and organizational activity of declining artisanal groups, the Italian clothing proletariat, with little experience of industrial life, much less of socialism, repeated a common pattern of first-generation immigrant submissiveness to factory routines and authority.

However, that pattern was punctuated by episodic outbursts of mass rebellion, analogous to the risings of the *fascio* in Sicily in the 1890s, that expressed long-accumulating hatreds with great energy. These outbreaks occurred sometimes under the auspices of the IWW or under the charismatic influence of free-lancing Italian anarcho-syndicalists, and left precious few organizational traces behind. Italian socialist and ACW organizer Frank Bellanca described the perennial rhythms of these industrial jacqueries: "Italians are impulsives, are easy to enthusiasm, but they are also easy to mistrust. And those who know Italians know also that it is more difficult to keep the organization among the Italians than organize themselves. Often is easy to organize the Italians; to call them in strike; but for to keep them, believe me, is necessary constancy, sacrifice, honesty, and big moral and material power."[42]

Even where these industrial syndicalists could be incorporated within the union's formal structure, they remained estranged from the union leadership by virtue of strong localist, not to say nationalist, sentiments. The leadership was often forced to concede the formation of entirely Italian locals, and even after joining the ACW Italian syndicalists continued to oppose not only the mechanisms of impartial arbitration but any form of binding contractual arrangement covering wages, hours, and conditions of work.[43]

The Italian problem for the union, however, was more often one of inactivity rather than hyperactivity. In every market where they were important, local union cadres reported extraordinary difficulties organizing Italians. Rochester, the most important center, remained unorganized until 1919, mainly because Italians in the coat trade and the Italian women were unreachable, especially those working for Hickey-Freeman, a company whose paternalist labor policies gave it a reputation as the "Paradise" of the industry. Rochester was eventually organized despite its heavily Italian work force because the city's manufacturing elite, prodded by Kirstein, finally saw the wisdom of unionization. Philadelphia, on the other hand, could not be organized until 1929, because it lacked such an elite, because Italian subcontracting padrones insulated female Italian homeworkers from union appeals, and because "the situation in the shops where the Italians are the dominant factor is bad."[44]

It was generally believed that if Italians were to be organized at all, they could not be recruited in ones and twos but only in large groups, and more often than not through the galvanizing effect of a mass strike. Indeed, for many Italian workers the concept of organization was synonymous with that of the strike. Whenever possible, Italian organizers used old ties of *campanilismo* and the ethos of *la famiglia* and were careful to observe the sexual and other cultural prohibitions. But even where organizing succeeded, the results were often ephemeral. Italian locals were soon nearly defunct or subject to rapid turnover, and in some cases the union "virtually forced the Italian to join" through the closed shop and compulsory dues check-off.[45] The ACW wrestled with an Italian work force for whom industrial and trade-union discipline were not yet second nature.

### The New Unionism and an Old Politics

The union's founding elite thus confronted a mélange of ethno-work cultures not yet sufficiently deracinated to be assimilated into the bureaucratic patterns of behavior expected of an industrial citizenry. To make citizens was not the work of a day. At every opportunity the union sought to promote that transformation by dissolving foreign language locals into mixed assemblies, merging older craft locals into larger industrial units, encouraging members to take out citizenship papers, and insisting that only English be spoken at union conventions. The union also used a broad program of general education to acquaint the rank and file with the operating assumptions of American life as well as with the particular requirements of the new unionism.[46]

In the long run, this diligence in the arena of cultural reform and reeducation helped instill in the rank and file a commitment to the principles and policies of social liberalism later effectively mobilized on behalf of the New Deal. Before that could happen, however, the new politics of industrial democracy had to contend against the still compelling political allegiances of artisanal and peasant syndicalists. Thus, while the new unionism may have originated in corporate headquarters, in union executive offices, and in the conference rooms of management consultants and lawyers, its future was decided on shop floors and in convention halls, where older forms of political radicalism had their last say.

During the 1920s all the needle-trades unions underwent a prolonged period of internal factional struggle. In most instances, a union leadership closely identified with if not in the Socialist party found its hegemony challenged by the new-born Communist party and its allies. Although not entirely dissimilar, the experience of the ACW was nonetheless unique and a premonition of political developments inside the mass industrial unions of the CIO a decade and more later.

Most remarkable was the fact that from 1920 through mid-1924, the Hillman elite allied with rather than against the CP on behalf of industrial democracy, while the SP found itself defending the remaining outposts of artisanal democracy against a union leadership it considered too independent, too heterodox, and above all too insensitive to the dangers of Bolshevism. After 1924, however, as the horizon of radical possibilities was drastically foreshortened by a global and domestic political thermidor, more conventional factional alignments were reestablished. The Hillman group then conducted a purge of the left, calling on their erstwhile opponents from the SP for assistance. However, while ideological and party lines shifted, the underlying social tensions remained the same. Only with the conclusion of this second phase of factionalism by 1928 was the victory of industrial democracy over artisanal democracy assured.

Organized factional strife began when the union leadership boldly took the initiative over the issue of production standards. The decision to promote industrywide standards of production was reached through the collective deliberations of union, managerial, and scientific management elites. Standards were to apply to distinct work groups and departments, only indirectly to individuals, and were to be established through the joint consent of labor and management, each armed with its own battery of technical experts. In many respects production standards made sound economic sense, not only from the standpoint of business, but as a device for fixing a limit to overexertion on the shop floor.[47]

However, the scheme also suggested a remodeled version of piecework and even a return to the loathsome "task system" in which manufacturers unilaterally raised the output demanded of teams of workers, which prevailed throughout the industry in the late nineteenth century. As such it outraged an artisanal sense of autonomy and fueled anxieties generated by the homogenizing and leveling tendencies represented by the new technologies, the new requirements thrown up by the expanding mass market for cheaper clothing, and the rationalizing practices of the new unionism. In New York particularly, it threatened to eliminate the system of "week work," which entailed the payment of weekly wages calculated on the basis of hours worked without precise regard for the quantity and pace of production. It thereby enhanced the power of informal work groups over the production process.[48]

Opposition to production standards was voiced principally through the union's foreign-language press. It centered among older groups of skilled workers, especially cutters, pressers, and children's clothing workers, some of whom had experienced the task system first hand. On the one hand, the creation of the union had fortified the position of these skilled work groups, reinforcing and formalizing their customary rights to regulate the pace of production, to control the level of expected output, to police the introduction of new machinery, and so on. Now, however, the same leadership for whom they otherwise displayed the greatest respect proposed a new system which seemed to be a kind of counterfeit piecework and all too reminiscent of what many characterized as an old "slavery." While by no means the only ones alarmed by the attempt to install standards, these particular older artisanal immigrants, concentrated in New York's contracting shops, were overwhelmingly Jewish and socialist.[49]

Torn between their unswerving commitment to trade unionism and their anxieties about the new unionism, this Jewish artisanal opposition remained organizationally and politically inchoate until the SP, and especially the circle of Jewish socialists gathered around the *Forward*, launched a campaign against production standards as part of a more general assault on the union leadership.

That the ACW should have to fend off attacks from this quarter was remarkable in the extreme since, like the rest of the needle unions, the ACW was founded by socialists and drew heavily on the SP, in particular the Jewish Socialist Federation (JSF) and the United Hebrew Trades (UHT), for funds, for organizational, administrative, and educational cadres, and for political support. In return, the union campaigned actively for local and national SP candidates.[50]

This relationship with organized socialism was not only instrumental, it was practically organic. For the mass of immigrant Jewish garment workers, socialism was a kind of secularized messianism, a religion of political solace and apocalyptic deliverance in which trade unionism counted as one of the rites of passage. The ACW elite had grown to political maturity in this atmosphere. Some had been active in Jewish revolutionary politics in the old country or members of their families had been. Whether members of the SP or not, they were firmly implanted in those traditions of the Second International which affixed the timing and tempo of socialism to the inexorable rhythms of industrial and social development under capitalism.[51]

Beneath this surface of ideological harmony and organizational co-operation, however, serious differences in political and industrial strategy as well as struggles for pelf and power made relations between the union and the party brittle from the ACW's inception. The ACW was, after all, an outlaw organization, guilty in the eyes of the AFL hierarchy of dual unionism for having dared to abandon the moribund but AFL-sanctioned UGW. The SP leadership was never entirely happy with this state of affairs, and Jewish socialists associated with the *Forward* and the UHT particularly attempted to heal the breach, sometimes with propositions that would have seriously compromised the autonomy and authority of the fledgling ACW. The party did so in the interests of maintaining its working relationship with the nation's only bona fide labor federation, but in the end only managed to inspire an abiding distrust of its intentions on the part of the young rebels in the men's clothing industry. For its part, the Hillman elite scrupulously guarded its organizational independence, quietly turned away invidious peace proposals, and opened up new lines of political communication and assistance into the wider circles of progressive reform.[52]

It was Bolshevism, however, that transformed a polite if edgy relationship into open antagonism. Hillman was determined, for reasons to be explained momentarily, to maintain the union's political friendship with the Russian revolution. By 1922, however, the *Forward* group had assumed a posture of militant anti-Communism and found Hillman's attitude insupportable. In a bitter contest for the loyalties of the Jewish rank and file, the contentious issue of production standards provided party apparatchiks a convenient stick with which to flay the union leadership. Indeed, the SP's most devoted followers included those most sensitive to the issue. Their artisanal ethos was responding to the pressures of new unionism by gradually succumbing to a sense of craft exclusiveness intent on defending parochial privileges. And despite the delirious enthusiasm with which they initially greeted the overthrow of the Russian autocracy, it was this group as well that was most prepared to follow the SP elite into the new politics of anti-Communism.[53]

For many others, however, Bolshevism remained a heroic crusade. Beginning in 1921, large segments of the JSF left the organization and reassembled either in the newly formed CP or in loosely allied anarcho-syndicalist groupings. Within the ACW they coalesced inside the CP's united-front trade-union formation, the Trade Union Educational League (TUEL). Drawn most heavily from the coat-making and tailoring trades, this Jewish left was somewhat younger and somewhat less skilled than the cutters and pressers of the right. But in a fundamental

sense the social makeup and motivation of the Jewish left was strikingly like that of the right. Not only did they display a similar artisanal
militance, but the shop-floor cadre of the TUEL was no happier about
the advent of production standards than its factional opponents from
the SP.[54]

The singular difference was that rank-and-file TUEL members accepted the political and organizational authority of a CP leadership
which supported the Hillman elite in its struggle against the right.
The price of such obedience was the muting of indigenous shop-floor
protest over production standards, an act of self-abnegation sometimes
proffered voluntarily, at other times only under the duress of party
discipline.[55]

Tactical advantages accrued to both Hillman and the CP so long as
the alliance lasted. The former could count on the TUEL's factional
support, on its core of experienced and dedicated organizers to help
domesticate the New York market then in a state of disintegration, and
on its ability to discipline segments of the membership otherwise apt to
oppose the continued rationalization of the industry. Most important,
the alliance meant that the Hillman elite, unlike its bureaucratic
colleagues in the rest of the needle trades, never had to face a united
factional opposition. In return, Hillman warmly endorsed the Russian
revolution and its Bolshevik leadership, mobilized political as well as
material aid on its behalf, and even entered into a joint agreement with
the Soviets to reconstruct the Soviet clothing industry along the most
modern lines of technology and labor relations. At the same time, the
union extended its administrative protection to a TUEL caucus under
attack by the SP right.[56]

If Hillman could befriend the Bolshevik experiment and Communists do likewise for the new unionism, it was not, however, merely a
case of mutual tactical advantage. Union and CP elites shared a perspective which included the elaboration of a system of rational and
democratic labor relations in an industry notoriously lacking them,
and the invention of machinery for the comanagement of the industry
in the interests of planned production and consumption. Indeed, party
propagandists argued that imposition of production standards was not
a concession to antilabor Taylorism, but that it was in fact compatible
with revolutionary principles of economics. Thus the party leadership,
if not its social constituency, was as receptive to strategies for rationalizing an underdeveloped clothing industry as the Bolsheviks were
fascinated by western administrative and technical practices that promised to modernize an underdeveloped country. The collaboration was
thus deep, if brief, and premised on a temporary affinity between
Bolshevik policy during the period of the New Economic Policy and

the policy of the new unionism. For Hillman, the NEP represented the seed of "state" or "cooperative capitalism," germinating within the soil of war communism, much as the new unionism represented the kernel of state capitalism concealed within the husk of free enterprise.[57]

An alliance predicated on such strategic agreement could not survive any unilateral alteration in outlook. It so happened that political questions, in particular presidential politics, rather than matters of trade-union or industrial perspective, proved to be the occasion for a parting of the ways. Thus the union elected to support the La Follette campaign in 1924 and not the efforts of the CP to establish an independent labor party. For the Hillman elite, the campaign represented the last best opportunity to extend both the labor and the more general reforms of the clothing industry into the mainstream of national policy-making. For the CP elite such developments signaled the restabilization of bourgeois politics and a closure of radical options.[58]

Once the La Follette decision was finalized, the TUEL emerged as the factional center of the left opposition, while the SP right abruptly made peace with union leaders, sensing the chance for a major assault on the CP. It was immediately clear, moreover, that the TUEL caucus combined so many disparate elements as to undermine its ability to challenge the Hillman leadership seriously.

To begin with, the CP elite, drawn from second-generation and "native" American milieux more attuned to the workings of corporate capitalism, did not entirely trust its own immigrant cadre on the shop floor. These workers, including not only Communists but clusters of Jewish anarchists as well, were too quick to act without regard for the strategic concerns of the party, too absorbed by the immediate problems of the shop floor, which the party was willing to neglect in favor of grander objectives. For these TUEL rebels in the shops the struggle was an age-old one against "bureaucracy" and "graft," whose basic contours had not changed any more than the populist allegory which gave such struggles their meaning. They articulated a traditional ideology whose values, myths, and nostalgic tone remained disconnected from the new processes and institutions of modern industrial society. Thus discarding the party's earlier commitment to production standards, they revived the old artisanal cry for shop-floor control and week work, thereby revealing that left politics and ideology had, in part, merely camouflaged a deeper if diminishing resistance to the institution and ethos of the new unionism.[59]

If the party faced problems disciplining its Jewish following, it found it even more difficult to strike dependable alliances with Italian and Lithuanian syndicalists who had their own reasons for opposing the ACW leadership. The Lithuanians were preoccupied with their own internecine nationalist struggles for control of the Lithuanian foreign-language locals. Moreover, their nationalism and latent anti-Semitism not only estranged them from the heavily Jewish union leadership, but for the same reason lent a tentative air to their relations with the TUEL. Their syndicalist traditions also made them reluctant participants in contractual commitments, which the party and TUEL had, in the end, come to accept as the essence of collective bargaining.[60]

Italian insurgents, who comprised the main body of factional opposition in Rochester especially, proved even more organizationally and politically unreliable. Leading Italian leftists, while associating with the TUEL, maintained a dual loyalty to the world of Italian radicalism which tended to reproduce a kind of *clientilissmo* politics on the left. Thus Italian organizers turned to General Executive Board member and socialist August Bellanca for protection against the more repressive maneuverings of the rest of the union leadership, and in return were willing to be guided by Bellanca's cautious advice, even if that meant strained relations with non-Italian comrades in the TUEL caucus. Relations with the left were further strained by Italians who posed as militants in order to cultivate a more traditional *personalissmo* politics among their ethnic brethren. Once such personal ties between leader and masses were established, alliances with the left proved unreliable in the extreme.

More fundamentally, as Bellanca well knew, Italian affiliation with the left was at most temporary. Indeed, the CP was forced to admit that its greatest weakness in all the needle unions was its lack of a secure foothold among the Italians. Italian workers who comprised the small armies of leftism were often as new to unionism as they were to radical politics. More often than not their anger with the union elite was sparked not by political differences but by a sense of ethnic discrimination and a general reluctance to submit to industrial routine, whether under union auspices or not. In a sense, the Italians had always been "anti-administration." But they were comfortable neither with the shop-floor perspective of artisanal democracy nor with the political vision of the CP.[61]

By 1927, the TUEL was forced to lead an underground existence. Internally divided and politically isolated, the status of the party in the ACW was soon reduced to that of a sectarian clique. Its voice was heeded by few as it enunciated the jeremiads of a bygone era and the belligerent platitudes of a revolutionary future not many thought necessary any longer. With its demise, the last serious opposition to the new unionism died also.

## Conclusion

Retrospective assessments of the union's formative years have recognized a premonition of the New Deal era. ACW commitments to industrial unionism and to social security constitute persuasive evidence offered in support of this judgment. That Sidney Hillman and the Amalgamated were to play a critical role in the founding of the CIO, that the ACW's Socialist rank and file became devoted to Roosevelt, and that Hillman assumed the major political and organizational responsibility for assimilating the new labor movement into the New Deal coalition, flowed more or less naturally from the historical momentum generated between the great Chicago strike of 1910 and the depression of 1929. This essay has made clearer the interconnections between the micro-politics of the shop floor and the macro-economics of a complex industrial society which prepared the ACW, and Hillman particularly, to perform as they did.

Thus the new unionism foreshadowed the CIO not simply because it adopted an industrial rather than a craft form of organization (in fact, cutters clung tenaciously to their exclusive craft prerogatives for quite some time). More significantly, the internal development of the ACW anticipated a range of problems that would subsequently confront the new unions of the 1930s. In the first instance, in the interests of internalizing a sense of industrial discipline, the union had to overcome the resistance of ethno-work cultures unaccustomed to the centralized, bureaucratic procedures which made industrial unionism a valuable asset to business as well as to labor. A similar process of resistance, rationalization, and cultural transformation accounted for the turbulence that characterized the early years of most of the new CIO unions.

In the second place, the role of the CP, while not as decisive in the development of the ACW as it would prove to be in the formation of the United Auto Workers, Transport Workers Union, or United Electrical Workers, was nonetheless analogous. Party cadres would prove to be among the most dedicated organizers and astute tacticians. More important, the party leadership shared a sense that craft practices constituted an obstacle to mass organization, and because the party's strategic orientation was ultimately political, it was prepared to discipline rank-and-file members more inclined to adopt craft or syndicalist solutions to problems on the shop floor. The harmony of outlook and interest that colored Hillman-CP relations from 1920 to 1924 was to be recovered not only with Hillman but with much of the CIO leadership in the "popular front" 1930s and again during World War

II. Finally, the severe political and industrial isolation of the CP following the La Follette campaign recurred in the aftermath of the Henry Wallace defeat of 1948 and suggests that the influence of political radicalism was always provisional and vulnerable, not so much because of its own strategic miscalculations but more because of the inherent historic limitations of the mass organizations and mass politics it attempted to direct.

In certain essential respects, then, the internal organizational and political dynamics of the industrial unionism of the 1930s recapitulated the experience of the new unionism in the Progressive era. Moreover, in both cases, the complex of behaviors associated with the shop floor was decisively transformed by a specific configuration of macrohistorical circumstances. Managerial practices, the activities of state agencies, the catalytic initiatives of political and union elites, as well as the more general elaboration of the culture of mass consumption and the political economy of Keynesian liberalism, qualitatively reshaped the motivations, organizational practices, and even the public language of shop-floor cadres in the ACW and in the principal CIO unions. With the advent of the new unionism, and especially with the eradication of the traditions of artisanal independence, the autonomy of the shop-floor perspective ceased to be anything more than a nostalgic conceit.

If the molecular processes of industrial unionism thus recapitulated, in certain essential respects, the internal dynamics of the new unionism, so, too, were both projects undertaken with an eye to their structure and function within the new order of mass consumption capitalism. When the General Executive Board told the assembled delegates at the 1928 convention that "factionalism in the Amalgamated has burned itself out," it was announcing the death of something more fundamental than intramural political squabbling. Politics itself, that is the politics associated with the traditional slogans and categories of the class struggle, was being interred as well. Gone were the millenarian enthusiasms and universalist yearnings that marked the union's founding era. Gradually they were replaced with conceptions of economic interest and political pluralism and with a concern for reform modulated by a sense of social responsibility.[62]

Just before the stock market collapsed, Hillman observed that "a high standard of living is no more a question of mere justice. . . . It is essential to our system of mass production to create a consumers' demand for almost unlimited output." Thus the new unionism, in keeping with broader currents of Progressive political and economic reform, had taken the first steps toward transmuting what had once been moral and political questions into matters of administration and social engineering. Poverty and exploitation had not only been adjudged inhumane but, in the eyes of some, were also seen as seriously destabilizing, and as such represented a menace to the smooth functioning of a complex industrial and democratic society.[63]

The ACW's pioneering innovations were undertaken from this standpoint. Indeed, by the mid 1920s Hillman was proselytizing for unemployment insurance not only for the benefit of the rank and file, not only as a device for moderating the seasonal fluctuations of the clothing industry, but as part of a broad program of national reform designed to sustain mass purchasing power to absorb the output of mass production industry.[64]

During the deceptively prosperous decade of the 1920s, however, the relative stability of the economic order relegated such programmatic innovations to the periphery of national politics. The depression changed all that. Those labor, industrial, and political elites who had spent the '20s monitoring developments in the provincial backwaters of the clothing industry and whose efforts to reconstitute bourgeois politics fizzled in the abortive La Follette campaign now reassembled in the anteroom of power as the old order collapsed. Hillman spent the period before the advent of the Roosevelt regime making and renewing political friendships with La Follette Jr., Frankfurter, Filene, Frances Perkins, Cooke, and Rexford Tugwell. Together they formulated proposals for a tripartite national economic council to plan economic development, and for a tripartite labor board modeled after the impartial arrangements of the clothing industry to regulate the conditions of labor. They sponsored legislative initiatives for minimum wages and maximum hours, for public works, and for unemployment insurance, all designed to promote recovery by restoring mass purchasing power.[65]

It was, of course, one thing to propose, quite another to dispose, and it was a few years before these architects of the Keynesian welfare state actually occupied the corridors of power. That they were ultimately able to do so was in no small measure attributable to the political mobilization of the new industrial unionism, an undertaking in which Sidney Hillman was instrumental. Like the ACW in an earlier era, the CIO became a consenting partner to a relationship which guaranteed it political legitimacy and material advantages, and to which it contributed its moral and institutional authority over a working class no longer amenable to traditional forms of patriarchal dependence. For all these reasons it may truly be said that the new unionism was a dress rehearsal for the New Deal.

## NOTES

A number of people read a considerably longer version of the present essay and made suggestions that proved enormously valuable in preparing the article that appears here. I wish to thank Jill Andresky, Eric Foner, Joshua Freeman, Peter Friedlander, Michael Frisch, Paul Milkman, and David Montgomery.

1. There is a considerable body of literature on the Jewish labor movement, and on the labor movement more generally, which examines the ACWA's contribution to the new unionism. In addition to numerous articles, the following books are especially useful: Matthew Josephson, *Sidney Hillman: Statesman of American Labor* (New York, 1952); Irving Howe, *World of Our Fathers: The Journey of the East European Jews to America and the World They Found and Made* (New York, 1976); Jesse Thomas Carpenter, *Competition and Collective Bargaining in the Needle Trades, 1910-1967* (Ithaca, N.Y., 1972); J. M. Budish and George Soule, *The New Unionism in the Clothing Industry* (New York, 1920); Charles Elbert Zaretz, *The Amalgamated Clothing Workers of America: A Study in Progressive Trades Unionism,* (New York, 1934); Irving Bernstein, *The Lean Years: A History of the American Worker, 1920-1933* (Boston, 1972); Chicago Joint Board ACWA, *The Clothing Workers of Chicago 1910-1922* (Chicago, 1922); Joel Seidman, *The Needle Trades* (New York, 1942); Melech Epstein, *Jewish Labor in the U.S.A.,* 2 vols. (New York, 1950); Melvyn Dubofsky, *When Workers Organize: New York City in the Progressive Era* (Amherst, Mass., 1968).

2. On the size, proliferation, and business practices of the petty garment manufacturer see: Howe, *World of Our Fathers,* pp. 156-59; Rosara Lucy Passero, "Ethnicity in the Men's Ready-Made Clothing Industry, 1880-1950: The Italian Experience in Philadelphia" (Ph.D. dissertation, University of Pennsylvania, 1978), pp. 110-12, 163; Harry A. Corbin, *The Men's Clothing Industry: Colonial through Modern Times* (New York, 1970), pp. 40-50. Jesse Eliphalet Pope's *The Clothing Industry in New York* (Columbia, Mo., 1905) is still the best single history of the industry in the nineteenth century and includes a description of its dualistic structure. Moses Rischin, *The Promised City: New York's Jews, 1870-1914* (New York, 1962), p. 255, notes the greater degree of capitalization of the men's as opposed to the ladies' garment industry, while remarking that the degree of incorporation was still remarkably low. Epstein, *Jewish Labor,* vol. 1, pp. 94-100, describes the familial and localist networks which comprised the casual labor market upon which contractors depended. Budish and Soule, *New Unionism,* pp. 33-37. The U.S. Census of Manufacturing for 1914 contains the statistical data on the value of annual product, the size distribution of enterprises by number of employees, etc., but the census figures often undercounted the number of inside contractors and subcontractors, and it was of course extremely difficult to measure the extent of homework. Abraham Cahan's novel, *The Rise of David Levinsky* (1917; reprint ed., New York, 1960) vividly depicts the competitive ethos of the petty garment manufacturer.

3. Robert J. Meyers and Joseph W. Bloch, "The Men's Clothing Industry," in *How Collective Bargaining Works: A Factual Survey of Labor-Management Relations in Leading American Industries,* ed. Twentieth Century Fund, Inc., Labor Committee (New York, 1942), p. 388; U.S. Foreign and Domestic

Commerce Bureau, "The Men's Factory-Made Clothing Industry," report in Misc. Series #34 (Washington, D.C., 1916), pp. 157-58.

4. Morris Cooke, "The Men's Ready-Made Clothing Industry," report appearing in *Waste in Industry* (New York, 1921), a study prepared by the Committee on Elimination of Waste in Industry of the Federated American Engineering Societies (hereafter Waste in Industry). Cooke's report was more broadly concerned with the causes of inefficiency in the industry for which he held management largely accountable, but he emphasized the critical role of the subcontracting system in defeating attempts at industrial planning, p. 113. "Collective Bargaining: Production Standards—Special Problems, 1919" and Testimony of Sidney Hillman and David Wolff, Joint Conference of the American Men's and Boy's Clothing Manufacturers Association and the ACWA, Jan. 1919, in Papers of the Amalgamated Clothing Workers of America (hereafter ACWA Papers). The papers of the ACWA and of Sidney Hillman have recently been acquired by the Labor-Management Documentation Center of the Martin P. Catherwood Library of the New York State School of Industrial and Labor Relations at Cornell University and are now in the process of being reorganized. Felix Frankfurter and Samuel Rosensohn, "Survey of the New York Clothing Industry," May 1920, ACWA Papers; "Men's Factory-Made Clothing Industry," pp. 157-58.

5. Passero, "Ethnicity in Men's Ready-Made Clothing Industry," provides the most thorough statistical analysis of the industry's structural differentiation according to regional market, see esp. pp. 162-64; "Reports on Working Conditions 1920," ACWA Papers; Zaretz, *Amalgamated Clothing Workers*, pp. 29-30.

6. Zaretz, *Amalgamated Clothing Workers*, pp. 23-24, 29-30; "From Pain to Victory," *Labor Age*, 33 (May 1924), 111-33; Passero, "Ethnicity in Men's Ready-Made Clothing Industry," p. 163; "Experience with Trade Union Agreements—Clothing Industries," report #38 prepared by the National Industrial Conference Board (hereafter NICB Report), June 1921. The need for a high volume of goods to move continuously through a plant in order to maximize the profitable use of fixed capital, materials, and energy, as noted by Alfred Chandler's *The Visible Hand: The Managerial Revolution in American Business* (Cambridge, Mass., 1977), was not unknown to the most modern clothing factories and their managements. N. I. Stone, labor manager for Hickey-Freeman, an elite Rochester firm, made precisely this point in a report prepared for the National Bureau of Economic Research, "Business Cycles and Unemployment" (1923). Stone noted that the normal pattern of intermittent, seasonal production was not only socially harmful, but also bad for businessmen who might otherwise benefit from continuous operations, especially those with "plants having a large overhead expense, a considerable part of which is in the nature of fixed charges which cannot be eliminated while the plant is temporarily shut down" (quoted in *Daily News Record* [hereafter *DNR*], 11/3/23).

7. Testimony of Walter Drew in 1919 before an advisory board composed of William Z. Ripley, Felix Frankfurter, and Louis Marshall (hereafter Frank. Adv. Bd.), quoted in Carpenter, *Competition and Collective Bargaining*, p. 475, as exemplary of a growing conviction by manufacturers that a union was not only necessary but that to function best in the interests of the industry it needed to be a strong union. "A Private and Confidential Memorandum

Regarding Review of Federal Income and Profits Tax Returns of Hart, Schaffner, and Marx for the 4 Fiscal Years ending 11/30/20," located in the Treasurer's Office, HSM headquarters in Chicago, dated 6/23/21. The *Chicago Tribune*, 11/23/23, reported that President Hart attributed the company's recent good profit performance to the greater efficiency of production coincident with the establishment of the ACWA. Shortly after the strike, several Chicago newspapers reported that Schaffner was contemplating an employee stock-purchase plan as it was just months after the strike ended that the company became a public corporation. Schaffner's testimony of April 1914 before the Industrial Commission, quoted by George Creel, "A Way to Industrial Peace," *Century Magazine*, July 1915. In the same testimony, Schaffner indicated that even before the strike ended the company had independently devised a plan for revamping its labor relations which ruled out any opposition to an independent union. *Final Report and Testimony Submitted to Congress by the Committee on Industrial Relations*, S. Doc. 415, 64th Cong., 1st Sess. (Washington, D.C., 1916), vol. 1, pp. 564-65.

8. Meyer Jacobstein, "Can Industrial Democracy Be Efficient?—The Rochester Plan," *Bulletin of the Taylor Society*, 5 (Aug. 1920), 153-77.

9. William E. Hotchkiss, "Collective Agreements in the Men's Clothing Industry," *Annals of the American Academy of Political and Social Science*, Mar. 1922; *DNR*, 11/27/14; Eli Strousse to Hillman, 10/3/19, Hillman Papers (see n. 4 for information on the Hillman Papers); Judge Jacob M. Moses, "Labor Agreements with a Powerful Union," *Annals of the American Academy of Political and Social Science*, Sept. 1919; NICB Report, quoted in Seidman, *Needle Trades*, p. 255.

10. Joseph Schlossberg to Hillman, 9/20/15, Hillman Papers; *Documentary History of the ACWA* (hereafter *Doc. Hist.*) *1918-1920* (New York, 1920) and *Proceedings of the 4th Biennial Convention of the ACWA* (hereafter *Conv. Proceedings*) (New York, 1920); Earl Dean Howard to Hillman, 8/1/19, ACWA Papers; Corbin, *Men's Clothing Industry*, p. 128; Major Gitchell to Hillman, 8/9/19, ACWA Papers; George Bell, "Agenda for a Conference of Impartial Chairmen and Labor Managers in the Clothing Industry at Cleveland, May 24, 1919" and "Proposal for a Survey of Wages and Hours," 1919, ACWA Papers; "Minutes of a Meeting between Mr. Lowenthal, Mr. Wolman, Mr. Szold, and Mr. Hotchkiss," 3/9/20, ACWA Papers.

11. The Filenes had earlier been instrumental in persuading Louis Brandeis to intervene during the 1910 New York cloak-makers strike out of which issued the famous Protocols of Peace; see Samuel Haber, *Scientific Management in the Progressive Era, 1890-1920* (Chicago, 1964), p. 97, and Louis Levine, *The Women's Garment Workers* (1924, reprint ed., New York, 1969) pp. 186-89, and Dubofsky *When Workers Organize*. On other occasions Hillman turned to Fashion Park in Rochester, Gimbels Brothers in New York, and Morris Rothschild in Chicago for similar help. Lazarus Marcovitz to Schlossberg, 2/1/17, Hillman Papers; General Executive Board Minutes, ACWA, Sept. 26-28, 1929, ACWA Papers (hereafter GEB Min.); *Doc. Hist. 1918-1920*. Kirstein's business connections were rather extensive, as he sat on the boards of Lee Higginson & Co. and Abraham and Strauss, and maintained close relations with Paul Mazur of Lehman Brothers; Edward Filene memo, 1/17/29, Edward A. Filene Papers, Bergengren Memorial Library, Filene House, Madison, Wis. (hereafter Filene Papers); interview with Abraham Chatman, 8/23/78.

12. Dubofsky, *When Workers Organize*, passim; Leo Mannheimer/Committee on Industrial Relations of the Jewish Community—Keillah—of New York to Hillman, 11/24/14, Hillman Papers; Ellen Gates Starr to Jacob Abt, 11/23/15, published in the *Chicago Tribune*, 11/26/15, in which Starr attempts to arouse (successfully as it later turned out) a sense of guilt in Mr. Abt by quoting from Isaiah and Ezekiel and reminding him of the persecution of Jews abroad; Norma Fain Pratt, *Morris Hillquit: A Political Biography of an American Jewish Socialist* (Westport, Conn., 1979); Newton Baker to Filene, 5/18/20, Filene Papers; Filene to Baker, 5/14/20, Filene Papers; David Eakins, "The Origins of Corporate-Liberal Policy Research 1916-1922," in *Building the Organizational Society: Essays on Associational Activities in Modern America*, ed. Jerry Israel (New York, 1972); James Gilbert, *Designing the Industrial State: The Intellectual Pursuit of Collectivism in America, 1880-1940* (Chicago, 1972), pp. 101-4; Charles Maier, "Between Taylorism and Technocracy: European Ideologies and the Vision of Industrial Productivity in the 1920's," *Contemporary History*, 5 (1970), 54-57.

13. Daniel Nelson, *Managers and Workers: Origins of the New Factory System in the United States, 1880-1920* (Madison, Wis., 1975), pp. 156-61; Stuart D. Brandes, *American Welfare Capitalism, 1880-1940* (Chicago, 1970), p. 127; Bruno Ramirez, *When Workers Fight: The Politics of Industrial Relations in the Progressive Era, 1898-1916* (Westport, Conn., 1978), pp. 171-72, 208; Jacob Potofsky Memoir, Oral History Collection of Columbia University (hereafter OHCCU), p. 103; *Doc. Hist. 1920-22*, appendices.

14. "Minutes and Reports"—Report of the Work of the Board of Control of Labor Standards for Army Clothing through December 15, 1917," ACWA Papers; Hillman to Walter Lippmann, 7/5/17; Hillman to Baker, 10/16/17; Florence Kelley to Lippmann, 6/26/17, all in ACWA Papers; Hillman to Samuel Levin, 7/11/17; Hillman to GEB, 8/31/17; Hillman to John Williams, 7/13/17, 7/11/17, 9/7/17, all in Hillman Papers; *The Survey*, 2/2/18.

15. *Doc. Hist. 1916-18*; Jacob Potofsky to Frank Rosenblum, 8/10/17; Hillman to Baker, 10/16/17; William Z. Ripley to Hillman, 8/23/18, 8/20/18; Ripley to William H. Wanamaker, 7/24/18; Richard Feiss to Hillman, 3/1/18; N. I. Stone telegram to Hillman, 3/30/18; Hillman telegram to Potofsky, 9/15/18 and 10/1/18; Hillman to Alex Cohen, 11/20/18; Sam Levin to Hillman, 8/6/18; Schlossberg to Stone, 5/7/18, 6/2/18, 6/5/18; Hillman to Ripley, 8/23/18; Aldo Cursi report to GEB, 1/12/18; Hillman to Louis Hollander, 7/9/18; Ripley to Kirstein, 7/2/18; Ripley to Hillman, 8/8/18, all in ACWA Papers; *Doc. Hist. 1918-20. The Advance*, 3/22/18, published a statement by Hillman and ACW General Secretary Schlossberg supporting the war against "German autocracy and the war aims of British labor and the inter-allied labor conference." "Statement by William M. Leiserson," 3/20/20, and testimony by Judge Moses and Hillman at hearings on the Michaels-Stern injunction against the ACWA, ACWA Papers; Hillman to the *New York Tribune*, 12/15/17, and to *New York Times*, 12/24/17.

16. "Wartime Policies on Wages, Hours, and Other Labor Standards in the U.S. 1917-18," prepared by the U.S. Department of Labor, Wage and Hour Division, Economics Branch, May 1942, Felix Frankfurter Papers, Box 125, Library of Congress (this report focuses specifically on the War Labor Policies Board); John S. Smith, "Organized Labor and Government in the Wilson Era, 1913-21: Some Conclusions," *Labor History*, 3 (1962), 277-78; James Augustine

Walsh, "The Political Ideas of Felix Frankfurter, 1911-39" (Ph.D. dissertation, American University, 1976), pp. 57, 69, 72-73; Gerald D. Nash, "FDR and the World War I Origins of Early New Deal Labor Policy," *Labor History*, 1 (1960), 46-51; *Doc. Hist. 1918-20*; Frank. Adv. Bd. Proceedings, ACWA Papers; Potofsky Memoir, OHCCU, p. 130; Frankfurter and Rosensohn, "Survey," ACWA Papers; "Plan for Establishing 'Inside Shops,'" Nov. 1919, and "Report on 'Inside Shops'" of Clothing Manufacturers Industrial Exchange and Clothing Trade Association, 11/21/19, and association memo, 7/7/20, all in ACWA Papers.

17. Josephson, *Sidney Hillman*, chs. 7 and 8. As it would for others who witnessed this first major experiment in government-organized economic activity, the wartime experience helped shape Hillman's attitude toward the problem of economic recovery during the early years of the depression and the New Deal.

18. Ramirez, *When Workers Fight*, pp. 4-5, sees an irresolvable conflict between collective bargaining and scientific management not borne out in the case of the ACWA; Gilbert, *Designing the Industrial State*, p. 104; Milton Derber, *The American Idea of Industrial Democracy, 1865-1965* (Urbana, Ill., 1970) pp. 134-36, 244-45, 265-66; Monte A. Calvert, "The Search for Engineering Unity; The Professionalization of Special Interest," in Israel, *Building the Organizational Society*, p. 50; Haber, *Scientific Management*, pp. 32-33, 122, 129-31, 144, 149-50; Jean Trepp McKelvey, *AFL Attitudes toward Production, 1900-1932*, Cornell Studies in Industrial and Labor Relations, vol. 2 (Ithaca, N.Y., 1952), pp. 19-22, 67; William E. Atkin, *Technocracy and the American Dream: The Technocratic Movement, 1900-41* (Berkeley, Calif., 1977), pp. 8, 36; Milton J. Nadworny, *Scientific Management and the Unions, 1900-32: A Historical Analysis* (Cambridge, Mass., 1955), pp. 98, 105, 110, 118-19, 126-28, 135; Carpenter, *Competition and Collective Bargaining*, pp. 100-101; *The World*, 7/11/20; interview with Beatrice Bornstein, 6/7/79; interview with Laurence Levin, 6/8/79; Morris Cooke to Hillman, 6/18/19; Cooke to Harlow Person et al., 6/18/20 and 6/22/20; Cooke to Hillman, 10/10/22, 6/7/19, 9/10/19, 4/15/20, all in Morris L. Cooke Papers, Box 9, Files 73-90, Franklin Delano Roosevelt Library, Hyde Park (hereafter Cooke Papers); Morris Cooke, "Worked Material Classification for Men's and Boy's Clothing," 4/9/20, Box 172, Cooke Papers; Jacobstein to Cooke, 3/13/20, 2/10/20, Box 21, File 211, Cooke Papers.

19. *Doc. Hist. 1920-22*; *New Republic*, 1/2/29, 5/19/20; *The Nation*, 6/5/20; Frankfurter to Hillman, 10/7/19, Box 125, Frankfurter Papers; Frankfurter speech to 1920 ACWA Convention, *Conv. Proceedings 1918-20*; Carl Sandburg in *Chicago Daily News*, 2/8/20; Daniel T. Rodgers, *The Work Ethic in Industrial America, 1850-1920* (Chicago, 1978), pp. 58-60; Derber, *American Idea*, pp. 171, 244-45; Hillman to Warren Stone, 4/16/20, Hillman Papers; *Felix Frankfurter Reminiscences: An Intimate Portrait*, ed. Harlan B. Phillips (New York, 1962), pp. 204-6; *Doc. Hist. 1920-22*; J. Michael Eisner, *William Morris Leiserson: A Biography* (Madison, Wis., 1967); Walsh, "Political Ideas of Felix Frankfurter," pp. 72-73; Robert Bruere to Hillman, 10/8/20, Hillman Papers; U.S. Senate Committee on Education and Labor, "Hearing on the Clothing Industry," 6/9/21, excerpted in ACWA Papers; Potofsky Memoir, OHCCU, pp. 120-21, 130; Hillman to Frankfurter, 3/29/20; Frankfurter to Hillman, 3/30/20, both in Box 67, Frankfurter Papers; Max Lowenthal to Frankfurter,

12/20/20, Box 125, and Frankfurter letter to *New Republic*, 1/12/21, in Frankfurter Papers.

20. Chicago Joint Board ACWA, *Clothing Workers of Chicago*, pp. 198, 230-31, 257-58 (*Cases* Part III); John R. Commons, "Legal and Economic Job Analysis," *Yale Law Journal*, Dec. 1927; *Hart, Schaffner, and Marx Labor Agreement—Cases Decided by the Board of Arbitration Direct and Appealed, 1913-1925* (hereafter *HSM Arbit.*), and *Board of Arbitration Men's Clothing Industry—Chicago Market, 1920-31* (hereafter *Chic. Arbit.*), both in Library of the Amalgamated Clothing and Textile Workers, New York.

21. Chicago Joint Board ACWA, *Clothing Workers of Chicago*, pp. 191, 230-31, emphasizes the transformation of "wage-servants" into "citizens" of industry, conscious of their rights and responsibilities. Ray Stannard Baker, "Shop Council Plan Covers the Entire Clothing Industry," *New York Evening Post*, 2/14/20; *New Republic*, 5/6/20; Paul Blanshard, "Industrial Government in Rochester," *The Outlook*, 2/23/21.

22. Ramirez, *When Workers Fight*, ch. 11: Budish and Soule, *New Unionism*, pp. 290-302; *New Republic*, 2/1/19; "The Conference Method of Handling Disputes in the Men's Clothing Industry," published by the American Council Institute of Pacific Relations, 1929; the transcript of Hillman's speech to Montreal workers appeared in *The Advance*, 2/8/18.

23. Hillman testimony before Chicago Board of Arbitration, 12/13/19, and Hillman speech to the annual convention of the Industrial Relations Association, May 1920, both quoted in ACWA Red Book, 1910-21, housed with ACWA and Hillman Papers.

24. McKelvey, *AFL Attitudes*; Bernstein, *Lean Years*; Ellis W. Hawley, *The Great War and the Search for a Modern Order: A History of the American People and Their Institutions, 1917-1933* (New York, 1979), pp. 91-94; Steven J. Scheinberg, "The Development of Corporate Labor Policy, 1900-40" (Ph.D. dissertation, University of Wisconsin, 1966), pp. 115, 149-50.

25. Epstein, *Jewish Labor*, vol. 1, pp. 224-36, 370-75; Rischin, *Promised City*, passim; Howe, *World of Our Fathers*, pp. 296-300 and passim; Will Herberg, "The Jewish Labor Movement in the U.S.," *American Jewish Year Book* (New York, 1952); Thomas Kessner, *The Golden Door: Italian and Jewish Immigrant Mobility in New York City, 1880-1915* (New York, 1977); John Commons, quoted in Herberg, *Jewish Labor Movement*, p. 5; Herberg, *Jewish Labor Movement*, p. 11.

26. *HSM Arbit.*, Cases Appealed to the Board of Arbitration, 8/13/17, 5/16/19; *Doc. Hist. 1926-28*.

27. Indeed, even before the first arbitration agreement was in place at HSM, rank-and-file opposition to such arrangements surfaced during the 1910 strike. "A Call for Action" issued by a "Committee of Italian Workers" probably affiliated with the IWW denounced the pending arbitration agreement— "Don't hesitate, Don't mediate, Don't arbitrate, Don't wait!" it cried, urging the workers not to be "whipped back to work under an arbitration agreement." In fact, some contemporary observers speculated later that had there been a vote the agreement would have been defeated, untitled leaflet in private possession of Beatrice Bornstein; and Agnes Nestor, *International Socialist Review*, 1/11/11; Howard Barton Meyers, "The Policing of Labor Disputes in Chicago: A Case Study" (Ph.D. dissertation, University of Chicago, 1929), pp. 695-96; *Chicago Daily Socialist*, 1/16/11; ACWA Minutes of Joint Boards and Locals, "Minutes:

Joint Board of HSM Employees," 10/23/12-5/19/13; Hillman report, 11/21/12, 12/11/12, 4/30/13, both in ACWA Papers; Chicago Joint Board ACWA, *Clothing Workers of Chicago*, pp. 50-56; *Chicago Tribune*, 11/7/11; Anzuino D. Marimpietri, *From These Beginnings*, ACWA Papers; Potofsky Memoir, OHCCU, p. 48; *HSM Arbit.*, 5/7/17.

28. Sam Levin to Hillman, 6/6/18; Hillman to Schlossberg, 5/10/17, both in Hillman Papers; *HSM Arbit.*, 2/21/20, 6/8/20, 1/20/19, 5/16/19; *Chic. Arbit.*, 5/26/21; *HSM Arbit.*, 4/22/21, 1/9/22; August Bellanca to Hillman, 3/16/17, ACWA Papers; David Saposs's interview with Elias Rabkin, 2/12/19, in David J. Saposs Papers, Box 21, Wisconsin State Historical Society, Madison (hereafter Saposs Papers).

29. Jacobstein, "Can Industrial Democracy Be Efficient?"; Rabkin interview, Saposs Papers.

30. These generalizations are based, in part, on an examination of the case records of the HSM and Chicago Boards of Arbitration, the number of exemplary cases being too numerous to list here. *Doc. Hist. 1916-18*; Earl Dean Howard to William Leiserson, 8/12/24, William M. Leiserson Papers, Box 17, Wisconsin State Historical Society, Madison (hereafter Leiserson Papers).

31. Sam Levin to Leiserson, 1924, Box 17, Leiserson Papers; "A Report on the Working Conditions of Steam Pressers in the Clothing Factories of Henry Sonneborn & Co., Baltimore," 5/22/26, ACWA Papers; William G. Haber, "Workers Rights and the Introduction of Machinery in the Men's Clothing Industry," *Journal of Political Economy*, 33 (Aug. 1925), 388-409; Frank. Adv. Bd. report, 3/4/19, on the introduction of new machinery, ACWA Papers.

32. Thomas W. Holland, "The X Plan in the Clothing Trade," *New Republic*, 8/7/29; *Doc. Hist. 1924-26*; *HSM Arbit.*, 6/17/15, 1/10/14; *Chic. Arbit.*, 12/12/21, 1/16/22; *Doc. Hist. 1920-22*, appendix chart on decisions of impartial arbitration boards.

33. Ripley to Hillman, 9/4/18, 9/20/18, 11/18/18; War Department to Hillman, n.d.; Frank Rosenblum to Potofsky, 9/3/20, 9/27/20, all in Hillman Papers; "Disposition of Strikes and Lockouts Pending 8/1/20," ACWA Papers; "Report of General Conditions in Contracting Shops Manufacturing Clothing for the U.S. Government," 10/7/18, Box A16, Louis Kirstein Papers, Baker Library, Harvard University; William Z. Ripley, "Loading the Olive Branch," *The Survey*, 9/1/22; William Z. Ripley, "Bones of Contention," *The Survey*, 4/29/22.

34. Ripley, "Bones of Contention"; Leon Mann to George Bell, 2/25/19, ACWA Papers; interviews with Nathan Katzman and Leopold Gross, 1/18/80; Samuel Liptzin, *Tales of a Tailor*, trans. Max Rosenfield (New York, 1965) pp. 68, 137; *Chic. Arbit.*, 5/27/20, 6/23/20; Cahan, *Rise of David Levinsky*, pp. 270-72; Epstein, *Jewish Labor*, vol. 1, pp. 98-99.

35. *Doc. Hist. 1920-22*; "Minutes: Joint Board of HSM Employees 1912-1913," ACWA Papers; "Baltimore Joint Board Minutes 1915-1916," ACWA Papers; "Notes on Frank Rosenblum," ACWA Papers; Boutelle E. Lowe, "Industry and Trade Unionism in an American City," n.d., ACWA Papers; Stephen Skala, "The Story of the Great Organizing Campaign in Chicago, 1915-19," ACWA Papers; *Garment Worker* (house paper of the United Garment Workers), Aug. 1901 and Aug. 1903; Frankfurter and Rosensohn, "Survey"; Ripley to Hillman, 8/18/18; L. Feldman to Schlossberg, 12/20/17, all in ACWA Papers; "Official Souvenir of the 4th Biennial Convention, 1920," local

history of the Boston ACWA, ACWA Papers; H. Meyers, "Policy of Labor Disputes in Chicago," p. 652; *Immigrants in Industries, Parts 5-7*, in *Reports of the Industrial Commission of Immigration*, extract from S. Doc., vol. 73 (Washington, D.C., 1909), pp. 387-88; "Trade Union Methods and Policies," in Saposs Papers, Box 21; *HSM Arbit.*, 2/6/20.

36. Rischin, *Promised City*, pp. 26, 45; Ezra Mendelsohn, *The Class Struggle in the Pale: The Formative Years of the Jewish Workers Movement in Tsarist Russia* (Cambridge, 1970), pp. 6-17, 59, 64, 82, 85; Howe, *World of Our Fathers*, passim; Nora Levin, *While Messiah Tarried: Jewish Socialist Movements, 1871-1917* (New York, 1977), pp. 219-39; Budish and Soule, *New Unionism*, pp. 51-52.

37. Nora Levin, *While Messiah Tarried*, passim; Arthur Liebman, "The Ties That Bind—Jewish Support for the Left," *American Jewish Historical Quarterly*, 66 (Dec. 1976), 290-94; Henry Tobias, *The Jewish Bund in Russia: From Its Origins to 1905* (Stanford, Calif., 1972), pp. 7-8 and passim; David Lane, *The Roots of Russian Communism* (University Park, Pa., 1968), p. 167.

38. Howe, *World of Our Fathers*, pp. 120, 292-95; Epstein, *Jewish Labor*, vol. 1, pp. 305, 350; Herberg, "Jewish Labor Movement"; Mendelsohn, *Class Struggle*, p. 88 and passim; Rischin, *Promised City*, pp. 150-60; interview with Nathan Katzman, 1/18/80; interview with Samuel Liptzin, 2/2/80; Liptzin, *Tales of a Tailor*; Joseph Schlossberg, *The Workers and Their World: Aspects of the Workers' Struggle at Home and Abroad* (New York, 1935); *Doc. Hist. 1914-16*.

39. Table 51, "Affiliation with Trade Unions of Males 21 Years of Age or Over," Extract from Senate Documents, vol. 73, *Immigrants in Industry, Parts 5-7*, pp. 316-18, in Saposs Papers; Passero "Ethnicity in the Men's Ready-Made Clothing Industry"; interview with Mini Corder, 4/5/79; Lazarus Marcovitz to GEB, 6/15/16; Frank Bellanca to Schlossberg, 3/7/15; P. Sinkus to Schlossberg, 11/2/15 and 10/21/15; Marcovitz to Hillman and Schlossberg, 8/20/15; Hillman to William Zuckerman, 11/28/25; Bekampis to GEB, 1/22/18 and 8/26/18; Dusevico to Hillman, 4/22/18; Dorothy Bellanca to Schlossberg, 11/27/16; Extract of Fiorello La Guardia report to New York Joint Board meeting, 2/19/16; August Bellanca to Schlossberg, 9/6/15 and 4/14/16; "Scabs and Scab Agencies: Proven Facts of the Scandalous Scabbism of the IWW," pamphlet, all in Hillman Papers; Madanick to Hillman, 11/1/15; "1916 Convention Materials (Resolutions, Drafts, Proceedings)," resolution by Lithuanian locals 54 and 58 of Brooklyn; Bellanca to Brais, 5/19/15; K. Jurgelianis to Potofsky, 1/20/19; Jurgelianis to Schlossberg, 8/31/19, all in ACWA Papers.

40. Passero, "Ethnicity in the Men's Ready-Made Clothing Industry," pp. 160-64, 151-56; Edwin Fenton, *Immigrants and Unions, A Case Study: Italians and American Labor, 1870-1920* (1957; reprint ed., New York, 1975), pp. 463, 467-68; David Saposs interview with Frank Bellanca, 3/29/19, Saposs Papers, Box 21; Schlossberg to Nicholas Klein, 3/8/16, ACWA Papers; Robert F. Foerster, *The Italian Emigration of Our Times* (1919; reprint ed., New York, 1969) pp. 347-48, 327; Kessner, *Golden Door*, p. 56.

41. Passero, "Ethnicity in the Men's Ready-Made Clothing Industry," pp. 151-56, 305-6, 314, 319; Fenton, *Immigrants and Unions*, pp. 462-63, 469. Fenton notes (p. 487) that the situation began to change with the creation of an Italian committee by the Women's Trade Union League in 1907; Foerster,

*Italian Emigration*, pp. 347-48, 381; Barbara Klacznska, "Why Women Work: A Comparison of Various Groups in Philadelphia, 1910-1930," *Labor History*, 17 (1976), 77-85; *Chic. Arbit.*, 2/27/20 and 8/23/21, for example; interview with Nora Piore, 5/21/79; Jacob Loft, "Jewish Workers in the New York City Men's Clothing Industry—Report of a Preliminary Study," *Jewish Social Studies*, 2 (Jan. 1940), 63-66.

42. Biographical sketches of Marimpietri, Joseph Catalanotti, Aldo Cursi, Ulisse De Dominicis, ACWA Papers; Fenton, *Immigrants and Unions*, pp. 16-18, 510-14, 467-68; Passero, "Ethnicity in the Men's Ready-Made Clothing Industry," pp. 315-18; *Chic. Arbit.*; Frank Bellanca to Schlossberg, 2/12/14, ACWA Papers.

43. Potofsky to Grandinetti, 1/19/21, Emilio Grandinetti Papers, Box 4, Immigration History Research Center Archives, St. Paul, Minn. (hereafter Grandinetti Papers); "Summary of the 1910 Strike," culled mainly from the *Chicago Daily Socialist* reports on the activity of a well-established Italian syndicalist current in persuading the rank and file to reject the arbitration agreement proposed at a 1/16/11 meeting, ACWA Papers; Minutes, Baltimore Joint Board, 1915-16, ACWA Papers; August Bellanca to Schlossberg, 9/6/15, ACWA Papers; Aldo Cursi to GEB, 1917; A. Bellanca to Schlossberg, 1915; Frank Bellanca to Schlossberg, 1/6/15, 2/4/15, 2/12/15, 3/7/15; Hillman talk with shop stewards in Baltimore, 1/15/18; F. Bellanca to Hillman, 6/15/19, all in Hillman Papers; *Doc. Hist. 1914-16*; GEB Minutes, July 1920 and July-Aug. 1924, ACWA Papers.

44. Paul Arnone to Schlossberg, 6/9/17; Louis Feldman to Schlossberg, 9/29/15; Feldman to Hillman, 12/28/15; Artoni to Schlossberg, 1918; Louis Feldman report, 6/30/18, from Rochester; Abraham Shiplacoff to Hillman, 6/5/16; Valenti to Schlossberg, 9/6/17; Cursi to Schlossberg, 8/23/17, all in Hillman Papers; Eli Oliver to Frank Rosenblum, 5/17/25, ACWA Papers; Grandinetti to Potofsky, 9/20/16, Jacob Potofsky Papers (now housed with ACWA Papers at Cornell) (hereafter Potofsky Papers); J. A. Bekampis to Schlossberg, 3/1/19, ACWA Papers; GEB Min., Sept. 1928 and Sept. 1929, ACWA Papers; Fenton, *Immigrants and Unions*, p. 471.

45. Valenti to Schlossberg, 9/6/17; Gillis to Hillman, 7/5/17; Valenti to Schlossberg, 12/28/17, all in Hillman Papers; GEB Min., May 1924; Fenton, *Immigrants and Unions*, pp. 477-80, 526-27; Foerster, *Italian Emigration*, passim; Anthony Capraro to Potofsky, 6/16/22 and 5/26/22, Anthony Capraro Papers, Box 3, Immigration History Research Center Archives, St. Paul, Minn. (hereafter Capraro Papers); "The Man without a Friend," leaflet by a contrite ex-scab describing the social ostracism he faced in his Italian community, Grandinetti Papers, Folder 11; strike leaflet, Box 4, Capraro Papers, which exhorted Italian workers "not to dishonor your name and that of your family" by scabbing; Fenton, *Immigrants and Unions*, pp. 509-10, 515-16, 520; Frank Rosenblum to Hillman, 12/6/16, ACWA Papers; "Official Souvenir of the 4th Biennial Convention 1920," ACWA Papers; Saposs interview with David Wolff, 3/1/19, Saposs Papers, Box 21.

46. Saposs interviews with Joseph Schlossberg, 2/27/19, and with Sam Levin, 12/26/18, Saposs Papers, Box 21; *Doc. Hist. (1918-20, 1920-22, 1922-24)*; David Saposs, "The Americanization Work of the ACW," Box 21, Saposs Papers. Saposs emphasized the efforts of the ACW leadership to "substitute the labor leader for the clan leader," which included attempts "to weaken the old national tie" and "to initiate members into the mysteries of self-government,"

along with efforts aimed at "specifically encouraging citizenship and developing an interest in American institutions." The end product was "a well controlled, orderly membership which is trained to keep its bargains with the employers, to refrain from impulsive action common to unassimilated foreigners."

47. Morris Cooke to Hillman, 6/18/20, and Cooke to H. S. Person et al., 6/18/20 and 6/22/20, Cooke Papers; "A Fight for Production Standards," *Evening Post*, 1/5/21; *Doc. Hist. 1920-22*; NICB Report; Hillman to New York Manufacturers Association, 12/8/20, ACWA Papers; Sidney Hillman, "Week Work with Standards," *The Advance*, 5/28/20; "Plan for Establishing Inside Shops," Nov. 1919, and Memo from New York Clothing Trade Association, 7/7/20, ACWA Papers; Frank. Adv. Bd., New York, 1919, ACWA Papers.

48. NICB Report; Max Friedman to Jacob H. Schiff, 12/19/18; Jacob Spitz to Potofsky, 1/24/20, ACWA Papers; Joseph Schlossberg, "Standards of Production," *The Advance*, 5/28/20; *Doc. Hist. 1916-18*; Herberg, "Jewish Labor Movement," pp. 38, 54.

49. *Doc. Hist. (1914-16* and *1918-20)*. The major fight over the issue took place at the 1920 convention and can be followed in *Convention Proceedings* for that year; GEB Min., May 1920, ACWA Papers; "Extraordinary Meeting of the GEB—Minutes," 12/18/20, ACWA Papers; *The Advance*, 5/28/20; *DNR*, 5/17/20, 5/21/20; Potofsky to Hillman, 6/10/24, ACWA Papers; Liptzin, *Tales of a Tailor*, pp. 256-57, 168-72; *Doc. Hist. 1920-22* (also *1922-24* and *1924-26*, as recalcitrant locals and joint boards continued to raise the issue); L. Marcovitz to Hillman, 3/13/20, Hillman Papers; Irving Howe interview with Israel Breslow, 1968, YIVO Archives, New York City; Leary to F. Rosenblum, 12/24/23, ACWA Papers; GEB Min., Dec. 1921, ACWA Papers; "Needle Trades—1920's", a précis of an article by Salutsky, "Constructive Radicalism in the Textile Industry," Daniel Bell Collection, Box 3, Tamiment Library, New York City (hereafter Bell Collection); GEB Min., May 1924, ACWA Papers.

50. GEB Min., Aug. 1922, ACWA Papers; Feldman to Schlossberg, 10/22/15, Hillman Papers; Melvyn Dubofsky, "Success and Failure of Socialism in New York City, 1900-18: A Case Study," *Labor History*, 9 (1968), 365-73; Howe, *World of Our Fathers*, passim; Rischin, *Promised City*, passim; Rochester Joint Board Report, 1918, ACWA Papers; Schlossberg to GEB, 1/2/16; Rosenblum to Schlossberg, 1916; A. Bellanca to Hillman, 7/10/16, all in ACWA Papers; *Doc. Hist. (1916-18, 1920-22, 1918-20)*; Saposs interview with David Wolff, 3/1/19, Box 21, Saposs Papers; Liptzin, *Tales of a Tailor*, pp. 167-72; Hillman to B. Charney Vladeck, 4/15/15 and 5/4/15, Baruch Charney Vladeck Papers, Tamiment Library, New York City (hereafter Vladeck Papers); Epstein, *Jewish Labor*, vol. 2, passim.

51. Many historians have noted the kinship between messianic traditions in the Old World and the Jewish socialist movement in the New, but Rischin, Howe, and Herberg do so emphatically. *Conv. Proceedings 1916*; Saposs interview with David Wolff, 2/27/19, Box 21, Saposs Papers; interview with Beatrice Bornstein, 6/7/79; interview with Laurence Levin, 6/8/79; Saposs interview with Hyman Schneid, 1919, Saposs Papers; interviews with Nathan Katzman and Leopold Gross, 1/18/80; biographical sketches of Potofsky, Rosenblum, Sander Genis, Bessie Abramovitz-Hillman, Louis Hollander, Dorothy Jacobs-Bellanca, J. B. S. Hardman/Salutsky, Joseph Schlossberg, Sam Levin, Lazarus Marcovitz, Jack Kroll, Charles Weinstein, and Hyman Blumberg, all in ACWA Papers; Josephson, *Sidney Hillman*, ch. 1.

52. The *Forward* group had, in addition, opposed the election of Schlossberg, a member of the Socialist Labor party, to the post of general secretary, and had always resented Hillman as an outsider to the closely knit circle of New York Jewish socialists who founded the other needle unions; GEB Min., 1922, ACWA Papers. Howe, *World of Our Fathers*, pp. 351-52; Chicago Joint Board ACWA, *Clothing Workers of Chicago*; Epstein, *Jewish Labor*, vol. 2, pp. 414-17; Herberg, "Jewish Labor Movement," p. 23; Hillman to Sam Levin, 11/12/14; Hillman to Rosenblum, 12/10/14 and 6/9/15, Hillman Papers; Brais to Schlossberg, 5/12/15, Hillman Papers; John Williams to Potofsky, 11/2/14, Potofsky Papers; Epstein, *Jewish Labor*, vol. 2, pp. 48-49.

53. Howe, *World of Our Fathers*, pp. 326-30; "Queries on the Political Committee and the TUEL, 1921-27," Box 8, Bell Collection; Harry Fleischman, *Norman Thomas: A Biography* (New York, 1964), p. 95; Memo on GEB meeting, 1/5/22, from GEB Min., ACWA Papers; GEB Min., May 1924, ACWA Papers; *Doc. Hist. 1920-22*; Hillman to Vladeck, 6/3/22, Vladeck Papers; Children's Joint Board Report to Schlossberg, 6/15/20, ACWA Papers. Anthony Capraro, onetime syndicalist, hero and near martyr of the 1919 Lawrence strike, ACW organizer and Workers Party-TUEL member, and later in the 1930s a management representative in labor negotiations, provides a fascinating critique of Josephson's account of the faction fight and Hillman's role, Box 5, Capraro Papers. GEB Min., Aug. 1922, ACWA Papers.

54. The standard accounts of the formative years of the Communist party are: Theodore Draper, *The Roots of American Communism* (New York, 1957); Irving Howe and Lewis Coser, *The American Communist Party* (Boston, 1957); and Bert Cochran, *Labor and Communism: The Conflict That Shaped American Unions* (Princeton, N.J., 1977). See also Howe, *World of Our Fathers*, pp. 325-40; Epstein, *Jewish Labor*, vol. 2, pp. 64-66, 110-11, 115, 123, 130-31, 163-68, and passim; Herberg, "Jewish Labor Movement"; interview with Sam Liptzin, 2/2/80; interview with Leopold Gross, 1/18/80; interview with Abe Chatman, 8/23/78; Zaretz, *Amalgamated Clothing Workers*, p. 258; Oral History Collection, Charles Zimmerman file, Box 6, 11/13/64, YIVO Archives (hereafter Zimmerman oral history); GEB Min., Nov. 1924, ACWA Papers; Liptzin, *Tales of a Tailor*, pp. 167-72; ACW "Diaries," file on meeting to investigate factionalism in local 5, ACWA Papers; "Amalgamated Clothing Workers of America," Box 5, Bell Collection; "Memo on Shopfloor Grievances and Stoppages, Rochester 1925-26" (hereafter Stoppages Memo), ACWA Papers.

55. Capraro to William Z. Foster, 7/18/22, Box 4, Capraro Papers; interview with Liptzin, 2/2/80; *Doc. Hist. 1924-26*; "Report of the National Committee, Needle Trades Section, TUEL, 1924," Box 45, Charles Zimmerman Records, ILGWU Archives, New York City (hereafter Zimmerman Records); Irving Howe interview with Charles Zimmerman, YIVO Archives; "TUEL 1923—Report of Secretary Joseph Zack, Secretary of the National Needle Trades Committee, to the National Committee of the TUEL," Bell Collection (hereafter Zack Report); Johnstone letters, 11/20/25 and 11/15/26, Box 3, Bell Collection; "Statement by Weinstein, Gitlow, and Lipshitz," Mar.-Apr., 1925, File 8, Box 40, Zimmerman Records; National Committee of Needle Trades Section TUEL letter, 5/13/25, File 8, Box 45, Zimmerman Records; Melech Epstein, *Profiles of Eleven* (Detroit, 1965), pp. 290-91.

56. *The Liberator*, July 1920, carried an article by Mike Gold defending week work with standards, and Gold's article in *The Liberator* of June 1922 described the recently concluded ACWA convention as preparation for "the red

dawn of labor." The Bell Collection contains much material that attempts to document the Byzantine factional alignments and realignments within the CP hierarchy which determined its shifting relations with the Hillman elite during the period—see especially the précis of Salutsky's article, "Needle Trades—1920's" in Box 3, written in 1922; Bell's interview with Earl Browder, 6/22/55, in Box 9, which examines the tensions between the party leadership and its caucus in the ACWA, especially over production standards; Bell's "Notes on TUEL Minutes, 1923-27," in Box 3, esp. 3/7/24, where Foster warns against any open break with the Hillman leadership; and Browder's minutes for 5/1/24, Box 3; *Conv. Proceedings (1918-20, 1920-22, 1922-24)*; *DNR*, 11/18/21; Hillman speech on his Russian trip at Carmen's Hall, 11/18/21; GEB Min., Aug. 1922, ACWA Papers; *Baltimore Evening Sun*, 1/5/23. The joint agreement with the Soviet Union was called the Russian-American Industrial Corporation, under whose auspices nine clothing and textile factories were established, to which the ACW contributed not only money but a complement of skilled cutters and industrial engineers; see Mary Agnes Hamilton interview with Hillman, *Contemporary Review*, vol. 1, 2/27/27, pp. 210-15; Hillman speech in Carnegie Hall, 12/1/22, Hillman Papers; *New York Call*, 11/22/21 and 7/15/22; GEB Min., Dec. 1921, ACWA Papers; *DNR*, 9/1/22, 11/26/23; *New York World*, 10/20/22; George Soule, letter in *New York Globe and Commercial Advertiser*, 11/18/22; *The Liberator*, Dec. 1923; *Daily Worker*, 1/22/24; Federal Bureau of Investigation, File # 61-9899, Internal Security File on Sidney Hillman, released under the Freedom of Information Act.

57. Hillman Carnegie Hall speech, 12/1/22, ACWA Papers; Hillman speech before the Foreign Policy Association, 2/3/23, ACWA Papers.

58. Zaretz, *Amalgamated Clothing Workers*, pp. 25-58; Herberg, "Jewish Labor Movement"; *Conv. Proceedings 1924*. To follow the extremely intricate maneuverings of both the ACWA and CP leaderships over the La Follette campaign, the Bell and Zimmerman collections are especially valuable, as are the papers of J. B. S. Hardman (housed at the Tamiment Library) and the Anthony Capraro Papers. In Capraro's case, much of the correspondence was written in Italian and I want to thank Nunzio Pernicone of New York City for graciously agreeing to translate some of this correspondence for me. See also: Draper, *Roots of American Communism*; Howe, *World of Our Fathers*; Howe and Coser, *American Communist Party*; and Hawley, *Great War*. Henry David, "Labor and Political Action after WWI, 1919-24," *Labor and Nation*, 2 (Feb.-Mar., 1946), pp. 27-32; Cochran, *Labor and Communism*; GEB Min. during 1924 are of course also valuable.

59. Interview with Liptzin, 2/2/80; Liptzin, *Tales of a Tailor*; Joseph Zack, "TUEL 1923—Report of the Secretary of the National Needle Trades Commission to the National Committee of the TUEL," 2/2/27, Box 2, Bell Collection; reports of "Trade Union Committee 1925-27," Box 3, Bell Collection; Howe interview with Paul Novick, 3/29/68, YIVO Archives; Howe interview with Charles Zimmerman, 4/13/68, YIVO Archives; "The Hillman-Beckerman Clique," leaflet, undated, Box 40, File 5, Zimmerman Records, ILGWU Archives; "Report of the National Committee, Needle Trades Section of the TUEL," Jan. 1925, Box 45, File 8, Zimmerman Records.

60. *Conv. Proceedings 1926*; Stoppages Memo, ACWA Papers; "An Appeal to the Lithuanian Amalgamated Tailors," issued by Lithuanian local 203 in Rochester, 2/22/21, ACWA Papers; K. Jurgelianis to Potofsky, 1/20/19; Jurgelianis to Schlossberg, 8/31/19; Resolution of Lithuanian Branches 54 and 58

in Brooklyn, Jan. 1921, demanding abolition of piecework and threatening to call a secessionist convention, all in ACWA Papers; De Luca to Schlossberg, 9/26/25; GEB Min., Aug. 1922; "1916 Convention Materials"; Bekampis to GEB, 1/22/18 and 8/26/18; GEB Min., Dec. 1925; Resolution of local 138, Philadelphia, 7/17/25, all in ACWA Papers.

61. Stoppages Memo, ACWA Papers; Tesso Tomassini, "Tactics and Methods of the ACWA," Box 3, Capraro Papers; Capraro to Giovanitti, 5/27/28, Box 1, Capraro Papers; unsigned letter to Gitlow, Krumbein, and William Weinstone, 8/11/26, commenting on Capraro's plan for organizing an Italian Trade Union Council of America (and draft of Capraro Plan), Box 1, Capraro Papers; correspondence between Capraro and August Bellanca, 4/14/28, 4/11/28, 3/30/28, 10/15/22, 8/23/23, 9/2/23, 9/10/23, 9/24/25 (trans. Nunzio Pernicone), Box 6, Capraro Papers; correspondence with Frank Bellanca, 8/22/25, 11/17/25, 1/17/24, and Capraro to Hillman, 8/8/26, Box 5, Capraro Papers; Peter Teem to Capraro, 1924?, Box 2, Capraro Papers; Capraro to Teem, 9/11/26, and Teem to Capraro, 9/7/26, Box 2, Capraro Papers; "Statement by Mr. Anthony Capraro, Secretary of Rank and File Committee of the Amalgamated," 1926?, Box 1, Capraro Papers; Dorothy Bellanca to Capraro, 6/14/28; A. Bellanca to Capraro, 5/4/22; A. Bellanca to Capraro, 6/30/25; A. Bellanca to Capraro, 10/26/23; A. Bellanca to Capraro, 11/2/23, all in Box 6, Capraro Papers; GEB Min., Feb. 1925, Dec. 1925, and Oct. 1927, ACWA Papers; "Report of Proceedings of the 4th Annual Conference, Needle Trades Section, TUEL-NYC, Jan. 1927," Box 45, Zimmerman Records; Zack Report, Bell Collection; "Report of the Secretary on Purposes of the Special Amalgamated Conference," 1/3/27, Box 45, Zimmerman Records; Hillman to Levin, 6/4/25, Hillman Papers; A. Bellanca to Capraro, 2/9/25; A. Bellanca to John Bongiovonni, 6/1/25, ACWA Papers; GEB Min., Aug. 1926, ACWA Papers; *Doc. Hist. 1926-28*; Peter Teem to Capraro, 1926?, Box 2, Capraro Papers; William Z. Foster, "Report to Trade Union Committee of the Central Executive Committee," 9/17/26 and 1/14/27, Box 3, Bell Collection. The Italian Labor Council of America noted the general problem of *personalissmo* politics where Italian labor bosses "see to it that no general interlocking movement among Italian workers developed and that whatever leadership was created should remain regionalistic, clannish, and almost feudal in its antiquated form and function." "What Is and Why an Italian Labor Council of America," Box 1, Capraro Papers.

62. *Doc. Hist. 1926-28*, p. 8.

63. *St. Louis Post-Dispatch*, 50th Anniversary Edition, 12/9/28, pp. 6-7.

64. Morris Cooke to Hillman, 4/15/20, Cooke Papers; Cooke to Hillman, 12/29/19, Jacobstein file, Cooke Papers; Sidney Hillman, "A Successful Experiment in Unemployment Insurance," *Annals of the American Academy of Political and Social Science*, Mar. 1931.

65. Sidney Hillman, "A Shorter Working Day and a Minimum Wage," *Harvard Business Review*, 11 (July 1933), 457-61; Sidney Hillman, "Unemployment Reserves," *Atlantic Monthly*, 148 (Nov. 1931), 661-69. Numerous Hillman proposals on unemployment insurance, on planning, on the creation of tripartite labor boards which foreshadowed the NRA arrangements can be found in the Hillman Papers; for example: Hillman testimony on Mastick-Steingut Unemployment Reserve Fund Bill, 3/18/31; Hillman testimony before the Senate Sub-Committee of the Committee on Manufacturers on establishing a National Economic Council, 1931, 1st Sess., 72d Cong., in which

Hillman criticized the Swope Plan; Hillman testimony before the Senate Finance Committee, Mar. 1933, on industrial planning; Sidney Hillman, "Labor Leads toward Planning," *Survey Graphic*, 21 (Mar. 1932), 586-88. Hillman's involvement in pre-New Deal policy formulation is suggested by the following: Leo Wolman to William Leiserson, 10/24/31, Box 1, Leiserson Papers; Frankfurter to Hillman, 1/5/33, Potofsky Papers; Potofsky Memoir, OHCCU, pp. 208-11, 230-34; Frances Perkins Memoir, OHCCU, vol. 4, pp. 302-21; Hillman to Perkins, 12/31/32, and memo, Special MS Collection, Part I, Letters to Frances Perkins, Frances Perkins Collection, Columbia University Archives, New York; GEB Min., June 1933, ACWA Papers.

# Catholics, Communists, and Republicans: Irish Workers and the Organization of the Transport Workers Union

## JOSHUA B. FREEMAN

Between 1933 and 1937, a newly formed union, the Transport Workers Union of America (TWU), succeeded in enlisting and winning contracts for some 30,000 New York transit workers, an impressive accomplishment in an industry with a half-century record of autocratic management, broken strikes, and defeated unions. The TWU, however, was soon known not only for its contractual gains, but also for its unusual combination of a heavily Irish membership and a leadership close to the Communist Party (CP). Although in some ways the TWU was exceptional, the role of Irish workers in the formation of the union, their interaction with the CP, and the impact of republicanism on both processes point to a general relationship between nationalism, unionism, and radicalism that helps explain the success and character of the CIO and, in turn, the popular base for the New Deal.

For generations, the New York transit industry, in one worker's words, was "a dumping ground for the Irish."[1] Although in both the popular image and the scholarly literature Irish immigration has been almost exclusively associated with the nineteenth century, a substantial if diminished migration across the Atlantic continued well into the twentieth century.[2] In every year but four between 1901 and 1930—excepting the wartime period from 1915 to 1920—over 20,000 Irish immigrants came to the U.S., for a thirty-year total of 705,837 arrivals. In 1930 there were 923,542 foreign-born Irish living in the U.S., about half the number a half-century earlier, but still a sizable group in absolute terms. Furthermore, the Irish were heavily concentrated in a few urban areas, with over a quarter living in New York City or neighboring Westchester County, so that in selected regions they formed a major component of the total immigrant population.[3]

Even in its late phase, Irish immigration was primarily a rural to urban migration. The Irish countryside was poor, backward, and overwhelmingly agricultural. Farms were small and by custom passed from father to but one son; other male children and daughters without dowries were forced to compete for the few available rural jobs, head to the cities, or emigrate. In a land of few opportunities and little wealth, the last option, for generations an established part of Irish life, continued to hold great attraction through the 1920s.[4]

With the exception of a minority of skilled workers leaving Irish cities, most Irish immigrants had few skills of value in the American urban labor market. As a result, Irish women who sought employment generally became domestic servants, with a smaller number taking office, teaching, or semiskilled factory jobs. Similarly, men tended to concentrate in jobs with few entrance-level skill requirements, generally poorly paid and nonunion. In New York, specific industries and even specific companies requiring large unskilled work forces became centers of employment for recent Irish arrivals: utilities, construction, trucking, the docks, American Express, Yonkers carpet factories, supermarkets, some city government jobs, and transit. Once established, these patterns tended to reproduce themselves as friends and relatives helped one another to find jobs, and word spread about where an Irishman off the boat could find work.[5]

In the early 1930s, although no firm statistics are available, the existing evidence suggests that foreign-born Irish made up roughly half of the New York transit work force, by far the largest ethnic group present, though varying in importance from job category to job category and company to company.[6] Transit jobs can be roughly divided along functional lines into three groups: transportation work, that is, actually operating buses, trolleys, subways, and subway stations; fixed location work, in shops, barns, and powerhouses; and maintenance of way, keeping up the various structures throughout the system. Transportation workers were the largest group and included motormen, switchmen, bus and trolley drivers, conductors, train guards, changemakers (called ticket agents), and porters. Their jobs generally required either relatively simple skills or skills that could be learned through on-the-job training. In many cases, however, at least some contact with the riding public was involved, therefore necessitating English-speaking workers. To meet this particular manpower need as cheaply as possible, it had become the long-established practice to hire large numbers of Irish immigrants, so that industrywide transportation workers tended to be heavily Irish, and in some companies almost exclusively so. In the interwar years, these were usually "country people" from the poorer counties of southern and western Ireland.

Shop, powerhouse, car barn, and maintenance of way jobs, on the other hand, did not involve public contact and varied greatly in required skill levels. As a result, this segment of the work force came from extremely varied backgrounds. Irish workers were well represented in some of the less-skilled categories, such as car cleaners and track workers, and some "city people" with industrial experience or vocational training in Ireland held skilled shop craft jobs. Overall, however, the Irish were but one of many ethnic groups represented in nontransportation work, and constituted only a relatively small minority of the workers.

Crosscutting this occupational distribution was an unequal distribution of Irish workers among companies. Of the three separate subway and el systems, only the largest, the Interborough Rapid Transit Co. (IRT), had an overall majority of Irish workers, although the Brooklyn-Manhattan Transit Co. (BMT) and the much smaller Independent Subway System (ISS) had sizable Irish minorities. By contrast, while some of the city's smaller bus and trolley companies had few if any Irish workers, the main Manhattan and Bronx lines—the Third Avenue Railway, the Fifth Avenue Coach Company, and New York City Omnibus—all were very heavily Irish, with probably well over three-quarters of their workers born in Ireland.[7]

For Irish transit workers, work was but one sphere of shared experience, one arena in which relationships formed, for they constituted a distinct social group situated in the dual setting of the transit industry and the New York Irish community. Many knew one another even before emigrating; others met in the Irish neighborhoods of New York where they found new homes. Most were Catholic, attended church with one another, and joined the same church-sponsored organizations. The numerous Irish fraternal and social groups, such as the Ancient Order of Hibernians and the county associations, had large transit-worker memberships. Athletic events and dances—the bread and butter of New York Irish social life—likewise brought together men who worked in the transit industry. So did the bars where Irish transit workers socialized, especially the single men who made up a large percentage of the work force. Others knew one another through the Democratic party or the many Irish nationalist organizations.[8]

Father Charles Owen Rice once described New York transit workers as part of "the industrial peasantry of the United States," a suggestive formulation at least when applied to the Irish immigrants among them.[9] Many Irish transit workers were but a few years removed from the Irish peasantry, and social, political, and characterological patterns forged in that old world continued in the new. Although generally literate, many Irish workers still had only a dim understanding of metropolitan life. Mike Quill, for example, who was to rise to the top of the TWU, first saw a telephone only on his arrival in New York. Although Quill quickly developed a lifelong fascination with telephones, airplanes, and other technical marvels of the late industrial age, many of his fellow immigrants remained deeply suspicious. It was common for Irish transit workers to send a neighbor or child with a message, rather than use a phone.[10]

More important, in many cases Irish workers had little if any experience with wage labor before their jobs in transit, and old systems of authority—deference, obligation, and repression—were reproduced on the transit lines. A large percentage of transit managers and supervisors, on all levels, were themselves Irish Catholic and jobs and promotions were often obtained through personal favor or even kinship networks. In an effort to ensure employee loyalty, transit companies sponsored extensive paternalistic programs and company unions, in some cases with a decidedly Irish flavor. At the same time, work regulations were detailed and strict, disciplinary procedures personalistic and often deliberately degrading, and punishments harsh. For most Irish workers, unionism was at best an alien notion, and displeasure with specific aspects of their jobs was matched by relief at simply having work, and the fear of losing it.[11]

The very act of emigration, of course, was the beginning of a break with the past. In Ireland, parental authority was strong and usually continued until marriage at a late age. In New York, Irish workers were on their own, freed from the constant surveillance of family and community, particularly since extended celibacy and late marriage continued to be typical. If on one hand this led to widespread loneliness, alcoholism, and neurosis, on the other hand it left men free of responsibilities and restraints. Having already left behind the tight, structured world of the Irish countryside, but not yet fully assimilated into the industrial world, these recently rural Irish immigrants faced the choice of either accepting a new way of life as they found it or helping to transform it.[12]

In the post-World War I years, the New York transit industry was, with some minor exceptions, nonunion. Working conditions were poor, hours extremely long, and pay rates for the most part low. In the transportation departments, twelve-hour days and seven-day weeks were not unusual for those with regular "tricks" or work assignments, while low-seniority "extras" faced the opposite misery of unsteady work and extensive, unpaid waiting time. In the shops and powerhouses hours were shorter, but still rarely fewer than fifty hours a week. Few workers had vacations or sick pay, and accident-caused injuries and deaths were frequent. Wage rates varied considerably, from very low for the unskilled to fairly high for top craftsmen and subway motormen. Although long hours helped bring up weekly earnings, the cost of required uniforms, pension deductions, and company union dues cut into pay packets. Most transit workers could afford to live only quite modestly, and indebtedness was widespread. Lower-paid workers often found themselves unable to afford marriage or families.[13]

As long as alternatives existed, transit labor turnover was high, with many men entering the industry only as a temporary expedient.[14] The depression, however, ended such fluidity, as other jobs became impossible to get. At the same time, a decline in ridership led the transit companies to undertake steep cost-cutting programs. By 1933 transit wage rates had generally been cut by 10 percent, most of the few existing benefits eliminated, and the work force reduced through extensive layoffs and an accompanying speedup. Earnings were further diminished by work-sharing programs and hours reductions.[15]

It was against this background of job immobility and deteriorating working conditions that the TWU was created. In some respects its origins were typical of new CIO unions, lying in both an incipient process of self-organization and externally initiated and directed activity, in this case by the CP. The integration and expansion of these two varieties of praxis, under Communist leadership, led to the formation of the union and the successful organization of the industry.

The CP began organizing New York transit workers in the second half of 1933 as part of a new, national industrial concentration policy. The Communist effort had two interrelated goals—the formation of an industrial transit-workers union in which the party would play a significant role, and the recruitment of transit workers into the party itself. Although the CP already had a few members and contacts in the industry, the party's main union-building strategy was intensive outreach at selected locations by "concentration units," teams of outside organizers.

The strongest response to the CP agitation came on the IRT, and in particular in the company's large repair complexes and powerhouses. In these facilities, men worked in constant proximity, often on interrelated tasks, and in some cases with considerable autonomy. Many strains of craft, union, and radical traditions were present: there were former UMW, AFL craft-union, and IWW members, veterans of the European trade-union movement, and a variety of leftists, including several Communists and members of Communist-affiliated fraternal groups. In several locations, informal groups of workers had already formed to discuss among themselves job conditions, and in some cases the possibility of unionization. Through the incorporation of these circles—what one TWU organizer aptly termed "discontent groups"—

and the recruitment of various individuals, by early 1934 the party-led union drive had developed an initial base from which to expand within and among work locations.[16]

The situation, however, was quite different among transportation workers, who on the IRT constituted two-thirds of the work force. These workers functioned in either virtual solitude or small, shifting teams, and previous union experience was unusual, largely limited to earlier failed transit drives that had left older workers fearful and divided. Furthermore, craft traditions, except among the self-defined elite of motormen, were largely absent. Although dissatisfaction was widespread, it had not generally led to the formation of "discontent groups." As a result, the union drive initially attracted only scattered adherents among the transportation workers.[17]

If the structure and composition of the work force outside of the shops and powerhouses at first inhibited organizing along the contours of the work process, however, the concentration of Irish in these very jobs facilitated union development along alternative lines, the contours of community. With so many transit workers, particularly in the transportation jobs, part of a well-defined, close-knit community of Irish immigrants, the whole historical problem of unionization overflowed the confines of work environment and brought into play preexisting patterns of acquaintance, leadership, and ideology developed in the context of a national experience. The creation of the TWU thus involved two different but interrelated processes. In the large, socially heterogeneous work locations, employing men of a range of skill levels, the union grew through the contacts and activities of outside CP organizers and, more important, by on-the-job expansion, with a series of escalating assertions of union strength shifting the center of authority from management to union.[18] Among the mass of unskilled or semiskilled transportation employees, an additional, parallel process of community mobilization came into play that helped to extend the union into one of the least proletarian sectors of the work force, the recently rural Irish immigrants.

Communist organizers were aware from the start that special measures would be needed to enlist the mass of Irish workers into a transit union. It was apparently with this in mind that the TWU's very name was chosen, closely resembling that of the Dublin transit union. Similarly, the decision not to affiliate the TWU with the Communist-dominated Trade Union Unity League was made out of the belief that Irish workers in particular would be reluctant to join a union with open Communist ties.[19] Nevertheless, the CP was ill equipped to organize Irish workers directly. It had few Irish or Irish-American members and little experience working within the Irish community.[20]

On one occasion in early 1934, when CP organizers did succeed in setting up a meeting with a small group of Irish transit workers, the problems became evident. According to one worker who was present, the CP members consisted "mainly of Jewish fellows . . . [and] the Irish are extremely nationalistic," and he warned party leaders that "if this thing continues, your union is going to go up in smoke."[21]

In the end, the crucial bridge, ideologically and organizationally, between the initial CP-led union core and the mass of Irish workers was Irish republicanism. Close to two dozen former Irish Republican Army (IRA) members working in transit can be identified playing key local or unionwide leadership roles in the period before the TWU won recognition and contracts, and in all likelihood this is but a partial count. In any case, the influence of these men, their movement, and their ideology was far greater than numbers alone would indicate. Retired transit worker Pat O'Connor echoed a commonly heard sentiment in recalling that in the early days of the union, "our greatest assets . . . were . . . the fighting and organizational ability of the ex-I.R.A. men [and] the help of the C.P."[22]

The republican transit workers had come to the U.S. as part of a general exodus of IRA members that formed a distinct substream within the larger flow of Irish emigration. Most had joined the IRA as young men either in the late stages of the Anglo-Irish conflict or during the subsequent civil war. Although generally too young to have played major roles in the fighting, they did include one former bombing expert, a participant in several prison escapes, and two hunger-strike veterans. As prospects for renewed struggle faded in the mid-1920s and the Irish economy stagnated, these IRA men emigrated to New York and, like so many others, quickly found jobs in the transit system, primarily with the IRT or the Third Avenue Railway. Since most had had little if any work experience in Ireland, with a few exceptions they ended up in transportation or maintenance-of-way jobs. At the time that the TWU was formed, the ex-IRA men generally had four or five years seniority, and numerous friends and acquaintances among their co-workers.

Although some of these latest nationalist emigrés, the so-called wild geese, abandoned active politics with their flight across the Atlantic, a significant number continued to participate in republican activities. The most important orthodox republican organization in the New York area was the Clan na Gael, whose roots extended all the way back to mid-nineteenth-century Fenianism. In the 1920s and '30s, the Clan was in effect the American arm of the IRA—a support group for those in Ireland who sought to sever the remaining ties between the southern Irish Free State and England and to drive the English out of northern

Ireland, thus creating a united Irish Republic. The group, dominated by exile rebels, was semiclandestine and probably had at most a few hundred members, but it commanded considerable respect and influence in the Irish community, particularly among recent immigrants. At least ten ex-IRA transit workers, perhaps more, were members of the Clan na Gael. Through old-country friendships, fraternal groups, dances, relatives, and neighborhood ties, they in turn knew other IRA veterans working in transit, forming something of a loose network interweaving the industry.[23]

In the winter and spring of 1934, members of this republican transit network and the Communist transit organizers came to know one another and rather quickly joined forces. Some contact was inevitable, since the CP-led union organizing group was throwing out as broad a net as possible. Of particular importance, however, was the independent action of a small group of IRT workers in the Clan na Gael. Sometime in 1933, before they had had any contact with the CP, these men had begun to discuss among themselves the possibility of forming a union, even approaching some non-Clan workers to join them.[24]

The decision of this relatively small group of republican transit workers to turn toward unionism at a time when few other Irish workers were doing so did not primarily reflect past personal experience with labor organizations. In fact, few of the ex-IRA men working in transit, and as far as can be ascertained none of the transit Clan members, had ever been in a union, and their contact with organized labor had been at most peripheral.[25] Rather, what distinguished them from their fellow Irish workers were matters of personality, politics, and ideology.

On the simplest level, the IRA men were a particularly tough group, men who had "gone through hell" together in Ireland. Having faced British and Irish guns, lived in flight, and in some cases gone to jail, they found company supervisors and their plainclothes agents, the much-hated "beakies," less intimidating than others might. Generally at an age when they hoped to begin families but still had few responsibilities, they were more willing than most to take their chances in trying to improve their lot. As Quill put it to another IRA veteran, in words used so many times before, "What the hell do we have to lose . . . [our] chains?"[26]

But more than courage, or recklessness, was involved in the break with the syndrome of repressed hatred, subservience, and fear that was all too often characteristic of pre-union transit workers. The Irish republican movement, in its decades of struggle, had borrowed, developed, and transmitted conceptions of politics and man that represented a break with earlier notions. Along with its formal program of national independence and revived heritage came a democratic vision and a generalized attack on privilege. Underlying both were broad new ideas about natural rights and possessive individualism, and a new style of instrumental politics that included the use of mass mobilization, a new language, and a revolutionary political personality. Together, these constituted the heritage of the prolonged fight against the British, and continued to be found wherever there were veterans of the struggle.

In the nineteenth century, as David Montgomery, Eric Foner, and others have shown, Irish nationalism helped to bring Irish workers in the United States into the main currents of western democratic liberal thought, and made possible their participation in a range of union and reform activities (which in turn transformed the shape of nationalism back at home). In the twentieth century the process continued, if in a more limited manner. Although second- and third-generation Irish-Americans had already gone far toward finding established places in the mainstream of the nation, be they AFL craft unionists or lace-curtain Irish, there remained a flood of new immigrants clustered in cultural and industrial ghettos. If post-1920 Irish republican emigrants are usually portrayed, with some truth, as a far less significant group than their predecessors, within the immigrant community they continued to serve as carriers of new political ideas and practices that sharply delimited them from both the less politicized arrivals and the established Irish-American community. Politics, for these standard-bearers of republicanism, was not the passive, personalistic enterprise that Irish and Irish-American political culture at its worst encouraged, but rather a creative instrument to transform the world in which they found themselves, a search for personal betterment and secular salvation through collective action. And unlike their fellow immigrant workers, they reacted to their plight not as isolated individuals but as part of a self-conscious, structured movement.[27]

Industrial unionism, like Irish nationalism, was an expression by excluded groups of the demand for the full rights of bourgeois citizenship, including an end to paternalistic systems of social control, individual and collective dignity and opportunity, minimal standards of economic security, and participation in economic and political decision-making. Thus the leap from nationalism to unionism, from IRA to TWU, was as much a change of arena as a shift of purpose. Beyond this, the republican movement, if not exposing its members to the actuality of unionism, had at least sympathetically exposed them to the idea of unions. During the Easter Rebellion of 1916, the republicans' one fighting ally, James Connolly's Citizen Army, had been drawn from the ranks of the labor movement. Although thereafter the ties between the two movements loosened, a respect for trade unions remained common in the IRA, particularly for Connolly's brand of militant industrial unionism, so similar to that advocated by the Communist transit organizers.[28] Thus in seeking a way out of their industrial degradation, unionism appeared as an obvious answer to the men of the Clan na Gael, in spite of their own nonindustrial origins.

In a sober and realistic assessment of their limited resources and experience and the difficulties ahead, the Clan group looked for outside help. According to IRT conductor Gerald O'Reilly, one of those involved, some men may have approached the AFL, but if so, no concrete aid resulted. Likewise, approaches to two mainstream Irish fraternal groups, the Hibernians and the Friendly Sons of St. Patrick, proved fruitless. While New York's Irish community provided a milieu in which a dense web of relationships among transit workers could develop, the main pillars of the community—the church, the Democratic party, the fraternal organizations, the Irish-American press— displayed little interest in the plight of transit workers as workers. Most Irish and Irish-American organizations cut across class lines and were dominated by middle-class leaders and middle-class views. In fact, some Irish transit executives were important figures in community and church organizations, including the Hibernians, the Ancient Sons, and the Knights of Columbus. Even unions that were Irish-led, for example some of the building trades, were generally conservative, craft-oriented, and had little interest in mass unionism. Having failed to find aid within the Irish community, the Clan group finally contacted the CP, perhaps by then knowing of its transit activities. A delegation including O'Reilly and Mike Quill, then an IRT ticket agent, met with Elizabeth Gurley Flynn, William Foster, and Israel Amter, and after considerable discussion the party agreed to support the Clan men, quickly integrating them into the existing transit drive.[29]

The Irish Workers Club (IWC) provided a second channel of contact between the CP and Irish republicans. Set up by the CP in 1932 in an effort to build support among Irish and Irish-American workers, the IWC sponsored athletic, social, educational, and cultural programs at several New York locations. Politically, the clubs stressed agitation around U.S. social and political issues and support for "complete [Irish] liberation . . . and the establishment of an Irish Workers' and Farmers' Republic." Although always remaining small, the IWC became something of a mixing ground for Irish radicals and republicans, including some ex-IRA men in touch with transit workers. It was through an IWC member, for example, that IRT turnstile mechanic Tom O'Shea, an IRA veteran and a Clan activist, met party transit organizers, and, at O'Shea's suggestion, an IWC leader, Austin Hogan, was assigned to join the small CP team leading the transit drive. (Hogan eventually became president of the TWU's New York local and part of the quadrumvirate that collectively constituted the union's top leadership between 1937 and 1948.)[30]

By the early spring of 1934, the alliance of Irish republicans and Communists—what was to be the distinctive political feature of the TWU—was already largely formed, even before the union itself was officially founded. In fact, it was the development of a working relationship with the republicans that gave the CP sufficient confidence to transform its transit organizing committee into a formal union, the TWU, in April 1934. In an early issue of the new union's newspaper, the social amalgam that had been midwife to the TWU's birth was tacitly acknowledged in a list of demands for IRT motormen: "no men . . . be discriminated against when they take off special holidays such as May 1, St. Patrick's Day, etc."[31]

The transit republicans' alliance with the CP was initially a by-product of the independent efforts of both groups to form a union, and the party's success in recruiting Irish members and supporters in the transit industry rested to a large degree on its role in the union drive. Had some other organization made an equivalent commitment to the organization of transit workers, the development and eventual character of New York transit unionism would have been very different. In this sense, Philip Carey of the Xavier Labor School was well justified in applying to the TWU John La Farge's dictum that "communism is a vacuum phenomenon."[32] But both the existence of a vacuum and the CP's willingness and ability to fill it were historical in character and appreciated as such by transit workers. Over and over again pioneer TWU members of varied political outlooks credit the party's contribution of money, personnel, and guidance, at a time others were unwilling to do the same, with playing a crucial, even decisive, role in the union's success.[33]

In spite of this shared recognition of the centrality of the CP's contribution, attitudes toward the party varied greatly. Many Irish workers, including some IRA veterans, disliked the CP. For others, the alliance was an issue-by-issue affair, even after years of close working relationships and deep personal friendships.[34] Even among those workers who actually joined the CP, their action did not necessarily represent any particular devotion to the general principles of the party.

Some workers joined the CP simply because they saw it as the strongest and most effective advocate of unionization. John J. Murphy, for example, by his own account one of the first transit workers to join the CP as a result of the TWU drive, later told the Dies Committee that

"I suppose I would not have joined the Communist Party if the American Federation of Labor had been on the job." In other cases, party membership was seen as a means of advancement within the union.[35]

Also at work was a categorical confusion between union and party that arose in some workers' minds. The idea of communism was unfamiliar to many newly arrived Irish workers, to the extent that it was sometimes referrred to as "communionism," and the nature of the CP itself was unclear.[36] Edward Maguire, an Irish-born ticket agent who enrolled in party in March 1934, apparently thought that the purpose of the group he had joined was simply to build a union. His confusion was still evident in his 1938 Dies Committee testimony, when he tellingly referred to the meetings of his CP unit as "union meetings."[37] Since most of the party transit recruits were initially in cells composed strictly of transit organizers and other transit workers, led by union leaders, whose immediate work was union-related, this confusion could go on for some time. When men like Maguire finally did realize that the CP was not simply a union-organizing group, their disillusionment was sharp, and Maguire and Murphy were among a group of Irish transit workers who joined and then rather quickly left the CP to become among its bitterest critics within the TWU.

Other Irish workers, however, developed deep and long-lasting ideological, organizational, and emotional ties to the party. Frequently these workers had already developed left-wing views within the republican movement before their first contact with the CP. Most republicans, like most Irish, were not radical in their social and political views, but the movement had always had a progressive wing, in the 1930s represented in Ireland by men like Paeder O'Donnell, George Gilmore, and Frank Ryan. Although long a tolerated minority current within the IRA, left republicanism was most influential in the 1930s, part of a general left-wing upsurge that also led to the founding of the Communist Party of Ireland in June 1933.[38] In a situation not uncommon among exiled nationalist groups, the New York Clan na Gael had a decidedly more leftist cast than the IRA itself, and most transit Clan members embraced a left republican outlook. Some had developed their views while still in Ireland, while others, like Quill, moved left only after coming to New York, probably in part as a result of their contact with left-wingers in the Clan and the IWC. It was from among this group, and like-minded individuals, that the CP recruited some of its most important transit members.[39]

In the early and mid-1930s, a variety of developments converged—the CP's outreach to Irish workers, the surge of left republicanism in Ireland and America, and the founding the of TWU—and in that moment emerged a political nexus, tying together union, party, and community, that lasted a decade and a half, until shattered by internal contradictions and the developing cold war. If the material basis for this convergence was economic depression on both sides of the Atlantic, its ideological expression and legitimacy came from Connolly. Left republicans in both the U.S. and Ireland saw themselves as the heirs of Connolly and the combination of Irish nationalism, industrial union- ism, and international socialism he had advocated. Quill, O'Reilly, and Hogan, for example, all credited their exposure to Connolly's writings with playing a major role in their political development. Clan members read, discussed, and preached Connolly, and IWC propa- ganda and education focused on Connolly, Larkin, and other Irish leftists, deliberately avoiding non-Irish Marxists or Marx himself. Later even the TWU claimed the mantle of Connolly, asserting that it had been built upon his principles and serving as one of the principal sponsors of the annual Connolly Commemorations, usually held in the union's Transport Hall.[40]

Among the broad mass of Irish transit workers Connolly was a widely revered figure but his socialist views were never generally adopted. Only a small number of Irish workers actively participated in the overlapping worlds of the Clan, the IWC, and the CP. In fact, among TWU members in general, the CP never succeeded in building a mass membership.[41] In a sense, it was this very failure that made the role of the left republicans so important. With their Communist ties generally kept secret—as O'Reilly put it, "of course we never went out and said we are here by the Party"—they continued to be viewed in the Irish community as representatives of the orthodox republican move- ment.[42] As such, they commanded considerable respect and could draw on the wide if sometimes shallow pool of Irish nationalist sentiment to confer legitimacy upon the TWU. At the same time, they were a valuable political asset for the CP both inside and outside of the TWU, helping the party to maintain organizational control of the union and providing it with a point of entry into the wider Irish community.

The story of the TWU's growth between its official founding and its recognition victories is a complex one, and the activity of Irish repub- licans is but one aspect. However, especially in the first two years of organizing when the union concentrated on the IRT, the republican workers played a critical role. The Clan na Gael group was strategically scattered throughout the IRT transportation department and provided the TWU with a strong starting point among ticket agents, platform men, guards, and conductors. In addition, individual Clan men in various maintenance-of-way subdepartments, such as track and structure, helped form union groups and provided local leadership.

The Clan men first recruited other ex-IRA men, but as the union grew they began to bring in trusted non-IRA workers. Some were men known from "the other side," while others were co-workers, neighbors, relatives, or acquaintances from Irish organizations or bars. Ex-IRA men and Clan members were widely known and highly respected in the Irish community, and their support for the TWU carried considerable weight. John Nolan, an ex-IRA ticket agent recruited for the union by Mike Quill, recalls that Irish workers "all wanted to know where the Clan na Gael were" and, as it became known that they were pro-union, movement towards the TWU accelerated. As Irish membership grew, the dynamic of growth took on a life of its own, as new members in turn brought in friends, co-workers, and acquaintances, widening the base of Irish support far beyond republican circles.[43]

Given the past history of broken unions, the existence of a company spy network, and the pervasive atmosphere of fear, TWU leaders felt that the union could survive and attract workers only if it could protect the identity of its membership. A structure was therefore devised to sustain covert status as long as possible, keep out company spies, and minimize the damage any infiltrator could do. Until the union was well established, most members had contact with the TWU only as part of a group of five to twenty unionists with whom they regularly met. A leader of each group in turn had contact with the rest of the union through the central leadership and a delegates' council. To further minimize possible exposure, meetings were held in scattered and changing locations, including various Irish halls, sometimes under the guise of social events. In at least one case, the union met under the cover of a local Holy Name Society.

This semiconspiratorial method of operation was seen by the ex-IRA men as an application of the tactics that they had developed in Ireland and, with their wealth of organizational experience, they were masters at it. According to Maurice Forge, one of the early TWU leaders, the union "practically had a network of organization with their help without any visible surface iceberg." The CP, of course, had also used similar tactics elsewhere, and this was one of several instances in which elements of the republican and communist traditions converged, enabling both groups to see TWU practice as an outgrowth of their past.[44]

The generally smooth working relationship between the Irish republicans and the Communist transit organizers was not without occasional tensions. In the summer and fall of 1934, for example, a disagreement arose over strategy toward the well-entrenched IRT company union, the Brotherhood of Interborough Rapid Transit Company Employees. The CP argued that because "there was still some illusions among the men as to the possibility of turning the company union into a fighting body," TWU activists should agitate within it and seek election to Brotherhood offices. Some active TWU members, however, including at least a few of the key republicans, wanted to abandon the Brotherhood immediately and boycott its elections. For the Irish republicans, this stand may well have reflected the deep-rooted Irish tradition of boycotting institutions viewed as illegitimate. The IRA itself had always taken this position which was the product of both a long history of trying to maintain Irish identity in an environment of foreign-imposed structures and the need to justify rebellion within the confines of a Catholic dogma which condemned the overthrow of any legitimate national government. Only after several meetings with top CP leaders did opponents of the party's strategy agree to work within the Brotherhood, and on the election issue a compromise was reached— the union opposed abstention but did not run candidates under its own banner.[45]

Agitation within the Brotherhood, in fact, proved to be a highly successful means of reaching nonunion workers, as did a rich array of on-the-job tactics developed by union members. Still, reaching all of the often isolated transit employees remained difficult, and to overcome the problem in the summer of 1934 the TWU began holding open-air meetings in neighborhoods with heavy concentrations of transit workers, particularly the Irish South Bronx. Held on Friday nights, these rallies sometimes attracted as many as a thousand people (including a few disrupters), making the TWU well known in the Irish community.[46]

The republicans, however, were not the only element in the Irish community influencing the attitude of transit workers toward the TWU, and from other quarters came opposition to the union. The TWU and the CP, and especially their Irish activists, had to work hard to undercut the community standing of Irish transit executives and to prevent their use of Irish organizations as anti-union forums, arguing repeatedly that these officials had little interest in the plight of common Irish workers. Executives were held personally responsible for company anti-union actions, and their homes, and in at least one case one of their churches, were picketed, a practice very much in line with the Irish tradition of publicly shaming transgressors of the community moral order. Perhaps sensitive to the divisive nature of the issue, most Irish organizations and the Irish-American press remained largely silent about the TWU until the union was close to victory, when some measured support for the transit group began to be expressed.[47]

The Catholic Church presented the greatest potential challenge to the TWU, both in its general stance and in its specific activities. Church condemnation of Communism and the hostility of part of the Church to militant industrial unionism tended in itself to inhibit workers from joining the TWU, and Gerald O'Reilly recalls that the early union adherents were generally less religious than the work force as a whole. In addition, there were sporadic efforts by some elements of the Church to directly intercede against the TWU. However, those opposed to the union were slow to see its significance and did not generally become active until after the IRT drive was well under way. Nevertheless, TWU leaders were very aware of the potential impact of Church opposition, and carefully avoided any direct confrontation. Furthermore, many TWU leaders were themselves practicing Catholics, and as Quill put it: "Our going to Church did no harm either. Many a fellow who thought me a dangerous agitator found me more to his taste after meeting with me at the Paulist Fathers."[48]

The republican efforts played an important part in the TWU's ever growing support among Irish IRT workers. This is not to say that the Irish were necessarily the first to join the union, or the strongest union supporters, although within some job categories such was the case. In fact, the union's greatest strength was always in the shops and power-houses, among the least Irish sectors, and, on a companywide basis, probably at no point were Irish workers disproportionately represented in the union. Still, in the end the Irish workers were the key to the TWU's success on the IRT, simply because of their numerical preponderance; without them there could be no union. Thus, although the earliest union members and the union leadership came from remarkably varied backgrounds, the Irish republicans assumed a disproportionately large number of key union positions, and from among them emerged the TWU's first two presidents, Tom O'Shea and Mike Quill.[49]

The respective careers of O'Shea and Quill illustrate both the delicate balance of ideological and cultural forces within the union and the manifold political tendencies within Irish republicanism. Tom O'Shea was given the title of union president in late 1934 or early 1935 by the core group of union organizers, which meant in effect the CP. Although O'Shea was in many ways a natural choice—one of the first Irish republicans to join the union, well known as an outspoken union advocate, and by then a member of the CP—a more immediate factor was also involved. O'Shea had been fired from his job for union activity, and after a major TWU campaign been rehired. He was therefore in the spotlight first as victim and then as victor.

Tom O'Shea turned out to be the TWU's Homer Martin; although a popular figure and an enthusiastic unionist, he proved to be a poor organizer, heavy drinker, and unable to operate well within the CP-dominated collective leadership. Perhaps even more important, it gradually became clear that O'Shea's whole approach to building the union significantly differed from that of the CP and most of the union's key activists. While many of the ex-IRA men sought to draw upon republican traditions and some specific tactical measures, such as cellular organization, O'Shea saw the entire TWU project as essentially analogous to that of the latter-day IRA. O'Shea, who in Ireland had helped bomb police stations, publicly and privately suggested the use of terrorist tactics, including threats to derail trains and the like. In this he was not unique; one or two others, including John Murphy, had advocated similar measures. Although these men were but a tiny minority, even among the ex-IRA men, they represented an aspect of Irish political culture that went all the way back to the pre-Famine rural terror bands and their urban counterparts, the Catholic Ribbon societies, and continued on strongly in the IRA.[50]

In the meantime, Mike Quill was becoming an ever more prominent figure in the union. Quill's family had been republican sympathizers, and their mountain farm in County Kerry a rebel hideout. Quill himself briefly served with the IRA but, after coming to New York in 1926, it was the Irish social world, not republican politics, into which he plunged. With his extraordinary energy, wit, and ability to put others at ease, Quill became a well-known figure in the Irish community and much in demand as a master of ceremonies for dances sponsored by county associations and other groups. In fact, he first became involved with the Clan na Gael when the group's members asked him to help run their Saturday night fund-raising dances. Although he soon became a member of the Clan and began steeping himself in Irish political writing, he never was a leader within the organization. Among the transit worker members alone, several men, including O'Shea, played more significant roles.

In the world of the TWU, however, Mike Quill came into his own. With hundreds of acquaintances and contacts from the dances he ran, with considerable oratorical and organizing abilities, and with a willingness to learn from and defer to Communist organizers, Quill soon became a key figure in the union. Although Quill quickly moved close to the CP, probably even becoming a formal member sometime in 1934, his political style remained intensely personal and highly theatric, owing at least something to the ways of Tammany. Perhaps his most potent weapon was his ability to ridicule those in authority, using the gift of gab to shatter psychological and social structures of deference. As a result, Quill was better able to bridge the gap between the union and the mass of relatively apolitical and conservative Irish workers than those republicans or Communists more ascetic in manner, more acclimated to operating within small, semiclandestine milieux, or more dogmatically devoted to Irish or Communist causes. It was the very complexity and contradictions of his personality—a committed left republican and a popular demagogue, deeply democratic and personally ambitious, a man of considerable moral vision but inordinate tactical flexibility and ruthlessness—that made Quill so able to thrive in and eventually dominate the complex social mix of the TWU.[51]

In the fall of 1935, CP organizers suggested electing Quill as union president, to replace O'Shea. At a series of meetings with key activitists that followed, some men objected but most agreed that regardless of whether or not they personally liked O'Shea, his personality and political world view were inappropriate to the tasks ahead. Realizing that he could not be elected by the delegates' council in whose hands the decision lay, O'Shea did not seek election. Quill thus became the first elected president of the TWU, a post he held until his death three decades later. O'Shea, on the other hand, after losing a tight and possibly rigged election for union business agent, left the CP and by 1937 was publicly denouncing Communist influence in the union. Increasingly bitter, he allied himself first with internal union dissidents and anti-Communist Catholic activists, and eventually with government investigators seeking to portray the TWU as a tool of international Communism.[52]

By the fall of 1936, although still representing only a minority of the workers, the TWU had established a solid organization on the IRT, and it began extending its organizing drive to other New York transit companies. In these latter campaigns, Irish republicanism was not as significant a direct factor. In some cases, such as on the BMT and ISS, the proportion of Irish workers was lower and there were few active republicans present. Even when the work force was heavily Irish, as on the Manhattan and Bronx trolley and bus lines, the union was no longer as dependent on republican ties, since its large and diverse existing Irish membership was able to supply numerous contacts. Furthermore, by then it was no longer necessary for the TWU to repeat the intricate process of social construction that had characterized its growth on the IRT. It was now an established institution, well known, experienced, with an existing leadership and proven organizing techniques, operating at the height of a national wave of union growth. In each successive campaign, starting points were easier to find, workers more willing to join. As a result, even though individual IRA veterans were again to be found among the most active unionists, the role of the republican movement as such was less crucial.[53]

At the same time, in late 1936 and 1937, the TWU faced more sustained and effective opposition from Church-affiliated groups, as it became obvious that the TWU was a growing, left-aligned power, and a potentially important force within the Irish community. Church activity was particularly strong in Brooklyn, where the diocese was among the most conservative and hostile to the CIO in the country. Father Edward Lodge Curran, an influential figure in the Brooklyn Church, a strong supporter of Father Coughlin, and the chaplain of the Brooklyn branch of the Ancient Order of Hibernians, vehemently opposed the TWU. With his support, a group called the American Association Against Communism worked against the TWU in the July 1937 BMT recognition election, supporting instead the Independent Traction Workers Union, a successor to the long-established company union, which was itself later found by the State Labor Relations Board to be company-dominated. Curran was known to visit transit workers on the job in an effort to enlist their opposition to the TWU, and some local priests, in Brooklyn and elsewhere, denounced the union from the pulpit. Holy Name Societies and the Knights of Columbus were apparently also used to build opposition to the union. Additionally, the influential and widely circulated Brooklyn diocesan newspaper, the *Tablet*, opened its pages to attacks on the TWU, calling for men to quit the union and vote against its selection as a bargaining agent.

Although these Church attacks on the TWU caused the union considerable difficulty, the anti-TWU campaign was weakened by divisions among local Catholic leaders, mirroring national Church disagreements over the CIO. Some elements of the Church, in fact, actively aided the TWU. As early as February 1936, Dorothy Day of the *Catholic Worker* advised Catholics to join the TWU, pointing out that since the majority of the work force was Catholic, "they can bring into the union Catholic principles of justice." The TWU was also able to quote attacks in *Commonweal* and *America* on red-baiting and company unions. Even more important, the newly formed Association of Catholic Trade Unionists (ACTU), an offshoot of the *Catholic Worker* and heavily Irish, came out in support of the TWU during the height of the Brooklyn campaign. Acting in response to the *Tablet* attack, ACTU handed out 10,000 leaflets urging BMT workers to vote TWU, arguing that the charges of Communist infiltration were pure allegations and that the opposition organization was a company union.[54]

Anticlerical attitudes among Irish workers also diminished the effectiveness of Church activities. During the Irish "troubles" the Church had condemned the use of force against the government, and in 1931 it forbade IRA membership. The resulting anticlerical reaction extended across the Atlantic and, though strongest among active republicans, was by no means restricted to them.[55] One Jesuit priest who tried his hand at working with TWU members in the late 1930s noted that "very many of the men bitterly resent the action taken by the Irish Bishops and the Irish Clergy during the trouble with England."[56]

Even among those for whom the priest remained a respected figure, there was a common belief that his authority was appropriate in church matters but not in political or social affairs. This attitude was reinforced among transit workers by their resentment over the Church's lack of interest in their plight as workers until the TWU came along. As one Irish Catholic motorman put it, "What the hell did the Church do for us? Not a god damn thing." With considerable caution, some unionists tried to build on existing doubts about Church interference by pointing out that it was the TWU, not the Church, that was fighting to get workers time off to attend church on Sundays and money enough to make a contribution to the weekly collection.[57]

The competing poles of Church and union caused considerable strain for some Catholic workers, in spite of union efforts to separate the spheres. One worker, for example, switched parishes after his priest denounced the TWU. Others deliberately chose not to inquire about the political beliefs and affiliations of union leaders, again to avoid being forced into an open choice between Church and union. Most, however, simply attended both church and union meetings and coped the best they could. In the end, the divided and belated Church response failed to dissuade significant numbers of workers from backing the TWU as their bargaining agent, except possibly on the BMT, where the TWU hold was weakest and its eventual margin of victory smaller than on the other major lines.[58]

The series of union recognition elections in the late spring and summer of 1937 marked the culmination of the TWU's four years of organizing. Except in one unit of largely female BMT ticket agents, the TWU won all of the major elections it contested, generally by overwhelming margins. By the fall it had signed union-shop contracts with all of the major New York transit lines except the city-operated ISS, where it nonetheless had considerable membership. At the same time, the TWU affiliated with the CIO as a new international union and began establishing locals in other towns and cities.[59] Fittingly, when TWU members marched into Madison Square Garden in October 1937 to celebrate their victories and open their first international convention, the band was playing "The Wearing of the Green."[60]

The TWU's victory was the beginning of transit workers' long march toward improved working conditions and higher living standards. Simultaneously, it brought an important block of workers into the organizational and political structures of the CIO and the New Deal. The creation of the TWU was as much a political watershed as an economic one. Though the TWU had enlisted Irish workers in part by mobilizing ties created in a shared national experience, the whole thrust of the union's development was away from the very parochialism that had been one source of its initial strength. Union leaders plunged into the American Labor party (ALP) as candidates and organizers, joined Popular-Front efforts of various kinds, and tried in numerous ways to bring their members into the left-liberal world of economic, political, and social reform.

In these efforts, the TWU achieved only partial success, and the contest between union leaders and other elements in the Irish community for the allegiance of transit workers intensified. In spite of the union's affiliation with the ALP and Quill's personal political success as an ALP city councilman, the Democratic party probably retained majority support among Irish transit workers. Efforts by TWU leaders to wield influence in Irish fraternal and nationalist groups also met with only mixed results. But in their own domain, TWU leaders remained firmly in control. For over a decade, successive Church-affiliated opposition groups, from the Christian Front on the right to the ACTU on the left, attempted to oust the union leadership, but in no case did they win enough support to pose a fundamental challenge.[61]

In the eyes of the union leadership, their very ability to maintain organizational hegemony was in part a measure of the political development of their Irish members. A 1944 letter from Mike Quill to Philip Murray announcing that the TWU had defeated a District 50 raid on the Third Avenue Railway analyzes the certification vote in almost strictly political terms: "The employees are a little better than 95% Irish Catholics and they [District 50] raised with them the 'Red' issue, the 'Black' issue, and, the whole question of President Roosevelt and Irish neutrality. This vote, to our minds, is an indication of how the Irish will vote in relation to Roosevelt and I can say, it is very encouraging."[62]

At least as important, however, in preserving the TWU's position was the gratitude of workers toward the institution that had finally begun to end their industrial misery, and toward those that had helped create it. It was a gratitude so great that, in spite of the long-standing lack of congruence between the beliefs of the bulk of the membership and those of the hierarchy, only internal divisions in the leadership after the collapse of the Popular Front finally brought a change in the political complexion of the union. As a priest involved in one of the many antileadership fights eloquently observed, "When you sow dragon's teeth, you reap a fearsome crop. . . . And when a Communist-dominated union, brushing aside all legal technicalities and niceties of ethical considerations did a bang-up job . . . could you blame the men for joining and thanking God that it had come to free them?"[63]

## NOTES

Steve Fraser, Nelson Lichtenstein, Deborah Bell, Michael Frisch, and Daniel Walkowitz read an earlier version of this article, and their comments and suggestions helped me to clarify my thinking and strengthened what follows. A summary of this article was presented at the Social Science History Association Annual Meeting in Rochester, New York, on Nov. 8, 1980.

1. Interview with Patrick Walsh, June 1, 1978. (Unless otherwise indicated, all interviews were conducted by, and are in the possession of, the author.)

2. For a good introduction to the literature on Irish immigrants, see Robert Sean Wilentz, "Industrializing America and the Irish: Towards a New Departure," *Labor History*, 20 (1979), pp. 579-95.

3. U.S. Department of Commerce, *Historical Statistics of the United States, Part I* (Washington, D.C., 1975), pp. 105, 117; U.S. Department of Commerce, Bureau of the Census, *Fifteenth Census of the United States: 1930*, vol. 3, part 2 (Washington, D.C., 1933), pp. 298-99, 302.

4. Conrad Arensberg, *The Irish Countryman* (1937; reprint ed., Garden City, N.Y., 1968), pp. 76-86; Conrad Arensberg and Solon Kimball, *Family and Community in Ireland* (Cambridge, Mass., 1940), pp. 98-99, 148-51, 224, 245-46, 252; Robert Kennedy, Jr., *The Irish: Emigration, Marriage, and Fertility* (Berkeley, Calif., 1973), pp. 93, 102, 106, 163; Paul O'Dwyer Memoir, Oral History Collection of Columbia University (hereafter OHCCU); interview with Gerald O'Reilly, July 11, 1979; City College Oral History Project (hereafter CCOHP), drawer 4, tapes 4 and 5 (Mar. 26, 1974).

5. Kennedy, *The Irish*, pp. 76-77; Ronald H. Bayor, *Neighbors in Conflict: The Irish, Germans, Jews and Italians in New York City, 1929-1941* (Baltimore, 1978), pp. 22-25; Paul O'Dwyer Memoir, OHCCU; interviews with Gerald O'Reilly, May 15, 1978 and July 11, 1979; John Gallagher, Apr. 20, 1979; John Nolan, June 1, 1979; and Patrick Reilly, Sept. 7, 1978; CCOHP, drawer 4, tapes 4 and 5.

6. The following discussion of the social composition of the transit work force is based on interviews with Maurice Forge, Jan. 7, 1979; Patrick Walsh, June 1, 1978; John Gallagher, Apr. 20, 1979; James Sullivan (pseud.), July 27, 1979; Gerald O'Reilly, May 15, 1978 and July 11, 1979; Philip Bray, Aug. 13, 1979; Peter MacLachlan, Feb. 25, 1979; John Plover, Feb. 20, 1979; Victor Bloswick, Jan. 23, 1979; and Joe Labash, Aug. 3, 1979; and Michael J. Quill to Philip Murray, Aug. 30, 1944, TWU file, box A7-34, CIO Papers, Catholic University, Washington, D.C.; Leo Huberman, *The Great Bus Strike* (New York, 1941), p. 8; and *Daily Worker*, Apr. 16, 1934, p. 4. Census figures are of relatively little use, since they use occupational categories that do not correspond to those in the transit industry.

Very few women worked in nonclerical transit jobs, and those that did were almost exclusively ticket agents for the BMT. Black workers were almost completely restricted to jobs as porters (cleaning stations) or cleaning buses. The only partial exception was on the ISS.

7. As of 1933, the IRT had 16,403 employees, the BMT 13,427, the Third Avenue Railway 3,687, and New York Railways (the predecessor of NYC Omnibus) and Fifth Avenue Coach each about 1,500. The ISS had 1,597 employees in 1933, but by 1938 this had risen to 5,171. See State of New York, Department of Public Service, Metropolitan Division, Transit Commission, *13th Annual Report for Calendar Year 1933* (Albany, 1934), pp. 250-51, 513 (hereafter Transit Commission, *1933 Report*); James J. McGinley, *Labor Relations in the New York Rapid Transit Systems, 1904-1944* (New York, 1949), p. 442.

8. Interviews with Gerald O'Reilly, May 15, 1978, Jan. 11, 1979, and July 11, 1979; Maurice Forge, Jan. 7, 1979; and Lewis Fraad, June 30, 1980; and CCOHP, drawer 4, tapes 4 and 5. In developing a general understanding of New York's Irish community, the following were particularly helpful: Bayor, *Neighbors in Conflict*; Robert D. Cross, "The Irish," in John Higham, ed., *Ethnic Leadership in America* (Baltimore, 1978); Andrew M. Greeley, *That Most Distressful Nation: The Taming of the American Irish* (Chicago, 1972); Lawrence J. McCaffrey, ed., *Irish Nationalism and the American Contribution* (New York, 1976); Nathan Glazer and Daniel Patrick Moynihan, *Beyond the Melting Pot: The Negroes, Puerto Ricans, Jews, Italians and Irish of New York City*, 2d ed. (Cambridge, Mass., 1970); Paul O'Dwyer Memoir, OHCCU; and issues of the *Irish World* from the late 1920s and early 1930s.

9. L. H. Whittemore, *The Man Who Ran the Subways: The Story of Mike Quill* (New York, 1968), p. 260.

10. Whittemore, *Man Who Ran the Subways*, p. 86; interviews with Maurice Forge, Jan. 7, 1979; and Lewis Fraad, June 30, 1980.

11. Interviews with Gerald O'Reilly, May 15, 1978; John Gallagher, Apr. 20, 1979; Peter MacLachlan, Feb. 25, 1979; John Nolan, June 1, 1978; Philip J. Carey, Oct. 13, 1977; Victor Bloswick, Jan. 23, 1979; and John Plover, Feb. 20, 1979; *Daily Worker*, June 8, 1934, p. 4; U.S. Department of Justice, Immigration and Naturalization Service, "Hearings in the Matter of Charges against Desideriu Hammer, alias John Santo," p. 863 (hereafter "Santo Deportation Hearings"); McGinley, *Labor Relations*, pp. 125, 209-11, 269-71; *B.M.T. Monthly*, 1933-35, passim; *I.R.T. News*, Aug. 26, 1927, p. 7; Oct. 20, 1928, pp. 1, 4; Apr. 29, 1929, p. 3; June 3, 1930, p. 4; Oct. 26, 1930, p. 4; *New York Post*, July 2, 1937, p. 4.

12. Arensberg and Kimball, *Family and Community*, p. 151; interviews with Maurice Forge, Jan. 7, 1979; Philip Bray, June 13, 1979; Lewis Fraad, June 30, 1980; and Gerald O'Reilly, May 15, 1978.

13. The best single source for information on New York transit working conditions is McGinley, *Labor Relations*. See also Transit Commission, *1933 Report*, pp. 260-63, 512-13, 562-63; TWU, *Proceedings of the Second Biennial Convention* (New York, 1939), p. 80; Michael J. Quill, "Memorandum on Bill Int. 879, Print 913," box 2642, Fiorello H. La Guardia Papers, New York City Municipal Archives (hereafter La Guardia Papers); and interviews cited in n. 6.

14. Emerson P. Schmidt, *Industrial Relations in Urban Transit* (Minneapolis, 1937), pp. 83-84; *Transport Workers Bulletin*, Aug. 1936, p. 3; *I.R.T. News*, July 19, 1928, p. 1; Apr. 29, 1929, p. 1.

15. *Tenth Annual Report of Brooklyn-Manhattan Transit Corporation for the Year Ended June 30, 1933* (New York, 1933), p. 5; Fifth Avenue Coach Company, *Annual Report for Year Ended Dec. 31, 1937* (New York, 1938), p. 4, *New York Times*, Dec. 10, 1934, p. 1; *I.R.T. News*, Dec. 23, 1931, pp. 1-2; interview with Patrick Walsh, June 1, 1978; *Daily Worker*, June 22, 1934, p. 3;

July 6, 1934, p. 4; Dec. 7, 1934, p. 4; June 7, 1935, p. 4; June 28, 1935, p. 4; McGinley, *Labor Relations*, pp. 171, 175, 526-27; *Transport Workers Bulletin*, Aug. 1934, p. 6; Nov. 1936, p. 6.

16. Charles Krumbein, "How and Where to Concentrate," *Party Organizer*, 4 (Aug.-Sept. 1933), 24-25; Louis Sass, "Harlem Concentration on Transport," *Party Organizer*, 7 (Mar. 1935), 23-24; "Small Progress in N.Y. District," *Party Organizer*, 6 (Nov. 1933), 18; "Report of Convention Section 15, District 2 CPUSA [Middle Bronx]," in Earl Browder Papers, microfilm ed., series 2-44, reel 3; Report of the New York Office, Sept. 10, 1943, Federal Bureau of Investigation files on Communist infiltration of the Transport Workers Union of America-CIO, released under the Freedom of Information Act (hereafter FBI-FOIA); "How TWU Really Came to Be," *Rank and File Transit News*, Mar. 1950, p. 3; *Transport Workers Bulletin*, Apr. 1934, p. 4; *Daily Worker*, Apr. 2, 1934, p. 2; May 1, 1934, trade-union section, p. 1; interviews with Maurice Forge, Jan. 7 and Aug. 8, 1979; John Gallagher, Apr. 20, 1979; Joseph Labash, Aug. 3, 1979; Victor Bloswick, Jan. 23, 1979; and John Plover, Feb. 20, 1979; *New York Herald Tribune*, Nov. 30, 1934. The term "discontent group" comes from Maurice Forge.

17. Transit Commission, *1933 Report*, pp. 250-51; interviews with Patrick Reilly, Sept. 7, 1978; John Nolan, June 1, 1978; and Maurice Forge, Jan. 7, 1979.

18. A more detailed discussion of the growth of the TWU among non-transportation workers, and among non-Irish workers in general, will appear in the author's forthcoming study of the TWU between 1933 and 1950.

19. Interviews with Maurice Forge, Jan. 7, 1979; and Gerald O'Reilly, Jan. 15, 1978; U.S. House of Representatives, Seventy-sixth Congress, 3d Sess., *Hearings before a Special Committee on Un-American Activities*, vol. 13 (Washington, D.C., 1940), pp. 7919-20 (hereafter *Dies Committee*, vol. 13); Report of the New York Office, Sept. 10, 1943, FBI-FOIA.

Both Forge and O'Reilly believe that the TWU name was chosen with an eye towards the Irish. "Transport" is a word rarely used in American English but standard in both English and Irish speech, and the similarity of the TWU's name to that of the Irish Transport and General Workers Union is striking. On the other hand, it should be pointed out that Communists had occasionally used the term *transport* well before the TWU had been established. See, for example, Krumbein, *How and Where to Concentrate*, p. 25.

20. Nathan Glazer, *The Social Basis of American Communism* (New York, 1961), pp. 87-89; interview with Abner Berry, Dec. 5, 1978.

21. Both quotes come from Thomas O'Shea, the first in *Dies Committee*, vol. 13, p. 7895, the second in "Santo Deportation Hearings," p. 603.

22. Identifications and information about ex-IRA transit workers came from interviews with Philip Bray, Aug. 13, 1979; James Sullivan, July 27, 1979; John Nolan, June 1, 1978; Patrick Walsh, June 1, 1978; Gerald O'Reilly, May 15, 1978, Jan. 11, 1979, and July 11, 1979; Jerry O'Brien, Sept. 12, 1979; and Philip Carey, Oct. 13, 1977; and *Transport Workers Bulletin*, Oct. 1937, p. 11; Apr. 1, 1936, p. 1; Oct. 1945, p. 4; "Santo Deportation Hearings," pp. 627-28; J. Bowyer Bell, *The Secret Army* (Cambridge, Mass., 1974), pp. 53-54, 69n. Pat O'Connor is quoted in an unpublished paper by Patrick Lynch, "Transport Workers Union—Dublin, New York and Chicago—An Analysis of Organization and Collective Bargaining" (1968), p. 9 (copy in possession of John Nolan).

23. For general background on the republican exodus and the Clan na Gael, see Bell, *Secret Army*, pp. 5, 7, 15n., 26, 50-51, 56-57, 74; Sean Cronin, *The*

*McGarrity Papers* (Tralee, County Kerry, Ireland, 1972), pp. 93-101, 138-39, 143-45, 161. On republican transit workers, see n. 22.

24. Interview with Gerald O'Reilly, May 15, 1978.

25. Interviews with Gerald O'Reilly, May 15, 1978, and July 11, 1979. See also sources cited in n. 22.

26. Interview with John Nolan, June 1, 1978 (includes quote); telephone interview with Sean Cronin, Apr. 9, 1979; Gustav Faber, *And Then Came TWU!* (New York, 1950), p. 27.

27. On Irish nationalism and republicanism in the United States, see Eric Foner, "Class, Ethnicity, and Radicalism in the Gilded Age: The Land League and Irish-America," *Marxist Perspectives*, 1 (Summer 1978), 5-66; David Montgomery, *Beyond Equality: Labor and the Radical Republicans, 1862-1872* (New York, 1967), pp. 126-34; Charles Callan Tansill, *America and the Fight for Irish Freedom, 1866-1922* (New York, 1957); and McCaffrey, ed., *Irish Nationalism.*

Useful and suggestive comments on Irish and Irish-American political culture appear in Cross, "The Irish"; Greeley, *Most Distressful Nation*, p. 30; Glazer and Moynihan, *Beyond the Melting Pot*, pp. 224-25; William V. Shannon, *The American Irish* (New York, 1962), pp. 17-19; and David E. Schmidt, *The Irony of Irish Democracy* (Lexington, Mass., 1973), esp. pp. 43-64. Also helpful were comments by Sean Cronin and Gerald O'Reilly in the previously cited interviews.

28. Arthur Mitchell, *Labour in Irish Politics, 1890-1930* (New York, 1974), pp. 47-54, 67-77, 81-85, 91-122, 144-70, 235-39; Bell, *Secret Army*, pp. 121-22.

IRA membership did not ensure sympathy for the TWU. IRA veteran Jeremiah Ryan, for example, an electrical foreman at the IRT 148th Street shop and a friend of both Tom O'Shea and the president of the IRT Brotherhood, opposed the TWU. See National Labor Relations Board, "Stenographic Report of Hearing in the Matter of the Transport Workers Union v. Interborough Rapid Transit Company, Oct. 31, 1934," p. 34, IRT Co. file #805, Records of the NLB and NLRB, Record Group 25, National Archives, Washington National Records Center, Suitland, Md. (hereafter NLRB, "Stenographic Report").

29. Interviews with Jerry O'Brien, Sept. 12, 1979; and Gerald O'Reilly, May 15, 1978 and July 11, 1979; TWU, *Report of the Proceedings of the Convention, 1937* (New York, 1937), Oct. 7 afternoon session, pp. 57-58 (hereafter *TWU 1937 Convention*); David Doyle, "The Irish and American Labour, 1880-1920," *Saothar*, 1 (May 1975), 50-52. Mike Quill gave a somewhat different, but not incompatible, account of the first CP-Clan contact in A. H. Raskin, "Presenting the Phenomenon Called Quill," *New York Times Magazine*, Mar. 6, 1950.

30. Glazer, *Social Basis of American Communism*, pp. 87-89; IWC leaflet, Jan. 19, 1936, copy in possession of the author; *Dies Committee*, vol. 13, pp. 7893-94, 7901, 7906, 7911; *Daily Worker*, Oct. 6, 1933, p. 4; Nov. 8, 1933, p. 4; May 14, 1934, p. 5; interviews with Gerald O'Reilly, May 15, 1978 and July 11, 1979; Sean Murray, *Ireland's Fight for Freedom and the Irish in the U.S.A.* (New York, 1934), pp. 14-16 (quoted phrase on p. 15).

31. Huberman, *Great Bus Strike*, pp. 10-12; *Dies Committee*, vol. 13, p. 7906; *Transport Workers Bulletin*, Apr. 1934, pp. 1, 3; May 1934, p. 2 (includes quoted passage). According to Tom O'Shea, at the time that the TWU was founded the transit organizing committee had about 100 members.

32. Philip J. Carey, S.J., to Maurice A. Walsh, Jr., Jan. 29, 1948, in "Correspondence-W" file, Archives of the Xavier Institute of Industrial Relations,

Archives of the New York Province (Jesuit), Bronx (hereafter Xavier Archives).

33. See, for example, interviews with John Gallagher, Apr. 20, 1979; Jerry O'Brien, Sept. 12, 1979, and Gerald O'Reilly, May 15, 1978.

34. Interviews with Philip Carey, Oct. 13, 1977; Philip Bray, Aug. 13, 1979; and James Sullivan, July 27, 1979; *Transport Workers Bulletin*, Apr. 1, 1936, p. 1; *Labor Leader*, Jan. 17, 1938, p. 2.

35. Murphy's statement appears in U.S. House of Representatives, *Hearings before a Special Committee on Un-American Activities*, 75th Cong., 2nd Sess., vol. 2 (Washington, D.C., 1938), p. 1040 (hereafter *Dies Committee*, vol. 2). See also *Dies Committee*, vol. 13, p. 7912; interview with Maurice Forge, Aug. 9, 1979.

Dies Committee testimony, perhaps more than most sources, has to be used with considerable caution; in the context in which they were given, statements like Murphy's were clearly self-serving. This alone, however, does not indicate untruth. Other TWU activists, including both long-time Communists and anti-Communists, advanced similar views on the party's attraction as a result of its role as a union advocate. See, for example, interviews with Gerald O'Reilly, May 15, 1978; Philip Bray, Aug. 13, 1979; and John Gallagher, Apr. 20, 1979.

36. Interview with Patrick Reilly, Sept. 7, 1978.

37. *Dies Committee*, vol. 2, p. 1070.

38. Bell, *Secret Army*, pp. 52, 73, 77-78, 101, 104, 106-7, 111, 117; Communist Party of Ireland (CPI), *Outline History* (Dublin, 197?), pp. 11-12, 22-24; telephone interview with Sean Cronin, Apr. 9, 1979.

39. Bell, *Secret Army*, pp. 81, 88; interview with Gerald O'Reilly, Jan. 11, and July 11, 1979; James Sullivan, July 27, 1979; telephone interview with Sean Cronin, Apr. 9, 1979. According to the CPI's *Outline History*, p. 4, "At all stages it would be true to say that there were more Irish Communists in countries outside Ireland [than in it]."

40. Telephone interview with Sean Cronin, Apr. 9, 1979; *TWU 1937 Convention*, Oct. 8 afternoon session, pp. 41-42; interviews with Gerald O'Reilly, Jan. 11, 1979; James Sullivan, July 27, 1979; Jerry O'Brien, Sept. 17, 1979; and Patrick Reilly, Sept. 7, 1978; *Daily Worker*, June 16, 1934, p. 4; June 22, 1934, p. 3; *TWU Express*, May 1964, p. 15; *Transport Workers Bulletin*, May 1939, p. 15; May 1940, pp. 3, 8; June 1941, p. 12; James Larkin, *Ireland and the Irish in the U.S.A.* (New York, 1947).

41. Interviews with Gerald O'Reilly, May 15, 1978; Maurice Forge, Dec. 30, 1978 and Jan. 7, 1979; and Martin Young, Nov. 15, 1978. For CP comment on this situation, see Max Steinberg, "Rooting the Party among the Masses in New York," *The Communist*, 17 (Sept. 1939), 831, 833, and Rose Wortis, "Organization Brings Results," *Party Organizer*, 10 (Aug. 1937), 40-41.

42. Interview with Gerald O'Reilly, May 15, 1978.

43. Interviews with Gerald O'Reilly, May 15, 1978 and July 11, 1979; Maurice Forge, Jan. 7, 1979; John Nolan, June 1, 1978; and Patrick Reilly, Sept. 7, 1978.

44. *Transport Workers Bulletin*, May 1934, p. 3; July 1934, p. 3; Sept. 1934, p. 8; Oct. 1934, p. 2; May 1940, p. 8; *Daily Worker*, Oct. 19, 1934, p. 4; NLRB, "Stenographic Report," pp. 32, 35; interviews with Maurice Forge, Jan. 7, 1979 (includes quote); Gerald O'Reilly, May 15, 1978; John Nolan, June 1, 1979; Patrick Reilly, Sept. 7, 1978; and Peter MacLachlan, Feb. 25, 1979. For an example of the CP's use of a similar organizational technique elsewhere, see *Daily Worker*, Mar. 26, 1934, p. 6.

45. On the IRT Brotherhood situation, see Sass, "Harlem Concentration," p. 25 (includes quote); *Daily Worker*, Feb. 1, 1935, p. 6; *Transport Workers Bulletin*, Oct. 1934, p. 7; Mar. 1935, p. 4; May 1, 1936, p. 6; *Dies Committee*, vol. 13, pp. 7913-14; and interviews with Patrick Reilly, Sept. 7, 1978, and Maurice Forge, Jan. 13, 1979.

On Irish abstentionism and boycotting, see interview with Philip Carey, Oct. 13, 1977; Paul O'Dwyer Memoir, OHCCU; and Bell, *Secret Army*, pp. 8, 16-19, 31-32, 54-55.

46. *Transport Workers Bulletin*, July 1934, p. 3; *Daily Worker*, Aug. 13, 1934, p. 3; interview with Maurice Forge, Jan. 7, 1979.

47. *Daily Worker*, July 27, 1934; *TWU 1937 Convention*, Oct. 7 afternoon session, pp. 57-58; interviews with Gerald O'Reilly, May 15, 1978; Jerry O'Brien, Sept. 12, 1979; Philip Carey, Oct. 13, 1977; John Nolan, June 1, 1978; and Maurice Forge, Jan. 27, 1979; *Transport Workers Bulletin*, May-June 1935, p. 6; Nov. 1, 1935, pp. 1, 7; Nov. 1936, p. 4; *New York Times*, Sept. 5, 1935, p. 8.

48. Interview with Gerald O'Reilly, May 15, 1978. Quill was quoted in the *New York Post*, July 2, 1937, p. 4.

49. Differential rates of organization on the IRT are discussed in Faber, *Then Came TWU!*, p. 29; *Transport Workers Bulletin*, Feb. 1935, pp. 1, 3; Dec. 1935, p. 1; Nov. 1936, p. 3; Jan. 1937, pp. 5, 8; and Feb. 1937, p. 2; TWU, "Minutes of Joint Executive Committees Meeting Held Monday, Sept. 15 [1936]," and various TWU leaflets from 1936 and 1937, copies in possession of the author; and interviews with Gerald O'Reilly, May 15, 1978; Maurice Forge, Jan. 7, 1979; and Joseph Labash, Aug. 3, 1979.

50. *Transport Workers Bulletin*, Sept. 1934, p. 3; Nov. 1934, p. 4; Dec. 1934-Jan. 1935, p. 1; Mar. 1935, p. 1; *Daily Worker*, Nov. 3, 1934, p. 2; interviews with Gerald O'Reilly, May 15, 1978 and Jan. 11, 1979; John Nolan, June 1, 1978; Maurice Forge, Jan. 7, 1979; Patrick Reilly, Sept. 7, 1978; and John Plover, Feb. 20, 1979; "Santo Deportation Hearings," pp. 627-28; *Dies Committee*, vol. 2, p. 1074; vol. 13, pp. 7893-7911. O'Shea himself denied having advocated terrorist tactics, but the weight of evidence seems strongly against him.

51. Raskin, "Quill"; *American Labor*, June 1971, p. 24; interviews with James Sullivan, July 27 and Aug. 16, 1979; Jerry O'Brien, Sept. 19, 1979; Gerald O'Reilly, Jan. 11, 1979; Patrick Reilly, Sept. 7, 1978; and Maurice Forge, Jan. 7, 1979; Len DeCaux, *Labor Radical* (Boston, 1970), pp. 425-26; *Dies Committee*, vol. 2, pp. 1044, 1069, 1071; vol. 13, pp. 7913-16, 8099, 8101-2. Quill repeatedly denied that he had ever joined the CP. However, available evidence suggests that he did in fact join in 1934, although after 1935 a certain distance was carefully maintained between Quill and the normal party apparatus. In any case, the issue is really of little importance, since there is no question that between 1935 and 1948 Quill worked closely with the CP and generally followed its positions on union and political issues.

52. See interviews cited in n. 50, and *Dies Committee*, vol. 13, pp. 7879, 7892-952; *Motorman, Conductor and Motor Coach Operator*, Aug. 1934, pp. 3-6; "Santo Deportation Hearings," pp. 597-628.

53. Interviews with Maurice Forge, Jan. 7 and Feb. 25, 1979; Peter MacLachlan, Feb. 25, 1979; Gerald O'Reilly, July 11, 1979; John Gallagher, Apr. 20, 1979; Patrick Walsh, June 1, 1978; and James Sullivan, Aug. 16, 1979.

54. *Labor Leader*, Jan. 3, 1938, p. 2; Aug. 1, 1938, p. 1; Mar. 11, 1940, pp. 1, 4, 8; Bayor, *Neighbors in Conflict*, p. 196; Sheldon Marcus, *Father Coughlin: The Tumultuous Life of the Priest of the Little Flower* (Boston, 1973), p. 293;

*Transport Workers Bulletin*, Nov. 1, 1935, p. 6; Dec. 1, 1935, p. 4; Feb. 1936, p.
5; May 1938, p. 1; Dec. 1938, p. 1; John K. Sharp, *History of the Diocese of
Brooklyn, 1853-1952*, vol. 2 (New York, 1954), p. 270; J., "The Daily Worker
Gave Me the First Break," *Party Organizer*, 11 (Apr. 1938), 43-44; *TWU 1937
Convention*, Oct. 7 afternoon session, pp. 57-58; *Tablet*, July 10, 1937; *Motor-
man, Conductor and Motor Coach Operator*, Aug. 1937, pp. 3-6; interviews
with John Nolan, June 1, 1978; John Plover, Feb. 20, 1979; Peter MacLachlan,
Feb. 25, 1979; Douglas Paul Seaton, "The Catholic Church and the Congress of
Industrial Organizations: The Case of Catholic Trade Unionists, 1937-1950"
Ph.D. dissertation, Rutgers University, 1975), pp. 1, 75-76.

On Catholic response to the CIO, see David J. O'Brien, *American Catholics
and Social Reform: The New Deal Years* (New York, 1968), and Neil Betten,
*Catholic Activism and the Industrial Worker* (Gainesville, Fla., 1976).

55. Interviews with Philip Carey, Oct. 13, 1977, and Gerald O'Reilly, May
15, 1978; Bell, *Secret Army*, p. 88.

56. Philip E. Dobson, S. J., "The Xavier Labor School, 1938-1939," pp. 271-
74 (quoted passage on p. 271), unidentified magazine clipping, in "History of
Labor School" file, Xavier Archives.

57. Greeley, *Most Distressful Nation*, pp. 84-85; interviews with Philip Bray,
Aug. 13, 1979 (includes quote), and John Nolan, June 1, 1978; P. Cacchione,
"A Foundation for Recruiting," *Party Organizer*, 10 (Dec. 1937), 13-14; Philip
Dobson, S.J., to Philip Carey, S.J., July 8, 1941, in "41-42" file, Xavier Archives;
Dobson, "Xavier Labor School," pp. 271-72; *Transport Workers Bulletin*, Apr.
1938, p. 12; May 1943, p. 10.

58. Interviews with John Plover, Feb. 20, 1979; Maurice Forge, Jan. 13, 1979;
and Peter MacLachlan, Feb. 25, 1979.

59. A summary of TWU accomplishments appears in the "Report of the
Executive Board," in *TWU 1937 Convention*.

60. Typescript transcript of the proceedings of the TWU's 1937 convention,
p. 40, copy in possession of the author.

61. *Transport Workers Bulletin*, 1937-48, passim; interviews with Gerald
O'Reilly, May 15, 1978; Patrick Reilly, Sept. 7, 1978; and Maurice Forge, Jan.
13 and Aug. 9, 1979; Michael J. Quill to Daniel Breen, Nov. 22, 1944, copy in
possession of the author; Michael J. Quill, *Justice . . . for Ireland* (New York,
1944); Paul O'Dwyer Memoir, OHCCU.

On Church-affiliated opposition efforts, see Dobson, "Xavier Labor School,"
pp. 266-74; interview with Philip Carey, Oct. 13, 1977; Jules Weinberg, "Priests,
Workers, and Communists," *Harper's Magazine*, Nov. 1948, pp. 49-56; Seaton,
*Catholic Church and the Congress of Industrial Organizations*, pp. 231-32, 241,
287, 303-5; and Betten, *Catholic Activism*, pp. 104-5, 138-41.

62. Michael J. Quill to Philip Murray, Aug. 30, 1944, TWU file, box A7-34,
CIO papers, Catholic University, Washington, D.C. The important question of
the relationship of the TWU to black workers is discussed in forthcoming
works by Mark Naison; August Meier and Elliott Rudwick; and the author.

63. Philip J. Carey, S.J., "Review of James J. McGinley, *Labor Relations in
the New York Rapid Transit Systems, 1904-1944*," p. 158, unidentified clipping
in "Rev. Philip Carey, S.J." file, Xavier Archives.

# Conflict over Workers' Control:
# The Automobile Industry
# in World War II

NELSON LICHTENSTEIN

During the 1930s and 1940s automobile industry workers played a key role in one of the most decisive battles waged between capital and labor in the twentieth century. In this most rationalized and integrated of all mass production industries, management's historic drive toward increasing Taylorization of the workplace encountered stiff resistance, and for a few years the balance of power in the sprawling production facilities of southeastern Michigan seemed to tip away from capital. The great sitdown strikes of 1937 and the consolidations of UAW power that followed have captured the most attention, but the decisive arena of struggle lay on the shop floor itself, where auto workers waged a protracted conflict with the bosses over control of the work routine and distribution of power in the factory.

Historians have long recognized that a considerable degree of autonomous worker self-activity accompanied the early years of industrial union growth, but they actually know little of the essential character of what they have conveniently labeled "working class militancy."[1] This essay takes a closer look at the dynamics of this shop-floor phenomenon, by focusing on the experience of automobile industry workers during World War II, when the conflict over the degree to which workers would exercise real power at the point of production reached a level of unsurpassed intensity. It first sketches the structural basis for the rise of shop-floor power and then explores the character of the extraordinary militancy of the World War II era. The essay also examines the obstacles to the institutionalization of workers' control and then briefly surveys the way in which managerial prerogatives in this area were firmly reestablished in the early postwar era.

The deployment of an assembly-line organization of work in the early twentieth century proved an important victory in the capitalist effort to win greater control of the production process. The radical subdivision of labor, the relentless flow of work, and the pattern of close supervision broke much of the power formerly wielded by skilled craftsmen in metal fabrication industries. The new factory regime abolished the stint, by which nineteenth-century craftsmen had openly and deliberately regulated output. An observer at Ford's pioneering Highland Park factory reported how the technology of work itself provided management with a new weapon in its arsenal of control: "The chain drive (continuous assembly) proved to be a very great improvement, hurrying the slower men, holding the fast men back from pushing work on those in advance, and acting as an all-around adjustor and equalizer."[2]

But management's success with the techniques of mass production did not end the chronic industrial war with their employees, rather it merely rearranged the battlefield. Although they had lost the power to formally determine their routine of work and quota of output, automobile industry workers never lost the capacity to exert some restrictions on the pace of production or some challenge to the prerogatives of management. Indeed the highly integrated character of the auto factory proved its Achilles' heel, for it gave the coordinated action of even a handful of unskilled workers the leverage to slow or stop production in a work area or department. In the 1920s Stanley B. Mathewson revealed that group efforts to retard production were commonplace even in nonunion shops, while in the next decade labor spies in auto plants found that the daily discussion of how many parts to put out each shift provided one of the main topics of workers' conversations. As David Montgomery has pointed out, the craftsman's stint had been an overt act of collective regulation by workers who directed their own productive operations, while the group regulation that replaced it in the twentieth-century factory represented a covert, underground effort, or as Montgomery puts it: "The stint had become sabotage."[3]

During the 1930s the structure of the work and the character of the work force together determined the location and timing of the militancy that burst forth in that decade. For the first time the Detroit working class had achieved a certain stability in the years since the birth of the automobile industry. The brutal layoffs of the early depression years eliminated many of the younger, unattached workers, the "suitcase brigade" of transient, seasonal workers from the rural South and upper Midwest. A smaller, older, somewhat more stable work force remained. Although frequently the victims of long layoffs and short work weeks, these predominantly married, male workers maintained a greater social and economic stake in their jobs than those employed in the industry during the second and third decades of the century. This commitment was reinforced by the far greater personal security the UAW seniority systems and grievance procedures brought to the industry after 1937.[4]

The informal work group provided the organizational basis for working-class militancy in the auto factories of the mid-1930s. Although the assembly line dominates the popular image of the production process, fewer than 20 percent of all employees worked directly on the main conveyor, while at least twice that number labored to manufacture stock or subassemblies to supply the needs of the final line. It was largely among the often tightly knit, long-service groups of somewhat higher skilled workers engaged in subassembly and benchwork that collective resistance to managerial authority centered in many plants. These workers maintained a high degree of verbal interaction and group identification, and they often retained a distinctive level of skill and collective experience. Workers of this sort were somewhat free of the harsh, mechanical work discipline imposed by the moving assembly line, yet they were so situated in the production process that a rapid and continuous flow of their work was essential to maintain overall output.[5]

Especially among the bodyworkers, who comprised about 15 percent of the work force, each man or work gang completed a substantial proportion of the production cycle on his particular job. Paid on a piecework or group incentive basis, these semiskilled production workers developed a strong sense of occupational loyalty and group solidarity. Trimmers, for example, were responsible for the upholstery of the car from one end to the other. The work was cramped and difficult, requiring considerable skill and mutual cooperation. In the 1930s changes in body style, a further subdivision of labor, and a tightening up of production standards brought trimmers into repeated conflict with their foremen in many auto factories. Thus, prior to the entrance of the union and then independently of the UAW, the effort by workers like the trimmers to limit management's unilateral right to set production standards became nearly synonymous with auto-worker militancy. Informal negotiations, slowdowns, and short stoppages to retime and reduce the pace of work were endemic in Detroit auto factories, especially at the beginning of the model year before the "grooving in" process was complete. Although less politically engaged or union conscious in the mid-1930s than the highly skilled maintenance and tool-and-die workers, the shop-floor militancy of trimmers and other semiskilled workers could be more explosive, first because of the key positions they occupied in the day-to-day production cycle and second because of their more frequent battles with management over the pace and content of their work.[6]

Union recognition initially increased the leverage of such combative, strategically located work groups. The contract gave workers, whatever their tactics, a measure of protection from arbitrary reprisal. At the same time few workers accepted the modern distinction between contract negotiation and contract administration, so shop-floor assemblies, confrontations, slowdowns, and stoppages proliferated after the sitdown strikes of 1937 and after UAW organization of the Rouge and other Ford plants in 1941. In these early years militancy and organization proved dialectically dependent, building confidence and hope in a new and powerful synthesis. Direct shop-floor activity legitimized the union's presence for thousands of heretofore hesitant workers who now poured into union ranks; and such job actions established a pattern of union influence and authority unrecognized in the early, sketchily written, signed contracts.[7] Such work groups often maintained what one industrial sociologist termed a "strategic" attitude toward the struggle with management: "They seemed to be shrewdly calculating pressure groups which never tired of objecting to unfavorable management decisions, seeking loop-holes in existing policies and contract clauses that would redound to their benefit. . . . They demanded constant attention for their problems and had the ability to reinforce their demands by group action."[8]

The union shop steward played a key role in the life of these groups. In the 1930s and early 1940s an extensive steward system roughly coincided with the organic leadership generated by the various work groups that composed the plant work force. Although stewards were generally not recognized in the usual collective-bargaining contract as part of the official grievance procedure, the UAW stewards were in fact the "cornerstone of union organization."[9] Elected by the rank and file, these stewards collected all union dues, heard rank-and-file complaints, and negotiated informally with immediate supervision. Their moral authority lay in the ability to maintain a unity of purpose with their workmates and win extracontractual concessions from foremen and other lower-level managers. When militancy and élan were high, as in the spring of 1937 or the summer and fall of 1939, stewards often orchestrated the "spontaneous" slowdowns and departmental work stoppages that consolidated the UAW's power and widened the area of workers' control and union influence on the shop floor.[10] Stewards focused the power of the work group, providing semiskilled machine-tenders and assemblers with the kind of leverage nineteenth-century craftsmen had once jealously guarded in the skill of their hands. "Once we got our first contract, we set about improving the working conditions," recalled a Dodge worker many years later. "First we had to cut down to size those hard-boiled foremen. . . . Sometimes foremen would jerk up the automatic conveyer a couple of notches and speed up the line. We cured them of that practice: we simply let jobs go by half-finished. Make no mistake about it; in those days our stewards had power."[11]

The stewards and other secondary-level union officers were also key elements in the life of the shop because they provided the social and cultural link between the often parochial, insular world of the factory and the larger, cosmopolitan realm of union politics and national affairs. These were the individuals, probably numbering between ten and twenty thousand, who provided the essential infrastructure without which the union simply could not function. A politicized minority were influenced by one or another of the active political groups within the UAW: the Socialists, the Communists, the Trotskyists, or even scattered elements of the Ku Klux Klan and the Black Legion.[12] During the union's entire first decade the largest political tendency of this sort was that of the Communists, who had played a central role in mobilizing and channeling the workplace militancy of the rank and file during the union-building era of the late 1930s. With about 600 members and a circle of fellow travelers several times that size, the Communists had an organized presence in almost every large factory. During World War II they doubled their membership in the auto/aircraft industry, but the party's role in advancing the shop-floor power then would prove far different from that which it played in the era of the first popular front.[13]

The localistic shop-floor militancy of the prewar era remained largely intact when the automobile industry began its transition to military production in 1941 and 1942. Of course, the overwhelming majority of American workers patriotically backed the president, the armed forces, and the war itself. They generally accepted the necessity for the no-strike pledge UAW leaders had offered the nation immediately after Pearl Harbor, and they were willing to give the complicated dispute-adjustment machinery established by the National War Labor Board a chance to work. Yet the wartime ideology of equal sacrifice, pushed by the UAW in its widely publicized "Victory through Equality of Sacrifice" program, made war workers extremely sensitive to the usual exercise of managerial authority or to what seemed inequitable burdens in their structure of work or wages. Told repeatedly that their production effort in the heart of the "arsenal of democracy" was equal to that of the fighting soldiers themselves, many workers resented all the more the petty discriminations of factory life: the abrupt changes in shift and work hours, no-smoking rules enforced in blue- but not white-collar work areas, dress codes unilaterally imposed by management. Veteran auto workers certainly did not believe that the wartime ideology of labor-management cooperation and full production had fundamentally altered old conflicts. Even as the conversion of Detroit auto factories was getting underway, a secret government survey in May 1942 revealed that fully half of all Motor City workers feared employers would try to use the wartime emergency as a means of destroying labor's recent victories.[14]

The changing political economy of the war era initially enabled workers to enhance their relative control of the shop-floor work environment. In the transition to war work, managers found the incentive toward low-cost production greatly reduced, the maintenance of the new and unfamiliar production schedules established by the military all important. Since no one in top management or government really knew the cost of a piece of war material rushed into production on a "cost-plus" contract, labor expenses were relatively uncontrolled in either Washington or Detroit. Meanwhile, a tight labor market gave individual workers unprecedented individual bargaining power, which was soon reflected by the steadily upward drift of wages and high rates of labor turnover. Despite manpower controls, wartime inflation and government wage ceilings, real auto industry wages increased by about 20 percent in the forty months after Pearl Harbor. Of course, for workers who migrated to the new employment opportunities from low-paying jobs outside the industry the shift to the higher-paying defense work could represent pay increases of 100 percent or more.[15]

The conversion of the auto industry to critical aircraft, gun, and tank production also set the stage for a substantial decline in factory discipline. Production for the war effort necessitated a modification of the technology of manufacture so as to enhance indirectly the relative degree of control auto workers held over their shop routine. Most military production, and especially that of such labor intensive items as heavy artillery, tanks, aircraft parts, engines and airframes, was not fully adaptable to prewar conveyor-line technology. Instead, much war work was individually paced, task-oriented, small-batch production. Airframe workers labored as a team, building—not assembling—each fuselage and wing section. Labor inside a B-24 had the feel of construction work, not machine-paced factory production. In aircraft engine plants a larger proportion tended grinding machines, drill presses, or other operator-controlled machine tools. The actual assembly of the engines—conveyor-line work—required about 50 percent less personnel than did the prewar auto engine.[16] Such changes in organization and technology did much to enable war workers to set informal production quotas and work norms on a group or individual basis. The change in production technique largely accounted for management's wartime campaign to abandon daywork and restore incentive pay. Plant supervisors recognized that with the assembly line in relative eclipse, only a return to some form of piecework could eliminate the need for stepped-up supervision and spur workers on to greater effort.[17]

The alienation of the foreman from the ranks of factory supervision proved another key element in the decline of factory discipline. Since early in the century this front-line lieutenant of management had lost much power and prestige as corporate personnel and engineering departments steadily assumed ever more of the foreman's traditional control of hiring, wages, and production. In the late 1930s the new CIO unions further restricted the foreman's authority when grievance procedures and seniority rules limited and regulated his unilateral disciplinary power. Caught between management's drive to maintain efficiency and the increasingly strong pressures from the rank-and-file work group to "get along," the foremen had become the "marginal men" of industry by the early 1940s.[18]

The war itself produced an additional, major drop in the status and managerial élan of this key figure in the factory hierarchy. In all the mass production industries, but especially the booming auto/aircraft plants, the dramatic expansion of employment forced managers to recruit thousands of ordinary workers into the supervisory ranks quickly. At General Motors 42 percent of its 19,000 foremen had been on the job less than a year in 1943. They complained that without overtime pay for themselves their average wage hovered little above those they supervised, and since foremen lost their union seniority when promoted from the ranks, they feared that without their own grievance procedure and seniority system they could be demoted to the production line or unemployment role when the postwar layoffs began.[19] Many, of course, had been union-conscious production workers before their promotion, and remained so afterwards. "They have not been properly trained or instructed in order to function efficiently," complained a middle-level supervisor at Packard, "nor have they the proper viewpoint of management toward their jobs."[20]

The Foremen's Association of America (FAA) built its spectacular wartime growth on this disenchantment. Beginning among veteran foremen at the Rouge shortly after the UAW success there in April 1941, the association signed up more than 33,000 by mid-1944. Although the FAA recruited well among the steel and rubber industries of Ohio and in several shipyards on the East Coast, about 80 percent of its members were in Detroit area auto/aircraft plants. Aside from the Rouge there were organized foremen in Briggs, Packard, Chrysler, and Murray Body. In the face of adamant opposition from management and a series of inconsistent administrative rulings from the National

Labor Relations Board and the War Labor Board, the ability of foremen to maintain their organization rapidly became dependent upon
the friendly neutrality of the UAW and the active goodwill of the rank-
and-file workers they supervised.[21]

Taken together, then, the conversion of factories to high-cost military
production, the new demand for labor, and the defection of the foreman, all created an environment on the shop floor which contributed
to an erosion of traditional factory discipline and the rise of worker
power at the actual point of production. At Packard, union committeemen prevented managers from making any new time-studies in the
Naval Engine Department and reached an agreement with foremen in
the overstaffed aircraft engine division that once the work quota for the
day had been fulfilled, the men could doze or play cards until quitting
time. At the Buick Motor Aluminum foundry in Flint workers making
Pratt and Whitney aircraft engines maintained a "peg" of twenty-two
cores per shift for several months despite management efforts to increase production.[22] "Rate busters" who violated informal work norms
were expelled by a New Jersey Ford local, while unionists at the Rouge
warned "reactionary" foremen that the local would veto their readmis-
sion if and when they were demoted during the postwar layoff.[23]

A major demographic convulsion shook the Detroit working class in
the first half of the war, helping to shape the particular character and
fate of this syndicalist impulse. By 1943 the war had shattered the
stability of the depression-era work force. As the draft took its toll,
about 30 percent of the half-million predominantly male factory workers of 1940 left the area. Their ranks were soon filled and then swelled
by the recruitment of some four hundred thousand additional workers,
so that by the end of 1943 about one out of two workers was new to the
industry. About half of these factory recruits were from the Detroit
metropolitan area itself, of the remainder about a third came from the
South, about two-fifths from the rest of Michigan and the Midwest.
Contrary to the popular impression, most of these workers had not
come directly from the farm; nevertheless, for more than half, war work
in Detroit proved their first factory experience.[24]

The massive employment boom pushed total UAW membership to
over 1.2 million, and profoundly altered the social composition of the
union. The expanded auto work force resembled that of the pre-
depression nonunion era when the seasonal migration of workers from
the rural South and upper Midwest made for a volatile but not particularly union-conscious proletariat. Meanwhile the UAW cadre became, like the IWW militants of the 1920s, a thin stratum, somewhat
older and more skilled than the mass of new recruits who had not
experienced the deeply transforming process of actually building the

unions of which they were now a part.[25] As a frustrated officer of the UAW's 42,000-member Willow Run local put it, "At the bomber local the majority are paying $1 a month for the privilege of working. They have no understanding at all of the union and are probably a little mystified as to how they ever got into it."[26]

One of the most notable features of this wartime employment surge was the substantial increase in the employment of women and blacks in the industry. Unlike the regional auto boom of the 1920s, the nationwide labor shortage in World War II ultimately forced the major corporations to recruit and upgrade workers who had heretofore been automatically excluded from most sections of the industry. Women's employment in the Detroit-Willow Run area more than doubled during the war, and in some of the newer plants—chiefly aircraft assembly—reached 40 percent of the factory work force. Of these women about 90 percent had never paid union dues before. In Detroit, as elsewhere, World War II proved a watershed in the history of women's work. Before the conflict the typical woman worker had been young and single; the well-paying job opportunities available during the war drew into the work force large numbers of older married women who had worked only intermittently or not at all.[27]

Of course, the new demand for women workers did not fundamentally alter the sexual division of labor in either the factory or the home. To most employers and male workers, and to many women themselves, the new job-openings of the 1940s came not as part of a general feminist advance, but rather as women's particular opportunity to aid the war effort and as a more effective way to contribute to the family economy. Thus, many of the jobs women war workers took over were now informally redefined as part of the new realm of "women's work." Aircraft riveting and wiring became predominantly female occupations at Willow Run, although the more highly skilled workers and the foremen in these departments were almost exclusively male. When they were considered an alien intrusion into formerly all-male departments, women suffered a good deal of petty harassment, but except for occasional protests over sexist clothing regulations, women participated in relatively few job actions as a group.[28] In part this may have derived from their concentration in aircraft assembly work, which foremen found difficult to supervise or time. Because of a complex pay scale imposed by the War Labor Board, all airframe plants generated an enormous number of individual wage grievances, but these disputes usually involved individual skill reclassifications that provided little basis for collective action. Outside of work, severe housing, transportation, and child-care shortages in the Detroit area made the traditional responsibilities women bore at home even more difficult. In general, women workers responded to the discrimination they found on the job and the difficulties they encountered in the wartime household economy on an individual basis. Absenteeism of women was about 50 percent greater than that of men, their rate of labor turnover more than double.[29]

Black participation in the Detroit labor force increased as rapidly as that of women, growing by almost 100,000 from 8 to 14.5 percent in the five years after 1940. Like women, blacks also began to move out of traditional occupational categories, in their case janitorial and foundry work, and into departments heretofore reserved for white men. But the upgrading of black workers proved a far more explosive phenomenon than that involving white women because it came as part of a larger program of aggressive civil-rights militancy that had begun to sweep the northern black community in the late 1930s and early 1940s. During the war most blacks adopted the ideology of the "Double V" campaign: victory over the nation's enemies abroad, victory over discrimination and segregation at home. The movement of blacks into new and better jobs would represent, therefore, not a temporary expedient to win the war but the clear start of a fundamental change in social relations.[30]

As blacks sought to move into "white" jobs, they encountered resistance from many workers and a policy of continued segregation or mere tokenism from key employers like Ford and Chrysler. As historians August Meier and Elliott Rudwick have recently shown, the UAW's well-known commitment to interracial solidarity at the leadership level often dissipated in the locals where seniority rules and informal agreements often sustained a pattern of white discrimination against black workers. Interracial conflict proved most intense in 1942 and 1943, when a well-coordinated effort by black UAW leaders, the local NAACP, and liberal elements of the federal bureaucracy and the UAW international leadership pushed for implementation of President Franklin Roosevelt's 1941 executive order banning discrimination in the defense industry. This effort was backed by the mobilization of thousands of black workers, who took part in numerous protest demonstrations and strike actions. One of the largest came at the foundry unit of the Rouge, a center of black militancy in auto, when 12,000 walked off the job in April 1943 to demand that Ford management accelerate the transfer and hiring of black workers to the corporation's expanded wartime facilities.[31]

Black mobility ushered in the era of Detroit's so-called hate strikes, which erupted when whites quit work to protest black integration of previously segregated departments. These stoppages reflected the racism endemic to large sections of the Detroit working class, but they also arose from the fear by many whites that factory managers would use the influx of black workers to erode work standards and dilute job security. Most of these strikes were "spontaneous" job actions taken by small groups of workers in a single department, though some of the larger stoppages seem to have been either condoned or led by local union officials, possibly in league with fundamentalist "worker-preachers" or Ku Klux Klan members in the plants. Such strikes reached a climax in June 1943 when 25,000 Packard workers walked off the job for a week after two blacks had been promoted to a grinding machine department.[32]

Such racially motivated strikes subsided thereafter, both because of increasingly firm opposition by UAW and government officials, and also because, after an initial period of racially tense integration, many white workers simply accepted blacks as part of the factory work environment. Although wildcat strikes over other issues increased enormously after the spring of 1943, the incidence of hate strikes declined almost to the vanishing point. At Timkin-Detroit Axle Company, for example, three wildcat strikes over racial issues accounted for almost half of all man-hours lost in the eleven work stoppages recorded before September 1943. Thereafter, the number of strikes more than tripled to thirty-six, but only one very minor departmental protest involved a racial dispute. Of course, Detroit remained a city of racial antagonisms, but for the next twenty years these no longer exploded primarily at the workplace.[33]

The decline in shop-floor racial antagonism coincided with an increase in the intensity of the conflict over the pace and the extent of managerial authority. As long as production had remained paramount and labor relatively scarce, there had been little factory managers could do about the loss of shop control they experienced in the early months of the war. Depending on the company, however, the opportunity for tightening up on discipline and abandoning the policy of making concessions to guarantee uninterrupted production came somewhere between mid-1942, when conversion problems were generally resolved, and the end of 1943, when output reached a high plateau and some layoffs began at individual factories. GM voiced management's new élan by repeatedly demanding that UAW locals "discontinue in official union papers, handbills and other literature attacks and accusations of 'speed up' on management efforts to increase production of war materials."[34] At Ford a fresh group of managers reorganized and centralized labor relations late in 1943. "Clearly defined policies were set out," reported a key executive, "particularly with reference to meting out of disciplinary action and enforcement of production and other similar items."[35] Leaders of the UAW local at the Rouge found evidence that mid-level managers there consciously procrastinated on grievances to discipline strike ringleaders and blacken the union's image with a patriotic public. Similarly, at Briggs, a supervisor increased production of some items to the prewar standard "only after successful application of disciplinary action and after a strike."[36]

Workers met this new managerial toughness with a dramatic increase in the number of strikes over production standards and workplace discipline. By 1944 one of every two workers in the auto industry took part in some sort of work stoppage, up from one in twelve in 1942 and one in four in 1943.[37] This was a level of strike participation that exceeded that of 1937. In 1944 a GM vice-president reported that most of the strikes in the corporation's plants were "caused by the refusal of small groups of workers to meet production standards." Of man-hours lost, almost 83 percent involved disputes over discipline, compared to 4 percent in 1940.[38]

Most of these strikes were so-called quickie stoppages, involving anywhere from half a dozen to a few hundred employees who halted work for a shift or less in duration. They typically began when management retimed an operation or changed a job assignment, then insisted that the employees meet the new standard or duty. If they refused or proved sluggish, managers took disciplinary action by either firing or suspending those who failed to meet the new level of work intensity. At this point the issue in the strike became less the original grievance than the discipline itself, and an entire department might go out in defense of those penalized.[39] The record of a couple of Chrysler quickies gives a hint of the character of these work stoppages: "Ten machine operators were sent home for refusal to operate two machines as instructed; 23 others walked out in sympathy, necessitating sending home 99 others." And in another instance: "Seven employees stopped work in protest of discharge of employee for refusing to perform his operation: five of seven were discharged when they refused to return to work: 320 employees then stopped work and left the plant." Both these strikes lasted but one shift.[40]

In strikes such as those described above, the wage issue was not of paramount concern, except insofar as in-plant wage inequalities exacerbated an already difficult situation. Conversely, among workers for whom production standards were not a pressing issue but who felt wages to be unsatisfactory, wildcat strikes were infrequent. For example, highly skilled tool, die, and maintenance workers controlled the pace of their own labor in an autonomous work environment. They were among the most union-conscious in the UAW. During the war their chief grievance revolved around the wage inequalities that the war economy generated in their trade: tool-and-die workers found their wages in the major "captive" shops like Fisher and Ford well below those commanded in the scattered "job" shops of the city. Likewise, maintenance men found their pay below that of AFL craftsmen who were sometimes assigned to their work. However, these skilled workers rarely took part in quickie strikes, but sought instead to migrate to the higher-paying job shops or, after the imposition of manpower controls, to use union channels aggressively to win a wage increase from the War Labor Board. Maintenance workers actually conducted a citywide strike in October 1944, but it was basically a political demonstration directed against the WLB and the UAW leadership, with few of the characteristics of the production standard job actions that so convulsed the industry.[41]

Struck by the dramatic demographic changes that engulfed the auto/aircraft industry, some observers have argued that the very absence of a union tradition among these several hundred thousand new workers gave rise to the breakdown of factory discipline so evident in these walkouts. The influx of these raw industrial recruits certainly disrupted the usual pattern of factory life, diluted union influence, and generated new racial and sexual conflicts within the work force. They increased the level of tension within the factory, but their presence alone hardly explains the intensity or the location of the shop-floor conflict that grew during the war. Of greater long-range import was an oppositional infrastructure and a preexisting tradition of struggle into which these new workers could be acculturated. Thus, the center of working-class militancy during World War II was not in the "cornfield factories" erected far from the older centers of UAW strength, but rather in the unionized shops of Detroit and other industrial centers.[42]

As the work force at factories like Briggs, Packard, Dodge, and Highland Park doubled and tripled in size, the influx of workers untutored in collective action disrupted traditions of departmental militancy and the pattern of steward-foreman accommodation. Often, this gave management the opportunity to restructure production and introduce higher output norms. It then fell to the relatively thin line of stewards and union militants to integrate these new workers into the shop-floor culture they hoped to sustain. Normally this took place in the day-to-day life of the factory, but sometimes this tradition was renewed in more dramatic fashion. Two sociologists who visited Detroit factories late in the war reported that "we were struck by the fact that several of the most paralyzing strikes were set off by the discharge of men who had been with companies for a long time. In one case a company had set an output standard in an operation on which a large number of inexperienced workers were employed and that the workers were about to make the standard. Whereupon an old-timer who was also important in the union had come to the youngsters and told them that they ought to stick together and turn out a good deal less. Then the old timer and some of the new men were fired and the strike was on."[43]

Job actions of this sort represented the class struggle at a fundamental level, but these same disputes over production standards and factory discipline were among the most difficult grievances to define or resolve; and given the unequal and imprecise distribution of work and authority in a factory, shop-floor problems might be intensely felt by some workers and not at all by others. Like the work stoppages which flared in the industry during the nonunion era, the wartime stoppages were often uncoordinated except on a department- or shiftwide level, short in duration, led by a shifting and sometimes unrepresentative leadership. Their timing and organization could prove awkward, thus providing management with an opportunity to take retaliatory action.[44]

Although usually led by stewards or popular union militants, these job actions lacked the overall union-building context that had given prewar strikes of this sort a more consistently progressive character. The presence of a large group of inexperienced workers had already diluted union consciousness in the work force; the UAW's formal no-strike pledge, and the increasingly heavy-handed efforts the leadership took to enforce it, also gave many of these stoppages a debilitating anti-union flavor. Although an increasing number of UAW shop-floor leaders defended these stoppages as part of a larger rank-and-file insurgency, the Communist grouping in the UAW threw its considerable weight resolutely against the coordination of these shop-floor eruptions, arguing instead for the maintenance of the cross-class unity the party thought necessary to win the war against fascism. Under such social and political conditions a union-organized factory could degenerate into a Balkanized set of rival work groups, each of which sought to make the best deal possible with management that reflected its own specific importance in the production cycle or its own particular degree of ethnic or occupational combativeness and solidarity.[45]

Disaffection of this sort put the secondary leadership of the UAW under enormous pressure. These were the experienced and committed union cadre—the stewards, committeemen, department chairmen, and local officials—who had built the UAW in the 1930s and who composed its essential organizational infrastructure for many years thereafter. Given the heterogeneous character of the new wartime work force and the growing management offensive, many of these unionists recognized that without some accommodation to the pressure from below they might lose the confidence of the rank and file, leading either to their ouster from office or to disintegration of the local. From the point of view of this stratum, the no-strike pledge, and to a lesser extent the government wage and manpower controls, robbed them of much of their effectiveness in the complicated game of thrust and parry, militancy and accommodation that composed so much of their day-to-day relationship with mid-level plant management. As a GM unionist in Flint put it, "the company took advantage of this situation. The fact that we had pledged that we would not strike meant that when we went in to negotiate something, a mere "no" was enough. There was nothing much that we could do about it. We had government agencies, of course, and long drawn-out procedures to seek relief but they were so time consuming and so detailed and very, very difficult."[46] As a result, wrote a Briggs local official in a similar bind, "workers began to ask each other, 'What good is our union? What are we paying dues for, anyway? Why do our leaders let us down like this?'"[47]

Beginning in 1943, a growing number of secondary leaders sought to restore meaningful unionism to the shop floor, not by championing these quickie strikes themselves, but by channeling the unrest they represented into a more unified and powerful movement. Especially when key union activists were fired the local leadership might "adopt" a departmental stoppage and authorize a plantwide closure. They did so to aggregate grievances, reintegrate their local unions, and "close the gap between the rank and file and their elected leadership."[48] There is considerable evidence that where a strong, union-conscious leadership conducted these organized wildcat strikes, and where the work force still retained a core of militants from the prewar union-building era, there were actually fewer uncoordinated short stoppages than otherwise. Among Chrysler corporation plants, the older and more militantly led locals at Dodge Main, Jefferson Avenue, and Dodge Truck, were the scene of relatively few quickies in the latter half of the war: instead each plant witnessed periodic well-organized wildcat strikes. In contrast, the war-born locals, such as the Tank Arsenal and the Dodge Chicago aircraft engine plant, were plagued with numerous uncoordinated quickie strikes.[49]

Although in clear violation of the wartime strike prohibition, these larger stoppages escalated in frequency and duration between 1942 and 1945. Such factorywide, even companywide walkouts, were often well-led affairs conducted with all the apparatus of the traditional strike. By 1944 there were some sixty-eight stoppages involving over 1,000 workers; in five of these more than 10,000 walked out. They averaged 3.5 days in length, less than in peacetime but more than twice the average length of wildcat strikes in the first years of the war.[50] In May 1943, for example, a citywide Chrysler work stoppage swept Detroit when management at the Dodge Main plant violated the seniority list and fired a steward. To protest this contract violation and break a grievance logjam that had kept the plants in turmoil for several months, officials of UAW Chrysler locals called mass meetings on May 20 to explain the issues, shut down the plants, and organize effective picket lines. "It was just like old times," reported one worker, "the stewards walked through the plant and announced the meeting, and in five minutes the plant was dead." Despite appeals by top UAW officials 24,000 strikers stayed out for four days, returning to work only after the WLB offered assurances of a timely hearing on the grievance problem and a rapid decision in the long pending Chrysler-UAW contract dispute.[51]

Naturally these wildcat strikes soon became a major issue within the UAW. Although the Communists and all elements of the international leadership continued to denounce these stoppages and support the no-strike pledge, a sizable minority of the secondary leadership soon favored outright repeal of the pledge. The implications of this movement were twofold: on one level it inaugurated a struggle with both the auto corporations and the government over the extent to which the union would continue to subordinate the immediate interests of its members to the politics of cross-class wartime unity; on another level, the repeal of the no-strike pledge would decentralize effective power in the union and help legitimize the combativeness of so many workers on the shop floor.[52]

Organized into a loose Rank-and-File Caucus, a coalition of local leaders and activists scored a stunning victory at the UAW's 1944 convention by pushing through a resolution authorizing a membership referendum on the question. The key organizers were socialist and Trotskyist militants who favored repudiation of the pledge as part of a larger defense of democratic values in American society. They were supported, in turn, by a much larger group of local union leaders who sided with these radicals, not out of any conscious commitment to socialist politics but because their day-to-day experience convinced them of the destructive impact continued adherence to the pledge might have on their locals.[53]

When referendum ballots were finally tallied in March 1945, less than 300,000 auto workers had voted, about 30 percent of union membership. Supporters of the pledge took a two-to-one lead over their opponents, though the contest came closer in Flint and Detroit, where anti-pledge votes reached almost 45 percent of all those cast. This relatively poor showing in the referendum did not mean that wildcat strikes and job actions subsided; on the contrary, they remained at a continuously high level. In UAW region 1 on Detroit's East Side, for example, only about 12 percent of the almost 200,000 workers there cast a vote against the no-strike pledge. But their region remained a hotbed of wartime strike activity, and numerous stoppages swept through the

Briggs, Packard, Hudson, and Chrysler plants early in 1945. The government reported more Detroit workers on strike than at any other time in the war.[54]

If there is any explanation for this seemingly dichotomous behavior it lies in the relationship between the inherent nature of the syndicalist impulse and the existing level of consciousness among wartime auto workers. To most the job actions and wildcat strikes of the era seemed a vital human response to shop conditions that violated their sense of dignity and fairness, but the day-to-day leadership they received subordinated the elemental resistance of these workers to the growing routinization of shop-floor labor relations and the maintenance of the no-strike pledge. Only rarely did rank-and-file workers find the kind of factory-level leadership that could have linked their inchoate rebelliousness with a more coherent and powerful social vision.

Although many wildcat strikes were led by union-conscious militants, the ideological left, which had played a central role in the legitimization of working-class insurgency in the previous decade, failed to influence this wartime movement to any significant degree. Socialists and Wobblies no longer had an organized presence in the UAW. The Trotskyists, who favored politicizing the wildcat-strike movement, played a larger role, but they were a relative handful who drew much of their support from middle-class people who had taken industrial jobs at the start of the war. Their sophistication and élan had enabled a high proportion to win secondary-level posts, but these were often in factories marginal to the older, decisive centers of union strength.[55]

Of considerably more importance were the Communists, who in the 1940s were by far the largest political faction within the UAW. During its ultrapatriotic wartime phase, the party staunchly opposed the wildcat-strike movement as an obstacle to full military production. This did not mean that individual Communists were not active and effective militants in the daily life of the shop, but it did throw the influence of the party against the effort to direct the wildcat-strike movement into something more organizationally stable.[56] By giving the war an uncritically progressive quality, the Communists provided the rationale for those auto workers who sought to reconcile the managerial offensive in the shops with their own radical and anticapitalist sensibilities. Thus a party leaflet for auto workers announced that "advocates of strike threats or strike actions in America in 1945 are SCABS in the war against Hitlerism, they are SCABS against our Armed Forces, they are SCABS against the labor movement." Such an orientation proved costly, and in the last half of the war party growth in auto halted and membership turnover increased. Communist leaders later concluded that its rigid wartime policy had "forfeited leadership to the Reuthers and other radical phrase-mongers."[57]

Finally, oppositional currents within the working class were weak because the war era inaugurated a quarter-century in which American culture seemed particularly homogeneous. In part this represented a major fruit of the social and political reforms of the late New Deal years, in part it reflected the extraordinary patriotic consensus of the home front during the most popular war in American history. In this conflict virtually every signpost of American culture and politics urged workers to consider themselves a part of the mainstream of national life. And like the flag and the uniform, the no-strike pledge held a powerfully symbolic content, representing an unquestionable affirmation of working-class patriotism and participation in the war-era celebration of American life. Caught between a chorus of condemnation that attacked wildcat stoppages as unpatriotic or even subversive and their own patriotic sensibility, most auto workers proved incapable of giving to their genuine shop-floor militancy a larger political and organizational meaning.

The end of the war dissipated the extremely favorable conditions under which auto industry workers had won even a measure of shop control. There was no postwar depression, but cutbacks and layoffs were severe in the reconversion-GM strike period. In a mood akin to that which had engendered the anti-union American Plan after World War I, auto company executives launched a campaign to rewin much of the shop-floor authority they had held in the nonunion era. Of course, they recognized that there was little chance to destroy the UAW itself, but sophisticated managers at Ford and GM were determined that in the postwar era "managers must manage" the production process in their facilities.[58] Under its new "whiz-kid" team recruited from the Air Force, Ford undertook a massive reorganization of production technology that eliminated many pockets of wartime workers' control, built new "automated" factories outside the center of union strength in Michigan, and bargained with the UAW to reimpose a uniform level of discipline throughout its plants. In the crucial 1946 contract negotiations Ford readily agreed to match the best contract the UAW could secure from strike-bound GM, but insisted upon a "company-security" clause codifying management prerogatives in elaborate detail. This included an almost unlimited right to set initial production standards and discipline those it considered guilty of unauthorized work stoppages.[59]

The next year Ford further increased its ability to enforce a greater level of work discipline when it broke the Foremen's Association established at the Rouge during the war. "We must rely upon the foremen to try and keep down those emotional surges of the men in the plants and urge them to rely on the grievance procedure," argued one Ford spokesman. "If we do not have the foremen to do that, who is going to do it?"[60] In the next few years management increased the loyalty of the several thousand foremen at the Rouge through a program that drew a sharp line between their status and that of the men they supervised. Foremen were put on salary, told to wear ties and white shirts, given desks and special parking privileges, and indoctrinated in management-oriented "human relations."[61]

Implementation of this new policy significantly weakened the union infrastructure at its lowest level. The transformation of the foreman into a simple disciplinarian and grievance "buck passer" necessarily diminished the independent leadership role of his counterpart, the union steward, who became at best a "referral agent" frequently bypassed in the actual working of the grievance procedure.[62] Once shop disputes were reduced to writing and began to make their way up the grievance ladder, they were out of the steward's control and subject to a body of lockstep precedent that increasingly defended management rights. "Time and again management does things that I know it has a right to do under the contract," reported one steward at Chrysler in the early 1950s, "but the men don't know it. If I explain to them that the company has the right under four or five rulings made previously they get sore at me." As a consequence, politically savvy stewards "become demagogues. They tend to fake on all this stuff. They write grievances when they know they shouldn't, the art of buck passing is developed to the nth degree."[63] Ultimately, the routinization imposed on all shop-floor bargaining relationships helped accelerate the demise of a vigorous steward system and transform local union officials into virtual contract policemen.

Political developments within the UAW itself reinforced this tendency. C. Wright Mills once called the trade-union leader a "manager of discontent," and Walter Reuther's union leadership during the mid-1940s offers graphic testimony to the validity of that aphorism. Reuther understood the tension under which the secondary leadership of the union had functioned during the war, and in the immediate aftermath of the conflict he sought to diffuse it through a major union offensive against General Motors. The success of this strategy lay in its ability to harness the restless energy of the auto workers, restore a measure of stability to the local unions, and at the same time advance Reuther's own fortunes in the internal union scramble for office. The key GM strike demand—for a 30 percent wage boost without an increase in the price of cars—boldly questioned management prerogatives in determining the relative distribution of its profits but ignored the intractable disputes over company discipline and production standards which had kept the union in turmoil for much of the war. "The GM strike was designed to take the ball out of the hands of the stewards and committeemen," recalled Victor Reuther, "and put it back in the hands of the national leadership."[64]

Wage increases demanded and won by the UAW in the postwar bargaining rounds unified rather than divided the work force, providing a readily available channel into which pent-up shop-floor grievances could be poured, as well as cutting off opportunities for their direct local expression. The elaborate UAW-GM contract of 1950 proved the apotheosis for this sort of bargaining. The union secured a wage escalator and annual improvement increase that guaranteed year-by-year growth in real pay, but in return agreed to an unprecedented five-year contract that made predictable GM labor costs during its mammoth expansion program of the early 1950s. "This kind of collective bargaining," observed the respected labor economist Frederick Harbison, "calls for intelligent trading rather than table-pounding, for diplomacy rather than belligerency, and for internal union discipline rather than grass roots rank and file activity."[65]

The renewal of companywide collective bargaining after the war coincided with the centralization of power in the UAW itself. Reuther's popular leadership of the GM strike provided the political basis for his election to the UAW presidency in early 1946, and in the eighteen months that followed his aggressive caucus eliminated all serious internal union opposition. Reuther's politics in this era have been the subject of much scrutiny, but the real significance of his victory lay as much in his faction's transformation of the union into an effective one-party administrative regime as in the anti-Communist social-democratic program his forces advanced.[66] The elimination of a unionwide opposition substantially reduced the relative freedom local union officers had enjoyed when two factions had competed for their allegiance. Although UAW locals still held formal rights to bargain and strike on work standards, the Reuther leadership approved stoppages over such issues only with the greatest reluctance, especially when they threatened to upset the union's national bargaining strategy or drain its limited resources.[67]

This study of auto worker militancy in World War II illustrates the extent to which shop-floor activism is a historically rooted phenomenon, defined in each era by a concrete set of social, technical, and ideological conditions that give it a unique imprint. In the early 1940s the expansion and conversion of the auto industry to military production generated a decline in factory discipline and a rise in the expectations of many workers over the degree to which they would control the

conditions of their labor. Favorable circumstances such as these enhanced the efficacy of the semiformal web of organization erected by
union-conscious workers, further tipping the power balance on the
shop floor and sustaining in a collective sense a very real element of
workers' control.

Although this wartime militancy drew much of its strength from a
favorable set of social and technological developments, its political
dimension proved far less stable. The extremely rapid demographic
and political changes of the 1940s diluted and fragmented the class
consciousness of the generation of auto workers who had built the
union in the previous decade; and without their more coherent polit-
ical-organizational leadership, the shop-floor militancy that did flourish proved unable to transcend its parochial and localistic focus when
it came under greater attack after 1944. Although wartime rebelliousness was often based upon the feeling that in a war effort which
required sacrifice from all the usual exercise of hierarchical authority
in the workplace rankled unfairly, the activism of this era lacked the
kind of larger ideological legitimacy, the oppositional social vision,
which had proven so essential in advancing the frontier of workers'
control in the 1930s. Given this weakness, the rank-and-file insurgency
of the early 1940s could not stand against the enormous conservative
pressures generated by the new structures of power and authority that
began to emerge in American industrial life.

UAW shop stewards and local officials were the natural leaders of
any workers' control movement, but maintenance of their independent
power threatened the ideology of patriotic unity in the war and undercut the larger collective bargaining regime the UAW and the auto
corporations sought to build in the postwar era. In most plants the
aggressive shop steward system of the union's first decade atrophied,
while the stratum of full-time local officials adopted a more bureaucratic orientation toward the mass of increasingly atomized workers.
With shop-floor channels of resistance and protest thus progressively
diminished, rank-and-file workers fell prey to an alternating pattern of
apathetic resignation and episodic militancy that provided little basis
for a sustained challenge to the managerial offensive of the postwar
years.

NOTES

I wish to thank Eileen Boris, David Brody, and Joshua Freeman for help in the
preparation of this essay.

    1. For the 1930s, the best recent studies are Peter Friedlander, *The Emergence*

*of a UAW Local* (Pittsburgh, 1975); Robert Zieger, *Madison's Battery Workers, 1934-1952* (Ithaca, 1977); and Ronald Schatz "American Electrical Workers: Work, Struggles, Aspirations, 1930-1950" (Ph.D. dissertation, University of Pittsburgh, 1977). For the most part the study of shop-floor relations in the years after 1940 has been left to the labor economists and industrial sociologists who have generated a rich but largely ahistorical and often management-oriented body of research on worker behavior in the unionized shop. The automobile industry alone has several very good studies. Among the best are Charles R. Walker and Robert Guest, *The Man on the Assembly Line* (Cambridge, Mass., 1952) and *The Foreman on the Assembly Line* (Cambridge, Mass., 1956); Ely Chinoy, *Automobile Workers and the American Dream* (New York, 1955); Leonard R. Sayles, *Behavior of Industrial Work Groups: Prediction and Control* (New York, 1958); and B. J. Widick, *Auto Work and Its Discontents* (Baltimore, 1976). Robert Blauner's *Alienation and Freedom: The Factory Worker and His Industry* (Chicago, 1964) compares the relationship of work process to consciousness in several industries, including auto.

2. The best overall studies of the impact of the managerial offensive on the organization of work in the early twentieth century are Harry Braverman, *Labor and Monopoly Capital: The Degradation of Work in the Twentieth Century* (New York, 1974); Daniel Nelson, *Managers and Workers: Origins of the New Factory System in the United States, 1880-1920* (Madison, Wis., 1975); Harry Edwards, *Contested Terrain: The Transformation of the Workplace in the Twentieth Century* (New York, 1979); and David Montgomery, *Workers' Control in America: Studies in the History of Work, Technology and Labor Struggles* (New York, 1979). Much of the recent periodical literature in the field is synthesized by Jeremy Brecher in "Uncovering the Hidden History of the American Workplace," *Review of Radical Political Economics*, 10 (1978), 1-23. The quote is taken from Edwards, *Contested Terrain*, p. 118.

3. Montgomery, *Workers' Control*, pp. 116, 155.

4. Sidney Fine, *Sit-Down: The General Motors Strike of 1936-37* (New York, 1970), pp. 59-60; see also the unpublished manuscript by Chris Paige, "Automobile Workers in the Depression," ch. 1, copy in author's possession.

5. Fine, *Sit-Down*, pp. 55-59; "Wage Structure of the Motor Vehicle Industry," *Monthly Labor Review* (hereafter *MLR*), 42 (Mar. 1936), 549-50. Industrial sociologists were particularly interested in the phenomenon. Donald Roy, "Efficiency and 'The Fix': Informal Intergroup Relations in a Piecework Machine Shop," *American Journal of Sociology*, 60 (1954), 255-65; James W. Kuhn, *Bargaining in a Grievance Settlement: The Power of Industrial Work Groups* (New York, 1961); William Foote Whyte, *Men at Work* (Homewood, Ill., 1961), pp. 179-98, 300-323; Walker and Guest, *Man on the Assembly Line*, pp. 66-80; and Sayles, *Behavior of Industrial Work Groups*, pp. 41-93.

6. Joe Brown, "Why Auto Body Workers Are More Militant than Other Auto Production Workers," in Brown Collection, Briggs Strike File, Archives of Labor History, Wayne State University, Detroit (hereafter ALHWSU); reminiscences of J. M. Waggoner, p. 130, Ford Motor Company Archives, Henry Ford Museum, Dearborn (hereafter FMC Archives). Good narrative accounts that reveal the power and solidarity of these work groups and the union leadership that emerged from them are by John W. Anderson (a metal finisher), "How I Became Part of the Labor Movement," in Alice and Staughton Lynd, eds., *Rank and File: Personal Histories by Working Class Organizers* (Boston,

1973), pp. 37-66; and Henry Kraus (describing the leadership of Bud Simons, a torch solderer), *The Many and the Few* (Los Angeles, 1947), pp. 48-54. Although Peter Friedlander sees much of the dynamic of union growth in ethnocultural terms, his own research finds early militancy centered in certain semiskilled occupational groups, especially torch welding. See "Emergence of a UAW Local: Midland Steel, 1933-1941" (paper delivered at the 1977 meeting of the Organization of American Historians).

7. Fine, *Sit-Down*, pp. 323-25; Friedlander, *Emergence of a UAW Local*, pp. 38-70; Harry Ross interview with Jack W. Skeels, July 10, 1961, transcript, pp. 6-18, ALHWSU; Monroe Lake interview with George Heliker, Mar. 12, 1954, transcript, n.p., Frank Hill Papers, FMC Archives.

8. Sayles, *Behavior of Industrial Work Groups*, p. 19.

9. William H. McPherson, *Labor Relations in the Automobile Industry* (Washington, D.C., 1940), p. 49.

10. Irving Howe and B. J. Widick, *The UAW and Walter Reuther* (New York, 1949), pp. 235-38; Edward Zeller, ed., "How to Win for the Union, A Handbook for UAW-CIO Stewards and Committeemen" (Detroit, 1945); McPherson, *Labor Relations*, pp. 48-68; Carl Hassler interview with Skeels, Nov. 27, 1959, transcript, p. 22; John Anderson interview with Skeels, May 21, 1960, transcript, p. 56, both ALHWSU.

11. As quoted in Frank Marquart, *An Auto Workers' Journal: The UAW from Crusade to One-Party Union* (University Park, Pa., 1975), p. 78.

12. Friedlander, *Emergence of a UAW Local*, pp. 93-131, provides a rich, if controversial, analysis of leadership culture and politics in one UAW local. See also Sidney M. Peck, *The Rank and File Leader* (New Haven, Conn., 1963), pp. 23-34, 319-58; and Leonard R. Sayles and George Strauss, *The Local Union: Its Place in the Industrial Plant* (New York, 1953), pp. 83-131 passim.

13. Roger Keeran, *The Communist Party and the Auto Workers Unions* (Bloomington, Ind., 1980), pp. 148-85 passim, 247.

14. A vigorous discussion of the meaning of the "Equality of Sacrifice" program is found in *Minutes of Proceedings, UAW War Emergency Conference*, Apr. 7-8, 1942, Detroit; Office of Facts and Figures, "Labor Morale in Detroit and Pittsburgh, Survey of Intelligence Materials No. 22," May 6, 1942, in Entry 35, Record Group 202, National Archives, Washington, D.C.

15. F. D. Newbury, "Wages and Productivity—The Problems Involved," *American Management Association Personnel Series*, no. 105 (1946), pp. 5-6; "Money and Real Weekly Earnings during Defense, War and Reconversion Periods," *MLR*, 63 (June 1947), 989; U.S. Congress, Senate Special Committee to Investigate the National Defense Program, 79th Cong., 1st Sess., *Manpower Problems in Detroit* (Washington, D.C., 1945), no. 28, pp. 13251-54, 13332-34, 13554-55.

16. Testimony of Harry W. Anderson, *Manpower Problems*, no. 28, pp. 13782-84; author's interviews with Tom Whelan, editor of UAW Local 887 *Propeller* (North American Aviation), Feb. 12, 1978; Erwin Bauer, former chief steward, UAW Local 306 (Budd Wheel), Aug. 12, 1978; Anthony Plasenti, grievance committeeman, UAW Local 927 (Fisher Body, Columbus) Mar. 12, 1979. The shifting character of wartime work is reflected in the accompanying table. Data calculated from "Hourly Earnings in Aircraft Engine Plants,"

|                          | Percent Employed in Automobile Industry | Percent Employed in Aircraft Engine Industry |
| ------------------------ | --------------------------------------- | -------------------------------------------- |
|                          | (June 1940)                             | (August 1943)                                |
| Drill Press Operators    | 2.6                                     | 7.4                                          |
| Grinding Machine Operators | 1.9                                   | 12.2                                         |
| Milling Machine Operators | 1.0                                    | 5.5                                          |
| Assembly                 | 18.0                                    | 12.2                                         |

*MLR*, 58 (Mar. 1944), 583-84; "Wage Structure of Motor Vehicle Industry," *MLR*, 54 (Feb. 1942), 300-301.

17. Robert M. Macdonald, *Collective Bargaining in the Automobile Industry* (New Haven, Conn., 1963), pp. 128-29; General Motors, *3 War Labor Reports* (Sept. 26, 1942), pp. 383-84.

18. Nelson, *Managers and Workers*, pp. 34-54, provides the best description of the vast powers of the foreman before the rise of scientific management. The declining status of the foreman in the late 1930s and early 1940s is recounted in "Foreman's Cases," *26 War Labor Reports* (July 23, 1945), pp. 666-67; F. J. Roethlisberger, "The Foreman: Master and Victim of Double Talk," *Harvard Business Review* (hereafter *HBR*), 23 (Spring 1945), 283-98; and Donald E. Wray, "Marginal Men of Industry: The Foremen," *American Journal of Sociology*, 54 (1949), 298-301.

19. U.S. House of Representatives, Committee on Military Affairs, Part 68, *Full Utilization of Manpower*, 78th Cong., 1st Sess., pp. 375-78; Earnest Dale, "The Development of Foremen in Management," *AMA Research Report*, no. 7 (1945), pp. 9-59; Herbert R. Northrup "The Foreman's Association of America," *HBR*, 23 (Winter 1945), 187-91.

20. *Manpower Problems*, p. 13730.

21. Charles P. Larrowe, "A Meteor on the Industrial Relations Horizon: The Foremen's Association of America," *Labor History*, 2 (1961), 259-87; "Foreman's Cases," *26 War Labor Reports*, pp. 655-66; testimony of Edward Butler, *Full Utilization of Manpower*, p. 91.

22. *Manpower Problems*, pp. 13576-609, 13786-87, for these and several other examples.

23. Local 600 Resolution (1945?), Ford-UAW Collection, Box 2, ALHWSU; Edgewater UAW Local 906's expulsion of the two "rate busters" is discussed exhaustively in "Umpire's Decision A-74 (Mar. 29, 1944)," in *UAW-Ford Motor Company Umpire Decisions* (privately printed, 1945), in FMC Archives. In this widely reported and precedent-setting case, Umpire Harry Shulman reinstated the employees over the strong objections of the local on the grounds that the union could not use its contractual right to determine "membership in good standing" to enforce work norms in violation of managerial efforts to increase the pace of work.

24. *Manpower Problems*, pp. 13525-32; Alan Clive, *State of War: Michigan in World War II* (Ann Arbor, Mich., 1979), pp. 170-74.

25. Joshua Freeman, "Delivering the Goods: Industrial Unionism during World War II," *Labor History*, 19 (Fall 1978), 574-91, provides a critique of the union movement that rests heavily on this social transformation.

26. Report of William McAulay, Administrator of Local 50 (Willow Run), June 3, 1942, Box 7, R. J. Thomas Collection, ALHWSU; a detailed statistical survey of the social and geographical origins of the Willow Run work force is found in Lowell Juilliard Carr and James Edson Stermer, *Willow Run: A Study of Industrialization and Cultural Inadequacy* (New York, 1952), p. 359.

27. Clive, *State of War*, pp. 185-89; Judy Rosen, "Women in the Plant, the Community, and the Union at Willow Run" (M.A. thesis, University of Pittsburgh, 1978), pp. 4-6; a good overall survey of the changes in women's employment wrought by World War II is found in William Chafe, *The American Woman: Her Changing Social, Economic and Political Roles, 1920-1970* (New York, 1972), pp. 135-50.

28. Rosen, "Women in the Plant," pp. 34-37; Lyn Goldfarb, *Separated and Unequal: Discrimination against Women Workers after World War II (the UAW 1944-1954)* (Washington, D.C., n.d.), n.p.; Martin Glaberman, *Wartime Strikes: The Struggle against the No-Strike Pledge in the UAW during World War II* (Detroit, 1980), pp. 21-24. A thorough and brilliant analysis of the persistence of a sexual division of labor is found in Ruth Milkman, "Redefining the Sexual Division of Labor: The Automobile Industry in World War II," *Feminist Studies*, 8 (Summer 1982).

29. Clark Kerr and Lloyd H. Fisher, "Effect of Environment and Administration on Job Evaluation," *HBR*, 27 (Dec. 1949), 77-96; Leonard G. Levenson, "Wartime Development of the Aircraft Industry," *MLR*, 59 (Nov. 1944), 917-29; Illia Edder, "Proposed North American Contract Would Hurt Unions," *Labor Actions*, June 21, 1943; *Manpower Problems*, p. 13789.

30. August Meier and Elliott Rudwick, *Black Detroit and the Rise of the UAW* (New York, 1979), pp. 108-74 passim; Clive, *State of War*, pp. 130-37.

31. Meier and Rudwick, *Black Detroit*, pp. 112-26; Clive, *State of War*, p. 141.

32. Meier and Rudwick, *Black Detroit*, pp. 162-74.

33. Clive, *State of War*, p. 142; *Manpower Problems*, pp. 13795-96. See also the excellent first-person account of Charles Denby, *Indignant Heart: A Black Worker's Journal* (Boston, 1978), pp. 87-109.

34. H. W. Anderson to Walter Reuther, Aug. 31, 1943, Box 1,UAW-GM Collection, ALHWSU; the best overall analysis of managerial ideology and politics during the war is found in Howell John Harris, *The Right to Manage: Industrial Relations Policies of American Business in the 1940s* (Madison, Wis., 1982).

35. Malcolm Denise, "Labor Relations and Implementation of Policy—1943, 1944, 1945," as quoted in George Heliker, "Report," in Hill Papers, FMC Archives, p. 303; see also Richard Deverall's 1943 series of Office of War Information reports on Chrysler labor relations in Deverall Notebooks, vol. 2, pp. 102-47, Catholic University Archives, Washington, D.C.

36. Joseph Twyman, "The President's Column," *Ford Facts*, Nov. 15, 1943; "Ringwald Criticized," *Ford Facts*, Dec. 15, 1943; "Ford Provokes Strikes," *Ford Facts*, Mar. 1, 1944, Mar. 4, 1944; S. Evans, Labor Relations Department, to all building superintendents, Rouge Plant, Apr. 4, 1944, in Box 13, R. J. Thomas Collection, ALHWSU. For a general overview of the stormy wartime labor relations at Ford, see Heliker, "Report," and Allen Nevins and Frank Ernest Hill, *Ford: Decline and Rebirth, 1933-62* (New York, 1962), pp. 228-51; and Keith Sward, *The Legend of Henry Ford* (New York, 1948), pp. 422-50. The quote is taken from *Manpower Problems*, p. 13558.

37. Data compiled from "Strikes in 1942," *MLR*, 56 (May 1943), 964; "Strikes in 1943," *MLR*, 58 (May 1944), 934; "Strikes and Lockouts in 1944," *MLR*, 60 (May 1945), 961; "Work Stoppages Caused by Labor-Management Disputes in 1945," *MLR*, 62 (May 1946), 726. In 1945 about 75 percent of all auto industry workers were involved in a strike, but this included the official General Motors work stoppage as well.

38. *Manpower Problems*, p. 13563; all statistics on such unauthorized strikes are necessarily imprecise, but the Bureau of Labor Statistics figures for auto, which only capture the larger and longer strikes (at least a shift in duration), show the same trend. Work stoppages to protest discipline, work assignments, and working conditions increased from 205 to 452 between 1943 and 1944 and increased as a percentage of all stoppages from 30 to 45 percent. "Strikes and Lockouts in 1944."

39. *Manpower Problems*, pp. 13576-603; Glaberman, *Wildcat Strikes*, pp. 35-50; author's interview with Erwin Bauer.

40. *Manpower Problems*, pp. 13619, 13624.

41. U.S. Department of Labor, *National War Labor Board Termination Report* (Washington, D.C., 1947), pp. 1134-36; Detroit Tool and Die Shops, *4 War Labor Reports* (Oct. 24, 1942), pp. 33-37; UAW International Executive Board Minutes, Oct. 6, 1944, UAW-IEB Collection, ALHWSU; "Maintenance Workers—Statement Issued by Presidents of Detroit Locals," Thomas Collection, Series I, Box 4, ALHWSU.

42. Glaberman, *Wartime Strikes*, pp. 34, 123-25; Freeman, "Delivering the Goods," pp. 584-89; Ed Jennings, "Wildcat! The Wartime Strike Wave in Auto," *Radical America*, 9 (July-Aug. 1975), 83-97. Although they differ in their evaluation of the social and political character of these strikes, all three writers emphasize the extent to which the influx of new workers, without a union tradition, may have been responsible for the increased number of stoppages.

43. Jerome F. Scott and George C. Homas, "Reflections on the Wildcat Strikes," *American Sociological Review*, 54 (June 1947), 281.

44. Author's interview with Erwin Bauer; author's interview with Jack T. Conway, June 19, 1980, Washington, D.C.; Scott and Homas, "Reflections on the Wildcat Strikes," pp. 283-84. For an example of Ford management's use of a wildcat strike to weaken a union, see "Complete Report of March 7 and March 14 Incidents," in UAW International Executive Board Minutes, Sept. 7-8, Box 5, UAW-IEB Collection, ALHWSU; "Council Upholds Aircraft Dismissals," *Ford Facts*, Apr. 1, 1944.

45. Kuhn, *Bargaining in Grievance Settlement*, pp. 111-43, 167-90, provides an excellent analysis of the problems inherent in what he calls "fractional bargaining" of this sort.

46. As quoted in Glaberman, *Wartime Strikes*, p. 44.

47. Jess Ferrazza, "Radio Address on Non-Strike Pledge," *Voice of Local 212*, Feb. 1, 1945.

48. "Revoke the No-Strike Pledge," *The Hi-Flyer* (UAW Local 6), Nov. 1944.

49. Data based on an analysis of 157 Chrysler Corporation strikes between July 18, 1944, and Mar. 22, 1945, in Robert W. Conder, Chrysler Labor Relations, to R. J. Thomas, Dec. 13, 1944, Apr. 16, 1945, in Thomas Collection, Box 5, ALHWSU. A good account of the way a militant leadership coordinated job actions and strike activity in UAW Local 365 at Brewster Aircraft is found

in Al Nash, "A Unionist Remembers: Militant Unionism and Political Factions," *Dissent*, 24 (Spring 1977), 181-89.

50. "Strikes and Lockouts in 1944," pp. 961-64; Jennings, "Wildcat!" p. 85.

51. The tense background of the Chrysler situation is reported in Chrysler Corporation, *3 War Labor Reports* (Oct. 2, 1943), pp. 451-64, and Chrysler Corporation, *10 War Labor Reports* (Aug. 27, 1943), pp. 552-56. Between December 1941 and January 1943 some sixty-six work stoppages took place in the corporation's plants. See also Deverall to Philo Nash, Dec. 23, 1942; Nash to A. H. Feller, Jan. 1943; Deverall to Clarance Glick, May 24, 1943, in Deverall Notebooks; the strike incident on May 20 was reported in Jack Webb, "The Whole Set-Up Has to Be Changed—Dodge Worker," *Labor Action*, May 31, 1943.

52. Nelson Lichtenstein, "Defending the No-Strike Pledge: CIO Politics during World War II," *Radical America*, 9 (July-Aug. 1975), 56-65.

53. Glaberman, *Wartime Strikes*, pp. 98-114, provides the fullest account of the convention battle. The growth and ideology of the caucus is discussed in the pages of *Labor Action*, *New International* and *Rank and Filer* in the fall of 1944 and the winter of 1945. See also Howe and Widick, *UAW and Walter Reuther*, pp. 120-23.

54. Glaberman, *Wartime Strikes*, pp. 115-20.

55. The Trotskyists were divided into two groups: the "orthodox" Socialist Workers Party and the "third camp" Workers Party. Together they had about 200 members in auto. The WP sparked formation of the Rank-and-File Caucus, and although it had gained some strength in Detroit and Flint, it also had disproportionate support in such war-baby locals as Brewster Local 365, Willow Run Local 50, Bell Aircraft Local 501 in Buffalo, and Chicago Buick Local 6. In some of these new locals young ideological radicals taking their first industrial jobs were able to win influence in the fluid political climate of these large locals. Jack T. Conway interview with Skeels, Mar. 27, 1963, transcript, pp. 4-5, ALWHSU; author's interview with John Zupan, Aug. 28, 1972, Detroit.

56. Bert Cochran, *Labor and Communism: The Conflict That Shaped American Unions* (Princeton, N.J., 1977), pp. 206-28 passim; Keeran, *Communist Party and the Auto Workers Union*, pp. 226-49 passim.

57. As quoted in Keeran, *Communist Party and the Auto Workers Union*, pp. 245, 248.

58. See for example Robert M. C. Littler, "Managers Must Manage," *HBR*, 24 (1946), 366-76; and Henry Ford II, "The Challenge of Human Engineering," *Vital Speeches*, 12 (Feb. 15, 1946), 271-74.

59. John S. Bugas to Richard T. Leonard, Dec. 12, 1945, Box 1, UAW-Ford Collection, ALHWSU; Benjamin M. Selekman et al., *Problems in Labor Relations* (New York, 1958), pp. 361-80, 391-97; James R. Bright, *Automation and Management* (Boston, 1958), pp. 59-64.

60. William T. Gossett, Ford Counsel, as quoted in Harris, *Right to Manage*, p. 85.

61. Larrowe, "Meteor on the Industrial Relations Horizon," pp. 287-99; Heliker, "Report," pp. 345-51; "General Motors Teaches Foremen 'Humanics,'" *Industrial Relations*, 5 (Apr. 1947), 34-37.

62. Sayles and Strauss, *Local Union*, pp. 27-42; Heliker interview with B. J. Widick, Mar. 6, 1954, Hill Papers, FMC Archives; Plasenti interview; see also Richard Herding, *Job Control and Union Structure* (Rotterdam, 1972), pp. 142-212.

63. Widick interview, Hill Papers, FMC Archives.

64. C. Wright Mills, *The New Men of Power* (New York, 1948), p. 9; Barton Bernstein, "Walter Reuther and the General Motors Strike of 1945-46," *Michigan History*, 49 (Sept. 1965), 260-77; author's interview with Victor Reuther, Sept. 25, 1979, Washington, D.C. For Walter Reuther's assessment of the union's internal crisis and his strategy for defusing it, see UAW Executive Board Minutes, Sept. 10-18, 1945, UAW-IEB Collection, ALHWSU.

65. Frederick Harbison, "The General Motors-United Auto Workers Agreement of 1950," *Journal of Political Economy*, 58 (Oct. 1950), 408. For a perceptive interpretation of the function of the wage demand, see Alvin W. Gouldner, *Wildcat Strike, A Study in Worker-Management Relationships* (Yellow Springs, Ohio, 1954), pp. 32-37.

66. Howe and Widick, *UAW and Walter Reuther*, pp. 149-71, 187-204; Cochran, *Labor and Communism*, pp. 248-68, 272-79; Jack W. Sheels, "The Development of Political Stability within the United Auto Workers" (Ph.D. dissertation, University of Wisconsin, 1957), pp. 275-349; Frank Emspak, "The Break-Up of the Congress of Industrial Organizations (CIO), 1945-1950" (Ph.D. dissertation, University of Wisconsin, 1972), pp. 159-82; William D. Andrew, "Factionalism and Anti-Communism: Ford Local 600," *Labor History*, 20 (1979), 227-55.

67. Jack Stieber, *Governing the UAW* (New York, 1962), pp. 131-57; William Serrin, *The Company and the Union* (New York, 1974), pp. 303-33; Herding, *Job Control and Union Structure*, pp. 131-59; Widick interview, Hill Papers, FMC Archive. An indication of the disruptive effect local strikes could have on national bargaining came in May 1949 when the Ford local at the Rouge conducted a lengthy strike over "speed-up" issues, nearly sidetracking Reuther's effort to secure companywide pensions in the national Ford-UAW negotiations that began the following month. See "Chronology of Labor Disputes Which Culminated in the May 1949 Strike," Box 204, Martindale Papers, FMC Archives; also "Labor Control of Production Standards Is Needed to Fight Speed-up," *Labor Action*, July 4, 1949.

# Notes on Contributors

SUSAN PORTER BENSON teaches history at Bristol Community College in Fall River, Massachusetts. She is completing a dissertation on the history of saleswomen, managers, and customers in American department stores, 1890-1940.

FRANCIS G. COUVARES is a member of the history faculty at Clark University, Worcester, Massachusetts, where he teaches social and cultural history. He received his Ph.D. from the University of Michigan in 1980; his book, a cultural history of industrializing Pittsburgh, is forthcoming.

LEON FINK is a member of the history faculty at the University of North Carolina at Chapel Hill. His book, *Workingmen's Democracy: The Knights of Labor and American Politics* is forthcoming from the University of Illinois Press.

ELIZABETH FONES-WOLF is an associate editor of the Samuel Gompers Papers at the University of Maryland. KENNETH FONES-WOLF is Assistant Curator at the Urban Archives at Temple University, where he is working on a dissertation on religion and organized labor. They have published essays in *Labor History* and *Industrial and Labor Relations Review*.

STEVE FRASER is Senior Social Science Editor with Basic Books. His essay is part of a broader study of the role of Sidney Hillman and the Amalgamated Clothing Workers in the creation of the New Deal and the CIO.

JOSHUA B. FREEMAN is presently teaching history at the College at Old Westbury/SUNY. He is completing a full-length study of the Transport Workers Union in New York City between 1933 and 1950.

NELSON LICHTENSTEIN teaches history at The Catholic University of America. He is the author of *Worker Insurgency, Union Security: The Congress of Industrial Organizations in World War II* (1982). He is currently working on a biography of Walter Reuther.

JONATHAN PRUDE is a member of the history faculty at Emory University, where he teaches social and labor history. He has published essays in the *Journal of American History, Labor History,* and *The New Republic,* and is the author of *The Coming of Industrial Order: A Study of Town and Factory Life in Rural Massachusetts, 1810-1860* (forthcoming).

CHRISTINE STANSELL teaches social and women's history at Princeton University. She is an active feminist and is currently writing a book on women of the laboring poor in New York City before the Civil War.

SEAN WILENTZ is a member of the history faculty at Princeton University. A contributor to several journals including *History Workshop* and *Labor History*, he is the author of the forthcoming *Chants Democratic: New York City and the Rise of the American Working Class, 1790-1865.*

MICHAEL H. FRISCH teaches in the history and American studies departments at SUNY-Buffalo, and has recently been a Research Associate at the University of Pennsylvania's Philadelphia Social History Project. He is the author of *Town into City* (1972) and numerous recent articles on urban history and issues in oral and public history.

DANIEL J. WALKOWITZ is a member of the history faculty and co-director of the Graduate Program in Public History at NYU. He served as Project Director for a film *The Molders of Troy* (PBS, 1980) based on his book, *Worker City, Company Town* (University of Illinois Press, 1978). He is presently at work on several labor history films, and conducting research on the proletarianization of professional workers.